Macrosystems
The Dynamics of Economic Policy

Elias Karakitsos

BLACKWELL
Oxford UK & Cambridge USA

First published 1992

Blackwell Publishers
108 Cowley Road
Oxford OX4 1JF
UK

Three Cambridge Center
Cambridge, Massachusetts 02142
USA

British Library Cataloguing in Publication Data

A CIP catalogue record for this book is available from the British Library.

Library of Congress Cataloging-in-Publication Data

Karakitsos, Elias.
    Macrosystems : the dynamics of economic policy / Elias Karakitsos.
      p.   cm.
    Includes index.
    ISBN 0–631–17297–1 (acid-free paper). – ISBN 0–631–18457–0 (pbk) (acid-free paper)
    1. Macroeconomics. 2. Economic policy. I. Title.
  HB172.5.K37 1992
  339.5 – dc20   91–45207 CIP

Typeset in 10½ on 12pt Times
by Colset Pte Ltd., Singapore
Printed in Great Britain by Biddles Ltd., Guildford, Surrey

This book is printed on acid-free paper

Contents

To my father, Demosthenes

Foreword

One of the toughest challenges facing the investor, individual or institutional, is how to keep abreast of developments in the economy and how to relate them to investment decisions. Investor attention tends to be heavily biased towards a multitude of macroeconomic factors which in turn cause short-term swings in asset prices. The matter is made even worse when the market participants become reactive to such economic data and lose touch with the more important long-term factors.

There has been a clear need for a systematic approach to analysis of economies, leading to a determination of the main variables. These, together with the market's expectations about their likely course, can explain moves in the asset prices in the world financial markets.

Macroeconomics offers an excellent opportunity to provide such an approach. However, experience shows that there are just a few good macroeconomists around. A great deal of the problem lies in the way economics is taught and consequently in the books available on macroeconomics. Economists are trained to answer any question in an ambivalent way: on the one hand this would happen, but on the other hand exactly the opposite would happen. An ambivalent answer hides not only the effects of uncertainty, which are inherent in any decision-making process, but also rival economic theories. Furthermore, the answer is usually based on a partial equilibrium analysis and this reflects the fact that economists are not well trained in providing a synthesis of how the economy works. The emphasis in the teaching of macroeconomics, reflected in the books available in the field, is on the understanding of competing theories. Moreover, economists usually choose their assumptions with a view to being consistent not with stylized facts, but with the school of thought to which they belong. However, in the real world, as President Truman put it, the need is for 'one hand economists'.

This book goes a long way in rectifying these deficiencies in the teaching of macroeconomics and providing 'one hand economists'. It avoids theoretical debates and controversies and offers a single view of how the economy works. The methodology employed is exemplary. A single and coherent structure is gradually built and the reader is guided through nine chapters to understand the constituent blocks of this structure. Furthermore, even this single structure is capable of generating wildly divergent results. What I like about this book is that although these ambiguities are very well explained the reader is not left in the dark as to what to expect in the real world, but is offered the most likely outcome. In this context, the simulation models, which are numerical analogues of the theoretical models, provide an illustration of the time profile of the likely effects to be observed in the real world. In addition, the simulation models enhance understanding of the underlying theoretical models and allow the study of those complex dynamics, which are usually inadequately treated in other books, but which are the backbone of the understanding of economic phenomena in the real world.

Last, but not least, I am convinced that the view that is put forward on how the economy works is consistent with what is observed in the real world. The author has been using these principles to analyse the four major economies (USA, Japan, Germany and the UK) and their financial markets. For the past three years, in which he has been acting as an adviser to Citibank/Citicorp Private Banking Group, his forecasts and analysis have been systematically correct. Over the past 12 months his analysis has been used as a core component of the Bank's investment decision-making process.

This book will be extremely useful to a class of readers: business studies students who need to have a coherent view of how the economy works; economics graduates who want to straighten their minds from rival economic theories; and professional economists who wish to become 'one hand economists'.

Farhan Sharaff
Vice President
Citibank Private Banking Group

Introduction

The Scope of the Book and the Issues in Macroeconomics

In this book we are concerned with two main issues in macroeconomics: first, what causes business cycles (that is, booms and recessions); and second, the role of the government. In particular, can policy-makers dampen business cycles by using stabilization policies, and especially demand management policies, or in their attempt to do so are they causing such cyclical behaviour? Macroeconomics has been in a state of flux for a very long time with respect to these two questions. How the economy works and the way it is affected by policy and exogenous variables is still an unsettled issue and economists are divided into different schools of thought. Central to this debate is the issue of *laissez-faire* versus intervention, which dates back to Adam Smith. The debate evolves through time as our understanding of the economy is enhanced and the issues are refined. Research in macroeconomics is conducted with theoretical and empirical (econometric) models. Although economists use scientific methods and approaches there are three main reasons why the debate is still open. First, in theoretical models it is not uncommon to find that the structure (defined as a set of equations with inequality constraints on the admissible range of parameter values) is chosen not to be as close an approximation to the real world as possible, but rather to reflect the point that needs to be proven, since policy issues in economics are related to political ideologies. Second, in many cases statistical analysis cannot discriminate between rival hypotheses and therefore the data corroborate more than one empirical model. Third, economists tend to dismiss or ignore the evidence from empirical models, since these models are usually not theoretically sound.

These problems gave rise to a new research initiative in the 1980s to provide the microfoundations of macroeconomics. *Ad hoc* theoretical models that are not based on optimizing behaviour on the part of households and firms have been criticized and to some extent abandoned as belonging to old-fashioned macroeconomics. Econometric models, which had been the backbone of empirical research for most of the period since the Second World War, are in decline as a result of the 'Lucas critique' and the criticism that such models lack microfoundations. However, in spite of the recent research in microfoundations and the significant contribution that it has made in enhancing our understanding of the underlying problems and issues, we are a long way from a complete and undisputed theory of macroeconomic behaviour. The two main schools of economic thought, 'new-classical' and 'new-Keynesian', have largely developed along different paths with different methodologies. To be fair, there is a small core of models accepted by both schools of thought, but on the two main issues of what causes business cycles and the role of the government the gap has widened rather than narrowed compared with the debate twenty years ago between monetarists and Keynesians.

Since the work of Frisch (1933) and Slutsky (1937), business cycles have been thought to be generated by shocks (called 'impulses') through distributed lag functions (called 'propagation' mechanisms). The impulses may be serially uncorrelated, but their effect on output is serially correlated. Within this framework the issues that divide economists as to the causes of business cycles are the precise functional relationship of the propagation mechanism and the sources of impulses. Are shocks originating from the private or the public sector, and are these real or monetary? Since permanent shocks give rise to a trend that is a non-stationary time series, while transitory shocks produce a cycle that is a stationary time series, the issues that divide the two schools can alternatively be expressed as relating to the decomposition of the fluctuations in output between trend and cycle.

In new-classical macroeconomics, business cycles can be characterized as a non-stationary process for output in which all shocks, including those arising from changes in productivity and tastes and shifts in the terms of trade, are permanent. In this framework, there are no transitory shocks and therefore actual and trend output are always the same. Recessions are not temporary and are caused by negative shocks. Booms are also not temporary and are caused by positive shocks. The cyclical fluctuations in output are produced by accumulated shocks. Growth in the economy exists because, on average, there are more positive than negative shocks.

By contrast, in Keynesian macroeconomics there is a distinction between actual and trend output. The trend in output is either smooth or, according to the more recent new-Keynesian view, stochastic. This arises from permanent shocks, such as changes in technology, improvements in labour productivity and increases in the labour force. However, the main cyclical fluctuations in output are caused by transitory shocks. Since most permanent shocks are coming from the supply side, the latter is responsible for shaping the trend in output. On the other hand, since most transitory shocks are coming from the demand side, the latter is mainly responsible for explaining business cycles.

When the issues that divide the two schools on the causes of business cycles are put into such a framework it is tempting to conclude that statistical inference should be able to pass a verdict on which model explains the data better. Unfortunately, and as is typical with most statistical analysis, in a comprehensive test designed to compare the two models Campbell and Mankiw (1987) concluded that both fit the data equally well.

If statistical inference is of no use, we must employ different criteria to choose between the two models. New-classical macroeconomics emphasizes a real business cycle approach with continuous market clearing in perfectly competitive markets. I find this approach unsatisfactory on various grounds. First, it does not provide a convincing explanation of why the adjustment in the goods and the labour markets falls on quantities rather than prices. For example, some of these models imply a high intertemporal substitutability of leisure, which is counterfactual. Second, the theory cannot explain lay-offs, with the implication that unemployment is voluntary. Third, the assumption of perfect competition is unrealistic. Even when this assumption is invoked on an 'as if' basis, namely that the economy is behaving as if it is perfectly competitive, I find its implications misleading, especially when it matters most, such as in predicting the turning point of a recession. Finally, I do not believe that recessions or booms are caused mainly by technological shocks. I admit that some of these arguments are subjective and therefore it seems unfair to dismiss the whole body of an important and influential literature in macroeconomics in one paragraph. However, in analysing real-world phenomena almost all economists are eclectic. I am no exception to this rule, because there is not yet a single accepted model for all purposes. My eclectic view of the world does not agree with the new-classical macroeconomics.

I prefer an alternative explanation based on the Keynesian view of absence of continuous market clearing due to a 'coordination failure' of micro-agents. However, the microfoundations of the new-Keynesian macroeconomics are both incomplete, in that they leave many questions unanswered, and unsatisfactory, in that many models fit the stylized facts. Therefore, we have to rely on *ad hoc* models for now, or even for ever, to answer different issues in macroeconomics. The justification for using such models is that they can explain one aspect of reality by making approximations to other aspects of the real world. The art in economics is to choose the assumptions that fit the stylized facts rather than our ideologies. What are these?

- Changes in nominal GNP are strongly correlated with changes in output (real GNP), but have little correlation with inflation (measured, for example, by the GNP-deflator). The implications are, first, that shocks in nominal demand have persistent effects on output and, second, that prices are sticky.
- Innovations in money supply are positively correlated with innovations in output. This suggests that changes in money supply may have large effects on output.
- There is very little correlation between real wages and output or employment, and this is pro-cyclical rather than counter-cyclical.
- Changes in the demand for labour produce large fluctuations in employment and small changes in the real wage rate. This means that wages are sticky. Unemployment is largely involuntary and unemployed people are unhappier than those employed.

These stylized facts are consistent with the view that is espoused in this book: that business cycles are caused by transitory shocks, which stem mainly from the demand side, but also from the supply side of the economy. Demand side shocks come predominantly from the private sector, from changes in autonomous consumption, investment or world trade as a result, for example, of changes in tastes or entrepreneurial expectations. However, there have been numerous occasions in many industrialized countries, like the boom in the UK in 1987–8 and the recession of 1990–1, where the amplitude of the cycles has been amplified by economic policies. Stop–go policies are usually contributing to the cyclical behaviour of the economy. The long and variable lags in the effects of economic policy and the lack of readily available information about the state of the economy make government attempts to stabilize the economy have exactly the opposite effect.

Some supply shocks, such as changes in technology and improvements in labour productivity, are permanent and therefore affect the trend in output. Since these are random, the trend in output is not expected to be smooth. However, other supply shocks, such as changes in the relative price of oil, affect mainly the cyclical behaviour of the economy.

Given the above eclectic view of business cycles and the role of the government, the book is structured in such a way as to allow the study of the effects of policy and exogenous variables, like world trade and the price of oil, on the main macroeconomic variables.

The Methodology of the Book

Three features form the basis of the methodological approach of this book. First, models of increasing complexity are developed, that are derivable from each other by altering assumptions. The simplest possible model is analysed first, and makes very crude assumptions about the real world. These assumptions are then systematically relaxed to construct more complex and more realistic models of the economy. This approach makes the structure explicit and therefore the reader can appreciate the assumptions upon which certain results depend and consequently their generality. Second, the economy is treated as a dynamic system. This *systems approach* to macroeconomics entails that *all* main macroeconomic variables are simultaneously determined within a structure in which the role of policy and exogenous variables is explicit.

The third feature of the book is that the models are analysed using simple quantitative techniques and the *simulation approach*. Study of the dynamic behaviour of the system in the short, medium and long run with simulation models is superior to that using analytical models because the latter suffer from a serious drawback. The short-run analysis – short-run comparative statics – covers too short a period for any practical purposes because the assumption that the state variables remain fixed can only be justified if the analysis is instantaneous. For example, state variables like real private sector wealth or expected inflation cannot remain fixed in an environment in which prices are changing. On the other hand, the long-run analysis – steady-state comparative statics – covers too long a period for practical considerations, since most econometric models show that ten years is not an unreasonably long time for the system to converge to long-run equilibrium. For all practical purposes, the interest lies in the dynamic effects of a policy over a period of one to five years, since such a time period also coincides with the political cycle. Even if the system has not yet converged to steady state it is desirable to know whether a large proportion of the total effect, say 70–80 per cent, of a given policy has worked itself out within such a period. This type of analysis cannot be accomplished with analytical models. Simulation models, which are numerical replicas of the analytical models, provide perhaps the best vehicle for studying the dynamic response of the system to a policy change over a given time, say five years.

On the other hand, the disadvantage of the simulation approach is that the results are coefficient-specific. The solution to this problem is to submit the system to extensive sensitivity analysis in order to examine the robustness of the results within a critical range, or the parameter values along which the results substantially change. The sensitivity analysis is conducted in such a way as to test whether the system behaves symmetrically to positive and negative shocks. The parameter range is chosen to reflect the divergence of known empirical estimates.

The distinction between analytical and simulation models should not be carried too far, since the two are complements rather than substitutes. Recognizing the importance of this point, the book is organized in such a way that to every self-contained analytical model there corresponds a simulation model.

The models that are simulated are not econometric models with fixed coefficients, but numerical analogues of theoretical models with flexible coefficients. This enables the study not just of a *single* model, as in the case of econometric models, but rather of a *class* of models that give rise to a particular set of results. Furthermore, unlike econometric models, simulation models have a malleable structure and can be defined as close to a theoretical model as one wishes. This allows the study of: the dynamic behaviour of the underlying theoretical model; the sensitivity of the dynamic adjustment to parameter variation; the effect of a different structure of one equation or even a whole sector on the dynamic adjustment of the system etc.

Outline of the Book

The book is organized in three parts, which constitute conceptual building blocks of the economic system. Part I is devoted to the study of aggregate demand and the way it is affected by fiscal and monetary policies. In this analysis prices are fixed and a change in aggregate demand leads to a change in output. This analysis is relevant if there are unutilized resources and excess capacity. Such conditions prevail if the economy is in recession or depression. Part II integrates aggregate supply with aggregate demand to provide a system of simultaneous determination of output, prices and the interest rate. This analysis is relevant if the rate of capacity utilization is in the normal or upper range. Part III integrates the open economy with the rest of the system under fixed and flexible exchange rates.

The first three models provide a review of the basic model of income determination, the role of fiscal policy in such a model and the integration of the goods and assets markets, the *IS-LM* model. All this is basic material and is covered in any main macroeconomics textbook. The next two chapters provide the core of part I. In model 4 the government budget constraint is integrated into a simple *IS-LM* model. This imposes a dynamic structure on to an otherwise static model. The dynamics of the system, called *intrinsic dynamics*, stem from the relationship between stocks and flows. Model 4 allows the study of the wealth accumulation process associated with the finance of a budget deficit.

Model 5 is the first simulation model, and is a numerical analogue of the theoretical model 4 with two added features. First, there is a differential speed of adjustment between the goods and the assets markets with the latter clearing faster than the former. Second, there are interest payments on government debt. These make the model non-linear and affect the dynamics of the system as well as its steady-state properties. These two features allow also the examination of fiscal and monetary policies in a system with richer and more realistic dynamics than model 4, which is the model that has been analysed a great deal in the literature and is also covered in many books. The importance of non-linearities is studied by comparing the behaviour of the model with and without interest payments.

At the end of this chapter there are three appendices. These purport to explain the extent to which the main macroeconomic relationships of consumption, investment and the demand for money, which form the core of part I, can be derived from optimizing behaviour on the part of households and firms.

Model 6 integrates the wage–price sector into model 4. This is the first attempt to provide a simultaneous determination of output and prices (inflation). Furthermore, this model allows the study of the effect of a demand or supply shock on both output and inflation. One of the main objectives of the analysis is to see how a government can influence the targets of economic policy, namely output and inflation, and to examine the possibility of trade-off between them. The dynamics of the system are described by the adjustment of expected to actual inflation, and the wealth accumulation process associated with balancing the budget through a first-order system of two differential equations.

Model 7 is a numerical analogue of model 6. In this model the emphasis is on the dynamic and long-run effects of fiscal policy under alternative finance rules. The dynamic and long-run effects of open market operations and supply shocks are also considered. Finally, the role of non-linearities both in dynamic adjustment and in steady state are analysed. At the end of this chapter there is another appendix, which deals with the microfoundations of the wage–price sector.

Model 8 is devoted to the study of an open economy under fixed exchange rates. In this framework the degree of sterilization of foreign reserves has important implications for the efficacy of monetary and fiscal policy. The aim of this chapter is to analyse the implications of the combined choice of sterilization and method of budget finance for the stability and effectiveness of fiscal and monetary policy and for shocks in exogenous variables, namely oil price and world trade. What determines surpluses or deficits in the current account of the balance of payments is also considered.

Model 9 deals with an open economy under flexible exchange rates. In the goods market there are exports and imports to and from the rest of the world and in the assets markets domestic residents can hold foreign bonds. The determinants of the exchange rate are explained and its role in the macroeconomy is analysed. The dynamics of the system are described by the adjustment of wealth in response to current account imbalances and the budget, and the adjustment of expected to actual inflation. In this chapter the emphasis is in the interactions of the exchange rate with the rest of the main macroeconomic variables in response to a change in economic policy or other exogenous variables. The dynamic adjustment of the economy from one steady state to another is affected by the way expectations in the foreign exchange market are formed. In this context a comparison is made between model-consistent (or rational) expectations and exchange rate expectations that are consistent with balancing the current account in the long run.

Who Should Read This Book

This book arose from a course on macroeconomic policy that I have been teaching at Imperial College to third-year science and engineering students since 1986 and to MBA students since 1987. These students have no prior knowledge of macroeconomics, but they are numerate and their scientific background allows them to familiarize themselves quickly with the concepts and methodologies used in economics, which are, in fact, mostly borrowed from science. The book is therefore most suitable for non-specialists who would be involved in decision-making in industry, commerce, banking, financial markets and government departments and for whom the macroeconomy forms the business environment. In this context the aim is not to provide the reader with an account of the different schools of economic thought at a principles or advanced level, nor with the most recent developments in macroeconomics. Instead, the aim is to explain the interrelationship of the main macroeconomic variables in business cycles: output, inflation, unemployment, interest rates, money supply, exchange rates, balance of payments, budget deficit, public debt and private sector wealth. The book also seeks to analyse how these variables are affected by policy variables, such as tax rates, and variables exogenous to the system under investigation, such as world trade and oil prices. It is hoped that the book will teach the reader the theory and the techniques required to analyse macroeconomic problems and conflicting views on policy issues covered in public debates, the daily press, news magazines, economic reports and economic forecasts, and to relate them to her or his own business environment or personal circumstances. From this perspective, the book is also suitable for final-year undergraduate or postgraduate students in economics.

Accordingly, an eclectic view of how the economy works is developed based on the stylized facts of industrialized economies. The emphasis is on the dynamic behaviour of the economic system. To achieve these objectives within a one-year course in macroeconomics an intuitive explanation of all basic macroeconomic relationships is offered. The models are therefore postulated rather than derived from optimizing behaviour. This approach provides a short-cut that allows us to concentrate on the main issues of the interrelationship of the main macroeconomic variables in the business cycles and the way they are affected by economic policy. In four appendices we discuss the extent to which these *ad hoc* relationships can be justified from optimizing behaviour.

Economics students do not need to read models 1 to 3, which are covered in any macroeconomics textbook. These students may find all the appendices most useful since their purpose is to put into perspective the models analysed in this book, along with their underlying microfoundations. Precisely for this reason these appendices may be too difficult for the non-specialist student. They can be omitted when reading the book, at least for the first time, without losing anything. A prerequisite for non-specialist students is an analysis of national income accounts. These are not covered because they are particular to specific countries.

Part I

Aggregate Demand

1

Model 1 The Basic Model of Income Determination

1.1 Assumptions

In this simplified economy there are only households and firms who transact in two markets – the goods market and the labour market. Households supply their labour services and demand the single output that is produced by firms. The latter demand labour services and supply the output. Labour and capital are the only factors of production. However, capital is fixed. Employing more labour is the only way of increasing production. Firms are owned by the households. There is no government sector and therefore households do not pay any taxes or receive any benefits (or transfers) from the government. Furthermore, there is no trade with the rest of the world, no foreign trade sector. Such an economy is usually called a *closed economy*. The output that is produced is used for consumption by households and for investment by firms. In this economy there is no money, no medium of exchange. Such an economy is usually called a *barter economy*. Households supply their labour services in exchange for the product that is produced.

The way the goods market works is portrayed in figure 1.1. Demand for the single output, usually called aggregate demand, varies inversely with its price. The higher the price the smaller the demand for the product by households. Supply, on the other hand, which is called aggregate supply, may be horizontal, upward sloping or vertical. The aggregate supply curve in figure 1.1 combines all three features. At low levels of output, where there are idle resources because capital is fixed, aggregate supply is perfectly elastic – the horizontal segment. Firms are willing to increase production, at the same level of prices P_0, by employing more labour. The level of output is determined by demand and prices are fixed. In the upward sloping segment, firms are willing to increase production if the price they charge also increases. An increase in demand is met partly by increasing production, and therefore employment, and partly by increasing prices. In the vertical segment supply is perfectly inelastic – firms are faced with bottlenecks and there is full employment. Any increase in demand is met with higher prices at an unchanged

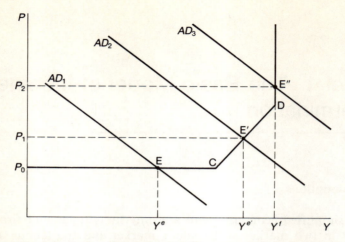

Figure 1.1 The determination of the general price level and output in the economy

level of production, Y^f, the full employment level.

In model 1, it is assumed that aggregate supply is perfectly elastic and therefore prices are fixed. Any change in demand is met by altering the level of production and employment. The assumption of a barter economy means that the prices of goods and services that comprise the GNP are relative prices expressed in terms of one particular good that acts as a numeraire. Moreover, the assumption of fixed prices means that nominal and real variables are the same.

1.2 The Model

The basic model of income determination is described by equations (1.1) to (1.4).

$$D = C + I \tag{1.1}$$

$$C = C_0 + C_y Y; \quad C_0 > 0, \quad 0 < C_y < 1 \tag{1.2}$$

$$Y = D \tag{1.3}$$

$$\dot{Y} \equiv \frac{\mathrm{d}Y}{\mathrm{d}t} = \alpha(D - Y); \quad \alpha > 0 \tag{1.4}$$

where D is aggregate demand; C is planned real consumer's expenditure (or consumption demand, or simply consumption); I is planned real investment expenditure (or investment demand, or simply investment); Y is output (gross domestic product, GDP) or factor incomes, or simply income. Factor incomes represent wages and salaries paid to households in their capacity as employees for their labour services, and profits paid again to households in their capacity as owners of capital and the firms. Because of the circular flow of income, output is always equal to income.

Equation (1.1) is a definitional equation. It defines aggregate demand as the sum of consumption and investment. This definition follows from the assumptions that the economy is closed with no government sector. Equation (1.2) is a behavioural equation. It describes the relationship between consumption and income and is called the *consumption function*. It asserts that consumption (or planned consumer expenditure) varies with income. The demand for consumption goods increases with income – households with higher income have higher levels of consumption. The parameter C_y is a constant and is called the *marginal propensity to consume*. It derives its name from the fact that $dC/dY = C_y$. This derivative shows the marginal (or infinitesimal) change in consumption for a given marginal change in income. Thus, if $C_y = 0.8$, then for a given increase in income of £1 consumption increases by £0.80. The marginal propensity to consume can take values between 0 and 1. It will differ from one economy to another or among different households. The restriction in the values of C_y is derived from the stability condition of the system (see below). The parameter C_0 is positive and is called the *autonomous consumption*. It shows the amount of consumption at a zero level of income. Obviously, autonomous consumption is financed in the short run from past savings. Equation (1.3) is an equilibrium condition and is derived from equation (1.4). It asserts that equilibrium in the goods market is obtained when demand equals supply.

The system of equations (1.1) to (1.3) determines the equilibrium values of the variables D, C and Y in terms of I. The dependent variables D, C and Y are usually called the *endogenous variables* of the system and the independent variable I is called *exogenous*. This model provides a theory for the determination of the equilibrium values of income. For a given value of investment, equilibrium income or output, Y, is determined such that demand equals supply in the goods market. Demand consists of two components – consumption and investment. The former depends on income, whereas the latter is exogenous to the system. Supply is demand-determined – whatever is demanded is immediately supplied at fixed prices. Equilibrium in this economy is obtained when demand equals supply.

Equation (1.4) describes the dynamic adjustment of the economy towards equilibrium. It asserts that profit-maximizing firms respond by increasing output (i.e. $\dot{Y} > 0$) whenever demand, D, exceeds supply, Y, at a rate that is proportional to excess demand. Similarly, when supply exceeds demand firms respond to unanticipated increases in stocks by cutting output and therefore income (i.e. $\dot{Y} < 0$), at a rate proportional to excess supply. The parameter α is positive and shows the extent to which output is adjusted for a given change in excess demand. The higher α is, the greater the response of output to a given change in excess demand. The equilibrium condition (1.3) is obtained from (1.4) by requiring stationarity, i.e. that in equilibrium $\dot{Y} = 0$. When demand is equal to supply ($D = Y$) there is no incentive for firms to change production (i.e. $\dot{Y} = 0$) and equilibrium in the economy is obtained. Thus, whereas the system of equations (1.1) to (1.3) determines the equilibrium values of income/output, Y, equation (1.4) describes the disequilibrium adjustment of Y.

1.3 The Determination of the Equilibrium Level of Income and Simple Comparative Statics

To obtain the equilibrium level of output, first substitute equation (1.2) into (1.1). This gives us the level of demand as a function of income and investment.

$$D = C_0 + C_y Y + I \tag{1.5}$$

Now substitute (1.5) into (1.3) and solve for Y to obtain the equilibrium level of income:

$$Y = \frac{1}{1 - C_y} (C_0 + I) \tag{1.6}$$

For given values of the parameters C_0 and C_y, (1.6) gives the equilibrium level of income as a function of investment. If investment follows a stochastic process, then income follows through (1.6) a stochastic process too. Thus, according to this model business cycles are caused by fluctuations in demand through changes in investment. If investment changes, the equilibrium level of income also changes. Thus, a change in investment equal to ΔI causes income to change by ΔY. This is approximately given by

$$\Delta Y = \frac{1}{1 - C_y} \Delta I \tag{1.7}$$

The derivative

$$\frac{\mathrm{d}Y}{\mathrm{d}I} = \frac{1}{1 - C_y} \tag{1.8}$$

is called the *multiplier*, since it shows by how much income will change for a given infinitesimal change in investment. The multiplier is denoted by κ and depends on the value of C_y:

$$\kappa = \kappa(C_y) \tag{1.9}$$

If $C_y = 0.8$, then $\kappa = 5$. Thus, if investment increases by £1 billion ($\Delta I = $ £1 billion), income will increase by £5 billion ($\Delta Y = $ £5 billion). It is obvious from (1.8) that κ is an increasing function of $C_y (\kappa' > 0)$. The higher the marginal propensity to consume, the greater the value of the multiplier.

The fact that the multiplier is so large limits the usefulness of this model as an explanation of business cycles because, according to the stylized facts, fluctuations in investment exceed those in output, while this model suggests the opposite.

1.4 Dynamic Adjustment to Equilibrium

To obtain the dynamic adjustment path towards equilibrium we substitute (1.5) into (1.4):

$$\frac{dY}{dt} + \alpha(1 - C_y) Y = \alpha(C_0 + I) \tag{1.10}$$

This is a first-order differential equation. The solution of the homogeneous part is

$$Y = x_0 e^{-\alpha(1-C_y)t} \tag{1.11}$$

where x_0 is an arbitrary constant to be determined by initial conditions. For stability we require that

$$- \alpha(1 - C_y) < 0 \Rightarrow C_y < 1 \tag{1.12}$$

Hence, provided the marginal propensity to consume is less than unity, the system will be stable. Alternatively, the expression $1 - C_y$ is the inverse of the multiplier. Hence, the system will be stable if the multiplier is positive and finite. Notice that the system is stable for any value of α provided this is positive; that is, firms respond to excess demand by increasing output and vice versa.

The particular solution of (1.10) is given by (1.6) since $\alpha (C_0 + I)$ is a constant. Denoting the equilibrium value of Y, which is given by (1.6), as Y^e the solution of (1.10) is

$$Y = x_0 e^{-\alpha(1-C_y)t} + Y^e \tag{1.13}$$

To find the value of x_0 given the initial value of Y, say Y_0, notice that when $t = 0$, (1.13) gives $Y_0 = x_0 + Y^e$. Using the latter (1.13) can be rewritten as

$$Y = (Y_0 - Y^e)e^{-\alpha(1-C_y)t} + Y^e \qquad (1.14)$$

If the system starts in equilibrium (i.e. $Y_0 = Y^e$), the first term of the right hand side of (1.14) is zero and the equation confirms that the system will continue to be in equilibrium. It is obvious from (1.14) that if the system starts in disequilibrium (i.e. $Y_0 - Y^e \neq 0$), it will return to equilibrium at a speed that varies along with α and inversely with the marginal propensity to consume. The higher the marginal propensity to consume or the lower the value of α, the slower the adjustment to equilibrium.

1.5 A Graphical Analysis of the Equilibrium Level of Income

The system of equations (1.1) to (1.4) is analysed in figure 1.2. On the vertical axis we measure aggregate demand and its components, consumption and investment; on the horizontal axis we measure output/income (i.e. aggregate supply). The 45° line, being the locus of points that are equidistant from the x and y axes, is a representation of the equilibrium condition of the goods market, that demand equals supply (equation 1.3). The consumption function, equation (1.2), is represented by the line $C = C_0 + C_y Y$. The intercept is C_0 and the slope is C_y. The restrictions that C_0 is positive and the marginal propensity to consume is less than unity imply that at levels of income below Y_1 consumption exceeds income and therefore households are dissaving, whereas at levels of income higher than Y_1 income exceeds consumption and therefore households are saving. This is a direct consequence of the fact that the consumption function is above and below the 45° line for levels of income lower and higher than Y_1 respectively.

Since investment does not vary with income, it can be represented as a horizontal line, cutting the y axis at a given level of investment. In terms of figure 1.2a, the investment level I_1 is given by the line $I = I_1$. To obtain the aggregate demand function we add, at each level of income, investment to consumption. Thus the AD curve is derived by a parallel shift of the C curve equal to the distance a, the level of investment I_1. The intercept of the aggregate demand function is therefore $C_0 + I_1$ and the slope is C_y. The dynamic adjustment equation (1.4) is represented in figure 1.2b as a negatively sloped line with intercept $\alpha + (C_0 + I_1)$ and slope $-\alpha(1 - C_y)$. The higher the value of α, the steeper the $\dot{Y}$ curve and therefore the faster the adjustment to equilibrium.

Equilibrium is attained when aggregate demand equals aggregate supply. This occurs at point E, corresponding to the output (and income) level Y^e. At levels of income higher than Y^e, such as Y_2, aggregate demand falls short of supply and there is excess supply equal to BB'.

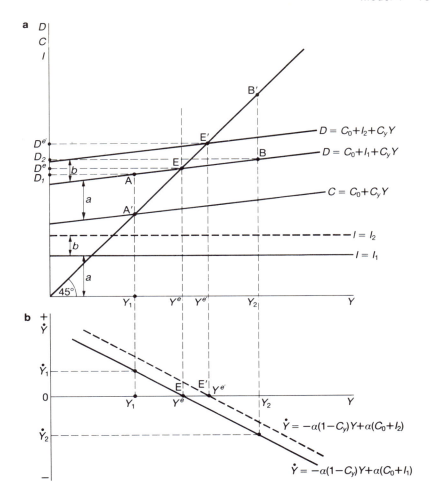

Figure 1.2 The determination of the equilibrium level of output (a) and the dynamics of the system (b)

Firms cannot sell all output produced and there is an unanticipated increase in stocks. Firms respond by cutting output at an initial rate equal to $\dot{Y}_2$. As output, and therefore income, is reduced, both demand for consumption by households and supply are decreased. However, supply falls at a faster rate than demand and therefore the gap between demand and supply is narrowed down. As long as income remains higher than Y^e, supply exceeds demand and firms continue to reduce output, albeit at a slower rate – we move along the $\dot{Y}$ curve towards point E, which corresponds to a zero rate of change of output. Similarly, at levels of income lower than Y^e, such as Y_1, aggregate demand exceeds supply by AA'. Firms find that there is an unanticipated decrease in their stocks and therefore respond by increasing output, at an initial rate equal to $\dot{Y}_1$, in order to replenish their stocks. As output and therefore income increase, both demand for consumption by households and supply increase. However, supply again increases at a faster rate than demand and therefore the level of excess demand is reduced. As long as income remains below Y^e, there is an excess demand and firms respond by increasing output, albeit at a reduced rate – we move along the $\dot{Y}$ curve towards the equilibrium point E.

It must have become apparent by now that the economy portrayed in figure 1.2 is stable; that is, once we move away from the equilibrium point E there are inherent market forces that tend to bring the system back to equilibrium. This system is stable because whenever there is excess demand or supply, output (or production) changes at a faster rate than demand. This is a direct consequence of the fact that the marginal propensity to consume is less than unity. Graphically, the system is stable if the AD curve is flatter than the 45° line. If $C_y > 1$, then demand changes more quickly than supply. In this case, if income is higher than Y^e, demand exceeds supply rather than the other way round. Firms respond by increasing output and therefore income, to which households respond by dissaving even more, thus increasing demand at an even higher rate than supply. Firms then find that the gap between demand and supply is increased rather than decreased and therefore the economy moves even further away from point E. If $C_y = 1$, then, except by sheer luck, equilibrium does not exist, because the AD curve is parallel to the 45° line.

1.6 A Graphical Analysis of Simple Comparative Statics

What will the equilibrium level of income be if investment changes? Suppose that the economy is initially in equilibrium at point E, with income level Y^e, corresponding to investment level I_1. Now, let us assume that investment rises to I_2. This causes an upward shift in the AD curve equal to the distance b – which represents the difference between I_2 and I_1. Equilibrium is now established at E', with a higher level of income, $Y^{e'}$. The rise in investment increases aggregate demand. Firms respond by increasing output and therefore income. Households increase consumption, which increases aggregate demand once again. This, in turn, increases output and income, and the process is repeated until the system converges to point E'. This process is called the multiplier. The system (or the economy) is guaranteed to converge, provided the marginal propensity to consume is less than one. In this case, in every round of increased income, aggregate demand increases only by a fraction – the value of C_y – thus ensuring convergence.

1.7 Summary and Limitations of Model 1

In this simplified economy demand is a function of income. When income increases, aggregate demand also increases. Equilibrium output/income is determined by the level of demand. Hence, fluctuations in demand cause fluctuations in output. Growth in the economy occurs only when demand grows. Equilibrium is attained when demand equals supply. The crude assumptions that have been made greatly restrict the usefulness of the model, but perhaps the greatest limitation of the model is that prices remain fixed, whatever the level of demand. In spite of these limitations the model is useful in illustrating the role of demand in determining the equilibrium level of output/income and emphasizing that business cycles (i.e. fluctuations in output/income) are caused by fluctuations in demand.

2

Model 2 Extension to the Government Sector: an Introduction to Fiscal Policy

2.1 Assumptions

In this model we extend the analysis to include the government sector. This will allow us to introduce fiscal policy and examine how a government can influence the equilibrium level of income/output. We continue with our assumptions of model 1, namely there are two factors of production – labour and capital – but the latter is fixed. There is a single output – GDP. There is no medium of exchange, that is, no money – this is a barter economy. There is no foreign trade – it is a closed economy. Supply is perfectly elastic. This allows us to keep prices fixed. All variables, like income and investment, are expressed in *real terms*. Until model 6, where the assumption of fixed prices is relaxed, there is no reason to distinguish between real and nominal variables. Thus, if on occasions the adjective 'real' is left out this is for convenience.

2.2 The Model

The model consists of equations (2.1) to (2.7).

$$D = C + I + G \tag{2.1}$$

$$C = C_0 + C_y YD; \quad C_0 > 0, \quad 0 < C_y < 1 \tag{2.2}$$

$$YD = Y + TR - T \tag{2.3}$$

$$T = t_0 + t_y Y; \quad 0 \le t_y \le 1 \tag{2.4}$$

$$psbr = G + TR - T \tag{2.5}$$

$$Y = D \tag{2.6}$$

$$\dot{Y} \equiv \frac{\mathrm{d}Y}{\mathrm{d}t} = \alpha(D - Y); \quad \alpha > 0 \tag{2.7}$$

where G is government demand for goods and services – the single product in our case – or planned (real) government expenditure on goods and services, or simply government consumption; YD is (real) disposable income; T is (real) income taxes paid by households to the government (or tax revenues or even tax receipts); TR is (real) transfer payments by the government to the private sector (such as unemployment benefits to households or investment subsidies to firms); $psbr$ is (real) public sector borrowing requirement, that is, what the government needs to borrow to cover the excess of its (real) expenditure over its (real) tax receipts.

The government collects taxes, pays transfers to the private sector and participates in the consumption of the single output produced by the firms. Equation (2.1) shows that the single output is demanded for consumption by households and the government, and for investment by the firms. Equation (2.2) differs from that in model 1 in that it is not total income that determines the level of consumption, but (real) disposable income. The latter is defined in (2.3) as the sum of factor incomes (wages, salaries and profits) and transfer payments received from the government, less income taxes paid to the government.

Equation (2.4) shows that income taxes are levied on factor incomes, Y. The coefficient t_0 can be positive, negative or even zero. When t_0 is positive, it represents lump sum taxes, that is taxes which do not vary with income, such as property taxes. When t_0 is negative, it represents income tax allowances. The coefficient t_y is called the *marginal tax rate*. It shows how much additional tax would have to be paid for a given (say, £1) increase in income. It derives its name from the fact that $dT/dY = t_y$. Equation (2.4), although a simple linear function, includes a variety of tax structures.

A tax structure is called *proportional* when taxes increase in the same proportion as income. A proportional tax structure is obtained when $t_0 = 0$. In this case, $t_y = T/Y$, that is, the marginal tax rate is equal to the average tax rate, T/Y. A tax structure is called *progressive* when taxes increase proportionately more than income. A progressive tax structure is obtained when $t_0 < 0$. In this case, $t_y > T/Y$. This is the most widespread tax structure in the real world. A tax structure is called *regressive* when taxes increase proportionately less than income. A regressive tax structure is obtained when $t_0 > 0$, and implies that $t_y < T/Y$.

Equation (2.5) defines the public sector borrowing requirement as the excess of total government expenditure $(G + TR)$ over tax receipts, T. Total government expenditure consists of government consumption and transfer payments. Equation (2.6) is the equilibrium condition of the goods market. It states that in equilibrium demand equals supply. Equation (2.7) describes the dynamic adjustment of income towards equilibrium. The last two equations are the same as in model 1.

Equations (2.1) to (2.6) determine, at any point in time, the equilibrium values of six endogenous variables (D, C, YD, T, *psbr* and Y) in terms of three exogenous variables (G, I and TR). The logic of the model is as follows. Firms hire the labour services of households to produce a single output. This product is demanded for consumption by households and the government, and for investment by firms. The only endogenous component of aggregate demand is private consumption, which depends on real disposable income – the after-tax income increased by any government transfers. Firms produce whatever is demanded at fixed prices. Equilibrium prevails when demand is equal to supply. The government does not produce anything. It taxes households and uses the proceeds to buy the single output that firms are producing. The government also provides transfer payments to the private sector (e.g. unemployment benefits and social security). If the economy is not in equilibrium, firms respond by increasing output when there is excess demand, and by cutting output when there is excess supply.

2.3 The Determination of the Equilibrium Level of Income

To obtain aggregate demand as a function of income substitute (2.3) into (2.2) and that into (2.1):

$$D = A + C_y(1 - t_y)Y \tag{2.8}$$

where

$$A = C_0 + I + G + C_y TR - C_y t_0 \tag{2.9}$$

The intercept of the aggregate demand function is A, which is defined in (2.9), and its slope is $C_y(1 - t_y)$. Since both the marginal propensity to consume and the marginal tax rate are less than unity the AD curve is flatter than the 45° line.

To obtain the equilibrium value of income substitute (2.8) into (2.6) and solve for Y:

$$Y = \frac{1}{1 - C_y(1 - t_y)} A \tag{2.10}$$

For given values of the parameters C_y and t_y, (2.10) gives the equilibrium level of income as a function of A. If any component of A, like I or G, changes, the equilibrium level of income also changes. The change is measured by the multiplier:

$$\kappa = \frac{\partial Y}{\partial I} = \frac{\partial Y}{\partial G} = \frac{1}{1 - C_y(1 - t_y)} > 0 \tag{2.11}$$

Thus, if $C_y = 0.8$ and $t_y = 0.25$, then $\kappa = 2.5$. This implies that if government expenditure increases by £1 billion ($\Delta G = £1$ billion), income will increase by £2.5 billion ($\Delta Y = £2.5$ billion). The multiplier is an increasing function of C_y and a decreasing function of t_y, i.e.

$$\kappa = \kappa(C_y, t_y); \quad \kappa_c > 0 > \kappa_t \qquad (2.12)$$

where κ_c and κ_t are the partial derivatives of κ with respect to C_y and t_y respectively. Equation (2.12) implies that the higher the marginal propensity to consume, or the lower the marginal tax rate, the greater the multiplier. Hence, business cycles can be caused if any component of A, such as I or G, follows a stochastic process. At the same time, however, the model illustrates the role of government in dampening business cycles. If fluctuations in demand through changes in investment cause business cycles, then fiscal policy can be used to stabilize output and reduce the amplitude of these cycles. The model therefore suggests that the observed fluctuations in output are consistent with larger fluctuations in investment (a large investment multiplier), which are partly offset by fiscal policy.

The effect on *psbr* is obtained by substituting (2.4) into (2.5):

$$psbr = G + TR - t_0 - t_y Y \qquad (2.13)$$

Thus an increase in G or TR increases *psbr*, while an increase in lump sum taxes, the marginal tax rate and income reduces *psbr*.

2.4 Dynamic Adjustment

To obtain the dynamic adjustment path towards equilibrium we substitute (2.8) into (2.7):

$$\frac{dY}{dt} + \alpha(1 - C_y(1 - t_y))Y = \alpha A \qquad (2.14)$$

This is a first-order differential equation. Its solution is

$$Y = (Y_0 - Y^e)e^{-\alpha(1 - C_y(1 - t_y))t} + Y^e \qquad (2.15)$$

where Y^e is the equilibrium value of income given by (2.10). For stability we require that

$$-\alpha(1 - C_y(1 - t_y)) < 0 \Rightarrow 1 - C_y(1 - t_y) > 0 \qquad (2.16)$$

The expression $1 - C_y(1 - t_y)$ is the inverse of the multiplier, $1/\kappa$. Therefore, the system will be stable provided the multiplier is positive. Equation (2.15) implies that whenever the system is in disequilibrium, it will return to equilibrium at a speed that depends on the inverse of the multiplier. The lower the marginal propensity to consume or the higher the marginal tax rate, the faster the speed of convergence.

2.5 A Graphical Analysis

The way model 2 works is analysed in figure 2.1. In figure 2.1a we measure aggregate demand and its components on the y axis and output/ income (or aggregate supply) on the x axis. The 45° line is a representation of the equilibrium condition in the goods market, equation (2.6).

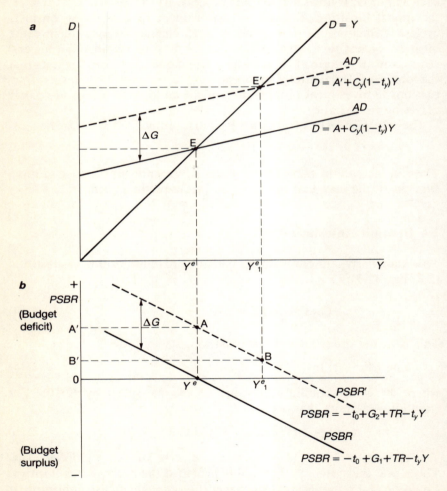

Figure 2.1 The effects of an increase in government expenditure on the level of output (a) and *psbr* (b)

Aggregate demand, equation (2.8), is represented by the AD curve, with intercept A and slope $C_y(1 - t_y)$. Since both C_y and t_y are less than unity, the AD curve is flatter than the 45° line. The AD curve shows the level of aggregate demand as a function of income. When income increases, aggregate demand also increases. The reason is that households are prepared to spend more on consumption as disposable income is increased. That the AD curve is flatter than the 45° line is a direct consequence of the fact that for any given increase in factor incomes consumers spend on consumption only a fraction of that increase. The rest is allocated to additional taxes and savings. This follows from the identity

$$YD \equiv C + S$$

where S is savings. This identity asserts that households either consume or save their disposable income. The household choice problem is how to allocate its given disposable income between consumption and savings. The first-order condition of this optimization problem is the consumption function.

The intersection of the AD curve with the 45° line determines the equilibrium level of income. At point E, aggregate demand equals aggregate supply in the economy. If income is greater than Y^e, supply exceeds demand, firms find that they cannot sell all output produced and therefore they respond by cutting production. As they do so, factor incomes are reduced and thus demand is also curtailed, but at a slower rate than production. We thus move towards the equilibrium point E. The flatter the AD curve, the smaller the decrease in demand for any given change in income. This guarantees fast convergence to equilibrium.

In figure 2.1b, we measure income/output on the x axis and *psbr* on the y axis. A positive *psbr* means that the budget is in deficit, and vice versa. The intercept of the $PSBR$ curve is $-t_0 + G + TR$, and its slope is $-t_y$. At the equilibrium level of income, Y^e, the $PSBR$ curve cuts the horizontal axis. This implies that at that level of income the budget is balanced and therefore *psbr* is zero.

2.6 Fiscal Policy

A government, or policy-maker, has four different ways of affecting the equilibrium level of income. It can change the level of government expenditure, G, lump sum taxes, t_0, the marginal tax rate, t_y, or even the amount of transfers, TR. These are called the instruments of fiscal policy. Any action by the government to change the values of these instruments is an implementation of fiscal policy. The government can change any single instrument or all of them in any particular combination. The choice depends on the government's objectives. For example, if the objective is to maximize the effect on income, the most effective instrument, as we shall see, is government expenditure. But if the objective is to stimulate the economy while reducing the size of the government sector (as measured by G/Y), the most effective policy is to reduce income taxes. The effectiveness of each instrument is measured by the corresponding multiplier. The higher the multiplier, the greater the effect on income.

Fiscal policy is said to be *expansionary* or *easy* if there is an increase in either government expenditure or transfer payments, or a decrease in the marginal tax rate or in lump sum taxes. Conversely, if there is a decrease in government expenditure or transfer payments, or an increase in the marginal tax rate or lump sum taxes, fiscal policy is said to be *contractionary* or *tight*. When more than one instrument changes at the same time and in conflicting ways, such as an increase in government expenditure and the marginal tax rate, then we need a more meaningful measure of the stance of fiscal policy. This is the change from year to year in the cyclically adjusted *psbr*. The change in *psbr* measures the importance of the change in the instruments. The cyclical adjustment is necessary because in a recession taxes fall and therefore *psbr* rises even though this is not the result of a discretionary change in the stance of fiscal policy. Similarly, in a boom taxes rise and therefore *psbr* falls. Again this is not the result of tight fiscal policy. The cyclically adjusted *psbr* can be measured in a simple way by the ratio of the year-to-year change in the *psbr* to nominal GNP or GDP. Alternatively, and perhaps more sophisticatedly, this can be measured by the change in *psbr* that is due to deviations of output from its potential path.

Increase in Government Expenditure

The government expenditure multiplier is obtained by partially differentiating (2.10) with respect to G and is given by (2.11). The size of the multiplier depends on the values of the marginal propensity to consume and the marginal tax rate. The way an increase in government expenditure affects the equilibrium level of income can be analysed with the help of figure 2.1. Such an increase shifts the AD and *psbr* curves upwards by an amount equal to ΔG. Equilibrium is established at E', the intersection of AD' with the 45° line, at a higher level of income, Y_1^e. The increase in government expenditure increases aggregate demand. At the initial level of income there is an excess demand in the goods market. Firms respond by increasing output. This leads to increased factor incomes and real disposable income. Households respond by increasing their consumption demand and this further boosts aggregate demand. The cycle is completed – an increase in government expenditure increases aggregate demand which, through an increase in income, leads to a second round of increased aggregate demand. This is the multiplier. It is effectively a process of repeated cycles of increases in aggregate demand and income. The process will converge provided the increase in aggregate demand in each round is smaller than the increase in real disposable income. This is guaranteed provided (2.16) holds. This will be the case if the government taxes income so that the increase in disposable income is less than the increase in income. An alternative condition is that households do not spend all the increase in income on consumption, that is, they save.

At the new equilibrium level Y_1^e, *psbr* is positive and therefore the budget is in deficit. However, the increase in *psbr*, at the new equilibrium, is not as big as ΔG. This implies that an increase in government expenditure is partly self-financed. At the initial level of income, Y^e, *psbr* is increased by ΔG. However, as income increases, tax revenues also increase, which brings down *psbr*: we move from A to B along the *PSBR'* curve. The degree of self-finance depends on t_y. The higher the marginal tax rate, the greater are taxes and therefore the smaller *psbr* at the new equilibrium. In terms of figure 2.1b, the higher t_y, the steeper is the *PSBR* curve and therefore, for any given level of income, the smaller *psbr*.

A government can stimulate the level of economic activity in the economy, measured by GDP, by boosting demand through increased government expenditure. This will reduce unemployment because the only variable factor of production is labour. That is, to meet the increased demand firms will have to employ more people to boost production. Conversely, if a government reduces its expenditure, the economy will be thrown into a recession. For most economies the government expenditure multiplier is slightly higher than unity. This implies that the rise in GDP will be proportionately larger than the increase in government expenditure. In the context of model 2 a typical value of the multiplier is 2.5, which is obtained when $C_y = 0.8$ and $t_y = 0.25$. This implies that if a government reduces (increases) its expenditure by £1 billion, income will fall (rise) by £2.5 billion. It therefore follows that, in the context of model 2, government decisions about the level of its expenditure can be very important in either causing or dampening business cycles.

Income Tax Cut

An income tax cut, in the context of model 2, takes the form of a decrease in either lump sum taxes, t_0, or the marginal tax rate, t_y. The effectiveness of each instrument is measured by the corresponding multiplier. These are obtained by partially differentiating (2.10) with respect to t_0 and t_y.

$$\frac{\partial Y}{\partial t_0} = \frac{-C_y}{1 - C_y(1 - t_y)} < 0 \qquad (2.17)$$

$$\frac{\partial Y}{\partial t_y} = \frac{-C_y Y}{1 - C_y(1 - t_y)} < 0 \qquad (2.18)$$

The effect of reducing the marginal tax rate is highlighted in figure 2.2. Initial equilibrium is at E, with income Y^e and the budget balanced. Now the government decides to reduce the marginal tax rate from t_y to t'_y. This has the effect of pivoting the *AD* and *PSBR* curves around the intercept, from *AD* and *PSBR* to *AD'* and *PSBR'* respectively in figure

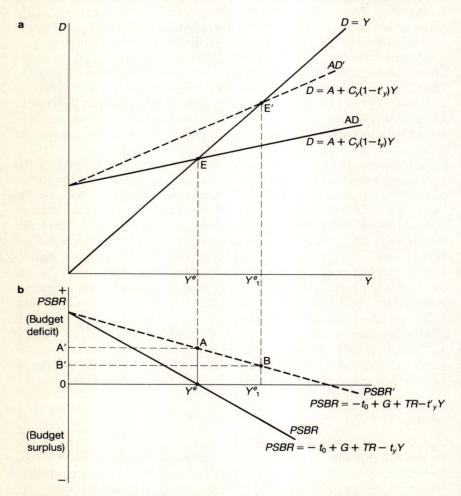

Figure 2.2   The effects of a cut in the marginal tax rate on the level of output **(a)** and *psbr* **(b)**

2.2 a and b. The new equilibrium is established at E', the intersection of the new AD curve with the 45° line. Income has increased from Y^e to Y^e_1.

The economic rationale of the increase in income is as follows. The income tax cut implies that real disposable income rises, which leads households to increase their consumption. This means that aggregate demand increases by the same amount. Firms respond to this excess demand by increasing output, which entails an equivalent rise in factor incomes. The latter leads to a second round of increase in real disposable income. The cycle is completed – an income tax cut leads to a rise in real disposable income, which through boosting demand leads to another rise in income and thus in real disposable income. The process repeats itself an infinite number of times, but each time the extra stimulus will progressively decline. Convergence is guaranteed because the government is subtracting a fraction t_y out of every extra pound in factor incomes and households spend only a fraction on consumption out of any extra pound in real disposable income. This fraction is measured by the marginal propensity to consume. The residual is saved. The total increase in income/output is measured by the size of the multiplier.

At the new equilibrium level of income, the psbr is OB' and the budget is in deficit. The income tax cut is partly self-financed. At the initial income level, *psbr* rises by OA'. However, as the economy is stimulated, more taxes are generated and therefore *psbr* is reduced, we move along the *PSBR'* curve from A to B.

2.7 Effectiveness of Fiscal Instruments

An instrument of fiscal policy is said to be more effective than another if it has a bigger effect on income. The effectiveness of each instrument is therefore measured by the corresponding multiplier. The income multipliers with respect to government expenditure, lump sum taxes and the marginal tax rate have already been obtained and discussed. These are given in (2.11), (2.17) and (2.18) respectively. The income multiplier with respect to transfers, TR, is obtained by partially differentiating (2.10) with respect to TR

$$\frac{\partial Y}{\partial TR} = \frac{C_y}{1 - C_y(1 - t_y)} > 0 \qquad (2.19)$$

An increase in transfers to the private sector (e.g. unemployment benefits) increases income/output. A cursory look at (2.17) and (2.19) reveals that the two multipliers are equal but of opposite sign. Thus, if the government were to increase transfers and lump sum taxes by an equal amount (i.e. $\Delta TR = \Delta t_0$), the effect on income would be zero.

Since C_y is less than unity, it follows, by comparing (2.11) with (2.17) and (2.19), that the government expenditure multiplier is greater than the transfers or lump sum taxes multipliers (in absolute terms). This implies that if the government has £X to spend, then an increase in government expenditure will have a bigger effect on income than either an increase in transfers or a decrease in lump sum taxes by the same amount (i.e. $\Delta G = \Delta TR = -\Delta t_0 = £X$). Therefore the most effective instrument of fiscal policy is government expenditure. Hence, if a government wants to reduce unemployment and has £X to spend for that purpose, it should use that money in the form of increasing government expenditure. Any other form of spending that money will have a smaller effect on income and therefore on employment.

2.8 Balanced-budget Multiplier

It has been shown that an increase in government expenditure or an income tax cut, although partly self-financed, lead to a budget deficit. The question therefore arises as to whether a government can still stimulate income if it does not want to run a budget deficit. In this case the government would have to raise taxes to cover the extra expenditure. Let us assume that the government decides to raise lump sum taxes. The effect on income of increasing both government expenditure and lump sum taxes is obtained by taking the total differential of (2.10) with respect to G and t_0.

$$\Delta Y = \frac{1}{1 - C_y(1 - t_y)} \Delta G + \frac{-C_y}{1 - C_y(1 - t_y)} \Delta t_0 \qquad (2.20)$$

If we increase lump sum taxes by the same amount as government expenditure (i.e. if $\Delta G = \Delta t_0$), the budget will end up in surplus. The reason is that as income rises more taxes are generated. The change in lump sum taxes will produce a change in total tax revenues equal to

$$\Delta T = \Delta t_0 + t_y \Delta Y \qquad (2.21)$$

which is obtained by taking the total differential of (2.4) with respect to t_0 and Y. Hence, if we increase lump sum taxes and government expenditure by the same amount, the surplus in the budget will be equal to $t_y \Delta Y$. In order to find by how much we need to increase lump sum taxes so that the budget will be just balanced (i.e. $\Delta G = \Delta T$), we solve (2.21) for Δt_0 and substitute into (2.20):

$$\Delta Y = \frac{1}{1 - C_y(1 - t_y)} \Delta G + \frac{-C_y}{1 - C_y(1 - t_y)} (\Delta G - t_y \Delta Y) \qquad (2.22)$$

Solving for ΔY and simplifying we obtain

$$\Delta Y = \Delta G \tag{2.23}$$

That is, income will increase by the same amount as government expenditure and the budget will be balanced in the new equilibrium. In other words, the balanced-budget multiplier is unity. This unit value is the result of the particular assumptions of this model. However, the balanced-budget multiplier is generally positive but less than unity in more complex models.

2.9 The Transmission of Fiscal Policy – a Summary

There are two routes via which the instruments of fiscal policy (G, TR, t_0 and t_y) affect the equilibrium level of income/output, Y. Box 2.1 provides a schematic representation of the transmission mechanism of fiscal policy.

Box 2.1 The transmission of fiscal policy

$$G\uparrow \Rightarrow D\uparrow \Rightarrow Y\uparrow \Rightarrow YD\uparrow \Rightarrow C\uparrow \Rightarrow D\uparrow \tag{a}$$

$$TR\uparrow \text{ or } t_0\downarrow \text{ or } t_y\downarrow \Rightarrow YD\uparrow \Rightarrow C\uparrow \Rightarrow D\uparrow \Rightarrow Y\uparrow \Rightarrow YD\uparrow \tag{b}$$

Government expenditure operates through route (a). Since G is a constituent part of D, we know from (2.1) that an increase in the former will lead to an increase in the latter ($G\uparrow \Rightarrow D\uparrow$). At the initial level of income there is an excess demand (i.e. $D - Y > 0$). From (2.7) we know that firms respond to an excess demand by increasing output and therefore income ($D\uparrow \Rightarrow Y\uparrow$). Assuming that the government does not tax away all the increase in income (i.e. $t_y < 1$), we know from equations (2.4) and (2.3) that YD will also rise ($Y\uparrow \Rightarrow YD\uparrow$). This leads, through (2.2), to an increase in C ($YD\uparrow \Rightarrow C\uparrow$). Finally, to complete the cycle, we know from (2.1) that C is a constituent part of D and therefore a rise in the former leads to a rise in the latter ($C\uparrow \Rightarrow D\uparrow$). From equation (2.7) we know that firms will continue increasing production (i.e. $dY/dt > 0$) as long as there is an excess demand. This tells us that the cycle just described will repeat itself until equilibrium is reached. This, we know from (2.6), will happen when demand equals supply.

Transfers, lump sum taxes and the marginal tax rate operate through route (b). We know from (2.3) and (2.4) that an increase in TR, a decrease in t_0 or a decrease in t_y will lead to a rise in disposable income ($TR\uparrow$ or $t_0\downarrow$ or $t_y\downarrow \Rightarrow YD\uparrow$). We also know from (2.2) that households respond to an increase in disposable income by increasing their consumption ($YD\uparrow \Rightarrow C\uparrow$). This leads, through (2.1), to an increase in aggregate demand ($C\uparrow \Rightarrow D\uparrow$). At the initial level of income there is an excess demand (i.e. $D - Y > 0$). Firms respond to an excess demand by increasing production and therefore income ($D\uparrow \Rightarrow Y\uparrow$). Provided the government does not tax away the whole increase in income, real disposable income wil rise ($Y\uparrow \Rightarrow YD\uparrow$). A cycle is completed – an initial increase in disposable income, caused by a change in one of the fiscal instruments (TR, t_0, t_y), leads, through an increase in demand, to another increase in disposable income. The process repeats itself for as long as there is an excess demand.

A comparison of the two routes explains why government expenditure has a greater impact on income than do the other instruments of fiscal policy. Government expenditure is a constituent component of aggregate demand and therefore an increase in the former leads to an equal increase in the latter. An increase in transfers or a cut in taxes by the same amount as the increase in government expenditure leads to a smaller boost in aggregate demand. The reason is that only a fraction of the increase in transfers or cut in income taxes is allocated to consumption; the rest is saved.

2.10 Summary and Limitations of Model 2

The logic of this model is very simple. The economy is in equilibrium when demand is equal to supply. The level of demand determines equilibrium income/output. Whenever there is excess demand firms respond by increasing output and therefore income. The role of fiscal policy follows from the above two propositions. Any action by the government that stimulates demand, either through increases in government expenditure and transfers or through tax cuts, will lead to higher income (i.e. growth) and lower unemployment. The implication of this model is therefore that the government should carry on stimulating demand. Obviously this is an erroneous conclusion, which follows from the assumption that supply continues to be perfectly elastic at all levels of demand. As demand increases, sooner or later bottlenecks will emerge, either through more intensive utilization of existing capital, which is fixed, or because labour becomes scarce as we approach full employment. Either way, firms will not be able to increase production at unchanged prices. It therefore follows that if the government carries on stimulating demand *ad infinitum*, it will just be feeding more and more inflation. Is the model therefore useless? The answer is no! If the economy is in recession, with under-utilization of its existing capital stock and unemployed labour, the government can stimulate demand

and therefore drive the economy out of the recession by using expansionary fiscal policy (i.e. increasing G or TR and cutting t_0 or t_y). The danger of generating inflation is very small because, at low levels of demand, like those in the 1930s and early 1980s, supply can be expected to be perfectly or near-perfectly elastic. The decomposition of the fiscal stimulus will be more on output than on inflation.

The model is also useful in suggesting that business cycles are caused by fluctuations in demand. The model suggests that the observed fluctuations in output are consistent with larger fluctuations in investment, which are partly offset by fiscal policy.

We have seen that a fiscal stimulus that relies on any single instrument alone, produces a budget deficit at the new equilibrium. The model ignores the consequences of financing this deficit for the equilibrium level of output. Nevertheless, one can argue that a combination of two instruments will bypass the problem of leaving behind a budget deficit – recall the balanced-budget multiplier.

We have singled out two important limitations of the model. It is obvious that all the simplifying assumptions we have made so far are limiting the usefulness of the model. In later chapters, we shall systematically relax these assumptions in an effort to build more realistic models.

3

Model 3 Extension to the Monetary Sector: an Introduction to Monetary Policy

The assumption of a barter economy is relaxed in this model. The introduction of a medium of exchange leads to an analysis of the role of money in the economy through an explicit consideration of the assets markets. This changes fundamentally the nature of the equilibrating process in the economy. In the models examined so far, equilibrium income/output is determined in the goods market alone by the condition that aggregate demand equals aggregate supply. The extension of the analysis to the assets markets implies that equilibrium income/output is determined through the interaction of the goods and assets markets. This will qualify the conclusions reached in model 2 about the role of fiscal policy. Model 3 will allow us to introduce monetary policy and examine how a government can influence the equilibrium level of income/output.

3.1 Assumptions

The only assumption we relax is that of a barter economy. All other assumptions made in model 2 still hold: there are two factors of production, labour and capital, but the latter is fixed; there is a single output, GDP; there is no foreign trade, a closed economy; supply is perfectly elastic. This means that prices remain unchanged whatever the level of demand. In considering the assets markets we have to introduce some extra assumptions. There are only two assets – money and government bonds. Private sector wealth is fixed.

3.2 The Model

The model consists of equations (3.1) to (3.15).

$$D = C + I + G \tag{3.1}$$

$$C = C_0 + C_y YD; \quad C_0 > 0, \quad 0 < C_y < 1 \tag{3.2}$$

$$I = I_0 + I_r r; \quad I_r < 0 \tag{3.3}$$

$$Y = D \tag{3.4}$$

$$YD = Y + TR - T \tag{3.5}$$

$$T = t_0 + t_y Y; \quad 0 \le t_y \le 1 \tag{3.6}$$

$$psbr = G + TR - T \tag{3.7}$$

$$m^d = M_y Y + M_r (r - r^d); \quad M_y > 0 > M_r \tag{3.8}$$

$$b^d = B_y Y + B_r (r - r^d); \quad B_y < 0 < B_r \tag{3.9}$$

$$m^d = m \tag{3.10}$$

$$b^d = b \tag{3.11}$$

$$v = m + b \tag{3.12}$$

$$v = m^d + b^d \tag{3.13}$$

$$\frac{dY}{dt} = \alpha_1 (D - Y); \quad \alpha_1 > 0 \tag{3.14}$$

$$\frac{dr}{dt} = \alpha_2 (m^d - m); \quad \alpha_2 > 0 \tag{3.15}$$

where m^d is demand for real money balances (demand for money); m is the real money stock (money supply); b^d is real demand for government bonds; b is the stock of government bonds (in real terms); r^d is the interest rate on deposits; r is the interest rate (yield) on government bonds, equal also to the interest rate charged by banks on loans; v is private sector real wealth (accumulation of past savings).

Equations (3.1) to (3.7) are the same as those used in model 2, with the exception of (3.3). Equations (3.1) to (3.4) describe the goods market. Equation (3.3) makes investment an endogenous variable determined by the interest rate. As the interest rate rises, the cost of finance increases and this deters new investment (i.e. $I_r < 0$). The coefficient I_r measures the interest rate sensitivity of investment. If investment is highly responsive to the interest rate, a small reduction in the interest rate will lead to a large increase in investment, and vice versa. The coefficient I_0 measures the degree of *autonomous investment*, that is, the part of investment undertaken at zero interest rate.

Investment also depends on demand conditions and therefore on income (or the change in income). However, the inclusion of income as a determinant of investment would not have changed qualitatively the results of model 3, because aggregate demand already depends on income through its effect on consumption.

3.3 The Assets Markets

Equations (3.8) to (3.13) describe the assets markets. We assume that there are only two assets, money and government bonds. Money is a difficult concept to define. The well known phrase that 'money is what money does' summarizes the principle that money is defined according to its functions. The problem with such an approach is that money plays more than one function and many assets fulfil, to a varying degree, these functions. The primary role of money is that of a medium of exchange or a means of payment. This implies that money is whatever can be generally accepted in settlement for purchases. This corresponds to the *narrow* definition of the money stock. The statistical definition that corresponds to the medium of exchange function of money is what is called M_1: currency (notes and coin in circulation) and demand deposits (current accounts) on which cheques can be written. But why stop there? Time deposits (or deposit accounts), especially at the short end, like those that operate on a seven-day notice, can also be used as a means of payment very easily and at little cost. The holder of such an account can write a cheque on his or her current account and instruct the bank to transfer this sum of money from the deposit to the current account at the cost of losing seven days' interest. This line of argument makes it very difficult to decide in practice where the dividing line between money and its close substitutes should be drawn. Since changes in statistical definitions occur less frequently than financial innovations, there will always be some dispute whether this or that asset should also be included in the medium of exchange function of money.

Money has another important function: it is a *store of value*. What distinguishes money from other financial assets, like bonds and equities, is that money has a fixed value, whereas the other assets do not. Their price is variable, it continuously fluctuates as demand conditions in the stock exchange are changing. Clearly, all forms of time deposits fulfil the store of value function of money. The appropriate definition is that of *broad* or *wide* money. In the UK, the inclusion, in addition to M_1, of 'time' or deposit accounts with the clearing banks and building societies corresponds to M_4 – the broad definition of the money stock. In this model the discussion on money applies equally to a narrow or wide definition of money.

The demand for money depends on the level of real income, Y, and the cost of holding money. The latter is the interest that is foregone by holding money and not higher interest earning assets (like bonds in the context of this model). The cost of holding money (also called the opportunity cost) is measured by the difference between the interest offered on government bonds, r, and the interest that money earns, r^d. The latter is zero for cash and most current accounts and positive, but less than r, for deposit accounts. The higher the interest rate on government bonds relative to the return on money, the more costly it is to hold money (i.e. $M_r < 0$). Thus, for a given interest rate on money, the demand for money will be lower, the greater the interest rate on government bonds. For a given interest rate on government bonds, the demand for money will be higher, the greater the interest rate on money. The coefficient M_r measures the interest sensitivity of the demand for money. The larger this coefficient is in absolute terms (i.e. $|M_r|$), the greater the sensitivity of the demand for money with respect to the interest rate on bonds relative to the return of money. If the demand for money is highly responsive to the interest rate, a small decline in the interest rate will lead to a large increase in the demand for money.

The demand for real money balances also depends on the level of income. The reason is that individuals hold money balances to finance their expenditure, which, in turn, depends on income. The higher the level of income is, the higher the level of expenditure and therefore the greater the demand for money. Hence, the demand for money is an increasing function of the level of income (i.e. $M_y > 0$). The coefficient M_y measures the income sensitivity of the demand for money. If the demand for money is highly responsive to income, a small increase in income will lead to a large increase in the demand for money.

The supply of money is assumed to be under the control of the central bank (the Bank of England in the UK or the Federal Reserve System in the USA). In our model this is reflected in the assumption that the supply of money, m, is exogenous. In the real world, however, the supply of money is an endogenous variable. A policy of monetary targets aims at controlling the money supply through other instruments, such as the discount rate or open market operations. A successful policy of monetary targets means that the money supply is under the control of the central bank and therefore corresponds to our assumption that it is exogenous.

The demand for government bonds depends on the level of income and the relative return on government bonds. For a given level of wealth, the higher the level of income is, the greater the transactions demand for money and the smaller the demand for bonds (i.e. $M_y > 0$ and $B_y < 0$). That is, in the short run (i.e. when wealth has not yet changed) an increase in the demand for money is financed by selling bonds. The relative return on government bonds is measured by the excess of the interest rate offered on bonds over the interest rate offered on money, $r - r^d$. In other words, the relative return on government bonds is equal, but of opposite sign, to the cost of holding money. Thus, an increase in the yield of bonds relative to the return of money leads to a higher demand for bonds and, as we have seen, to a lower demand for money (i.e. $B_r > 0$ and $M_r < 0$).

As we shall see later on, the supply of government bonds is determined by considerations on how to finance the government's budget deficit. These are outside the scope of the present model and we shall therefore assume that the supply of government bonds, b, is exogenously determined. The bond market is in equilibrium when demand equals supply (equation 3.11).

We have seen that changes in income and interest rates cause the demand for money and bonds to change in opposite directions. The relationship between the two demand functions can better be seen through the definition of private sector wealth, equation (3.12). This states that real financial wealth consists of real money balances and real bonds in existence. But this is an accounting identity, it must always hold. It says nothing as to whether individuals are happy to hold these stocks. At any point in time, individuals have to decide how to allocate a given size of wealth between money and bonds. This is a *portfolio decision* and is summarized by (3.13), which is the *wealth budget constraint*. This states that the demand for real money balances and the demand for real bond holdings must add up to the real private sector financial wealth. However, the two decisions about how much to hold of each asset are not independent. Since wealth is fixed, a decision to hold so much in terms of money implies a decision about how much to hold in bonds. That is, once a decision is made about how much to hold in terms of one of the assets, the demand for the other is obtained as a residual from the wealth budget constraint. Thus, the portfolio choice problem is well specified in terms of one asset demand function and the wealth budget constraint. The other demand function is redundant and therefore can be dropped. We choose to cast the discussion in terms of the money market and hence we drop the bond market. The wealth budget constraint implies a relationship between the two markets in both equilibrium and disequilibrium. This can be seen if we subtract (3.12) from (3.13):

$$(m^d - m) + (b^d - b) = 0 \qquad\qquad (3.16)$$

The first term represents excess demand for money and the second excess demand for bonds. Equation (3.16) implies that when the money market is in equilibrium the bond market is also in equilibrium. Similarly, when there is excess demand for money there is an excess supply of bonds, and vice versa.

The dynamic adjustment of the money market towards equilibrium is described by equation (3.15). What it says is that the interest rate rises when demand exceeds supply in the money market and vice versa. The rate at which the interest rate adjusts is proportional to the excess demand/supply. The equivalence of the two markets implies that the dynamic adjustment of the interest rate could have been expressed in terms of an excess demand/supply of bonds. In this case, the interest rate rises (and the price of bonds falls, see note 1) whenever there is an excess supply of bonds.

3.4 A Summary of the Model

Given our earlier analysis of the equivalence of the money and bonds market, and the simplifying assumptions that wealth and the interest rate on money are fixed, the model can be reduced to the following equations:

$$D = C + I + G \tag{3.17}$$

$$C = C_0 + C_y YD; \quad C_0 > 0, \quad 0 < C_y < 1 \tag{3.18}$$

$$I = I_0 + I_r r; \quad I_r < 0 \tag{3.19}$$

$$Y = D \tag{3.20}$$

$$YD = Y + TR - T \tag{3.21}$$

$$T = t_0 + t_y Y; \quad 0 \leq t_y \leq 1 \tag{3.22}$$

$$psbr = G + TR - T \tag{3.23}$$

$$m^d = M_y Y + M_r r; \quad M_y > 0 > M_r \tag{3.24}$$

$$m^d = m \tag{3.25}$$

$$\frac{dY}{dt} = \alpha_1 (D - Y); \quad \alpha_1 > 0 \tag{3.26}$$

$$\frac{dr}{dt} = \alpha_2 (m^d - m); \quad \alpha_2 > 0 \tag{3.27}$$

These are reproduced here for convenience.

The model can be solved in two different ways, according to the conduct (*modus operandi*) of monetary policy:

1 A policy of monetary targets – endogenous interest rates. The authorities set a target for the money supply, for example x per cent growth from year to year, or a target range for the rate of growth, say between 4 and 6 per cent. The central bank attempts to control the supply of money through the discount rate (the rate at which it provides liquidity to commercial banks) or open market operations (i.e. buying or selling of government bonds through the government broker in the stock exchange).[1] In this case the government decides on the amount of bonds and the market determines the price (and therefore the interest rate) at which it wants to hold this stock of bonds. The assumption that the central bank can control the supply of money

in the real world through open market operations is obviously a heroic one! A successful policy of monetary targets is represented in this model by assuming that the money supply, m, is the instrument of monetary policy and the interest rate, r, is an endogenous variable.

2 A policy of interest rate targets – endogenous money supply. The authorities decide on the price (and thus the level of the interest rate) at which government bonds will be sold and the market determines the stock of bonds it wishes to hold at that price. In other words, the authorities control the interest rate by supplying whatever amount of bonds the private sector wishes to hold. In this case the instrument of monetary policy is the interest rate and the money supply, m, and hence the stock of bonds, b, are market determined, that is endogenous variables.

In the real world the central bank may have some target range for the money supply and also a target for a key short-term interest rate, like the three-month interbank rate in the UK or the Fed funds rate in the USA, provided these are chosen consistently, i.e. they represent a point on the *LM* curve (see below). However, interest rates at the long end of the market, like r in our model, are still market-determined. The central bank may wish to influence the long end of the market by making the supply of bonds, and therefore the interest rate, perfectly elastic at a given price. However, the central bank is very much restricted in its ability to control the long-term interest rate because in modern financial markets, where capital is perfectly mobile, this rate cannot deviate a lot and for a long time from the international rate.

The set of equations (3.17) to (3.25) determines, at any point in time, the equilibrium values of D, C, I, Y, YD, T, $psbr$, m^d, and m or r according to the *modus operandi* of monetary policy. Finally, equations (3.26) and (3.27) describe the adjustment of the economic system to equilibrium.

3.5 The Determination of Income and the Interest Rate

The equilibrium condition of the goods market can be obtained as follows. Substitute (3.22) into (3.21) and that into (3.18). Substitute the resulting equation and (3.19) into (3.17). We thus obtain

$$D = C_0 + I_0 + G - C_y t_0 + C_y TR + I_r r + C_y (1 - t_y) Y \qquad (3.28)$$

Aggregate demand depends positively on income and negatively on the interest rate. Thus, an increase in income stimulates aggregate demand, whereas a rise in the interest rate causes a decline in aggregate demand.

Since the interest rate is affected by monetary policy, the latter has an indirect effect on aggregate demand. Fiscal policy also has an effect on the level of aggregate demand in the economy through the level of expenditure on goods and services, G, transfer payments, TR, and the tax rates, t_0 and t_y. An increase in either G or TR causes an expansion in aggregate demand, whereas a rise in either t_0 or t_y produces a contraction.

Equilibrium in the goods market is obtained when demand equals supply. We can therefore substitute (3.28) into (3.20) and solve for Y. We thus obtain

$$(1 - C_y(1 - t_y))Y = C_0 + I_0 + G - C_y t_0 + C_y TR + I_r r \qquad (3.29)$$

It is obvious from (3.29) that whenever the interest rate changes, the equilibrium level of income changes, too. Since the interest rate is affected by conditions in the money market, it follows that the goods market cannot be in equilibrium unless the money market is also in equilibrium. In technical terms we have two endogenous variables, Y and r, and only one equation. It is customary to solve (3.29) with respect to the interest rate. This relationship is called the IS curve.

$$IS: r = -\frac{1}{I_r}(C_0 + I_0 + G - C_y t_0 + C_y TR) + \frac{1 - C_y(1 - t_y)}{I_r}Y \qquad (3.30)$$

The IS curve is the locus of points (Y, r) such that the goods market is in equilibrium. The slope of the IS curve is

$$\left.\frac{\partial r}{\partial Y}\right|_{is} = \frac{1 - C_y(1 - t_y)}{I_r} = \frac{1}{\kappa I_r} < 0 \qquad (3.31)$$

where κ is the simple fiscal multiplier of model 2

$$\kappa = \frac{1}{1 - C_y(1 - t_y)} \qquad (3.32)$$

Since κ is positive but I_r is negative, it follows that the slope of the IS curve is negative. The economic rationale is that a reduction in the interest rate stimulates investment, aggregate demand expands and therefore firms respond by increasing output/income. In the (Y, r) space, the smaller κ and/or $|I_r|$ is (i.e. the smaller the multiplier and/or the less the interest sensitivity of investment), the steeper is the IS curve.

The position of the IS curve depends on fiscal policy. A shift to the right or an anti-clockwise rotation implies easy fiscal policy. A shift to the left or a clockwise rotation implies a tight fiscal policy. Neutral fiscal policy means that the IS curve remains fixed at its initial position.

For example, an increase in government expenditure stimulates, at any given interest rate, demand and therefore income. This is reflected as a rightward shift in the *IS* curve and represents easy fiscal policy. Similarly, at any given interest rate, an increase in transfers causes a rise in disposable income. This stimulates demand and therefore income through increased consumption. Hence, an increase in transfers causes a rightward shift in the *IS* curve and thus represents easy fiscal policy. A fall in lump sum taxes raises disposable income, hence consumption and demand and accordingly income/output. Thus, at a given interest rate the *IS* curve shifts to the right as a result of a fall in lump sum taxes – fiscal policy is easy. A change in the marginal tax rate, however, affects the slope rather than the position of the *IS* curve. A fall in the marginal tax rate results in an anti-clockwise pivoting of the *IS* curve with respect to the vertical axis. At a given level of interest rates, reduced taxes imply higher disposable income and thus increased consumption, demand and income. Fiscal policy is again easy.

The way the money market behaves is obtained by substituting (3.24) into (3.25) and solving for *r*. The relationship between income and the interest rate that describes assets markets equilibrium is called the *LM* curve.

$$LM: r = \frac{1}{M_r} m - \frac{M_y}{M_r} Y \tag{3.33}$$

The *LM* curve shows combinations of income and the interest rate such that the assets markets are in equilibrium. (Recall that when the money market is in equilibrium the bond market is in equilibrium too.) The slope of the *LM* curve is

$$\left. \frac{\partial r}{\partial Y} \right|_{lm} = - \frac{M_y}{M_r} > 0 \tag{3.34}$$

Since M_y is positive and M_r is negative, it follows that the *LM* curve is positively sloped. The economic rationale is that as income rises the demand for money for transactions purposes increases. People need more money to finance an increased volume of transactions. For a given money supply, there is an excess demand for money at the increased level of income and the interest rate has to rise to keep the assets markets in equilibrium. In the (Y, r) space, the larger M_y and the smaller $|M_r|$ are (i.e. the greater the income sensitivity of the demand for money and the smaller, in absolute terms, the interest sensitivity of the demand for money), the steeper is the *LM* curve.

The position of the *LM* curve depends on the level of the money supply, *M*. At any given level of the interest rate, as the money stock in the economy is increased people hold more money and therefore they are able to finance an increased volume of transactions, thus causing a rise in income. Alternatively, at any given level of income, an increase in the money supply implies an equivalent excess demand for bonds, which requires an increase in the price of bonds and thus a drop in the interest rate. This is reflected as a shift to the right in the *LM* curve. Hence the position of the *LM* curve is affected by monetary policy. An *easy monetary policy* (i.e. an expansion in the money supply) causes a rightward shift in the *LM* curve. A *tight monetary policy* (i.e. a contraction in the money supply) causes a leftward shift in the *LM* curve. *Neutral monetary policy* means that the *LM* curve remains fixed at its initial position.

It is obvious from (3.33) that the *LM* curve is one equation in two unknowns or endogenous variables, r and Y. If conditions in the goods market change, income will change and this will affect conditions in the money market, as a result of which the interest rate will change, too. We have also seen that the *IS* curve is one equation in two endogenous variables, r and Y. If conditions in the assets markets change, the interest rate will change and this will affect conditions in the goods market, as a result of which income will change too. It therefore follows that the goods market cannot be in equilibrium unless the assets markets are also in equilibrium. Equilibrium in the economy therefore requires the simultaneous equilibrium of all markets. Thus, the equilibrium values of income and interest rates are obtained by simultaneously solving the *IS* and *LM* equations (i.e. the goods and assets markets).

In technical terms, we have two equations (the *IS* and *LM* curves) and

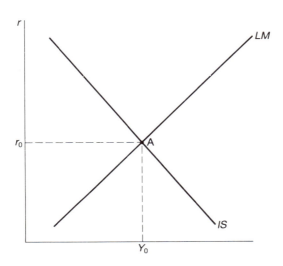

Figure 3.1 The determination of the equilibrium level of output and the interest rate

two endogenous variables (r and Y). To find the equilibrium values of income and the interest rate we have to solve equations (3.30) and (3.33) simultaneously. The equilibrium income/output is

$$Y = \frac{1}{1 - C_y(1 - t_y) + I_r\dfrac{M_y}{M_r}} A + \frac{\dfrac{I_r}{M_r}}{1 - C_y(1 - t_y) + I_r\dfrac{M_y}{M_r}} m \quad (3.35)$$

where $A = C_0 + I_0 + G - C_y t_0 + C_y TR$. In terms of figure 3.1 equilibrium is established at point A, the intersection of the *IS* with the *LM* curve; equilibrium income is Y_0 and the equilibrium interest rate is r_0.

If m or any component of A follows a stochastic process, then income will follow a stochastic process, too, through (3.35). Hence, in this system business cycles are caused by fluctuations in demand, which in turn reflect shocks in either the goods market or the assets markets. Fluctuations in demand arise from either the private sector (shocks in autonomous consumption or autonomous investment, or shocks in the demand for assets) or the government (in the operation of fiscal and monetary policy). The government may be trying to stabilize the economy but because of lags in the effects of policy and/or miscalculation of the correct dosage may cause rather than dampen business cycles.

3.6 Monetary Policy

Monetary policy can be neutral, easy (or accommodating) and tight (or contractionary). A neutral monetary policy means that the real stock of money is kept unchanged and the *LM* remains fixed. A tight monetary policy implies a reduction in the real stock of money and is represented as a shift to the left of the *LM* curve. An easy (or accommodating) monetary policy means an increase in the real stock of money and therefore a shift to the right of the *LM* curve.

Sometimes the *modus operandi* of monetary policy is confused with the stance of policy. If the authorities pursue a policy of monetary targets, then tight monetary policy means a reduction in the target rate of growth of the money supply (or its level in the context of model 3) and easy (or accommodating) monetary policy means an increase in the target. If, however, the central bank is operating a policy of interest rate targets, then tight monetary policy means higher interest rates and easy monetary policy lower interest rates. In both cases a tight monetary policy implies a leftward shift of the *LM* curve and an easy or accommodating monetary policy a rightward shift.

Monetary policy is powerful if the effect of a given change in the money supply on income is strong. This is measured by the money multiplier, κ_m, which is obtained by partially differentiating (3.35) with respect to m:

$$\kappa_m = \frac{\partial Y}{\partial m} = \frac{\dfrac{I_r}{M_r}}{1 - C_y (1 - t_y) + I_r \dfrac{M_y}{M_r}} > 0 \qquad (3.36)$$

Since both M_r and I_r are negative, while M_y is positive, it follows that the money multiplier is positive. That is, an increase in the money supply will raise income and therefore create growth whereas a decrease in the money supply will create recession. The higher the multiplier, the greater the effect on income and therefore the more effective is monetary policy.

The way an increase in the money supply affects the equilibrium level of income can be analysed with the help of figure 3.2. Initial equilibrium is at A, with income Y_0 and interest rate r_0. The increase in the money supply from m_0 to m_1 shifts the LM curve from $LM(m_0)$ to $LM(m_1)$. At any given level of income, the interest rate falls. The extent of the vertical shift is equal to

$$\Delta r = \frac{1}{M_r} \Delta m \qquad (3.37)$$

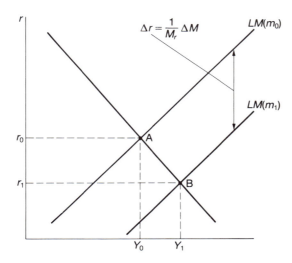

Figure 3.2 The effects of easy monetary policy (increase in the money supply) on output and the interest rate

and is obtained by partially differentiating r with respect to m in (3.33).

The new equilibrium is established at point B, the intersection of the *IS* curve with the new *LM* curve. At the new equilibrium, income rises from Y_0 to Y_1 and the interest falls from r_0 to r_1. The transmission of monetary policy is summarized schematically in box 3.1.

Box 3.1 The transmission of monetary policy

$$m\!\uparrow \,\Rightarrow\, r\!\downarrow \,\Rightarrow\, I\!\uparrow \,\Rightarrow\, D\!\uparrow \,\Rightarrow\, Y\!\uparrow \,\Rightarrow\, \begin{cases} YD\!\uparrow \,\Rightarrow\, C\!\uparrow \,\Rightarrow\, D\!\uparrow \\[1ex] m^d\!\uparrow \,\Rightarrow\, r\!\uparrow \,\Rightarrow\, I\!\downarrow \,\Rightarrow\, Y\!\downarrow \end{cases}$$

The economic rationale is as follows. The monetary authorities engage in open market purchases of government bonds. This allows the money supply to expand. The excess demand for bonds implies a rise in their price and thus a drop in the interest rate (the yield on government bonds; see note 1). This is summarized as $m\!\uparrow \Rightarrow r\!\downarrow$. Lower interest rates mean that the cost of borrowing has been reduced and therefore firms are induced to expand their investment programmes $r\!\downarrow \Rightarrow I\!\uparrow$). Since investment is a component of aggregate demand, the latter rises as a result of expanded investment activity ($I\!\uparrow \Rightarrow D\!\uparrow$). At the initial level of income, Y_0, there is an excess demand in the goods market. Firms respond by increasing output and therefore factor incomes ($D\!\uparrow \Rightarrow Y\!\uparrow$). The latter implies that disposable income rises too ($Y\!\uparrow \Rightarrow YD\!\uparrow$). Households respond by increasing consumption ($YD\!\uparrow \Rightarrow C\!\uparrow$), which in turn stimulates aggregate demand once more ($C\!\uparrow \Rightarrow D\!\uparrow$). This cycle is repeated until equilibrium is achieved. In every cycle the stimulus becomes smaller because the government takes away a fraction of the increase in income in the form of taxes and households save another fraction. In addition, the rise in income results in an increased demand for money to finance an increased volume of transactions ($Y\!\uparrow \Rightarrow m^d\!\uparrow$; see the lower channel of box 3.1), thereby reversing the interest rate fall ($m^d\!\uparrow \Rightarrow r\!\uparrow$), thus reducing the stimulus to investment ($r\!\uparrow \Rightarrow I\!\downarrow$) and income ($I\!\downarrow \Rightarrow Y\!\downarrow$).

It can be verified from (3.36) that the value of the money multiplier depends on all the parameters of the model. In other words, the money multiplier is a function of the marginal propensity to consume, C_y, the marginal tax rate, t_y, the interest sensitivity of investment, I_r, the income sensitivity of the demand for money, M_y and the interest sensitivity of the demand for money, M_r:

$$\kappa_m = \kappa_m\left(C_y, t_y, M_y, |I_r|, |M_r|\right) \tag{3.38}$$

$$\frac{\partial \kappa}{\partial C_y} > 0, \quad \frac{\partial \kappa}{\partial t_y} < 0, \quad \frac{\partial \kappa}{\partial M_y} < 0, \quad \frac{\partial \kappa}{\partial |I_r|} > 0, \quad \frac{\partial \kappa}{\partial |M_r|} < 0$$

The money multiplier is an increasing function of the marginal propensity to consume: the higher the marginal propensity to consume, the greater the multiplier. The reason is that, for a given increase in disposable income, the higher the marginal propensity to consume, the greater is the stimulus to consumption and aggregate demand in every round of the multiplier process, *ceteris paribus*. The multiplier is a decreasing function of the marginal tax rate: the higher the marginal tax rate the lower the multiplier. For a given increase in factor incomes, the greater the marginal tax rate is, the smaller the rise in disposable income and thus the lower the stimulus to consumption, demand and income, other things being equal.

The third derivative in (3.38) implies that the multiplier is a decreasing function of the income sensitivity of the demand for money. A given increase in income raises the demand for money and hence the interest rate. This tends to offset the initial drop in the interest rate and thus reduces the overall stimulus of monetary policy to income. The higher the income sensitivity of the demand for money is, the greater the increase in the demand for money and the interest rate and therefore the smaller the money multiplier.

The fourth derivative in (3.38) indicates that the multiplier is an increasing function of the interest sensitivity of investment. Other things being equal, the higher the interest sensitivity of investment is, the greater the multiplier will be. For a given reduction in the interest rate, the higher the interest sensitivity of investment, the greater is the stimulus to investment and therefore to income. Finally, the last derivative in (3.38) indicates that the multiplier is a decreasing function of the interest sensitivity of the demand for money. For a given increase in the supply of money, the greater the interest sensitivity of the demand for money, the smaller is the fall in the interest rate and hence the smaller the stimulus to investment and income.

3.7 Fiscal Policy

In this section we re-examine fiscal policy in the context of model 3. The introduction of the assets markets qualifies the conclusions reached on the efficacy of fiscal policy in model 2. We shall consider the effects of only two instruments of fiscal policy: government expenditure and the marginal tax rate. The effectiveness of the other instruments is left as an exercise for the reader. The efficacy of fiscal policy depends on the type of monetary policy pursued: neutral, easy (or accommodating) or tight.

Increase in Government Expenditure under Neutral Monetary Policy

The government expenditure multiplier under neutral monetary policy, κ_g, is obtained by partially differentiating (3.35) with respect to G:

$$\kappa_g = \frac{\partial Y}{\partial G} = \frac{1}{1 - C_y(1 - t_y) + I_r \dfrac{M_y}{M_r}} > 0 \tag{3.39}$$

Since M_r and I_r are negative whereas all the other parameters are positive, it follows that the government expenditure multiplier is positive. This implies that an increase in government expenditure stimulates the overall level of economic activity in the economy (i.e. GDP) and therefore creates growth, whereas a decrease in government expenditure creates a recession. Qualitatively, this is the same conclusion that was reached in model 2. However, a careful examination of fiscal policy will reveal fundamental differences in terms of both the nature of the new equilibrium and the size of the multiplier. A casual inspection of the fiscal multiplier in models 2 and 3 (relationships 2.11 and 3.39) reveals that they differ with respect to the term $I_r M_y / M_r$. Since this is positive it follows that the government expenditure multiplier in model 3 is smaller than in model 2. The economic reasoning is explained with the help of figure 3.3.

Initial equilibrium is at A, the intersection of the $IS(G_0)$ and $LM(m_0)$ curves. The government increases its expenditure from G_0 to G_1. This shifts the IS curve in figure 3.3a to the right. At any given level of income, the vertical shift is equal to

$$\Delta r = -\frac{1}{I_r} \Delta G \tag{3.40}$$

which is obtained by partially differentiating (3.30) with respect to G. Alternatively, at any given level of the interest rate, the horizontal shift in the IS curve is equal to

$$\Delta Y = \kappa \Delta G \tag{3.41}$$

where κ is the simple fiscal multiplier of model 2. This is obtained by partially differentiating Y with respect to G in (3.30). The increase in government expenditure also shifts the $PSBR$ curve in figure 3.3b to the right. At any given level of income the vertical shift is equal to ΔG. The new equilibrium is established at B, the intersection of $IS(G_1)$ and $LM(m_0)$. At the new equilibrium, the level of income rises from Y_0 to Y_1, but the interest rate also rises from r_0 to r_1. Assuming that in the initial equilibrium the budget is balanced, the increase in government

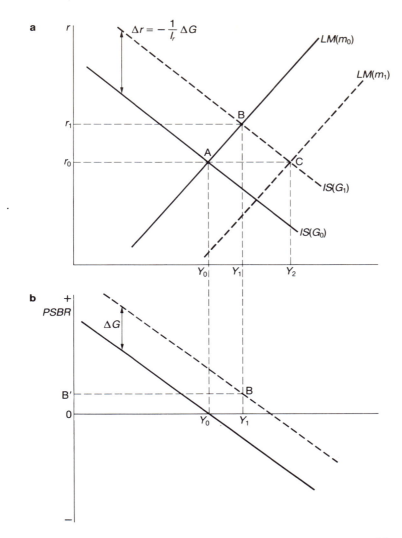

Figure 3.3   The effects of an increase in government expenditure on output and the interest rate (**a**) and *psbr* (**b**) under neutral and accommodative monetary policy

expenditure results in a budget deficit and thus a positive *psbr* equal to OB′, in figure 3.3b. OB′ is smaller than ΔG and therefore the increase in government expenditure is partly self-financed. At the initial level of income, Y_0, *psbr* increases by an amount equal to ΔG. However, as income rises more taxes are collected and therefore *psbr* falls. The degree of self-finance depends on the marginal tax rate. The higher the marginal tax rate, the greater the extent of self-finance.

The way the increase in government expenditure affects income and interest rates is further elucidated in box 3.2, which presents a schematic approach to the transmission mechanism.

Box 3.2 The transmission of fiscal policy (government expenditure)

$$G\uparrow \Rightarrow D\uparrow \Rightarrow Y\uparrow \Rightarrow \begin{cases} YD\uparrow \Rightarrow C\uparrow \Rightarrow D\uparrow \Rightarrow Y\uparrow \\ \\ m^d\uparrow \Rightarrow r\uparrow \Rightarrow I\downarrow \Rightarrow D\downarrow \Rightarrow Y\downarrow \end{cases}$$

The increase in government expenditure raises aggregate demand ($G\uparrow \Rightarrow D\uparrow$). At the initial level of income Y_0, there is an excess demand in the goods market and hence firms respond by increasing output/income ($D\uparrow \Rightarrow Y\uparrow$). The increase in income has two effects. On the one hand, it increases disposable income. This is represented by the top line in box 3.2 ($Y\uparrow \Rightarrow YD\uparrow$). Households respond by increasing consumption ($YD\uparrow \Rightarrow C\uparrow$). This raises aggregate demand even further ($C\uparrow \Rightarrow D\uparrow$), which leads to another round of excess demand. Firms then respond by increasing output/income ($D\uparrow \Rightarrow Y\uparrow$). This part of the transmission mechanism is the same as in model 2. However, the consideration of the assets markets gives rise to the second leg of the transmission mechanism, represented by the lower line in box 3.2. The rise in income leads to an increased demand for money to finance an expanded volume of transactions ($Y\uparrow \Rightarrow m^d\uparrow$). Now the assumption that the monetary authorities are pursuing a neutral monetary policy of keeping the money supply fixed becomes very important. With unchanged money supply, there is an excess demand for money and the interest rate has to rise to equilibrate the assets markets ($m^d\uparrow \Rightarrow r\uparrow$). The rise in the interest rate deters new investment expenditure as the cost of finance is increased ($r\uparrow \Rightarrow I\downarrow$). Since investment expenditure is a constituent part of aggregate demand, the latter falls ($I\downarrow \Rightarrow D\downarrow$). Firms respond to the fall in demand by cutting output ($D\downarrow \Rightarrow Y\downarrow$).

We thus have an expansionary force represented by the upper route and a contractionary force represented by the lower route of the transmission mechanism in box 3.2. It is conceivable that the expansionary effect may be completely offset by the contractionary effect, thus leaving income unchanged. This situation is called *complete crowding out*, because the increase in government expenditure displaces (or crowds out) an equal amount of private investment expenditure. The fall in private investment expenditure occurs because the monetary authorities pursue a policy of keeping the money supply fixed. If the money supply were allowed to expand to meet the excess demand for money, then the interest rate would have remained unchanged and therefore there would have been no fall in investment.

If we ignore, for the time being, the lower part of the transmission mechanism and concentrate on the upper route only, income will rise to Y_2 in figure 3.3. The increase is measured by the simple multiplier of model 2 and is given by (3.41). This we know from the fact that, by ignoring the lower route of the transmission mechanism, the interest rate remains unchanged, at the level r_0. However, point C cannot be in equilibrium. With fixed money supply the interest rate has to rise to equilibrate the assets markets. As it does so, private investment expenditure is cut, income falls and we move towards point B with income Y_1 and interest rate r_1. The reduction in private expenditure and especially investment, associated with the increase in government expenditure is called crowding out. Some degree of crowding out is always inevitable. This is associated with the lower route of the transmission mechanism in box 3.2 or the term $I_r M_r / M_y$ in (3.39). In terms of figure 3.3 the degree of crowding out is measured by $Y_1 - Y_2$. The government expenditure multiplier, given by (3.39), measures the ratio $(Y_1 - Y_0)/(G_1 - G_0)$. Alternatively, the degree of crowding out can be measured by the size of the fiscal multiplier. The closer the multiplier is to zero, the greater the degree of crowding out. Full crowding out occurs when the fiscal multiplier is zero.

It can be verified from (3.39) that the fiscal multiplier depends on all the parameters of the model:

$$\kappa_g = \kappa_g \left(C_y, t_y, M_y, |I_r|, |M_r| \right) \tag{3.42}$$

$$\frac{\partial \kappa}{\partial C_y} > 0, \quad \frac{\partial \kappa}{\partial t_y} < 0, \quad \frac{\partial \kappa}{\partial M_y} < 0, \quad \frac{\partial \kappa}{\partial |I_r|} < 0, \quad \frac{\partial \kappa}{\partial |M_r|} > 0$$

The fiscal multiplier is an increasing function of the marginal propensity to consume and a decreasing function of the marginal tax rate and the income sensitivity of the demand for money for the same reason as the money multiplier. The fiscal multiplier is a decreasing function of the interest sensitivity of investment. Other things being equal, the higher the interest sensitivity of investment, the greater is the degree of crowding out and therefore the smaller the effect on income. Finally, the fiscal multiplier is an increasing function of the interest sensitivity of the demand for money. For a given increase in income, the higher the interest sensitivity of the demand for money, the smaller is the increase in the interest rate required to equilibrate the assets markets, and so the smaller is the degree of crowding out and consequently the larger the effect on income.

Increase in Government Expenditure under Accommodating Monetary Policy

An easy or accommodating monetary policy implies an increase in the supply of money. The policy is called accommodating because the government accommodates the increased demand for money by supplying the extra money.

The increase in government expenditure under an accommodating monetary policy is illustrated in figure 3.3. Initial equilibrium is at A, with income Y_0 and interest rate r_0. The increase in government expenditure from G_0 to G_1 shifts the IS curve from $IS(G_0)$ to $IS(G_1)$. Accommodating monetary policy implies that the money supply increases from m_0 to m_1 to keep the interest rate unchanged at r_0. This means that the LM curve shifts to the right from $LM(m_0)$ to $LM(m_1)$ and equilibrium is established at C with income Y_2 and interest rate r_0. The increase in income is measured by the total differential of (3.35) with respect to G and m and is equal to the simple multiplier (3.41). When the government is following an accommodating monetary policy, there is no crowding out. Private expenditure, and especially investment, is not reduced because the interest rate is not allowed to rise. The excess demand for money is met by an increase in the money supply.

Income Tax Cut under Neutral Monetary Policy

The income tax cut we consider is of the form of a decrease in the marginal tax rate, t_y. The effect of an income tax cut on income under neutral monetary policy is obtained by partially differentiating (3.35) with respect to t_y:

$$\kappa_t = \frac{\partial Y}{\partial t_y} = \frac{-C_y}{1 - C_y(1 - t_y) + I_r \dfrac{M_y}{M_r}} \quad Y < 0 \tag{3.43}$$

Since the denominator is positive, the income tax multiplier is negative. This implies that an income tax cut stimulates the overall level of economic activity in the economy and therefore creates growth, whereas a rise in income tax creates a recession. A comparison of the income tax multipliers in models 2 and 3 (relationships 2.18 and 3.43) reveals that they differ with respect to the term $I_r M_y / M_r$. Since this term is positive, the income tax multiplier in model 3 is smaller than that in model 2. This is the term that gives rise to the crowding-out effect, which we also found in the context of the government expenditure multiplier.

The way the income tax cut affects income/output is illustrated in

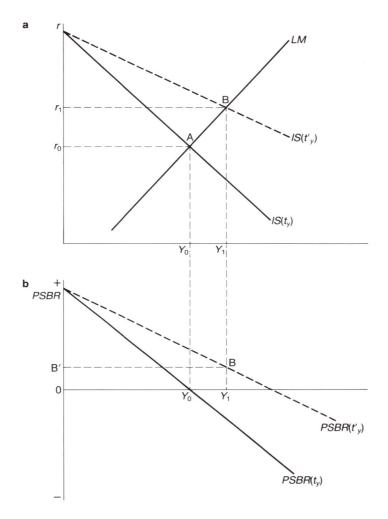

Figure 3.4   The effects of a cut in the marginal tax rate on output and the interest rate (a) and *psbr* (b) under neutral monetary policy

figure 3.4. Initial equilibrium is at A with income Y_0 and interest rate r_0. The income tax is reduced from t_y to t'_y. This results in an anti-clockwise rotation of the *IS* curve from $IS(t_y)$ to $IS(t'_y)$. The new equilibrium is established at B with higher income (Y_1) and higher interest rate (r_1).

The transmission mechanism of fiscal policy in the context of an income tax cut is highlighted in box 3.3. The reduction in the income tax rate results in an increase in real disposable income ($t_y\downarrow \Rightarrow YD\uparrow$) as households pay less taxes. The increase in real disposable income leads households to increase their consumption ($YD\uparrow \Rightarrow C\uparrow$) and consequently aggregate demand rises, since consumption is a constituent component of aggregate demand ($C\uparrow \Rightarrow D\uparrow$). At the initial level of output, Y_0, there is an excess demand in the goods market and firms respond by increasing output as they see their stocks depleted ($D\uparrow \Rightarrow Y\uparrow$). As in the case of government expenditure, there are now two opposite forces. The increase in output implies an equivalent increase in factor incomes and therefore real disposable income ($Y\uparrow \Rightarrow YD\uparrow$). We are now tracing the upper channel of the transmission mechanism in box 3.3. This stimulates for a second round consumption ($YD\uparrow \Rightarrow C\uparrow$) and therefore aggregate demand ($C\uparrow \Rightarrow D\uparrow$). Firms then respond by increasing output yet again ($D\uparrow \Rightarrow Y\uparrow$). The upper channel therefore represents the expansionary effect on income. However, as income rises the transactions demand for money increases too, as the private sector needs more money to finance an increased volume of transactions ($Y\uparrow \Rightarrow m^d\uparrow$). With unchanged money supply (recall our assumption of neutral monetary policy), there is an excess demand for money. The interest rate has to rise to equilibrate the assets markets ($m^d\uparrow \Rightarrow r\uparrow$). However, this implies that the cost of finance is increased as banks adjust their interest rates on loans to the yields on government bonds. This deters private investment expenditure ($r\uparrow \Rightarrow I\downarrow$). In other words, the income tax cut also leads to crowding out of private investment expenditure through the resulting interest rate rise, as in the case of a government expenditure increase. The fall in investment leads to a drop in aggregate demand by the same amount, as investment is a constituent component of aggregate demand ($I\downarrow \Rightarrow D\downarrow$). Firms respond by cutting output ($D\downarrow \Rightarrow Y\downarrow$). This is the contractionary effect of fiscal policy associated with the crowding-out effect and represented by the lower channel of the transmission mechanism in box 3.3. As in the case of government expenditure, the degree of crowding out depends on the parameters of the model.

Box 3.3 The transmission of fiscal policy (income tax cut)

$$t_y\downarrow \Rightarrow YD\uparrow \Rightarrow C\uparrow \Rightarrow D\uparrow \Rightarrow Y\uparrow \Rightarrow \begin{cases} YD\uparrow \Rightarrow C\uparrow \Rightarrow D\uparrow \Rightarrow Y\uparrow \\ \\ m^d\uparrow \Rightarrow r\uparrow \Rightarrow I\downarrow \Rightarrow D\downarrow \Rightarrow Y\downarrow \end{cases}$$

3.8 The Relative Effectiveness of Fiscal and Monetary Policy

The effectiveness of fiscal and monetary policy depends on all the parameters of the model. This can be verified by taking the partial derivatives of the two multipliers (3.36 and 3.39) with respect to the parameters of the model. These derivatives are summarized for the money and government expenditure multipliers in (3.38) and (3.42) respectively. An increase in the marginal propensity to consume raises the size of both multipliers. An increase in the marginal tax rate lowers the size of both multipliers. An increase in the income responsiveness of the demand for money lowers the size of both multipliers. An increase in the interest rate responsiveness of investment raises the size of the money multiplier, but reduces the size of the fiscal multiplier. Finally, an increase in the interest rate responsiveness of the demand for money reduces the money multiplier but increases the fiscal multiplier.

It therefore follows that the effectiveness of fiscal relative to monetary policy depends on the interest rate sensitivities of investment and the demand for money. This can also be seen if we take the ratio of the two multipliers (3.36) and (3.39):

$$\frac{\dfrac{\partial Y}{\partial G}}{\dfrac{\partial Y}{\partial m}} = \frac{\kappa_g}{\kappa_m} = \frac{M_r}{I_r} \tag{3.44}$$

This means that the higher the interest sensitivity of the demand for money and the lower the interest sensitivity of investment, the more effective is fiscal policy relative to monetary policy, and vice versa.

It is instructive to examine the size of the fiscal and money multipliers for certain extreme values of the interest sensitivity of investment and the demand for money. The first case is when the interest sensitivity of the demand for money tends to infinity. This is known as the *liquidity trap*.

$$\lim_{|M_r| \to \infty} \frac{\partial Y}{\partial G} = \frac{1}{1 - C_y(1 - t_y)} \tag{3.45}$$

$$\lim_{|M_r| \to \infty} \frac{\partial Y}{\partial m} = 0 \tag{3.46}$$

As the interest sensitivity of the demand for money becomes infinitely large, the fiscal multiplier tends to the simple fiscal multiplier in model 2, whereas the money multiplier tends to zero. In this case fiscal policy is most effective and monetary policy is completely impotent. *Crowding out is zero.*

The opposite polar case is when the interest sensitivity of the demand for money tends to zero.

$$\lim_{|M_r| \to 0} \frac{\partial Y}{\partial G} = 0 \qquad (3.47)$$

$$\lim_{|M_r| \to 0} \frac{\partial Y}{\partial m} = \frac{1}{M_y} \qquad (3.48)$$

As the interest sensitivity of the demand for money becomes infinitely small, the fiscal multiplier approaches zero in the limit, whereas the money multiplier tends to the inverse of the income sensitivity of the demand for money. Now fiscal policy is totally impotent, while monetary policy is most effective. This is the case where *full crowding out* takes place.

The third case is when the interest sensitivity of investment tends to zero.

$$\lim_{|I_r| \to 0} \frac{\partial Y}{\partial G} = \frac{1}{1 - C_y(1 - t_y)} \qquad (3.49)$$

$$\lim_{|I_r| \to 0} \frac{\partial Y}{\partial m} = 0 \qquad (3.50)$$

In this case the fiscal multiplier approaches the value of the fiscal multiplier in model 2, whereas the money multiplier tends to zero. Fiscal policy is most effective, while monetary policy is completely impotent. *Crowding out is zero*.

The special cases when fiscal policy is most effective and monetary policy is completely impotent are known as the *Keynesian cases*. On the other hand, the special case when fiscal policy is totally impotent but monetary policy is most effective is known as the *classical case*.

The special cases are analysed graphically in figures 3.5 to 3.7. The liquidity trap arises when the interest sensitivity of the demand for money becomes infinitely large. This results in a horizontal *LM* curve, as can be seen from (3.33). Initial equilibrium is at A, with income Y_0 and interest rate r_0, in figure 3.5a. Now the government increases its expenditure from G_0 to G_1. This shifts the *IS* curve from $IS(G_0)$ to $IS(G_1)$. The new equilibrium is established at B, with higher income, Y_1, and the same interest rate, r_0. The increase in income, $Y_1 - Y_0$, is equal to the full multiplier effect of model 2. If the government uses monetary policy to stimulate the economy, it will fail to do so. Initial equilibrium is at A, with income Y_0 and interest rate r_0, in figure 3.5b. The increase in the money supply from m_0 to m_1 will not shift the *LM* curve and consequently income will remain unchanged. Monetary policy is totally ineffective.

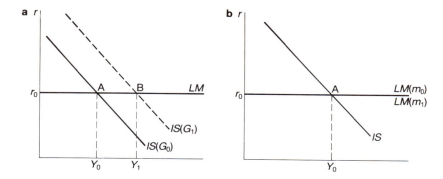

Figure 3.5 The effects of easy fiscal policy (a) and easy monetary policy (b) on output and the interest rate under the extreme case of a liquidity trap

The economic rationale of the policy implications of the liquidity trap is as follows. The infinite responsiveness of the demand for money to changes in the interest rate implies that people always prefer to hold money rather than bonds in their portfolios (i.e. they are trapped in liquidity). This will certainly occur when the yield on bonds is zero. In this case there is no incentive in holding any bonds because money, which may also not earn any interest, has the advantage that it can be used directly as a medium of exchange and in addition it does not bear the risk of a capital loss. However, can there be a liquidity trap at a low but positive interest rate? This will imply that people do not expect the price of bonds to go any higher than its current level or, therefore, the yield to fall any further. Any extra demand for bonds by the government through open market purchases will be met immediately by the private sector, which will be willing to sell at the existing price. People's expectations about the price of bonds will not be affected in spite of an active government campaign to change that by buying government bonds. In the real world this situation is highly unlikely.

It is now easy to understand why monetary policy is totally ineffective in the case of the liquidity trap. Any increase in the money supply by the government is met by an equal supply of bonds by the private sector at an unchanged price. People want to get rid of bonds and the government is offering to buy them. Since the interest rate does not fall, in spite of the increase in the money supply, investment is not stimulated and consequently income remains unchanged. On the other hand, an increase in government expenditure stimulates demand and therefore income. The increased demand for money for transactions purposes is met at an unchanged interest rate through the ample liquidity that exists. People hold more money than is actually needed for transactions, because they have switched their portfolios out of bonds and into money. Since the interest rate does not rise there is no fall in investment and therefore no contractionary effect on income through the crowding-out effect.

The opposite polar case arises when the interest sensitivity of the demand for money is zero. This implies that the *LM* curve is vertical, as can be seen from (3.33). This case is portrayed in figure 3.6. Initial equilibrium is at A, with income Y_0 and interest rate r_0. The increase in government expenditure from G_0 to G_1 shifts the *IS* curve to the right in figure 3.6a. This results in a higher interest rate, r_1, at an unchanged income, Y_0. Fiscal policy is completely ineffective. On the other hand, an increase in the money supply from m_0 to m_1 shifts the *LM* curve to the right in figure 3.6b. The interest rate falls from r_0 to r_1 and income rises from Y_0 to Y_1. Monetary policy has its maximum effect on income/output in the economy.

The zero interest rate sensitivity of the demand for money implies that the economic system is block recursive. This means that the equilibrium level of income and the interest rate are not simultaneously determined by the interaction of the assets and the goods markets. The system can be dichotomized. The assets markets determine the equilibrium level of output, *Y*. The goods market determines the interest rate. The way the system is solved is as follows. First, solve for the level of income from the money market equilibrium condition, the first block of the system. Then use that value of income in the goods market equilibrium condition to determine the interest rate.

In the classical world of zero interest sensitivity in the demand for money, an increase in government expenditure by ΔG results in a rise in the interest rate which curtails private investment expenditure by an amount equal to ΔG, so that income remains unchanged – full crowding

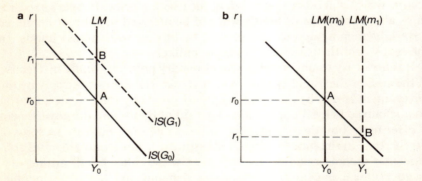

Figure 3.6   The effects of easy fiscal policy (**a**) and easy monetary policy (**b**) on output and the interest rate under the extreme case of zero interest rate elasticity of the demand for money

out. On the other hand, an increase in the money supply stimulates the level of economic activity because people hold money only for trans- actions purposes. As the money supply is increased people can finance an increased volume of transactions and this raises Y. The assump- tion of a zero interest sensitivity of the demand for money is extreme. Changes in the interest rate do induce portfolio shifts. However, the interest elasticity of the demand for money is rather small.

The third special case arises when the interest sensitivity of investment is zero. This implies that the IS curve is vertical, as can be established from (3.30). This situation is portrayed in figure 3.7. Initial equilibrium is at A, with income Y_0 and interest rate r_0. The increase in government expenditure from G_0 to G_1 shifts the IS curve to the right and the new equilibrium is attained at B, with higher income Y_1 and higher interest rate, r_1, figure 3.7a. Fiscal policy has its maximum effect on income equal to the full multiplier effect, as given by (3.41). On the other hand, an increase in the money supply from m_0 to m_1 shifts the LM curve to the right and the new equilibrium is established at B, with the same level of income, Y_0, but lower interest rate, r_1, in figure 3.7b. Monetary policy has no effect on income.

The zero interest sensitivity of investment implies that the system is again block recursive, but now the other way round relative to the classical world. In this Keynesian world, the level of income is deter- mined in the goods market, whereas the interest rate is determined in the assets markets. The economic system is solved in a recursive manner. First, we solve for the level of income from the equilibrium condition in the goods market. Then we use this value of income to determine the level of the interest rate from the money market equilibrium condition.

In the Keynesian world of zero interest sensitivity of investment, an increase in government expenditure stimulates demand and therefore

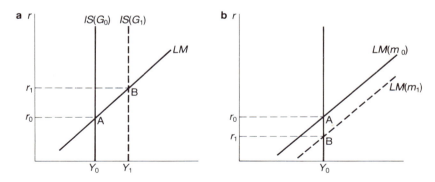

Figure 3.7 The effects of easy fiscal policy (**a**) and easy monetary policy (**b**) on output and the interest rate under the extreme case of zero interest rate elasticity of investment

income. The latter leads to an increased demand for money for transactions purposes, which results in a rise in the interest rate, for a given money supply. The interest rate rise, however, has no effect on investment (i.e. no crowding out) because of the hypothesized zero interest sensitivity of investment. Thus, fiscal policy has its maximum effect on income. The reason why monetary policy is completely ineffective is also easy to understand. The increase in the money supply leads to a fall in the interest rate, as in normal conditions, but since investment is insensitive to changes in the interest rate, there is no expansionary effect and therefore income remains unchanged.

The assumption of a zero interest sensitivity of investment is again extreme. Changes in the interest rate do affect investment expenditure. The interest elasticity of investment is, however, rather small.

3.9 Dynamic Adjustment

Until now we have considered how the equilibrium level of income and the interest rate are determined and how such an equilibrium is affected by fiscal and monetary policies. However, we have ignored the nature of the dynamic adjustment path from one equilibrium to the other. This is the task of this section.

The disequilibrium dynamics are described by the system of equations (3.26) and (3.27). To examine the properties of this system substitute (3.24) into (3.27) and (3.28) into (3.26), making use of the definition of A in (3.35). The system now becomes

$$\begin{bmatrix} \dot{Y} \\ \dot{r} \end{bmatrix} = \begin{bmatrix} -\alpha_1(1 - C_y(1 - t_y)) & \alpha_1 I_r \\ \alpha_2 M_y & \alpha_2 M_r \end{bmatrix} \begin{bmatrix} Y \\ r \end{bmatrix} + \begin{bmatrix} \alpha_1 A \\ -\alpha_2 m \end{bmatrix} \quad (3.51)$$

or

$$\dot{\mathbb{X}} = \mathbb{B}\mathbb{X} + \mathbb{C}$$

in matrix notation. A dot (·) over a variable denotes its time derivative. For the system to be stable what is required is that the trace of matrix $\mathbb{B}$, denoted by $\mathrm{tr}\mathbb{B}$, must be negative and that the determinant of $\mathbb{B}$, denoted by $\mathrm{det}\mathbb{B}$, must be positive (necessary and sufficient conditions).

$$\mathrm{tr}\mathbb{B} = -\alpha_1(1 - C_y(1 - t_y)) + \alpha_2 M_r < 0 \quad (3.52)$$

The element $(1, 1)$ in matrix $\mathbb{B}$ is the product of the speed of adjustment in the goods market, α_1, times the numerator of the slope of the *IS* curve. Hence, a sufficient condition for the trace to be negative is that *IS* is negatively sloped. The condition that

$$\det \mathbb{B} > 0$$

requires that

$$-\frac{M_y}{M_r} > \frac{1 - C_y(1 - t_y)}{I_r} \tag{3.53}$$

The term on the left hand side is the slope of the *LM* curve (see 3.34) and the term on the right hand side is the slope of the *IS* curve (see 3.31). Thus, (3.53) can be written as

$$\left.\frac{\partial r}{\partial Y}\right|_{is} - \left.\frac{\partial r}{\partial Y}\right|_{lm} < 0 \tag{3.54}$$

That is, the system will be stable if the *IS* curve is negatively sloped and the *LM* curve is positively sloped (i.e. if they have the usual slopes).

If both *IS* and *LM* are positively sloped, the system will be stable provided the former is flatter than the latter. In other words, for the system to be stable the slope of *IS* must be smaller than slope of LM:

$$\left.\frac{\partial r}{\partial Y}\right|_{is} < \left.\frac{\partial r}{\partial Y}\right|_{lm}, \quad \text{if } \left.\frac{\partial r}{\partial Y}\right|_{is} > 0 \tag{3.55}$$

The disequilibrium dynamics are analysed in figure 3.8. Points on the *IS* curve reflect equilibrium in the goods market. Points above and to the right of the *IS* curve correspond to an excess supply of goods, ESG. Let us consider point A. At the level of the interest rate r_0, demand is Y_0, while output is Y_1. There is an excess supply equal to $Y_1 - Y_0$. Output has to fall to equilibrate the goods market. The falling output is represented by leftward-pointing arrows.

Similarly, points below and to the left of the *IS* curve correspond to excess demand for goods, EDG. Consider point B. At the level of interest

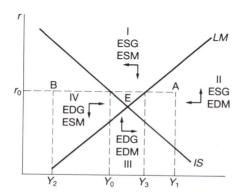

Figure 3.8 The disequilibrium dynamics of output and the interest rate

rate r_0, demand is equal to Y_0, but output is only Y_2. There is an excess demand equal to $Y_0 - Y_2$. Output has to rise to equilibrate the goods market. The rising output is represented by rightward-pointing arrows.

Points on the LM curve correspond to equilibrium in the assets markets. Points below and to the right of the *LM* curve correspond to excess demand in the money market, EDM. Consider point A. With money supply fixed and equal to m_0, the demand for money for transactions purposes that is consistent with the interest rate r_0 is Y_3. However, at that level of interest rate, income is actually Y_1 and therefore there is an excess demand for money for an increased volume of transactions. The interest rate has to rise to equilibrate the money market. The rising interest rates are represented by upward-pointing arrows.

Points above and to left of the *LM* curve correspond to excess supply in the money market, ESM. Consider point B. With fixed money supply at m_0, the demand for money for transactions that is consistent with interest rate at r_0 is Y_3. However, at that level of the interest rate, income is only Y_2 and therefore there is an excess supply of money. The interest rate has to fall to equilibrate the money market. The falling interest rates are represented by downward-pointing arrows.

The whole area in the (Y, r) space can be divided by the *IS* and *LM* curves into four different regions. In region I there is an excess supply of goods and an excess supply of money. In region II there is an excess supply of goods and an excess demand for money. In region III there is an excess demand for goods and an excess demand for money. In region IV there is an excess demand for goods and an excess supply of money.

Given our assumptions about the slopes of the *IS* and *LM* curves, the dynamic adjustment to equilibrium, described by point E in figure 3.8, is stable. Given that in the real world financial markets adjust more quickly than the goods market, we can speculate about the nature of the

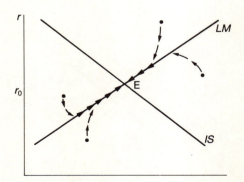

Figure 3.9 The dynamic adjustment of the economy when the assets markets clear more quickly than the goods market

dynamic adjustment path. Figure 3.9 portrays the dynamic adjustment to equilibrium E from four different points, each one belonging to a different region.

If we assume that the assets markets adjust instantly, and the goods market sluggishly, we can be much more specific about the nature of the adjustment path. Such an assumption may appear extreme, but it is not unreasonable in the modern world of electronic information with 24-hour stock exchange markets around the world. The implication of the assumption that assets markets clear instantly is that the dynamic adjustment path is always along the *LM* curve, since points along this curve represent equilibrium in the assets markets.

Figure 3.10 illustrates the dynamic adjustment under a monetary contraction. Initial equilibrium is at E, with income Y_0 and interest rate r_0. The reduction in the money supply shifts *LM* to the left from $LM(m_0)$ to $LM(m_1)$. Final equilibrium is established at E', with higher interest rate, r_1, and lower income, Y_1. The dynamic adjustment path is depicted by the arrows. The monetary contraction shifts the LM curve immediately. Given our assumption that the money market clears instantly, the interest rate rises immediately from r_0 to r_2, at the original level of income Y_0. Thus, we move from E to E". The interest rate rise deters private investment and this gradually reduces income. As income falls the demand for money for transactions is also reduced and this puts a downward pressure on the interest rate. From E" to E', both income and the interest rate are falling gradually along the *LM* curve, at a speed that depends on the slope of *LM*.

Figure 3.11 illustrates the dynamic adjustment under a fiscal expansion. Initial equilibrium is at E. The government increases its expenditure from G_0 to G_1 and this results in a shift to the right in the *IS* curve. The new equilibrium is attained at E', with higher income and interest rate.

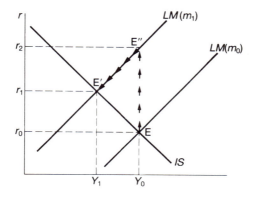

Figure 3.10 The dynamic adjustment of the economy to monetary contraction when the assets markets clear instantly and the goods market clears sluggishly

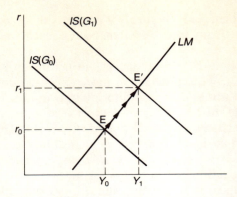

Figure 3.11 The dynamic adjustment of the economy to a fiscal expansion when the assets markets clear instantly and the goods market clears sluggishly

The dynamic adjustment is illustrated by the arrows and is along the *LM* curve. Initially, there is no change either in income or in the interest rate. However, at the initial level of income there is an excess demand in the goods market and firms respond by gradually increasing output. As income rises, the transactions demand for money increases and this gradually pushes the interest rate up.

3.10 The Policy Mix and the Composition of Output

Let us assume that the economy is in equilibrium at less than full employment, Y_0 in figure 3.12. Full-employment income is $\bar{Y}$. This is consistent with a wide range of interest rates. The choice of the level of the interest rate has implications for the composition of output (i.e. the contribution of the private and the public sector to GDP). The government has two extreme policy options to reach full employment. On the one hand, expansionary fiscal policy (such as an increase in government expenditure) can be used, while monetary policy remains unchanged. The required increase in government expenditure is such as to cause the *IS* curve to shift until equilibrium is reached at E_1, the intersection of the *LM* curve with the $\bar{Y}$ line. At E_1, income is at full employment and the interest rate is r_1. On the other hand, expansionary monetary policy (via an increase in the money supply) can be used, while fiscal policy remains unchanged. The required increase in the money supply is such as to cause the *LM* curve to shift until equilibrium is reached at E_2, the intersection of the *IS* curve with the $\bar{Y}$ line. At E_2, income is again at full employment but the interest rate is only r_2. The nature of the equilibrium at E_1 differs from that at E_2. In the former, the government

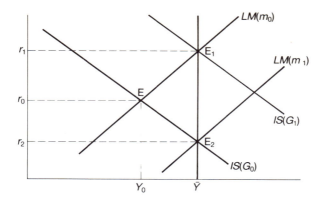

Figure 3.12 The effects of easy fiscal and monetary policy on the composition of output

sector, as measured by the G/Y ratio, expands at the expense of the private sector, as measured by the I/Y ratio. At E_2, the opposite is true. Which equilibrium point will be selected between E_1 and E_2 is a matter of political choice. Any such choice requires a particular policy mix (i.e. a specific combination of fiscal and monetary policy).

3.11 Summary and Limitations of Model 3

Model 3 differs substantially from the first two models in that income/ output is no longer determined in the goods market alone via the equality of demand for and supply of goods. The introduction of assets markets implies that both income and the interest rate are simultaneously determined by the interaction of the goods and the assets markets.

Both fiscal and monetary policies affect the level of income and the interest rate. Fiscal policy directly affects aggregate demand through government expenditure. Furthermore, fiscal policy indirectly affects consumption and therefore aggregate demand through the effect of lump sum taxes, marginal tax rate and transfer payments on disposable income. Monetary policy affects the interest rate and through that private expenditure, especially investment, and hence aggregate demand.

The special cases of liquidity trap and zero interest rate sensitivities of the demand for money or investment are theoretical cases with little relevance to the real world. Nevertheless, they help in our understanding of the factors that affect the relative effectiveness of fiscal and monetary policy. They also explain why policy (fiscal or monetary) may be more effective in one country than another. The policy mix, that is the appropriate combination of fiscal and monetary policy, is of enormous importance in deciding the proportion of consumption relative to investment and the desirable size of the government sector relative to the private sector.

The use of fiscal policy to stimulate economic activity leads to higher interest rates and therefore to crowding out of private investment. This results in an expansion of the government sector at the expense of the private sector. This is a problem because of the general belief that the government sector is very inefficient compared to the private sector. However, crowding out need not occur. It is the combination of neutral monetary policy with easy fiscal policy that results in some degree of crowding out. If accommodating monetary policy is instead used with easy fiscal policy then no crowding out will occur. This is a very important conclusion, but its validity depends on a crucial assumption that underlies all the models we have so far analysed; namely, that prices remain unchanged whatever the level of demand. This is a justified assumption if the economy is in recession with a lot of idle resources in the capital stock, excess capacity and unemployed labour. Such conditions prevailed in the 1930s.

As we shall see later, the degree of crowding out and the effectiveness of fiscal policy also depend on inflation, the degree of openness of the economy and the constraint of the balance of payments.

Model 3 goes some way towards an explanation of the causes of business cycles and the stabilization role of the government. Fluctuations in output are caused by fluctuations in demand, which arise from the private sector or even from the government. The instability of the private sector and therefore its stochastic behaviour may arise from shocks in the goods market (autonomous consumption or autonomous investment) or shocks in the assets markets (the demand for money or bonds). The government may also cause instability and therefore fluctuations in output because of miscalculations about when and by how much to change economic policy.

Note

1 A bond is a type of security that can be bought or sold at the Stock Exchange. A bond is a promise by a borrower to pay the lender the amount borrowed, called the principal and usually equal to £100 per bond, at a specified date, which is called the maturity date of the bond. In addition the lender receives an annual interest, called the coupon, C. When this is a fixed amount, the securities are called fixed interest bonds. The way the price of a bond, P, is related to the interest rate (or more properly the redemption yield), r, can be seen through the following equation:

$$P = \frac{C}{(1 + r)^1} + \frac{C}{(1 + r)^2} + \cdots + \frac{C}{(1 + r)^n} + \frac{100}{(1 + r)^n} \tag{A.1}$$

Since at any point in time P, C and n are given, (A.1) determines the redemption yield, which equates the revenue, given as the present value of all future income streams, with the cost of a bond, being the price. It also follows from (A.1) that the price of a bond varies inversely with the interest rate. The above relationship simplifies in the case of undated bonds, otherwise called perpetuities, to

$$P = \frac{C}{r} \tag{A.2}$$

If $C = 1$, (A.2) implies that the price of a bond is the inverse of the interest rate.

4

Model 4 A Long-run Model with Asset Accumulation: the Dynamics of Budget Finance

In this model we relax the assumption that private sector wealth is fixed. A budget deficit implies that the government has to print money or issue bonds to provide finance for its deficit. In the case of a surplus the government retires debt or reduces the supply of money. A budget deficit or surplus changes the stock of private sector wealth, which in turn affects consumption and the demand for assets. Equilibrium in the goods and assets markets cannot be established unless private sector wealth has ceased changing. This can only happen if the budget is balanced. The consideration of budget finance introduces a distinction between short-run and long-run equilibrium. In model 3 private sector wealth is fixed and equilibrium in the economy is attained by the condition that demand equals supply in the goods and assets markets. In the context of model 4, this is only a short-run (or instantaneous) equilibrium because private sector wealth is fixed. Long-run equilibrium is attained when all markets are in equilibrium and wealth is stationary. The latter occurs when the budget is balanced.

4.1 Assumptions

The only assumption that is relaxed in this model is that private sector wealth is fixed. All other assumptions made in model 3 still hold true. In particular, we continue our analysis by assuming that prices are fixed. This implies that the economy is operating on the horizontal part of the aggregate supply curve. The model is therefore valid in conditions of low capacity utilization, such as those that prevail during a recession, as in the early 1980s. There are only two assets in the economy: money and government bonds. In this model the only reason wealth is changing is because the stock of money and bonds changes as a result of the budget not being balanced. The economy is assumed to be closed: there is no trade with the rest of the world. Finally, it is assumed that the government does not make any interest payments on its debt.

4.2 The Model

The model consists of equations (4.1) to (4.11).

$$D = C + I + G \tag{4.1}$$

$$C = C_0 + C_y YD + C_v v_{-1}; \quad C_0 > 0, \quad 0 < C_y, C_v < 1 \tag{4.2}$$

$$I = I_0 + I_r r; \quad I_r < 0 \tag{4.3}$$

$$Y = D \tag{4.4}$$

$$YD = Y + TR - T \tag{4.5}$$

$$T = t_0 + t_y Y; \quad 0 \le t_y \le 1 \tag{4.6}$$

$$psbr = G + TR - T \tag{4.7}$$

$$m^d = M_y Y + M_r r + M_v v_{-1}; \quad M_y > 0, \quad M_r < 0, \quad 0 < M_v < 1 \tag{4.8}$$

$$m^d = m \tag{4.9}$$

$$v = m + b \tag{4.10}$$

$$\Delta b + \Delta m = psbr \tag{4.11}$$

where v_{-1} is the value of private sector real wealth at the beginning of the current period. Wealth at the end of period t, v_t, is equal to the wealth of the previous period, v_{t-1}, plus the savings that accrue during the period $(t - 1, t)$, S_t. That is,

$$v_t = v_{t-1} + S_t.$$

All other symbols are defined as before. However, whereas in model 3, m applied equally to a narrow or wide monetary aggregate, in model 4 and all subsequent models m is simply the monetary base, or high-powered money. This is defined as the sum of notes and coins in circulation plus the reserves of the commercial banks.

The introduction of wealth changes the consumption function and the asset demand functions. Consumption demand depends on real disposable income and real wealth at the beginning of the period. This is the wealth that has been accumulated until the current period and is available to finance consumption demand. The importance of the wealth effect is measured by the coefficient C_v. The higher the value of C_v the greater the importance of wealth in consumption. An increase in wealth raises consumption, but not by the full amount, i.e. $0 < C_v < 1$. This implies that a given increase in wealth is not solely allocated to increase consumption, but also to increase the demand for assets – money and bonds. Thus, an increase in wealth leads to increased demand for consumption, money and bonds. The latter is not shown here because, as we have shown in the context of model 3, the two asset demand functions are not independent. The portfolio decision involves a choice for one asset while the other is obtained as a residual from the wealth budget constraint. The importance of the wealth effect in the demand for money is measured by the coefficient M_v. For a given increase in wealth, the higher the value of M_v the greater the increase in the demand for money. M_v must also be less than unity for the same reason that C_v is less than unity. It can be shown (see chapter 6) that the sum of the wealth effects must add to unity (i.e. $C_v + M_v + B_v = 1$). This condition guarantees that an increase in wealth is allocated to increased consumption, money or bonds.

Private sector wealth (equation 4.10) consists of the stock of money and government bonds, which are the liabilities of the government. It follows from (4.10) and (4.11) that a change in wealth occurs only when *psbr* changes

$$\Delta v = \Delta m + \Delta b = psbr \qquad (4.12)$$

Equation 4.11 states that the budget deficit can be financed either by printing money or by issuing new bonds. This equation can be solved in two different ways depending on the way the budget is financed.

Bond finance: solve equation (4.11) with respect to b.

$$b = b_{-1} - \Delta m + psbr \qquad (4.11a)$$

In this case the stock of bonds, b, becomes an endogenous variable and the stock of money, m, is the instrument of monetary policy. The government adjusts the stock of bonds by issuing new bonds when the budget is in deficit or retiring old stock when the budget is in surplus. Changes in the stock of money represent a change in monetary policy.

Money finance: solve equation (4.11) with respect to m.

$$m = m_{-1} - \Delta b + psbr \qquad (4.11b)$$

In this case the stock of money, m, becomes an endogenous variable and the stock of bonds, b, is the instrument of monetary policy. The government prints more money to finance its budget deficit or withdraws money if the budget is in surplus. Changes in the stock of bonds represent a change in monetary policy.

4.3 Short-run (Instantaneous) Equilibrium

The system of equations (4.1) to (4.10) determines for a given value of wealth the following set of endogenous variables: $D, C, I, T, YD, psbr,$

Y, r, m^d, and b or m according to whether the system is solved under bond or money finance. Since the system is solved for a given value of wealth, the equilibrium is short run (or instantaneous). This equilibrium is obtained when the goods and assets markets are simultaneously in equilibrium. The system can be reduced to the *IS–LM* equations in the usual way. Substitute (4.6) into (4.5) and that into (4.2). Substitute the latter and (4.3) into (4.1). Finally, substitute (4.1) into (4.4) and solve for r to obtain the *IS* curve.

$$r = -\frac{1}{I_r}(C_0 + I_0 - C_y t_0 + C_y TR + G) + \frac{1 - C_y(1 - t_y)}{I_r}Y - \frac{C_v}{I_r}v_{-1}$$

$$(4.13)$$

In the (Y, r) space the *IS* curve has the usual negative slope. The *IS* curve of model 4 differs from that of model 3 with respect to the last term in (4.13), which arises from the influence of wealth on consumption. Since I_r is negative, the last term is positive, implying that, at the same level of income, an increase in wealth raises the interest rate. In other words, an increase in wealth shifts the *IS* curve upwards and to the right. The economic rationale is that an increase in wealth increases consumption and, at the same level of income, investment must be reduced if equilibrium in the goods market is to be maintained.

If the budget is not balanced, say because of an increase in government expenditure, the *psbr* will rise and this will increase private sector wealth (see 4.12). This will increase consumption and cause rightward shifts in the *IS* curve. These shifts will persist for as long as the budget is in deficit.

To obtain the *LM* curve substitute (4.8) into (4.9) and solve for r.

$$r = \frac{1}{M_r}m - \frac{M_y}{M_r}Y - \frac{M_v}{M_r}v_{-1} \qquad\qquad (4.14)$$

In the (Y, r) plane the *LM* curve has the usual positive slope. The *LM* curve of model 4 differs from that of model 3 with respect to the last term in (4.14), which arises from the wealth effect in the demand for money. Since M_v is positive and M_r is negative, an increase in wealth raises the interest rate. This implies that an increase in wealth shifts the *LM* curve upwards and to the left. The economic rationale is that an increase in wealth leads to an increase in the demand for money and the interest rate has to rise if equilibrium in the assets markets is to be maintained at the same level of income.

If the budget is not balanced, say because of an increase in government expenditure, the *psbr* will rise and this will increase private sector wealth (see 4.12). This will increase the demand for money and will produce leftward shifts in the *LM* curve for as long as the deficit persists.

To obtain the short-run equilibrium level of output we can solve the *IS* and *LM* curves simultaneously

$$Y = \kappa_g (C_0 + I_0 - C_y t_0 + C_y TR + G) + \kappa_m m + (C_v \kappa_g - M_v \kappa_m) v_{-1}$$
$$(4.15)$$

where

$$\kappa_g = \frac{1}{1 - C_y(1 - t_y) + I_r \dfrac{M_y}{M_r}} \qquad (4.16)$$

is the *fiscal multiplier* of model 3 and

$$\kappa_m = \frac{\dfrac{I_r}{M_r}}{1 - C_y(1 - t_y) + I_r \dfrac{M_y}{M_r}} \qquad (4.17)$$

is the *money multiplier* of model 3. The equilibrium level of income given in (4.15) is short-run because it is obtained for a given value of wealth. In terms of figure 4.1 short-run equilibrium is attained at A, the intersection of the $IS(v_0)$ with the $LM(v_0)$ consistent with a level of wealth equal to v_0. The short-run equilibrium level of output/income is Y^e and the interest rate is r^e.

4.4 Fiscal Policy under Bond Finance

In the context of model 3, the efficacy of fiscal policy is measured by the corresponding income multiplier, for example the government expenditure multiplier. This is obtained by differentiating the equilibrium level of income/output with respect to government expenditure. In the context of model 4 this procedure provides only the short-run multiplier, that is the effect on income/output for a given value of wealth. The long-run consequences of fiscal policy are obtained by allowing wealth to change in accordance with the method of financing the budget deficit. We study this dynamic process for only one instrument, namely government expenditure. In this section it is assumed that the government finances the whole of the deficit by issuing bonds – *pure bond finance*. The alternative of financing the deficit by printing money – *pure money finance* – is examined in the next section. Of course, in practice the government can use any particular combination of bond and money to finance its deficit. In this and the following section, however, it is assumed that the government resorts to either bond or money finance so that the differences between the two methods can be appreciated. The

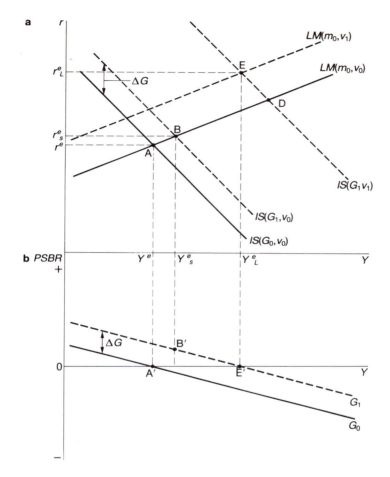

Figure 4.1 Bond finance of ΔG A → B, simple fiscal multiplier; A → D, bond finance, wealth effect on C; A → E, bond finance, wealth effect on C and m^d

bond finance of government expenditure is analysed with the help of figure 4.1.

Initial long-run equilibrium is at A, the intersection of $IS(G_0, v_0)$ and $LM(G_0, v_0)$. The long-run equilibrium income and the interest rate are Y^e and r^e respectively. The long-run equilibrium wealth is v_0. The position of the IS and LM curves is determined by this value of wealth. Point A defines a long-run equilibrium because at that value of income the budget is balanced and the *psbr* is zero. Now let us suppose that the government increases its expenditure by ΔG, from G_0 to G_1. This causes a shift to the right in the IS curve from $IS(G_0, v_0)$ to $IS(G_1, v_0)$. It also shifts the *PSBR* curve upwards from $PSBR(G_0)$ to $PSBR(G_1)$. At the initial level of income Y^e, *psbr* increases by the full amount, ΔG. In the short run private sector wealth is fixed and equilibrium would be established at B, with income Y_s^e. The increase in income is given by the simple fiscal multiplier of model 3.

In the context of model 4, B cannot be a long-run equilibrium. At income level Y_s^e the budget is in deficit, although not by the full initial amount, ΔG. The rise in income from Y^e to Y_s^e raises taxes and therefore some of the increase in the *psbr* is self-financed. The government issues more bonds to finance the deficit. This increases private sector wealth from v_0 to v_1. If we allow for the wealth effect in the consumption function, the *IS* curve will shift further to the right from $IS(G_1, v_0)$ to $IS(G_1, v_1)$. At the same level of interest rate, the increase in wealth implies a higher level of consumption and therefore of income. If we ignore, for the time being, the wealth effect in the demand for money, equilibrium would be established at D, with higher income and interest rates relative to B. The interest rate rise leads to further crowding-out effects. Thus, the wealth effect in the consumption function leads to an income expansion but also to higher interest rates and consequently to crowding out.

The increase in wealth also increases the demand for money. This causes a shift to the left in the *LM* curve, from $LM(m_0, v_0)$ to $LM(m_0, v_1)$. Final equilibrium is established at E, the intersection of $IS(G_1, v_1)$ with $LM(m_0, v_1)$. Notice that since the deficit is solely financed by bonds the money supply remains fixed at its initial value m_0. Point E is a long-run equilibrium because the budget is again balanced and the *psbr* is back to zero. Wealth rises sufficiently to balance the budget at the new equilibrium level of income, Y_f^e. At E, income is lower and the interest rate is even higher relative to D. The wealth effect in the demand for money raises the interest rate and therefore results in some further crowding out.

The total effect on income is obtained by totally differentiating (4.15) with respect to G and v_{-1}.

$$\Delta Y = \kappa_g \Delta G + C_v \kappa_g \Delta v_{-1} - M_v \kappa_m \Delta v_{-1} \qquad (4.18)$$

We can thus decompose the total effect (from A to E) of an increase in government expenditure under bond finance into three separate effects:

1 The direct expansionary effect of the increase in government expenditure. This results in a shift in the *IS* curve from $IS(G_0, v_0)$ to $IS(G_1, v_0)$. The effect on income, ΔY, is measured by the simple fiscal multiplier, $\kappa_g \Delta G$. The economy moves from A to B.
2 The indirect expansionary effect of any increase in consumption associated with the increase in wealth arising from the issue of more

bonds to finance the budget deficit, $C_v\kappa_g\Delta v_{-1}$. This effect moves the economy from B to D.

3 The indirect contractionary effect of any increase in the demand for money associated with the increase in wealth arising from the budget deficit, $-M_v\kappa_m\Delta v_{-1}$. This effect moves the economy from D to E.

It follows that the two wealth effects are working in opposite directions. The wealth effect in the consumption function is expansionary, whereas the wealth effect in the demand for money is contractionary. Whether point E lies to the right or to the left of B depends on the relative importance of the two wealth effects. A very strong wealth effect in the demand for money that outweighs the wealth effect in consumption implies that point E lies to the left of B. As we shall see below this is the case in which bond finance is unstable. On the other hand, a strong wealth effect in consumption that outweighs the wealth effect in the demand for money implies that point E lies to the right of B. Here the case of instability is not automatically ruled out. However, for certain parameter values the system is stable. If the economy is stable, point E implies higher income and higher interest rates relative to point B.

The overall long-run effect on income is greater than the short-run effect provided the economy is stable: in other words, Y_l^e lies to the right of Y_s^e. The long-run effect on the interest rate is also greater than the short-run effect (compare point E with point B). It must be noted that the decomposition of the total effect from A to E is conceptual and does not represent a possible time profile for income or the interest rate.

4.5 Fiscal Policy under Money Finance

In this section we consider the effects of an increase in government expenditure under pure money finance; that is, the whole deficit is financed solely by printing more money. The analysis is illustrated with the help of figure 4.2. Initial long-run equilibrium is at A, the intersection of $IS(G_0, v_0)$ and $LM(G_0, v_0)$. Point A defines a long-run equilibrium because the budget is balanced and the *psbr* is zero. The initial long-run level of output/income and the interest rate are Y^e and r^e respectively. Now the government increases its expenditure by ΔG, from G_0 to G_1. This shifts the IS curve from $IS(G_0, v_0)$ to $IS(G_1, v_0)$. At the same level of interest rate, there is an excess demand for goods and firms respond by increasing output. If we ignore the finance implications of the deficit, the wealth effects in consumption and the demand for assets – money and bonds – equilibrium would be attained at B, the intersection of $IS(G_1, v_0)$ and $LM(m_0, v_0)$. However, at B the budget

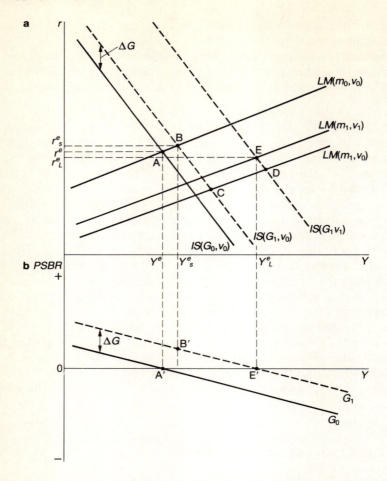

Figure 4.2   Money finance of ΔG A → B, simple fiscal multiplier; A → C, money finance, but no wealth effects; A → D, money finance, wealth effect on C; A → E, money finance, wealth effect on C and m^d

is in deficit, although not by the full initial amount, ΔG. The rise in income from Y^e to Y^e_s raises taxes and therefore some of the increase in the *psbr* is self-financed. The deficit is financed by printing more money and the stock of money is increased from m_0 to m_1. This causes the *LM* curve to shift to the right, from $LM(m_0, v_0)$ to $LM(m_1, v_0)$. At the initial level of income, there is an excess supply of money and the interest rate has to fall to equilibrate the assets markets. If we thus ignore the wealth effects in consumption and the demand for assets, but we consider the money finance implications of the budget deficit, equilibrium would be attained at C, the intersection of $IS(G_1, v_0)$ and $LM(m_1, v_0)$.

At C, output is even higher than at B and the interest rate is, most likely, lower than at B.

The increase in the stock of money from m_0 to m_1 also raises the value of private sector wealth, from v_0 to v_1. This leads households to increase their consumption expenditure. The increase in private sector wealth shifts the *IS* curve from $IS(G_1, v_0)$ to $IS(G_1, v_1)$. At the same level of interest rate, there is an excess demand for goods, because of increased consumption, which leads firms to increase production. If we ignore the wealth effect in the demand for money, but we consider the finance implications of the deficit and the wealth effect in consumption, equilibrium would be attained at D, with higher income and interest rates than at C. The rise in the interest rate associated with the wealth effect in consumption leads to some crowding out.

The rise in wealth also increases the demand for money. This causes the *LM* curve to shift upwards and to the left, from $LM(m_1, v_0)$ to $LM(m_1, v_1)$. At the same level of income, the rise in wealth creates an excess demand for money and the interest rate has to rise to equilibrate the assets markets. The final long-run equilibrium is attained at E, the intersection of $IS(G_1, v_1)$ with $LM(m_1, v_1)$. Income falls relative to D to Y_f^e and the interest rate rises to r_f^e. The interest rate rises even more relative to D. The wealth effect in the demand for money results in a further rise in the interest rate, which intensifies the crowding-out effects. The overall effect on the interest rate is uncertain: point E can be higher or lower than point A, depending on the relative importance of the wealth effects in consumption and the demand for money, and the extent of the increase in the money supply needed to finance the deficit. The overall effect on income is positive and greater than the short-run effect. Point E is a long-run equilibrium because the budget is balanced and the *psbr* is back to zero.

The total effect on income is obtained by totally differentiating (4.15) with respect to G, m and v_{-1}.

$$\Delta Y = \kappa_g \Delta G + \kappa_m \Delta m + C_v \kappa_g \Delta v_{-1} - M_v \kappa_m \Delta v_{-1} \tag{4.19}$$

We can thus decompose the total effect (from A to E) of an increase in government expenditure under money finance into four separate effects:

1 The direct expansionary effect of the increase in government expenditure. This results in a shift in the *IS* curve from $IS(G_0, v_0)$ to $IS(G_1, v_0)$. The effect on income, ΔY, is measured by the simple fiscal multiplier, $\kappa_g \Delta G$. This effect is common between money and bond finance. The economy moves from A to B.

2 The expansionary effect of any increase in the money supply associated with financing the budget deficit. This results in a shift in the

LM curve from $LM(m_0, v_0)$ to $LM(m_1, v_0)$. The effect on income, ΔY, is measured by $\kappa_m \Delta M$. The economy moves from B to C.

3 The expansionary effect of any increase in consumption associated with the increase in wealth arising from the budget deficit. This results in a shift in the IS curve from $IS(G_1, v_0)$ to $IS(G_1, v_1)$. The effect on income is measured by $C_v \kappa_g \Delta v_{-1}$. The economy moves from C to D.

4 The contractionary effect of any increase in the demand for money associated with the increase in wealth arising from the budget deficit. This results in a shift in the LM curve from $LM(m_1, v_0)$ to $LM(m_1, v_1)$. The effect on income is measured by $-M_v \kappa_m \Delta v_{-1}$. The economy moves from D to E.

It follows, as in the case of bond finance, that the two wealth effects are working in opposite directions. The wealth effect in consumption is expansionary, whereas the wealth effect in the demand for money is contractionary. Whether point E lies to the right or to the left of point B depends on the relative importance of the two wealth effects. These two effects were also present in the case of bond finance. However, under money finance there is one more expansionary effect in operation. This arises from the fact that the increase in the money supply, apart from its effect on wealth, also shifts the LM curve to the right. This reduces the interest rate and stimulates private investment expenditure.

4.6 Long-run (Steady-state) Effects of Fiscal Policy

We have considered up to now the effects of fiscal policy (in particular an increase in government expenditure) under bond and money finance. The question is which of these two policies is more expansionary in the long run, meaning at the new steady state. Initial equilibrium is at A and final long-run equilibrium is at E in terms of figures 4.1 and 4.2. The question therefore is whether $\Delta Y = Y_f^e - Y^e$ under bond finance (see figure 4.1) is greater or smaller than $\Delta Y = Y_f^e - Y^e$ under money finance (see figure 4.2). If we compare (4.18) with (4.19) we see that the former has three effects, two expansionary and one contractionary, while the latter has four effects, three expansionary and one contractionary. Thus, one would be tempted to say that money finance is more expansionary than bond finance. However, the long-run effects of fiscal policy (say, government expenditure) can be analysed very easily as follows. Substitute (4.6) into (4.7) and that into (4.11):

$$psbr = G + TR - t_0 - t_y Y \tag{4.20}$$

The condition for long-run equilibrium is that the budget is balanced and *psbr* is zero. From (4.12) we know that when the budget is balanced private sector wealth is stationary. This, in turn, implies that equilibrium in the goods and assets markets is no longer disturbed. Hence, the long-run effects of a change in government expenditure on income/output are obtained by differentiating (4.20) with respect to G and Y and setting the differential with respect to *psbr* equal to zero:

$$\Delta Y = \frac{1}{t_y} \Delta G \qquad (4.21)$$

The long-run effect of government expenditure on income/output is therefore independent of the mode of finance and is equal to the inverse of the marginal tax rate. Bond and money finance are equally expansionary in the long run. Thus, if the marginal tax rate $t_y = 0.25$, the long-run government expenditure multiplier is 4. The long-run multiplier is substantially higher than the short-run multiplier given by (4.16).

4.7 Stability under Bond and Money Finance

Substitute (4.15) and (4.10) into (4.20). Under bond finance this defines a first-order difference equation in terms of b:

$$b = (1 - t_y(C_v \kappa_g - M_v \kappa_m)) b_{-1} - (1 + t_y \kappa_m) m$$
$$+ (1 - t_y(C_v \kappa_g - M_v \kappa_m)) m_{-1} + (1 - t_y \kappa_g) G$$
$$+ (1 - C_y t_y \kappa_g)(TR - t_0) - t_y \kappa_g (C_0 + I_0) \qquad (4.22)$$

For stability under bond finance we require that the coefficient of b_{-1} lies within the unit circle. This implies that

$$\frac{C_v}{M_v} > \frac{\kappa_m}{\kappa_g} \qquad (4.23)$$

However, from (3.44) we know that the ratio of the two short-run multipliers (monetary to fiscal) is equal to the ratio of the interest rate sensitivity of investment, I_r, over the interest rate sensitivity of the demand for money, M_r. Making use of this last relationship, (4.23) becomes

$$C_v > \frac{I_r}{M_r} M_v \qquad (4.24)$$

Thus, for the system to be stable under bond finance, the wealth effect in the consumption function must be greater than the wealth effect in the demand for money by a factor that measures the relative effectiveness of monetary-to-fiscal policy. Figure 4.3 illustrates the case of instability under bond finance.

Under money finance, m is endogenous and b is exogenous. Hence (4.22) is solved for m. This defines a first-order difference equation in terms of m:

$$m = \frac{1}{(1 + t_y\kappa_m)} \left((1 - t_y(C_v\kappa_g - M_v\kappa_m))m_{-1} \right.$$

$$- (1 - t_y(C_v\kappa_g - M_v\kappa_m))b_{-1} + (1 - t_y\kappa_g)G$$

$$+ (1 - C_y t_y\kappa_g)(TR - t_0) - t_y\kappa_g(C_0 + I_0)) \tag{4.25}$$

For stability under money finance we require that the coefficient of m_{-1} lies within the unit circle. Making use of (3.44), this implies that

$$C_v > \frac{I_r}{M_r}(M_v - 1) \tag{4.26}$$

Since $0 < C_v, M_v < 1$ and both I_r and M_r are negative, (4.26) will always hold true. That is, with the usual restrictions on parameters, the system is stable under money finance.

Figure 4.4 plots the two stability conditions under bond and money

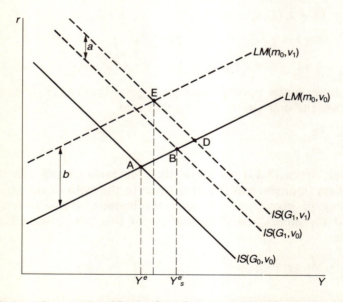

Figure 4.3   Instability under bond finance Point E lies to the left of B; *a* is less than *b*

finance (4.24 and 4.26). As can be seen from figure 4.3, the case of instability arises only under bond finance. For reasonable parameter values, money finance is always stable. Why is bond finance more likely to be unstable than money finance? The answer lies in (4.18) and (4.19). Under bond finance, there are two expansionary effects and one contractionary. Under money finance, there are three expansionary effects and one contractionary. We also know from (4.21) that the long-run effect on income of an increase in government expenditure is the same under bond and money finance. Yet there are fewer expansionary forces under bond than money finance. This implies that the possibility of reaching the new long-run equilibrium is smaller under bond than money finance.

In economic terms, the increase in government expenditure under bond finance implies an increase in the interest rate, which crowds out private expenditure and especially investment. The wealth effects in consumption and the demand for money lead to a further increase in the demand for money for transactions, which, for a given supply of money, implies an even higher interest rate. This leads to further crowding out relative to model 3. It is this crowding out that introduces the

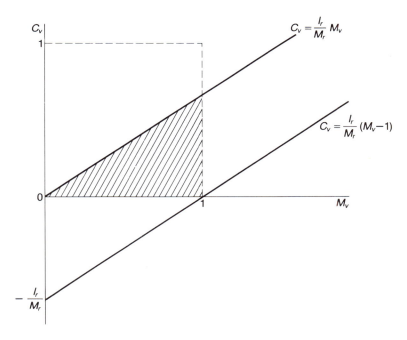

Figure 4.4   The shaded area illustrates instability under bond finance

possibility of instability under bond finance. This happens because, for the economy to be stable, income must rise by the inverse of the marginal tax rate. But a strong crowding-out effect may deny such an increase in income. This will certainly happen if the wealth effect in the demand for money is very strong. The interest rate rise leads to a fall in aggregate demand and therefore in income. Tax receipts decline along with income and this means that the deficit widens. The government has to issue more bonds to finance an enlarged deficit, which increases private sector wealth even more. The latter leads to even higher interest rates, which in turn crowd out private investment. As a result income falls and the deficit widens even more. Income continues to decline and the deficit is enlarged *ad infinitum*. This is the case of instability.

Money finance is stable because the possibility of crowding out is reduced by allowing the money supply to increase to provide finance for the budget deficit. The increase in the money supply results in an interest rate fall, rather than rise, and this reduces the possibility of crowding out. The interest rate fall implies that investment rises. This does not lead to a greater overall expansion under money finance, because the long-run effect is the same under both modes of finance. It simply increases the probability of stability under money finance.

4.8 The Transmission of Fiscal Policy

It is instructive to examine how the transmission mechanism of fiscal policy that we have been building up in the last three models is affected in the context of model 4, which allows for the dynamics of budget finance and the presence of wealth effects. Box 4.1 provides a schematic approach to the transmission mechanism of fiscal policy under bond finance. An increase in government expenditure raises aggregate demand ($G\uparrow \Rightarrow Y\uparrow$). For a given level of output, there is an excess demand for goods and firms respond by increasing output ($D\uparrow \Rightarrow Y\uparrow$). The increase in factor incomes leads to a rise in disposable income ($Y\uparrow \Rightarrow YD\uparrow$). Households respond by increasing consumption ($YD\uparrow \Rightarrow C\uparrow$). Since the latter is a constituent part of aggregate demand there is a further stimulus in demand ($C\uparrow \Rightarrow D\uparrow$), to which firms respond by increasing output yet again – route (a). But as income rises the transactions demand for money also increases ($Y\uparrow \Rightarrow m^d\uparrow$). With a given money supply, there is an excess demand for money and the interest rate has to rise to equilibrate the assets markets ($m^d\uparrow \Rightarrow r\uparrow$). The interest rate rise crowds out private investment ($r\uparrow \Rightarrow I\downarrow$). This leads to a fall in aggregate demand ($I\downarrow \Rightarrow D\downarrow$), to which firms respond by cutting output ($D\downarrow \Rightarrow Y\downarrow$) – route (b).

This part of the transmission mechanism is exactly the same as the

Box 4.1 The transmission of fiscal policy (government expenditure) under bond finance

$$G\uparrow \Rightarrow \begin{cases} D\uparrow \Rightarrow Y\uparrow \Rightarrow \\ \\ psbr\uparrow \Rightarrow b\uparrow \Rightarrow v\uparrow \Rightarrow \end{cases} \begin{cases} YD\uparrow \Rightarrow C\uparrow \Rightarrow D\uparrow \Rightarrow Y\uparrow & \text{(a)} \\ \\ m^d\uparrow \Rightarrow r\uparrow \Rightarrow I\downarrow \Rightarrow D\downarrow \Rightarrow Y\downarrow & \text{(b)} \\ \\ C\uparrow \Rightarrow D\uparrow \Rightarrow Y\uparrow & \text{(c)} \end{cases}$$

one derived in the context of model 3. The increase in government expenditure, however, leads to a budget deficit and a rise in *psbr* ($G\uparrow \Rightarrow psbr\uparrow$). Under bond finance, the government issues more bonds to finance its deficit ($psbr\uparrow \Rightarrow b\uparrow$). This increases private sector wealth ($b\uparrow \Rightarrow v\uparrow$), which in turn stimulates consumption ($v\uparrow \Rightarrow C\uparrow$), aggregate demand ($C\uparrow \Rightarrow D\uparrow$) and income ($D\uparrow \Rightarrow Y\uparrow$) – route (c).

As wealth rises, however, the demand for money increases ($v\uparrow \Rightarrow m^d\uparrow$) and with a fixed money supply there is an excess demand for money. The interest rate has to rise to equilibrate the money (and bond) market ($m^d\uparrow \Rightarrow r\uparrow$). This crowds out private investment ($r\downarrow \Rightarrow I\downarrow$), which depresses aggregate demand ($I\downarrow \Rightarrow D\downarrow$) and therefore income – route (b). Thus, there are two sources of crowding out in the context of model 4: the traditional income effect in the demand for money, which was analysed in model 3, and the wealth effect in the demand for money, which is the new element that is introduced in model 4. These two effects reinforce one another, thereby strengthening the crowding-out effect.

The transmission mechanism of fiscal policy under money finance is discussed with the help of box 4.2. The first route is the same as under bond finance and follows the principles of model 3. The increase in government expenditure leads to a budget deficit and a rise in *psbr* ($G\uparrow \Rightarrow psbr\uparrow$). Under money finance, the government prints more money to provide finance for the deficit ($psbr\uparrow \Rightarrow m\uparrow$). This creates an excess supply of money and the interest rate falls to equilibrate the assets markets ($m\uparrow \Rightarrow r\downarrow$). The fall in the interest rate stimulates investment ($r\downarrow \Rightarrow I\uparrow$), aggregate demand ($I\uparrow \Rightarrow D\uparrow$) and therefore income ($D\uparrow \Rightarrow Y\uparrow$) – route (b).

The increase in the stock of money also increases private sector wealth ($M\uparrow \Rightarrow v\uparrow$). Households respond to the increase in wealth by spending more on consumption ($v\uparrow \Rightarrow C\uparrow$). This stimulates demand and therefore income ($C\uparrow \Rightarrow D\uparrow \Rightarrow Y\uparrow$) – route (c). However, the increase in wealth also increases the demand for money ($v\uparrow \Rightarrow m^d\uparrow$). This tends to offset the excess supply of money, thereby reversing the interest rate adjustment process. This process is further intensified through the increase in

Box 4.2 The transmission of fiscal policy (government expenditure) under money finance

$$G\uparrow \Rightarrow \begin{cases} D\uparrow \Rightarrow Y\uparrow \Rightarrow \begin{cases} YD\uparrow \Rightarrow C\uparrow \Rightarrow D\uparrow \Rightarrow Y\uparrow \quad \text{(a)} \\ \\ m^d\uparrow \end{cases} \\ \qquad\qquad\qquad\qquad \Downarrow \\ psbr\uparrow \Rightarrow m\uparrow \Rightarrow \begin{cases} r\downarrow > r\uparrow \Rightarrow I\uparrow \Rightarrow D\uparrow \Rightarrow Y\uparrow \qquad \text{(b)} \\ \qquad\qquad \Uparrow \\ v\uparrow \Rightarrow \begin{cases} m^d\uparrow \\ \\ C\uparrow \Rightarrow D\uparrow \Rightarrow Y\uparrow \qquad\qquad \text{(c)} \end{cases} \end{cases} \end{cases}$$

the demand for money due to the income rise. The overall effect on the interest rate is uncertain because there are two forces that tend to raise the interest rate – income and wealth – while there is one force that tends to lower the interest rate – supply of money. In an economy where assets markets clear faster than the goods market, however, the interest rate adjustment process is one in which the interest rate initially falls and then gradually rises. Whether in the new long-run equilibrium the interest rate is higher or lower relative to the initial rate depends on parameter values.

4.9 Summary and Limitations of Model 4

Model 4 introduces a distinction between short-run and long-run equilibrium. The equilibrium condition in model 3, that demand equals supply in the goods and assets markets, defines only a short-run (or instantaneous) equilibrium in the context of dynamic model 4. A budget deficit or surplus implies a change in private sector wealth, which disturbs equilibrium in the goods and assets markets. Long-run equilibrium is obtained when wealth becomes stationary. This occurs when the budget is balanced.

The long-run effect of a fiscal expansion on income is greater than the short-run effect. The increase in private sector wealth associated with financing the budget deficit is highly expansionary, provided the system is stable. However, the long-run effect on the interest rate depends on the mode of finance. Under bond finance, the interest rate rises relative to the initial equilibrium. The long-run effect is higher than the short-run; that is, interest rates rise in the long run even more than in the short run.

Under money finance, on the other hand, the effect on the interest rate is uncertain. If the wealth effect in the demand for money is weak, then the most likely long-run effect is a drop in the interest rate. The interest rate rises in the long run relative to the short run.

The long-run effects of fiscal policy on income/output are independent of the mode of budget finance. An increase in government expenditure raises income by the inverse of the marginal tax rate under either bond or money finance. However, the mode of finance has implications for the composition of output. Bond finance implies higher interest rates and therefore an expansion of the public sector at the expense of the private sector through crowding out. Money finance, on the other hand, leads to lower interest rates relative to bond finance, if not relative to the initial equilibrium, too. This allows for a higher contribution of the private sector to GDP than with bond finance.

Bond finance is more likely to be unstable than money finance. This possibility arises because bond finance may, through crowding out, deny the expansion in income that is necessary for long-run equilibrium. A substantial rise in the interest rate crowds out private investment and leads to a fall rather than a rise in aggregate demand and consequently income. This reduces tax receipts and the deficit widens instead of narrowing down. This forces the government to issue even more bonds, which raise private sector wealth even further. This leads to even higher interest rates, which through crowding out lead to a further decline in income. The budget deficit widens even further and leads to another round of income fall. This is the case of instability under bond finance. Income keeps on falling.

It would therefore appear that, on the stability criterion if not also on the grounds of the composition of output, money finance is preferable to bond finance. However, as we shall see in the next two chapters, this conclusion will be qualified in the presence of interest payments on government debt and when prices are allowed to change. Nevertheless, if the economy is in recession with a lot of excess capacity a money finance fiscal stimulus must be preferred to bond finance.

5

Model 5 A Simulation Model with Asset Accumulation and Interest Payments

In this model the assumption that there are no interest payments on government debt is relaxed. Bonds are assumed to be fixed-price–variable-coupon with a maturity of one quarter. Interest is paid on maturity. The introduction of interest payments makes the model non-linear. Instead of linearizing the model along a given path, or long-run equilibrium, and studying it analytically, we prefer to solve it numerically by assigning plausible numerical values to the coefficients of the model. This approach has the advantage that it enables the study of the dynamic adjustment of the system from one long-run (steady-state) equilibrium to another. There are three sources of dynamics in this model: first, wealth accumulation dynamics arising from the finance of a budget deficit; second, dynamics arising from a different speed of adjustment between the goods and assets markets; third, dynamics arising from the fact that the effect of the explanatory variables on the economic system is not instantaneous, but is distributed through time.

The introduction of interest payments changes the conclusions of model 4 about the efficacy of fiscal policy under bond and money finance and the stability of the system. Furthermore, the effectiveness of fiscal policy along the transient dynamic path from one steady state to another under the two modes of finance is compared. Finally, the dynamic effects of open market operations are considered.

5.1 Assumptions

The assumptions made in the context of model 4 also hold in model 5. In particular, it is assumed that prices are fixed. There are only two assets in the economy: money and government bonds. Physical capital is fixed and therefore changes in investment do not affect the stock of capital. The only effect of investment is on the level of aggregate demand. The economy is closed. To keep the number of cases we analyse within reasonable limits, we assume that the goods market adjusts sluggishly, whereas the assets markets adjust instantly. Furthermore, in order to simplify comparisons with model 4 we abstain from the dynamics that arise from the distributed lag effects of the explanatory variables. Instead, it is assumed that the total effect of the explanatory variables is felt instantly. Alternative assumptions regarding the differential speed of adjustment of the goods and assets markets and the time profile of the effect of the explanatory variables on the system are left as exercises for the interested reader.

5.2 The Model

The model is assumed to be quarterly and consists of equations (5.1) to (5.12).

$$D = C + I + G \tag{5.1}$$

$$C = \mathcal{U}(\delta_{CY})\{\alpha_{CY} YD + \alpha_{Copi}(1 - HRT)opi\}$$
$$+ \alpha_{Cr}\mathcal{U}(\delta_{Cr})r + \alpha_{Cv}\mathcal{U}(\delta_{Cv})v_{-1} + \alpha_{CC}C_{-1} + \gamma_C \tag{5.2}$$

$$\alpha_{Cr} < 0, \quad 0 < \alpha_{CY}, \alpha_{Copi}, \alpha_{Cv}, \alpha_{CC} < 1$$

$$I = \alpha_{IY}\mathcal{U}(\delta_{IY}) Y + \alpha_{Ir}\mathcal{U}(\delta_{Ir})r - \alpha_{IK}K_{-1} + \alpha_{II}I_{-1} + \gamma_I \tag{5.3}$$

$$\alpha_{IY} > 0, \quad \alpha_{Ir} < 0, \quad 0 < \alpha_{IK}, \alpha_{II} < 1$$

$$Y = D \tag{5.4}$$

$$YD = (1 - SRT) Y \tag{5.5}$$

$$opi = ((1 + r_{-1})^{1/4} - 1)b_{-1} + \gamma_{opi} \tag{5.6}$$

$$m = \alpha_{MY}\mathcal{U}(\delta_{MY}) Y + \alpha_{Mv}\mathcal{U}(\delta_{Mv})\frac{v_{-1}}{CPI} + \alpha_{Mr}\mathcal{U}(\delta_{Mr})r + \gamma_M \tag{5.7}$$

$$\alpha_{MY} > 0, \quad \alpha_{Mr} < 0, \quad 0 < \alpha_{Mv} < 1$$

$$psbr = G + ((1 + r_{-1})^{1/4} - 1)b_{-1} - T - HRTopi + \gamma_{psbr} \tag{5.8}$$

$$T = SRT\,Y \tag{5.9}$$

$$m = m_{-1} + \alpha_{monfin}\,psbr + \Delta mb \tag{5.10}$$

$$0 < \alpha_{monfin} < 1$$

$$b = b_{-1} + (1 - \alpha_{monfin})psbr + \Delta omo \tag{5.11}$$

$$v = m + b + K \tag{5.12}$$

	Variable definition	Initial steady-state value
b	= real stock of government bonds	50
C	= real consumer expenditure	65
D	= aggregate demand	100
G	= real government expenditure	25
HRT	= higher rate of income tax on other personal income	0.6
I	= real gross investment expenditure	10
K	= capital stock	200
m	= real money stock, currency in circulation (notes and coin)	10
mb	= real autonomous monetary base	0
omo	= open market operations instrument	0
opi	= real other personal income (interest income)	2.0768
$psbr$	= real public sector borrowing requirement	0
r	= interest rate (yield) on government bonds	0.1
SRT	= standard rate of income tax	0.25
T	= total tax revenues, in real terms	25
v	= real stock of private sector wealth	300
Y	= real gross domestic output, GDP, real income	100
YD	= real disposable income	75

$$\mathcal{U}(\delta)X = \sum_{i=0}^{3}\delta_i X_{-i} / \sum_{i=0}^{3}\delta_i \text{ is a unitary moving average operator.}$$

In the exercises reported below $\mathcal{U}(\delta) = (1\,0\,0\,0)$, i.e. the total effect is distributed instantaneously.

Coefficient	Value
α_{CY}	0.35
α_{Copi}	0.5
α_{Cr}	−25
α_{Cv}	0.15
α_{CC}	0.5
γ_C	−36.25
α_{IY}	0.0775
α_{Ir}	−25
α_{IK}	0.05
α_{II}	0.0

γ_I	14.75
α_{MY}	0.075
α_{Mr}	-50
α_{Mv}	0.001
γ_M	7.2
γ_{PSBR}	0.04
α_{monfin}	1.0

Equation (5.1) defines aggregate demand. Consumption demand (5.2) depends on real disposable income, other personal income, the interest rate and private sector wealth. The influence of the interest rate arises from the definition of consumption as the sum of expenditure on non-durables and durables. A large part of the expenditure on durables is financed by credit and therefore changes in the terms of credit affect consumer expenditure. Hence, a rise in the interest rate deters consumption.

The model distinguishes between earned and unearned income. Real disposable income represents earned income that is generated by the participation of the factors of production (labour and capital) in the production of total output, GDP. Unearned income, called other personal income (*opi*), is the interest income that accrues to the holders of government bonds.

Actual consumption adjusts partially to desired consumption. The adjustment of actual consumption from one quarter to the next, $C_t - C_{t-1}$, is proportional to the desired adjustment, $C_t^* - C_{t-1}$. The partial adjustment hypothesis can be stated as

$$C_t - C_{t-1} = (1 - \alpha_{CC})(C_t^* - C_{t-1}) \qquad (5.13)$$

The coefficient α_{CC} measures the speed of adjustment and varies between zero and unity. Small values of α_{CC} imply quick adjustment, and vice versa. If $\alpha_{CC} = 0$, the adjustment is instantaneous. If $\alpha_{CC} = 1$, no adjustment takes place. Desired consumption is a function of real disposable income, other personal income, the interest rate and private sector wealth:

$$C^* = C(YD, opi, r, v_{-1}) \qquad (5.14)$$

Substituting (5.14) and (5.13) eliminates the unobserved variable C^*. Equation (5.2) and the other functions are derived in this manner.

The effect of disposable income on consumption is measured by the coefficient α_{CY}. The unitary moving operator $U(\delta)$ implies that the total effect α_{CY} is distributed through time according to the values of δ_i, and similarly for all other variables. In the current version of the model this effect is assumed to be instantaneous.

The coefficient α_{CY} is the short-run marginal propensity to consume. The long-run marginal propensity to consume is given by

$$\frac{\alpha_{CY}}{1 - \alpha_{CC}}$$

This is obtained by partially differentiating C with respect to YD in steady state. The latter is attained when $C = C_{-1}$ and $YD = YD_{-1} = \ldots = YD_{-4}$.

The model distinguishes between the marginal propensity to consume out of earned and unearned income, α_{CY} and $\alpha_{Copi}(1 - HRT)$, with the former being greater than the latter. This reflects the hypothesis that wage earners (low income groups) save a smaller fraction of a given increase in income than bond holders (high income groups).

An increase in the interest rate affects consumption through two channels. First, it raises the terms of credit and therefore deters consumer expenditure and in particular expenditure on durables. Secondly, it increases interest payments on government debt and therefore raises other personal income, which in turn stimulates consumption. Given that in the real world the proportion of bond holders is small and that their marginal propensity to consume out of unearned income is less than that out of earned income, it is plausible to assume that the overall effect on consumption of an increase in the interest rate is negative.

Private investment expenditure (5.3) depends on income/output, the interest rate and the stock of capital. Hence, the investment function in model 5 differs in two respects from model 4. First, it makes investment a function of income/output. This stands as a proxy for demand. As demand for the output produced in the economy rises, firms respond by increasing investment to expand capacity to meet future demand. The implicit assumption here is that firms expect the increase in demand to be permanent rather than temporary. Thus, it is possible that firms do not increase their investment expenditure, in spite of a rise in current demand, if it is perceived as temporary. Ideally, it is firms' expectations about future demand that affect current investment, since the latter alters capacity with a lag that varies from one to five years according to the industry. However, it is reasonable to assume that firms look at the current and past levels of demand, among other things, in forming expectations about future demand. In this model, however, we abstract from such complications and assume that an increase in current demand leads firms to increase their investment expenditure. This effect is measured by the coefficient α_{IY}.

The second difference between model 5 and model 4 is that investment also depends on the stock of capital. This approximates the effect of capacity utilization on investment. Other things being equal, an increase in the capital stock leads to an increase in productive capacity and hence to a decrease in capacity utilization. The latter deters, *ceteris paribus*, new investment expenditure.

Equation (5.4) asserts that equilibrium in the goods market is obtained when aggregate demand equals aggregate supply. Real disposable income (5.5) is defined as factor incomes net of income taxes. Factor incomes are taxed with a proportional tax rate, which is called the standard rate of income tax, *SRT*.

Government bonds are of the fixed-price–variable-coupon variety and they mature in one quarter. Other personal income, interest income, is defined in (5.6) as the product of the interest that accrues in a quarter times the stock of government bonds in existence.

The demand for money (5.7) depends on income, the interest rate and private sector wealth, as in model 4. The income, interest rate and wealth sensitivity of the demand for money is measured by α_{MY}, α_{Mr} and α_{Mv} respectively.

The public sector borrowing requirement, *psbr*, is defined in equation (5.8). Government expenditure includes spending on goods and services and interest payments on the existing stock of government debt, represented by the second term on the right hand side of (5.8). Tax revenues arise from two sources. The government is taxing factor incomes at the standard rate of income tax, *SRT* (5.9). The government is also taxing other personal income at a much higher rate of income tax, *HRT*.

The government can finance a budget deficit through printing money or issuing bonds. Indeed, the government can choose any combination it wishes between money and bond finance. This is controlled by the coefficient α_{monfin}, which varies between zero and one. The higher the value of α_{monfin}, the greater the degree of money finance. The smaller the value of α_{monfin}, the greater the extent of bond finance. At the extremes, if $\alpha_{monfin} = 1$, the deficit is purely money-financed. An increase in the *psbr* leaves the stock of government bonds unchanged (see 5.11), whereas the money supply increases, initially, by the full extent of the *psbr* (see 5.11). If $\alpha_{monfin} = 0$, the deficit is wholly bond-financed. The money supply remains unchanged, whereas the stock of bonds increases, initially, by an amount equal to the rise in *psbr*.

The government may change the quantity of money in the economy for reasons other than those relating to the finance of the budget. This reflects a change in monetary policy and is implemented in the context of model 5 by changing the value of the autonomous monetary base, *mb*. An increase in *mb* implies an expansionary (easy) monetary policy, which will lead to lower interest rates. A decrease in *mb* implies a contractionary (tight) monetary policy, which leads to higher interest rates. Similarly, the government may also change the stock of government bonds for reasons other than those relating to the finance of the budget.

This also reflects a change in monetary policy and is implemented here through a change in *omo*. An increase in *omo* implies a tight monetary policy and vice versa.

Finally, equation (5.12) defines private sector wealth as the sum of the stock of money, the stock of government bonds and capital stock.

5.3 Monetary Policy

Two aspects of monetary policy are considered: a straight increase in the supply of money and an open market purchase. The former is unrealistic because it means that people find themselves unexpectedly with more money (money from heaven). However, it corresponds to the money multiplier of models 3 and 4 and therefore is a useful experiment for comparison purposes. An open market purchase is a much more realistic exercise. It means that the government increases the supply of money by reducing the stock of government bonds by the same amount. Therefore it is a transaction in the stock exchange. The dynamic as well as the steady-state effects of the monetary expansion depend on the type of monetary policy pursued. We distinguish two cases: first, a policy of monetary targets, according to which after the initial shock the money supply is kept unchanged at the higher level; second, a policy of debt targets, according to which the stock of bonds is kept unchanged after the shock.

Increase in the Money Supply

Box 5.1 provides a schematic approach of the main channels through which an increase in the supply of money influences the economy. The initial effect is a fall in the interest rate, as the latter responds to clear the money market from an excess supply of money ($m\uparrow \Rightarrow r\downarrow$). The decline in the interest rate implies lower borrowing costs for firms and this stimulates investment and consumption ($r\downarrow \Rightarrow I\uparrow$ and $C\uparrow$), as a result of which aggregate demand increases ($I\uparrow$ and $C\uparrow \Rightarrow D\uparrow$). At the initial level of output, this creates an excess demand in the goods market, to which firms respond by increasing production ($D\uparrow \Rightarrow Y\uparrow$). This part of the transmission mechanism, route (a), is identical to the one in model 3. However, in the context of model 5 the fall in the interest rate implies, at the initial stock of government bonds, lower interest payments. Since other personal income consists exclusively of the coupon from bonds, it follows that the fall in the interest rate diminishes other personal income ($r\downarrow \Rightarrow opi\downarrow$). This reduces consumption, which in turn depresses aggregate demand and consequently income – route (b).

The reduction in interest payments implies that the deficit is diminished

Box 5.1 The transmission of monetary policy (increase in money supply)

$$I\uparrow \text{ and } C\uparrow \Rightarrow D\uparrow \Rightarrow Y\uparrow \tag{a}$$

$$m\uparrow \Rightarrow \begin{cases} r\downarrow \Rightarrow \begin{cases} opi\downarrow \Rightarrow C\downarrow \Rightarrow D\downarrow \Rightarrow Y\downarrow & \text{(b)} \\ \\ v\uparrow < \quad v\downarrow \Rightarrow C\downarrow \Rightarrow D\downarrow \Rightarrow Y\downarrow & \text{(c)} \end{cases} \end{cases}$$

and thus *psbr* falls. Now, the central bank has an option: to retire debt from the market or cut the money supply. If the government pursues a policy of monetary targets, the supply of money will remain fixed after the initial shock and the central bank will reduce the stock of government bonds, which in turn lowers private sector wealth. Thus, $r\downarrow \Rightarrow v\downarrow$. This induces households to spend less on consumption ($v\downarrow \Rightarrow C\downarrow$), which in turn depresses aggregate demand ($C\downarrow \Rightarrow D\downarrow$) and therefore income ($D\downarrow \Rightarrow Y\downarrow$) – route (c).

If the government follows debt targets, the stock of government bonds will remain fixed and the central bank will cut the supply of money. The latter reverses the interest rate adjustment process. The system will finally return to its original long-run equilibrium. The initial increase in the stock of money raises private sector wealth. However, as we have just seen, the fall in the interest rate leads to a decline in private sector wealth. Which of these effects dominates, depends on the type of monetary policy. Under monetary targets, the most likely effect is an ultimate fall in private sector wealth. Under debt targets, the fall in private sector wealth exactly offsets the initial increase and the economy returns to the original steady state.

An illustration of the various forces that work in the transmission of monetary policy is provided by simulating model 5 numerically under monetary targets. This is achieved by setting $\alpha_{monfin} = 0$ and implies that the only increase in the money supply is due to the policy shock induced by the central bank. The implications of this policy action on the budget and *psbr* are felt through changes in the stock of government bonds (see equations 5.10 and 5.11).

Figures 5.1 to 5.3 present the results for income, the interest rate and wealth, respectively, of simulating a permanent increase in the stock of money by £1 billion. The policy shock in the supply of money is induced via an increase in autonomous monetary base, *mb*. Initially, income rises rapidly, reaching its peak by the end of the first year with a multiplier of 2.3. However, after the first year income declines continuously. In

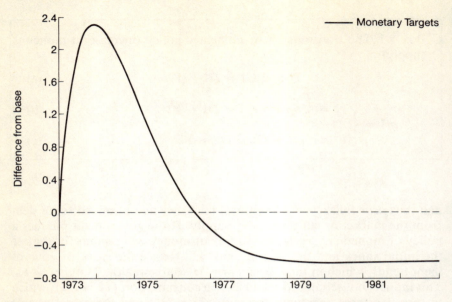

Figure 5.1 Output response to a step increase in the money supply under monetary targets

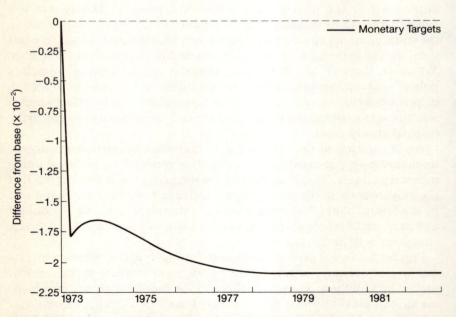

Figure 5.2 Interest rate response to a step increase in the money supply under monetary targets

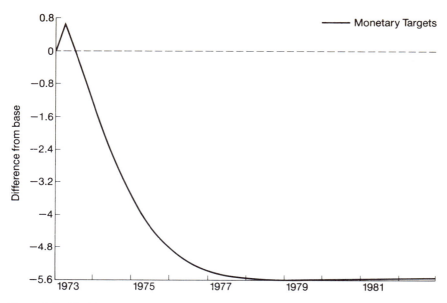

Figure 5.3 Wealth response to a step increase in the money supply under monetary targets

the new steady state income is lower than in the original steady state. The interest rate falls on impact by 1.8 percentage points; it then rises for the next two quarters, before it settles down to even lower than the impact level. Wealth rises only in the first quarter and then continuously declines, reaching a new steady state after five years at a much lower level than the initial steady state.

The initial fall in the interest rate is caused by the excess supply of money. This stimulates both consumption and investment, thus causing the upswing phase of the business cycle. The reduction in the interest rate, however, lowers interest payments on the existing stock of government bonds, hence cutting the budget and *psbr*. Under monetary targets, the government retires bonds from the market and this reduces private sector wealth, thus causing income contraction. Since the wealth effect works much more slowly than the interest rate effect on expenditure, the income contraction is not immediate. The ultimate income contraction is due to a strong wealth effect on consumption. However, unless there is such a strong wealth effect, the economy is unstable.

Open Market Purchase

Box 5.2 provides a schematic view of the main channels through which an open market purchase influences the economy under monetary

Box 5.2 The transmission of monetary policy (open market purchase) under monetary and debt targets

$$I\uparrow \Rightarrow D\uparrow \Rightarrow Y\uparrow \tag{a}$$

$$\Delta m\uparrow = -\Delta b\downarrow \Rightarrow r\downarrow \Rightarrow \begin{cases} opi\downarrow \Rightarrow C\downarrow \Rightarrow D\downarrow \Rightarrow Y\downarrow & \text{(b)} \\[2mm] psbr\downarrow \Rightarrow \begin{cases} b\downarrow \Rightarrow v\downarrow \Rightarrow C\downarrow \Rightarrow Y\downarrow & \text{(c1)} \\[2mm] m\downarrow \Rightarrow r\uparrow \Rightarrow I\downarrow \Rightarrow Y\downarrow & \text{(c2)} \end{cases} \end{cases}$$

and debt targets. An open market purchase implies that the central bank buys government bonds. This increases the supply of money and reduces the stock of bonds by the same amount ($\Delta m\uparrow = -\Delta b\downarrow$). The interest rate falls to equilibrate the money market. The interest rate affects the economic system through three channels. The first effect of the interest rate fall is to stimulate demand and therefore income – route (a). Second, the interest rate fall reduces other personal income, which induces households to spend less on consumption; hence aggregate demand, and therefore income, decline – route (b).

The third effect of the interest rate fall is a reduction in debt service and consequently in *psbr*. It is at this stage that the type of monetary policy being pursued by the government matters. The central bank has the option to retire debt or reduce the supply of money. Under monetary targets, the money supply remains fixed and the stock of bonds is reduced. This leads to a fall in private sector wealth, which depresses consumption and therefore income – route (c1). With debt targets, however, the central bank keeps the stock of government bonds fixed and reduces the supply of money. This reverses the adjustment process and the interest rate rises. Investment expenditure is deterred and therefore income declines – route (c2).

The effects of an open market purchase under monetary and debt targets are simulated through model 5 and the results are presented in figures 5.4 to 5.6 for income, interest rate and wealth, respectively. The open market purchase is simulated by setting $\Delta mb = -\Delta omo = £1$ billion.

Income initially rises and then declines under both policies. However, the rise in income is greater and lasts for one year under monetary targets, whereas it is much smaller and lasts for only one quarter under debt targets. In the new steady state income is lower relative to the initial steady state under both policies. The lowest income occurs under monetary targets. The interest rate falls on impact. With debt targets

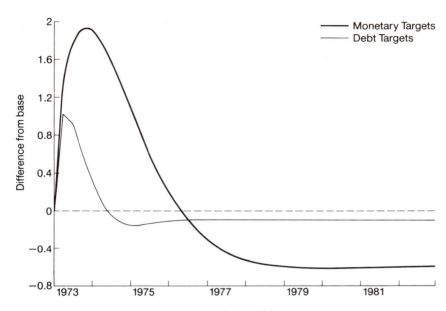

Figure 5.4 Output response to an open market purchase

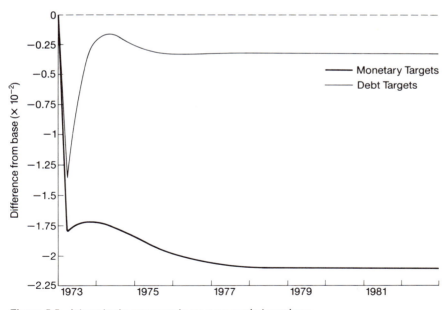

Figure 5.5 Interest rate response to an open market purchase

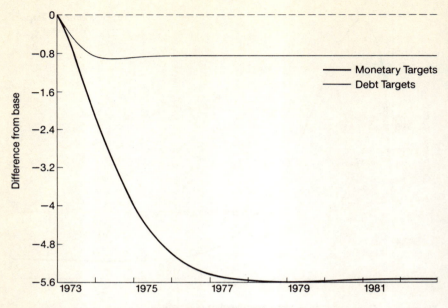

Figure 5.6 Wealth response to an open market purchase

there is an initial overshooting of the new long-run equilibrium. In contrast, the interest rate undershoots its new steady state under monetary targets. Wealth declines monotonically. The biggest fall occurs under monetary targets.

The initial stimulus to the economy comes from the impact fall in the interest rate. With debt targets the reduction in the interest rate leads to a decline in *psbr* and the central bank reacts by cutting the money supply. This reverses the adjustment process and the interest rate rises. However, with monetary targets the central bank retires debt from the market, private sector wealth is reduced and therefore income declines. As a result, the demand for money falls and the interest rate is reduced again. This causes a further decline in *psbr* and the central bank retires even more debt from the market, which in turn causes a further drop in private sector wealth.

5.4 The Long-run Effects of Fiscal Policy

The long-run effects of fiscal policy can be analysed by substituting (5.9) into (5.8) and noting that the second term on the right hand side of (5.8) is equal to *opi*:

$$psbr = G - SRT\,Y + (1 - HRT)opi \tag{5.15}$$

The condition for long-run equilibrium is that the budget is balanced. The long-run effect of a change in government expenditure on income is obtained by differentiating (5.15) with respect to G and setting $\mathrm{d}psbr = 0$:

$$\frac{\mathrm{d}Y}{\mathrm{d}G} = \frac{1}{SRT} + \frac{1 - HRT}{SRT}\frac{\mathrm{d}opi}{\mathrm{d}G} \tag{5.16}$$

The inclusion of interest payments on government debt changes the conclusions reached in model 4 on the efficacy of fiscal policy. In that model the long-run effect of a change in government expenditure on income/output is independent of the mode of finance and is equal to the inverse of the marginal tax rate. This is given by the first term on the right hand side of (5.16). In model 5, the long-run effect on income/output differs from that in model 4 by the second term on the right hand side of 5.16. This represents the effect of government expenditure on interest payments (debt service) or other personal income, since the private sector holds only government bonds. This is certainly affected by the mode of finance. Thus, the inclusion of interest payments makes the long-run effects of government expenditure on income/output dependent on the mode of finance.

The effect of government expenditure on *opi* is obtained from (5.6). Substituting this into (5.16) and remembering that time subscripts can be dropped since we are dealing with steady-state effects, we get

$$\frac{\mathrm{d}Y}{\mathrm{d}G} = \frac{1}{SRT} + \frac{1 - HRT}{SRT}\left(\frac{1}{4}(1 + r)^{-3/4}b\frac{\mathrm{d}r}{\mathrm{d}G}\right.$$
$$\left. + ((1 + r)^{1/4} - 1)\frac{\mathrm{d}b}{\mathrm{d}G}\right) \tag{5.17}$$

Hence, the long-run income multiplier consists of three effects: first, the effect obtained in the context of model 4, which is equal to the inverse of the marginal tax rate; second, the long-run effect of government expenditure on the interest rate; third, the long-run effect of government expenditure on government debt. Under bond finance, the interest rate rises unambiguously in the long run and hence the second term on the right hand side of (5.17) is positive. Furthermore, the effect of increasing government expenditure is to raise the stock of government bonds and therefore the third term in (5.17) is also positive. Thus, the long-run income multiplier in model 5 is greater than that in model 4 by the last two terms in (5.17).

Under money finance, on the other hand, the last term in (5.17) is zero, whereas the second term is most likely negative. Thus, the inclusion of interest payments makes bond finance more expansionary than money finance in the long run.

5.5 The Transmission of Fiscal Policy under Bond and Money Finance

We have seen that the inclusion of interest payments changes the conclusions reached about the efficacy of fiscal policy in the long run. In this section we examine the transition from one steady state to another. In other words, the focal point of the analysis is the dynamics of the system under bond and money finance. Box 5.3 provides a schematic view of the main channels through which an increase in government expenditure affects the economic system. It must be stressed that only primary forces within one cycle are analysed and feedback effects are for simplicity ignored.

Box 5.3 The transmission of fiscal policy (increase in government expenditure) under bond finance

$$
G\uparrow \Rightarrow
\begin{cases}
D\uparrow \Rightarrow Y\uparrow \Rightarrow
\begin{cases}
YD\uparrow \Rightarrow C\uparrow \Rightarrow D\uparrow \Rightarrow Y\uparrow & \text{(a)} \\
I\downarrow \Rightarrow D\downarrow \Rightarrow Y\downarrow & \text{(b)}
\end{cases} \\
psbr\uparrow \Rightarrow b\uparrow \Rightarrow v\uparrow \Rightarrow
\begin{cases}
m^d\uparrow \Rightarrow r\uparrow \Rightarrow
\begin{cases}
opi\uparrow \Rightarrow C\uparrow \Rightarrow Y\uparrow & \text{(c)} \\
\end{cases} \\
v\uparrow \Rightarrow C\uparrow \Rightarrow Y\uparrow & \text{(d)} \\
C\uparrow \Rightarrow D\uparrow \Rightarrow Y\uparrow & \text{(e)}
\end{cases}
\end{cases}
$$

An increase in government expenditure raises aggregate demand ($G\uparrow \Rightarrow D\uparrow$). At a given level of output, there is an excess demand in the goods market and firms respond by increasing output and therefore factor incomes ($D\uparrow \Rightarrow Y\uparrow$). This has two effects. First, it leads to a rise in disposable income ($Y\uparrow \Rightarrow YD\uparrow$) which, in turn, induces households to spend more on consumption ($YD\uparrow \Rightarrow C\uparrow$). This stimulates output in the economy by leading to yet another increase in aggregate demand ($D\uparrow \Rightarrow Y\uparrow$). This is the usual expansionary effect of model 2 – route (a).

The second effect of the initial rise in income is to increase the demand for money to finance an increased volume of transactions ($Y\uparrow \Rightarrow m^d\uparrow$). With an unchanged money supply, there is an excess demand for money

and the interest rate rises to equilibrate the assets markets ($m^d\uparrow \Rightarrow r\uparrow$).
This has three effects. First, it leads to crowding out of private invest-
ment expenditure ($r\uparrow \Rightarrow I\downarrow$), which, in turn, by cutting aggregate
demand ($I\downarrow \Rightarrow D\downarrow$) leads to a fall in income ($D\downarrow \Rightarrow Y\downarrow$). This is the traditional contractionary effect of model 3 – route (b). The second effect of
the rise in the interest rate is to increase interest payments on the existing stock of government debt. This is the new element that is introduced
in the context of model 5. Higher interest rates boost other personal
income (unearned income) for a given level of government bonds. Thus,
$r\uparrow \Rightarrow opi\uparrow$. This stimulates consumption, aggregate demand and therefore income – route (c). The third effect of the interest rate rise is to raise
private sector wealth. Increased debt service results in a wider budget
deficit, which in turn leads to a rise in *psbr*. The government issues
more bonds to finance the enlarged deficit and this increases private
sector wealth ($r\uparrow \Rightarrow psbr\uparrow \Rightarrow b\uparrow \Rightarrow v\uparrow$). The latter results in a rise in
consumption expenditure, aggregate demand and therefore income
($v\uparrow \Rightarrow C\uparrow \Rightarrow Y\uparrow$) – route (d).

The initial increase in government expenditure also leads to a budget
deficit and a rise in *psbr* ($G\uparrow \Rightarrow psbr\uparrow$). The government finances this
deficit through issuing bonds ($psbr\uparrow \Rightarrow b\uparrow$), which in turn increases
private sector wealth ($b\uparrow \Rightarrow v\uparrow$). The latter has two effects. First, it raises
the demand for money and therefore it leads to an interest rate rise,
since the money supply remains fixed. This intensifies the effects that
work through routes (b), (c) and (d). The second effect of the rise in
private sector wealth is to raise consumption, aggregate demand and
hence income – route (e). Routes (b) and (e) were also present in model
4. Thus, the inclusion of interest payments introduces two more channels
(routes c and d) through which an increase in government expenditure
under bond finance affects the economic system.

Box 5.4 provides a schematic view of the main channels through which
an increase in government expenditure under money finance affects the
economic system. The rise in government expenditure leads to a budget
deficit and an increase in *psbr* ($G\uparrow \Rightarrow psbr\uparrow$). The government prints
money to finance its deficit ($psbr\uparrow \Rightarrow m\uparrow$). At the initial level of income,
this creates an excess supply of money and the interest rate falls to
equilibrate the assets markets ($m\uparrow \Rightarrow r\downarrow$). This results in three effects.
First, the reduction in the interest rate encourages private investment
expenditure ($r\downarrow \Rightarrow I\uparrow$) and this stimulates income through its effect on
demand – route (b). Second, for a given stock of government bonds, a
fall in the interest rate reduces other personal income by cutting interest
payments on government debt ($r\downarrow \Rightarrow opi\downarrow$). This effect works through
route (c). Third, a reduced debt service implies a reduction in the budget
deficit and hence a cut in *psbr* ($r\downarrow \Rightarrow psbr\downarrow$). This allows the government
to retire debt from the market ($psbr\downarrow \Rightarrow b\downarrow$), which in turn implies a fall

Box 5.4 The transmission of fiscal policy (government expenditure) under money finance

$$G\uparrow \Rightarrow \begin{cases} D\uparrow \Rightarrow Y\uparrow \Rightarrow \begin{cases} YD\uparrow \Rightarrow C\uparrow \Rightarrow D\uparrow \Rightarrow Y\uparrow & (a) \\ \\ m^d\uparrow \end{cases} \\ \\ \Downarrow \\ \\ r\downarrow > r\uparrow \Rightarrow \begin{cases} I\uparrow \Rightarrow D\uparrow \Rightarrow Y\uparrow & (b) \\ opi\downarrow \Rightarrow C\downarrow \Rightarrow Y\downarrow & (c) \\ v\downarrow \Rightarrow C\downarrow \Rightarrow Y\downarrow & (d) \end{cases} \\ \\ psbr\uparrow \Rightarrow m\uparrow \Rightarrow \begin{cases} \Uparrow \\ m^d\uparrow \end{cases} \\ \\ v\uparrow \Rightarrow \begin{cases} \\ C\uparrow \Rightarrow D\uparrow \Rightarrow Y\uparrow & (e) \end{cases} \end{cases}$$

in private sector wealth ($b\downarrow \Rightarrow v\downarrow$). The latter leads to a fall in consumption and therefore income – route (d).

The initial effect of the increase in government expenditure works via route (a). This is the same as under bond finance and arises out of the stimulus that government expenditure provides, since it is a constituent component of aggregate demand. The rise in income leads to an increase in the demand for money. This tends to offset the initial excess supply of money that was created through the financing of the budget. This is the effect that was introduced in the context of model 3.

The initial increase in the supply of money raises private sector wealth ($m\uparrow \Rightarrow v\uparrow$), which in turn leads to an increase in the demand for money ($v\uparrow \Rightarrow m^d\uparrow$), as households reallocate their portfolios. This, too, tends to offset the initial excess supply of money. Thus, there are two forces that increase the demand for money: the rise in income and the rise in wealth. This introduces some ambiguity as to the effect of a fiscal expansion on the interest rate. However, in an economy where assets markets clear faster than the goods market, there is an initial excess supply for money, which is gradually reduced as income and private sector wealth rise and the demand for money is increased. Thus, the initial effect is a fall in the interest rate, which is gradually reversed ($r\downarrow > r\uparrow$). Whether in the new long-run equilibrium the interest rate falls or rises relative to the initial steady state is ambiguous and depends on parameter values.

The final channel through which a fiscal expansion affects the economic system is the traditional wealth effect – route (e). The increase in private sector wealth, which results from the increase in the supply of money, stimulates demand and therefore income.

A comparison of the transmission mechanism of government expenditure under bond and money finance indicates a difference in the effect on the interest rate. Under bond finance the interest rate will certainly rise and under money finance it will fall, at least in the initial phase of the adjustment process. This has implications for the dynamic effects of government expenditure on income/output. The interest rate rise under bond finance leads the economy to expansion through routes (c) and (d). Under money finance, however, the interest rate fall leads to contraction through routes (c) and (d). These channels describe the effects of the interest rate on *opi* and private sector wealth. These channels were not present in model 4, in which interest payments on government debt were ignored.

A second difference between money and bond finance is the quantitative importance of the overall wealth effect. There are two channels through which wealth affects the economic system – routes (d) and (e). The former arises from the effect of interest rate changes on the budget, whereas the latter arises from the effect of government expenditure on the budget. Under bond finance, both channels work in the same direction. Under money finance, however, these two channels counteract each other, at least in the short run. The reason is that bond finance implies higher interest rates, whereas money finance implies, at least in the short run, lower interest rates.

5.6 The Dynamics under Bond and Money Finance

In this section we solve the model numerically to analyse the dynamic effects of a fiscal expansion under bond and money finance. The fiscal expansion takes the form of a permanent increase in government expenditure equal to £1 billion throughout the ten-year horizon. Figures 5.7 to 5.9 present the results of this simulation under pure money finance and pure bond finance for income, the interest rate and wealth, respectively. The economy is initially in a long-run equilibrium, with income being £100 billion, the interest rate 10 per cent and wealth £300 billion. Government expenditure is increased by £1 billion to £26 billion and is equal to 1 per cent of GDP. The deviation of the dynamic path under money and bond finance from the horizontal line (initial steady state) measures the corresponding dynamic multiplier (i.e. the value of the multiplier through time).

In the first period income rises from 100 to 101.3 under bond finance, thus giving a multiplier for the first period equal to 1.4. Under money finance, however, income rises from 100 to 200 in the first period, giving a multiplier of 2. Thus, an increase in government expenditure is more expansionary under money finance than under bond finance. In the second period the bond finance multiplier is 1.7, whereas the money

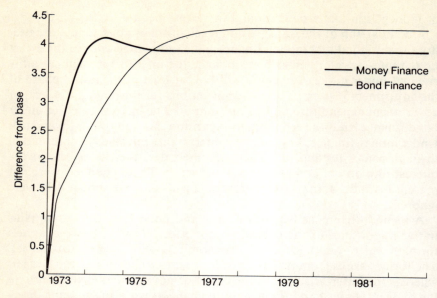

Figure 5.7   Output response to a step increase in government expenditure

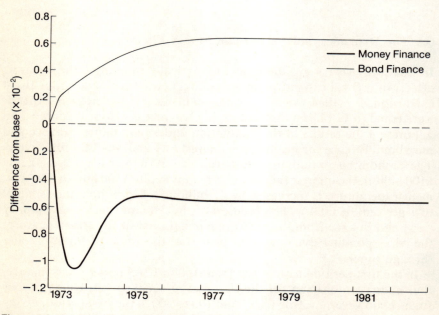

Figure 5.8   Interest rate response to a step increase in government expenditure

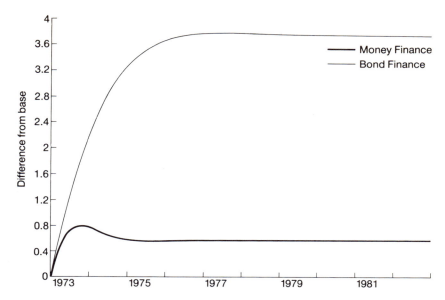

Figure 5.9   Wealth response to a step increase in government expenditure

finance multiplier is 2.9. Income rises more quickly under money finance for the first two and a half years, but more slowly thereafter. The new long-run equilibrium is reached after four years. The long-run income multiplier is 4.3 under bond finance, whereas under money finance it is only 3.9. Thus, money finance is more expansionary than bond finance in the short run, but less expansionary in the long run.

The numerical results conform with our theoretical expectations. Since the standard tax rate, *SRT*, is 0.25, the long-run multiplier in a numerical analogue of model 4 is 4, irrespective of the mode of finance. This compares with model 5, which includes interest payments, with 4.3 under bond finance and 3.9 under money finance. Thus, not only is bond finance more expansionary than money finance in the long run in the context of model 5, but it is also more expansionary relative to model 4. Furthermore, money finance in model 5 is less expansionary than model 4.

The interest rate falls in the first three quarters and then gradually rises under money finance. In the new steady state the interest rate is lower than in the initial steady state by half a percentage point. Under bond finance, the interest rate rises monotonically until it reaches a new long-run equilibrium at a higher level. Thus, bond finance implies higher interest rates both in the adjustment process and in the new steady state, whereas money finance implies lower interest rates in the new steady state, with an initial overshooting of the new long-run equilibrium.

Private sector wealth rises monotonically under bond finance. In the new steady state wealth has risen by £3.7 billion. Under money finance, however, wealth initially rises and then declines. In the new long-run equilibrium wealth is higher by only £0.5 billion.

Why is money finance more expansionary than bond finance in the short run and less expansionary in the long run? There are two basic reasons. First, under money finance there is an initial excess supply of money and, since the assets markets adjust instantly whereas the goods market adjusts sluggishly, the interest rate falls to equilibrate the assets markets. This stimulates investment and consumption and leads to income expansion. As income and wealth rise, however, the demand for money increases and the excess supply is progressively reduced. This reverses the interest rate adjustment process. The interest rate, after a fall in the first three quarters, rises until it reaches the new steady state. The interest rate rise dampens the effect on demand and therefore retards the income expansion. Under bond finance, however, the initial stimulus due to fiscal expansion creates an excess demand for money and the interest rate rises to equilibrate the asset markets. This leads to crowding out of private expenditure, which moderates the rise in income. Thus, the first reason why money finance is more expansionary than bond finance in the short run is the different behaviour of the interest rate, which rises under bond finance but falls under money finance. As the initial interest rate fall is reversed under money finance the stimulus in aggregate demand is weakened.

Second, the increase in money supply under money finance initially raises private sector wealth. However, the interest rate fall implies that debt service is reduced. This means that the budget deficit narrows down and *psbr* is reduced. The government retires debt from the market and this reduces, after the third quarter, private sector wealth. Under bond finance, however, the interest rate rise implies an increased debt service, a larger budget deficit and a rise in *psbr*. The government issues more bonds and this increases private sector wealth. However, the effect of wealth on consumption works through the system gradually. Thus, the second reason why money finance is more expansionary than bond finance in the short run and less expansionary in the long run is that the increase in wealth is substantially smaller in the former than in the latter, but these effects take time to work themselves out.

The numerical results provide an indication of the quantitative importance of the channels through which a fiscal expansion affects the economic system under the two modes of finance. This is done by comparing routes (a) to (e) in boxes 5.3 and 5.4. First, there is a qualitative difference between bond and money finance in that route (b) is contractionary in the former and expansionary in the latter. Second, route (c) is expansionary under bond finance, but contractionary under money finance. The quantitative importance of this channel is not large, because the proportion of households with unearned income is small and the marginal propensity to consume out of this source of income is low. Third, the overall wealth effect, routes (d) and (e), is much stronger under bond than money finance. The reason is that under bond finance routes (d) and (e) reinforce each other, whereas under money finance these two channels work in opposite direction. Under most parameter values, however, route (e) dominates route (d).

5.7 Sensitivity of Fiscal Policy Multipliers to Parameter Variation

Since the model is used with a specific set of parameter values, it is natural to ask how robust the results are to parameter variation. The approach adopted here is to examine the sensitivity of the fiscal multipliers under bond and money finance with respect to each coefficient separately. In perturbing a coefficient we also vary the constant in that equation to maintain the scaling of the equation. Table 5.1 presents the results of doubling and halving a few critical coefficients. These are the interest sensitivities of consumption, investment and demand for money; and the wealth effects on consumption and demand for money. Table 5.1 provides the impact and steady-state multipliers under bond and money finance. The impact multiplier is the first year multiplier, which is the average of the first four quarters. A measure of the sensitivity of the multipliers is provided by the corresponding elasticity. This is calculated as follows:

$$e = \frac{\dfrac{\Delta k}{k}}{\dfrac{\Delta a}{a}} \tag{5.18}$$

where k is the value of the multiplier in the base run; Δk is the change in the multiplier value due to a coefficient perturbation; a is the value of the perturbed coefficient in the base run and Δa is the perturbation in the coefficient. The denominators for doubling and halving a certain coefficient are 1 and -0.5, respectively. The elasticity shows the percentage change in the multiplier for a given percentage change in the coefficient. The elasticity, in absolute terms, is a measure of the sensitivity of the multipliers and allows for a comparison of coefficients with respect to their contribution to the multiplier change. A value of the elasticity near zero indicates that this parameter does not contribute a lot to the multiplier change; conversely, the greater the elasticity, the more sensitive the multiplier. This, in turn, implies that the results of the

Table 5.1 Sensitivity of fiscal multipliers to parameter variation

Perturbed coefficient		Bond finance		Money finance	
		Multiplier	Elasticity	Multiplier	Elasticity
Interest sensitivity of consumption, C_r					
Doubled, $C_r = -50$	Impact	1.75	0.074	3.30	0.065
	Steady-state	4.32	0.012	3.93	0.008
Halved, $C_r = -12.5$	Impact	1.97	0.085	2.93	0.110
	Steady-state	4.25	0.009	3.86	0.021
Interest sensitivity of investment, I_r					
Doubled, $I_r = -50$	Impact	1.79	0.053	3.23	0.042
	Steady-state	4.30	0.007	3.92	0.005
Halved, $I_r = -1.25$	Impact	1.94	0.053	3.00	0.065
	Steady-state	4.26	0.005	3.88	0.010
Interest sensitivity of demand for money, M_r					
Doubled, $M_r = -100$	Impact	2.02	0.069	2.82	0.090
	Steady-state	4.17	0.023	3.91	0.003
Halved, $M_r = -25$	Impact	1.67	0.233	3.30	0.065
	Steady-state	4.50	0.108	3.89	0.005
Wealth effect on consumption, C_v					
Doubled, $C_v = 0.30$	Impact	2.14	0.132	3.18	0.026
	Steady-state	4.19	0.019	3.93	0.008
Halved, $C_v = 0.075$	Impact	1.76	0.138	3.05	0.032
	Steady-state	4.44	0.080	3.88	0.010
Wealth effect on demand for money, M_v					
Doubled, $M_v = 0.002$	Impact	1.89	0	3.10	0
	Steady-state	4.27	0	3.90	0
Halved, $M_v = 0.0005$	Impact	1.89	0	3.10	0
	Steady-state	4.27	0	3.90	0

analysis critically depend on the value of the coefficient. The multiplier is inelastic or elastic according to whether the elasticity is less than or greater than unity.

The results in table 5.1 illustrate a number of points. First, all elasticities are less than unity, thus implying that the multipliers are inelastic to all perturbed coefficients. This increases our confidence in the numerical results. Second, the steady-state multipliers are less sensitive to parameter variation than the impact multipliers. Thus, the most sensitive multiplier is obtained under bond finance by halving the interest sensitivity of the demand for money. The elasticity of the steady-state and impact multipliers are 10.8 per cent and 23.3 per cent, respectively. Third, the coefficients can be classified according to the sensitivity they cause to the steady-state fiscal multipliers. Under bond finance the order of the coefficients, starting from the maximum sensitivity, is as follows: the interest sensitivity of the demand for money, the wealth effect on consumption, the interest sensitivity of consumption, the interest sensitivity of investment and the wealth effect on the demand for money. Under money finance the order of the coefficients is as follows: the interest sensitivity of consumption, the interest sensitivity of investment and the wealth effect on consumption (equal in second place), the interest sensitivity of the demand for money and the wealth effect on the demand for money.

The impact and steady-state multipliers in the base run are 1.89 and 4.27 under bond finance and 3.10 and 3.90 under money finance. These values provide a benchmark for comparison with the multipliers obtained with perturbed coefficients. Thus, by inspection of table 5.1 we see that doubling the sensitivity of consumption causes a fall in the impact multiplier under bond finance from 1.89 to 1.75. Hence an increase in the interest sensitivity of consumption reduces the impact multiplier under bond finance. Table 5.2 summarizes the signs of the partial derivatives of the impact and steady-state multipliers under bond and money finance with respect to a change in a number of coefficients, on the assumption that the system is stable. The direction of change of a multiplier in response to either doubling or halving a coefficient is the same and therefore table 5.2 provides only one sign for each coefficient.

In model 3 we examined the partial derivatives of the multipliers with respect to the parameters of the system. These multipliers can be interpreted as the impact multipliers in the context of model 5. It is therefore instructive to compare the signs of the partial derivatives of the multipliers between models 3 and 5. This provides a test of robustness of the results of model 3. The impact multiplier under bond finance behaves like the fiscal multiplier in model 3. In the latter, an increase in the interest sensitivity of investment reduces the fiscal multiplier. The reason is that the higher the interest sensitivity of investment, the greater is the degree of crowding out and the smaller the fiscal multiplier. This result holds true in the context of model 5. An increase in the sensitivity of

Table 5.2 Numerical evaluation of the signs of partial derivates of fiscal multipliers with respect to critical parameters

Perturbed parameter	Bond finance		Money finance	
	Impact	Steady-state	Impact	Steady-state
C_r	−	+	+	+
I_r	−	+	+	+
M_r	+	−	−	+
C_v	+	−	+	+

Note: + indicates that an increase in the coefficient increases the multiplier; − indicates that an increase in the coefficient reduces the multiplier.

investment or consumption (qualitatively they are the same because they both work through aggregate demand) reduces the impact multiplier under bond finance.

An increase in the interest sensitivity of the demand for money increases the fiscal multiplier in model 3. The reason is that the higher the interest sensitivity of the demand for money, the smaller is the increase in the interest rate required to clear the assets markets, and hence the smaller is the degree of crowding out and therefore the greater the fiscal multiplier. This result also holds true in the case of model 5. An increase in the interest sensitivity of the demand for money increases the impact multiplier under bond finance.

The impact multiplier under money finance behaves like the money multiplier in model 3. In the latter, an increase in the interest sensitivity of investment causes an increase in the money multiplier. The reason is that, for a given reduction in the interest rate, the higher the interest sensitivity of investment, the greater is the stimulus to investment and therefore to income. This holds true in model 5. An increase in the interest sensitivity of investment or consumption causes an increase in the impact multiplier under money finance.

In model 3, an increase in the interest sensitivity of the demand for money causes a reduction in the money multiplier. The reason is that, for a given increase in the supply of money, the greater the interest sensitivity of the demand for money, the smaller is the fall in the interest rate and hence the smaller the stimulus to investment and income. This principle applies to model 5. An increase in the interest sensitivity of the demand for money reduces the impact multiplier under money finance.

In model 4, an increase in the wealth effect on consumption increases the impact multiplier under bond and money finance. The reason is that the larger the wealth effect, the greater is the stimulus to demand and income. This result also holds true in the context of model 5. An increase in the wealth sensitivity of consumption increases the impact multiplier under bond and money finance.

In all cases the steady-state multiplier under bond finance has the opposite sign to the impact multiplier. The reason lies in the interest payments on government debt. The slower the speed of convergence to a new steady state, the higher are the interest payments under bond finance, because of higher interest rates in both the adjustment process and the new steady state. If the system is stable, any parameter perturbation that reduces the impact multiplier slows down the speed of convergence and raises interest payments, thereby increasing the steady state multiplier. This point is further illustrated by examining in more detail the results of halving the wealth effect in consumption. Figures 5.10 and 5.11 present the trajectories of income and wealth multipliers for the base run ($C_v = 0.15$) and the new run with the wealth effect being half

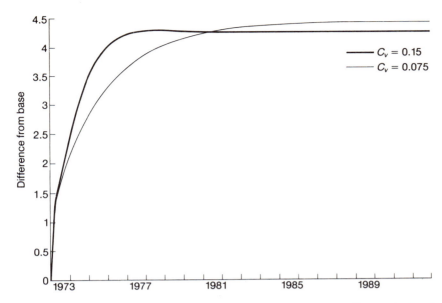

Figure 5.10 Output response to a step increase in government expenditure under bond finance for different values of the wealth sensitivity of consumption

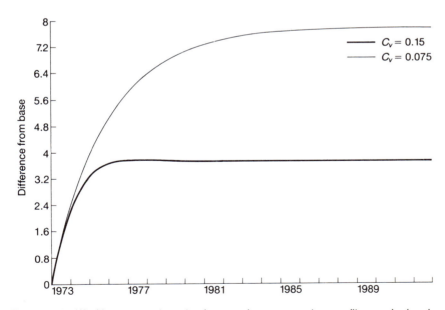

Figure 5.11 Wealth response to a step increase in government expenditure under bond finance for different values of the wealth sensitivity of consumption

$(C_v = 0.075)$. The impact multiplier in the new run is 1.76, down from 1.89 in the base run. The steady-state multiplier in the new run rises to 4.44 from 4.27. Long-run equilibrium is attained in 19 years in the new run, but in only four years in the base run. Increased interest payments on government debt cause wealth to rise by £7.78 billion in the new run, whereas it only rises by £3.7 billion in the base run.

5.8 The Stability of Bond and Money Finance

The striking result of the sensitivity analysis of table 5.1 is that bond finance is always stable. This is in contrast to the conclusion we reached in model 4, in which bond finance may be unstable. The stability of bond finance in model 5 is the result of the inclusion of interest payments on government debt combined with a very strong wealth effect in consumption and a very weak wealth effect in the demand for money. We have seen that bond finance implies increased interest payments because of

Table 5.3 Sensitivity of fiscal multipliers to parameter variation assuming C_v = 0.075 and M_v = 0.06

		Bond finance		Money finance	
Perturbed coefficient		*Income multiplier*	*Wealth multiplier*	*Income multiplier*	*Wealth multiplier*
Interest sensitivity of consumption, C_r					
Doubled, C_r = −50	Impact	Unstable		3.23	0.62
	Steady-state			3.93	0.53
Halved, C_r = −12.5	Impact	1.77	1.50	2.85	0.82
	Steady-state	4.90	12.01	3.83	0.78
Interest sensitivity of demand for money, M_r					
Doubled, M_r = −100	Impact	1.84	1.46	2.73	0.93
	Steady-state	4.51	8.73	3.89	0.93
Halved, M_r = −25	Impact	Unstable		3.25	0.55
	Steady-state			3.88	0.49
Wealth effect on consumption, C_v					
Doubled, C_v = 0.15	Impact	1.80	1.50	3.07	0.71
	Steady-state	4.49	5.56	3.90	0.59
Halved, C_v = 0.0375	Impact	Unstable		3.00	0.74
	Steady-state			3.87	0.68
Wealth effect on demand for money, M_v					
Doubled, M_v = 0.12	Impact	Unstable		2.99	0.75
	Steady-state			3.88	0.69
Halved, M_v = 0.03	Impact	1.71	1.53	3.04	0.73
	Steady-state	4.73	11.64	3.88	0.63

Table 5.4 Direction of change of fiscal multipliers to parameter variation with $C_v = 0.075$ and $M_v = 0.06$

Perturbed parameter	Bond finance		Money finance	
	Impact	Steady-state	Impact	Steady-state
C_r	−	+	+	+
M_r	+	−	−	+
C_v	+	−	+	+
M_v	−	−	−	0

Note: + indicates that an increase in the coefficient increases the multiplier; − indicates that an increase in the coefficient reduces the multiplier.

higher interest rates. If this boosts consumption, it can be highly expansionary, thus eliminating the possibility of instability. This can happen via two routes: other personal income and private sector wealth. In model 5 a very strong wealth effect in consumption ($C_v = 0.15$) and a very weak wealth effect in the demand for money ($M_v = 0.001$) are assumed.

Table 5.3 presents the sensitivity of fiscal multipliers to parameter variation for a base run in which the wealth effects on consumption and demand for money are $C_v = 0.075$ and $M_v = 0.06$. Table 5.4 shows the direction of change of fiscal multipliers. Now bond finance is unstable in four cases, whereas money finance is, as usual, stable. Even when bond finance is stable, it produces unrealistically long convergence (20 years) and unrealistic expansion in private sector wealth. In contrast, money finance converges in one year and wealth rises by less than £1 billion. In a model with interest payments, like model 5, the stability issue depends, as in model 4, on the interrelationship between the wealth effects on consumption and demand for money and the interest sensitivity of aggregate demand and demand for money. The condition for stability, though, is not as precise as in model 4, because the model is non-linear. In model 4, the higher the interest sensitivity of investment or the wealth effect in the demand for money and the lower the interest sensitivity of the demand for money or the wealth effect in consumption, the greater is the chance of instability under bond finance. This principle also applies to model 5. The cases of instability under bond finance are obtained when doubling the interest sensitivity of consumption, halving the interest sensitivity of the demand for money, halving the wealth effect in consumption and doubling the wealth effect in the demand for money.

Figure 5.12 illustrates the instability of bond finance for one of the above cases, that of increasing the wealth effect in the demand for money from $M_v = 0.06$ to $M_v = 0.13$ for a given value of the wealth effect in consumption, $C_v = 0.075$, and the other parameters. For $M_v = 0.13$

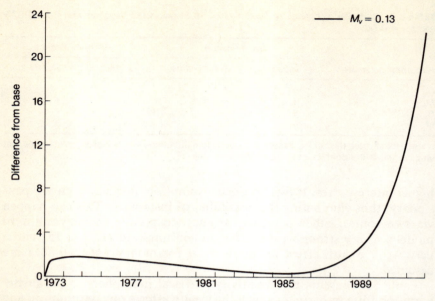

Figure 5.12 Unstable response of output to a step increase in government expenditure under bond finance ($M_v = 0.13$)

wealth and the interest rate rise monotonically. After 20 years wealth has risen by £357 billion (i.e. more than double) and the interest rate by 89 percentage points. The income multiplier after a gentle oscillation explodes upwards.

The role of interest payments in the stability of the system under bond finance is now obvious. If the system is marginally unstable, the inclusion of interest payments will make it stable.

5.9 Summary and Limitations of Model 5

The numerical simulations have allowed us to analyse the dynamic effects of monetary policy and fiscal policy under bond and money finance on the assumption that the assets markets clear more quickly than the goods market. The inclusion of interest payments on government debt changes the dynamic and steady-state effects of fiscal and monetary policies. A straight increase in the supply of money temporarily stimulates income/output. In the absence of interest payments income returns to its original equilibrium. With interest payments, income is lower in the new steady state. The effects of an open market purchase depend on whether the government is following monetary or debt targets. The initial stimulus is higher and the decline in income in steady state is larger under monetary than debt targets.

Without interest payments, fiscal policy is equally expansionary in the long run under bond and money finance (model 4). With interest payments, bond finance is more expansionary than money finance and more expansionary than model 4. Money finance with interest payments is less expansionary in the long run than model 4. In model 5, money finance is more expansionary than bond finance, in the short run.

The impact and, in particular, the steady-state multipliers are very insensitive to large parameter variation, thus increasing our confidence in the numerical results. The sensitivity analysis allows us to evaluate the signs of the partial derivatives of the multipliers in model 5 with respect to the parameters of the system. The impact multiplier under bond finance behaves like the fiscal multiplier in model 3, whereas the impact multiplier under money finance behaves like the money multiplier in model 3. This shows that the signs of the partial derivatives of the multipliers of model 3 remain robust to more elaborate model specification.

The stability of the system depends on the interrelationship of the wealth effects in consumption and the demand for money and the interest sensitivity of aggregate demand and demand for money. A strong wealth effect in consumption relative to the demand for money makes bond finance stable and vice versa. The inclusion of interest payments makes a marginally unstable system under bond finance stable. Money finance is much more stable than bond finance irrespective of the inclusion of interest payments. With interest payments, even when both are stable, money finance converges more quickly than bond finance.

The conclusion in models 4 and 5 that fiscal policy is more powerful in the long run than in the short run is a consequence of the assumption that prices are fixed and therefore there are no bottlenecks in expanding output. The other feature that limits the usefulness of this model is the assumption that the economy is closed.

Appendix 5.1 Further Reading on Consumption

In the various chapters of this book consumption is a function of disposable income, interest income, the interest rate and wealth, with all variables being expressed in real terms. This general specification appears to be *ad hoc* and the question arises of how it compares with the relationship that is derived from optimizing behaviour on the part of households and firms.

The theories of consumer behaviour developed in the 1950s – the permanent income hypothesis (PIH) and the life cycle hypothesis (LCH) associated with Friedman (1957), Modigliani and Brumberg (1954) and Ando and Modigliani (1963) – were primarily concerned with reconciling the positive relation between the saving ratio and income observed in cross-sectional data and the constancy of the saving ratio observed in long-run time-series data. According to the LCH, consumption depends on expected life-time resources based on expected income and non-human wealth during the consumer's lifetime. According to the PIH, consumption depends on average expected income over a long period, which Friedman called 'permanent income'. Both theories emphasize that consumers smooth out the effects of fluctuations in current income on consumption by maintaining a stable relationship between consumption and life-time resources or permanent income, rather than between consumption and current income. Thus, the implication of both theories is that current income is not so important in explaining consumption. However, recent research has challenged this result and suggests that current income has a stronger influence on consumption than the permanent income hypothesis predicts (see Campbell and Mankiw, 1989; Caroll and Summers, 1989; Flavin 1981; Hall and Mishkin, 1982). The importance of current income in consumption is also stressed in disequilibrium models (e.g. Barro and Grossman, 1976). With fixed or slowly adjusting prices, when individuals find themselves unable to sell their desired labour services (i.e. when they are off their 'notional' supply curves), they respond to this unexpected fall in their current income by reducing their effective demand for goods, thus spilling over these effects back to the labour market. The implication is that in disequilibrium models consumption is based on current income.

In the original formulation permanent income was proxied by current and past (real disposable) income with exponentially declining weights. Through a Koyck transformation, consumption becomes a function of real disposable income and lagged consumption. However, this formulation made the theory empirically indistinguishable from other theories, which stressed, for example, 'habit' persistence (e.g. Brown, 1952), or that consumers attempt to maintain their consumption patterns according to the income bracket in which they belong (social class) or according to their peak income levels (Duesenberry, 1949). An alternative approach of estimating permanent income is to use rational expectations (Hall, 1978). The implication of this formulation is that consumption follows a martingale process: the best predictor of tomorrow's consumption is today's consumption – no other variable known at time t is needed.

Both the LCH and the PIH are primarily based on partial equilibrium analysis, where income and wealth are mainly exogenous variables. The question then arises as to what the determinants of consumption are in a general equilibrium analysis in which decisions on consumption, saving and investment are taken interactively by households and firms. Ramsey (1928) has answered this problem in the case of a central planner who maximizes social welfare. It can easily be proved (see e.g. Blanchard and Fischer, 1990) that the optimality conditions in the Ramsey model are the same as those of a decentralized economy under the conditions of certainty, infinitely living individuals, rational expectations, perfectly competitive markets that clear instantaneously and no money, where firms maximize their value under constant returns to scale in production.

It is difficult in general to solve for the level of consumption from the Euler equation, which describes the first-order condition that has to be satisfied along the optimal path, since this determines only the rate of change of consumption and not the level of consumption. However, this can be done easily if a particular functional form for the utility function is assumed, although this diminishes the generality and importance of the results. Thus, with an isoelastic utility function in which, as the name implies, the elasticity of substitution between consumption at any two points in time is constant, consumption is a linear function of wealth, human (the present value of labour income) and non-human. The marginal propensity to consume out of the two components of wealth is the same and depends on the expected path of interest rates. In general, the effect of the interest rate on consumption is ambiguous.

What is the role of fiscal policy in the Ramsey model? Given the underlying assumptions, it is not surprising that fiscal policy is completely ineffective. A bond finance fiscal stimulus in the form of either increased government expenditure or an income tax cut completely crowds out private consumption (often called 'debt neutrality' or the 'Barro–Ricardo equivalence theorem'). The reason for this result is intuitively easy to understand. The intertemporal government budget constraint implies that a decrease in taxes now should be offset by higher taxes later on. The intertemporal household budget constraint implies that the increase in income now is exactly offset by a decrease in income later on. Accordingly, households save the entire increase in current income, thereby leading to full crowding out of the fiscal stimulus. For the same reason the balanced-budget multiplier of government expenditure with lump-sum taxes is also zero. An alternative way of expressing the Barro–Ricardo equivalence theorem is that government bonds are not part of private sector wealth (Barro, 1974).

These results are in sharp contrast with the ones obtained in chapter 2. Although we do not believe that the Ramsey model can explain reality it is nevertheless useful as a benchmark model with which to compare other models of consumer behaviour. The strong results concerning the ineffectiveness of fiscal policy can weaken in the context of the overlapping-generations model of Allais (1947), Samuelson (1958), Diamond (1965) and Blanchard (1985), where the assumption of infinitely living individuals is dropped. It is intuitively easy to understand why the debt neutrality proposition fails in this model. If individuals are not infinitely living and the benefits and burden of tax cuts are borne by different generations (one generation receives the benefits while another bears the burden of paying it back) then there is no reason to assume that all or even part of the government dissaving will be offset by increased saving by individuals.

Barro (1974) has argued that the existence of bequests is prima facie evidence that people care about the welfare of their children. Kotlikoff and Summers (1981) find that more than 70 per cent of personal sector wealth in the USA can be accounted for by bequests rather than life-cycle savings. The bequest motive makes the overlapping-generations model behave like the Ramsey model, in which people would regard lower current taxes as equivalent to higher future taxes (hence the name 'equivalence theorem'). However, the existence of bequests does not necessarily imply that people care about the welfare of future generations. Instead, bequests may be accidental, resulting from uncertainty about the time of death and the lack of annuity markets (see Abel, 1985, and Blanchard, 1985, for such a model). For example, in the latter model individuals face a constant probability of dying. In this model, although individuals do not care about the welfare of future generations, when dying they leave unintended bequests. The Ricardian equivalence theorem fails in this life-cycle model and aggregate consumption is a linear function of wealth, non-human and human (the present discounted value of future labour income). An evaluation of the pros and cons of Ricardian equivalence is provided by Bernheim (1987).

Until now the determinants of consumption were examined in a deterministic framework. How are these determinants affected in the presence of uncertainty? The problem of choosing a consumption/saving plan under uncertainty was studied by Samuelson (1969) and Merton (1969). In principle, consumption under uncertainty depends on the same variables as under certainty: labour income, wealth, current and anticipated rates of return. However, to be more specific about the role of each variable we have to make some further simplifying assumptions because, in general, we cannot solve from the first-order conditions explicitly for the level of consumption. If labour income is risk diversifiable or the utility function is quadratic, consumption is a linear function of total wealth, human and non-human, as under certainty. The marginal propensity to consume is equal to the rate of interest (the subjective discount rate). However, the simplifying assumptions are not realistic. The whole of the labour income risk cannot be diversified and a quadratic utility function means increasing absolute risk aversion, which is an unreasonable behaviour towards risk because it implies that people are prepared to pay more to avoid risk as wealth increases. With more plausible utility functions, it can be shown that uncertainty about labour income leads consumers to be more prudent and accordingly to consume less and save more (see e.g. Leland, 1968; Dreze and Modigliani, 1972; and for a comprehensive analysis Blanchard and Fischer, 1990). The implication of uncertainty is that the marginal propensity to consume out of current income is higher than that implied by the LCH or the PIH.

The importance of current income in explaining consumption is also supported by the presence of 'liquidity constraints' due to imperfections in credit markets (see Hayashi, 1985). Individuals cannot borrow as much as they like when their current income falls, as the LCH or the PIH would predict, because banks will be unwilling to lend to them.

This brief survey of the microfoundations of consumer behaviour highlights the difficulties in determining the exact role of each variable in the consumption function. Although there is some comfort from the fact that the general specification of the consumption function used in this book is compatible with the underlying theoretical models, there should be some concern that the importance of each variable is essentially *ad hoc*. This does not mean that we should refrain from using models of consumption until an undisputed theoretical model emerges. The need to provide policy advice or to analyse other issues, such as the interrelationship of the main macroeconomic variables, means that we may have to rely on *ad hoc* models for a long time, possibly for ever.

In this survey we have omitted all empirical work that attempts to distinguish between rival theories of consumer behaviour and the associated problems thereof. The reader is referred to Hadjimatheou (1987) for a comprehensive and critical review of the literature.

Appendix 5.2 Further Reading on Investment

In this book investment is generally specified as a function of output and the real interest rate. In this appendix a brief survey of the underlying theories of investment is provided so that the reader can put in perspective the functional form that is used in this book.

Early theories of investment were based upon an empirical relationship first observed by J.M. Clark (1917) between the level of boxcar production and the previous change in railroad traffic. This has led to the formulation of the accelerator theories of investment. In its 'simple' or 'naive' form, the *level* of investment depends on the *change* in output (in the last period). In the 'flexible' accelerator version, investment is a distributed lag function of changes in output (i.e. it depends on current and past changes in output). There are at least two explanations that are consistent with this empirical relationship. According to the first the desired level of the capital stock is proportional to output (i.e. the desired capital–output ratio is fixed), but firms are constrained in achieving their desired levels because of delivery lags in investment goods. In the second explanation of the flexible accelerator firms adjust instantaneously to their desired level of capital stock, which, however, depends on expected output, with expectations being formed adaptively.

Thus, output or demand is the crucial determinant of investment in the accelerator model, but the reason is unclear. It may be because of delivery lags in the capital goods supplying industry or firms forming expectations adaptively about expected output (or demand). The appealing feature of the accelerator theory is that empirically it performs reasonably well and this has motivated some research into its underlying microfoundations. The accelerator can easily be derived from a cost-minimization process, on the assumption that firms are constrained in selling their desired output (non-market clearing), and that the underlying technology is characterized by a fixed-coefficients production function with constant returns to scale. In this formulation there is no role for the relative prices of the factors of production (i.e. wages and interest rates) in explaining fluctuations in investment.

The neo-classical theory of investment, developed by Jorgenson and his associates (see, e.g., Jorgenson, 1963, 1967, 1972; Jorgenson and Siebert, 1968), was the first theory to be based on microfoundations. Under perfect competition in *all* markets (output, input and capital, including second-hand capital markets), perfect foresight (which under no uncertainty is equivalent to rational expectations) and no adjustment costs, a firm that is optimizing the future discounted cash flows will employ labour up to the point where the marginal product of labour is equal to the real wage rate and capital up to the point where the marginal product of capital is equal to the user cost of capital. From these first-order conditions the demand for labour and capital are derived. But, as pointed out by Haavelmo (1960), investment demand cannot be derived from the demand for capital without any further assumptions. Demand for more capital stock can lead to any rate of investment from almost zero to infinity, depending on the extra assumptions, such as delivery lags and costs of adjustment. Jorgenson sidesteps this problem by comparing two alternative dynamic paths for capital (comparative dynamics) and assuming that the rate of change of expected prices of capital goods compensates variations in the interest rate so that the cost of capital is left unchanged. In this manner investment demand is derived, which is a function only of relative prices (interest rates, prices of capital goods, wages and output prices) and not of output. However, as Tobin (1967) pointed out, the assumption that the prices of capital goods decline when the demand for investment rises in response to lower interest rates is implausible.

The first-order conditions of the neo-classical model have been criticized as being myopic in the sense that they depend only on variables known currently and not on expected variables. This implies that the firm can ignore the future in making optimal investment decisions. In this world 'a restaurateur . . . who had more customers on weekends as opposed to weekdays would be observed to buy a small restaurant for weekdays but would sell it on Friday nights and purchase a large restaurant for the weekend, reselling it on Monday mornings' (Nickell, 1978, p. 9). It has been argued that these myopic decisions are the result of assumptions on technology, perfect markets and no adjustment costs. Capital is homogeneous in the sense that it has the same productive characteristics irrespective of its age and can be substituted for labour in production both *ex ante* and *ex post* (i.e. before and after capital is installed). There are no adjustment costs either in the sale or purchase of capital or in its installation. The implications of these myopic rules can be altered in at least three ways by relaxing on each occasion a different assumption.

Consider first the assumption on technology. In the accelerator model the production function is characterized by fixed technology. There is no substitution of labour for capital and the isoquants are right angle, implying that investment depends solely on output. In the neo-classical model capital is substituted for labour in production, the isoquants are continuous and convex and investment is a function only of relative prices and not output. It has been argued, however, that both models are extremes. The accelerator model has a 'clay-clay' technology in the sense that the capital–labour ratio is fixed both *ex ante* and *ex post* (i.e. before and after the installation of capital), while the neo-classical model has a 'putty-putty' technology in which the firm can change the capital-labour ratio both *ex ante* and *ex post* in response to changes in relative prices. However, the real world resembles neither of these models. Instead, technology is of the 'putty-clay' variety. This means that the firm can choose technology and therefore a capital–labour ratio at the planning stage (i.e. *ex ante* technology is putty), but once capital is installed technology is fixed and the capital ratio cannot be altered (i.e. *ex post* technology is clay). Thus, the neo-classical model is relevant *ex ante*, while the accelerator model is relevant *ex post*. The implications of the putty-clay model are, first, that the myopic decision rules are replaced with forward-looking rules in which expectations are important for optimal investment decisions. Second, both output and relative prices play a role as determinants of investment. However, the response of investment to changes in relative prices is slower than output because capital would have to become obsolete before the firm can change the capital–labour ratio to take advantage of the changed relative prices.

Empirical evidence (see, e.g., Bischoff, 1969, 1971; Eisner and Nadiri, 1968; and especially Hausman, 1973, for a comprehensive test of all three models) seems to support the view that both output and relative prices are important determinants of investment and that the response of investment is faster to changes in output than to changes in relative prices. Moreover, the neo-classical model when estimated on relative prices alone performs very badly (see Brechling, 1975). However, these results are not necessarily evidence in support of a putty-clay model. As Abel (1981) has shown, the neo-classical theory of investment with a putty-putty technology but with the extra assumption of convex costs of adjustment is capable of producing the same relative speeds of adjustment as the putty-clay model. Furthermore, the decision rules (first-order conditions) are no longer myopic as they allow for a significant role for expectations. The implication of the Abel analysis is that the myopic behaviour of the original neo-classical model is due to the assumption of zero costs of adjustment and not necessarily to a putty-putty technology.

The third way in which Jorgenson's myopic decision rules can be altered is by relaxing the assumption that the prices of capital goods remain unchanged. This assumption is reasonable at the micro-level when the firm is facing perfect markets, as is assumed by Jorgenson. However, in deriving an investment function at the macro-level it is not plausible to assume that the prices of capital goods would remain unchanged when all firms expand their capacity in response to, say, an anticipated cut in the interest rate. Thus, as Precious (1987) has suggested, Jorgenson's decision rules based on putty-putty technology with decreasing returns to scale, perfect markets, rational expectations and no adjustment costs can be viewed, appropriately aggregated, as describing only the demand side of capital goods. If the supply of capital goods at the industry level is assumed to be upward-sloping, an assumption consistent with perfect competition, then equilibrium in the capital goods industry requires the equality of demand and supply and a change in demand would lead to higher prices. In this framework the decision rules are no longer myopic despite a putty-putty technology and despite the assumption of no adjustment costs because forward-looking behaviour is allowed through both the entire path of capital goods prices and their rate of change (expected capital gains on capital goods). The price of capital goods rises initially in response to increased demand caused by, say, an anticipated decrease in the interest rate and falls thereafter as the supply of capital goods is increased. This type of adjustment, called 'saddlepoint solution', where the price jumps initially to the unique stable path and then gradually declines to the new higher steady state, is characteristic of rational expectations models. This type of adjustment overcomes Tobin's earlier criticism, salvaging the neo-classical theory of investment.

Therefore, investment is a function of current and expected output and current and expected relative prices, with a higher relative speed of adjustment for the former than the latter. However, the underlying reasoning is unclear. It may be because firms face constraints in various markets (non-market clearing), in which case the problem is posed as an intertemporal cost-minimization problem with a putty-clay technology. Alternatively, firms may not face any constraints, in which case the problem is posed as an intertemporal profit-maximization problem with putty-putty technology but with convex costs of adjustment. Thus there are three issues that seem to divide the theories of investment: market conditions (cost-minimization or profit-maximization), technology (putty-putty or putty-clay) and the nature of expectations (myopic or forward-looking decisions rules).

The theory of investment that has dominated the literature in the past ten years is Tobin's 'q' theory (Tobin and Brainard, 1977). In its initial formulation the theory lacked microfoundations but nevertheless had a great attraction because it appealed to common sense that investment depends positively on 'q', which is defined as the market value of capital relative to its cost. For example, if the price of houses rises relative to their building cost, then residential investment is increased. The early empirical formulation of the theory in terms of *average* 'q', defined as the ratio of the stock market value of the firm to the replacement cost of its capital, seemed to avoid the issues that divided the other theories of investment, namely market conditions, technology, and the nature of expectations, on the grounds that these are captured in the market valuation of the stock value of the firm.

Tobin recognized, however, that it is *marginal* rather than *average* 'q' that determines investment. This is defined as the ratio of the discounted value of marginal benefits or profits from one unit of capital goods to their replacement cost (i.e. the price of capital goods). When defined in this way Tobin's 'q' theory can be derived from the neo-classical theory of investment, with a putty-putty technology but with convex costs of adjustment (see Abel, 1979; Yoshikawa, 1980). It is intuitively easy to see how this is done. The first-order conditions of the neo-classical theory of investment relate the marginal benefits to the marginal costs of investment. The firm will go on investing until the marginal benefit is equal to the marginal cost of investment. When the price of capital goods is taken as the numeraire and therefore set equal to unity the marginal benefit of investment is equal to marginal 'q' and the marginal cost is equal to the price of capital plus the marginal cost of adjustment. Hence, the neo-classical theory of investment augmented by adjustment costs provides a determinate rate of investment, which is an increasing function of marginal 'q'.

The formulation of the 'q' theory in terms of microfoundations destroyed its original attraction – that it does not depend on market conditions, the nature of expectations and technology. The reason is that the empirical formulation of the theory is based on average 'q' while its theoretical formulation is based on marginal 'q'. The two are equal only under the conditions of a putty-putty technology, constant returns to scale and perfect competition (see Hayashi, 1982). The discrepancy between marginal and average 'q' reflects the extent of rationing in the goods, labour and capital goods markets (see Precious, 1987, for a generalization of the Hayashi result). Thus, the 'q' theory of investment is not immune to market conditions, technology and the nature of expectations. Investment depends on current and expected market conditions and the form of the investment function depends on technology and whether the firms face constraints in the goods, labour and capital goods markets.

The extension of the theory of investment under uncertainty is not straightforward – see Driver and Moreton (1991, 1992) for a comprehensive analysis and the problems arising therefrom. Part of the problem stems from the role of non-linearities in computing the expected value of the utility of profit. This expectation is, in general, not equal to the value obtained when all stochastic variables are set equal to their mean values (i.e. certainty equivalence does not hold) because of non-linearities in either the profit function or the utility function (e.g. risk aversion). In general, investment depends on current and expected demand and cost conditions, but an explicit solution can be obtained only under very restrictive assumptions. One such case arises when the profit function is linear in capital, as it is for a firm that operates under constant returns to scale in competitive markets (Abel, 1983). Another case is when the profit and adjustment cost functions are quadratic under risk neutrality, with constant interest rates and price of capital (Blanchard and Fischer, 1990).

The irreversibility of investment becomes very important under conditions of uncertainty (see, e.g., McDonald and Siegel, 1986; Nickell, 1978; Pindyck, 1988). Irreversibility arises because capital is industry- or firm-specific and therefore cannot be used elsewhere, so that investment expenditures are considered as sunk costs. In this case the optimal investment rule must take into account the opportunity cost of delaying investment, which can be thought of as the price of 'exercising' an option. Thus, for a firm considering a capacity expansion problem (rather than discrete projects) the optimal investment rule is to expand capacity up to the point where the expected cash flow from an additional unit of capacity is just equal to the sum of the purchase price, the installation cost and the price of exercising the option to invest (Pindyck, 1988).

An important issue is the relationship between investment and uncertainty. Under risk aversion and incomplete markets an increase in uncertainty is likely to lead to lower investment (i.e. a negative relationship) (see, e.g., Craine, 1989). However, under risk neutrality the relationship between uncertainty and investment is ambiguous – see Driver and Moreton (1992) for a taxonomy of the factors that affect this relationship. Hartman (1972) and Abel (1983, 1984, 1985) found a positive relationship under symmetric and convex costs of adjustment, perfect competition and a convex profit function. On the other hand, the literature on irreversible investment with asymmetric costs of adjustment and imperfect competition (e.g. Pindyck, 1988) suggests a negative relationship between investment and uncertainty.

Caballero (1991) has provided an explanation of these conflicting results. Asymmetric adjustment costs are not sufficient for a negative relationship between uncertainty and investment. However, when combined with imperfect competition they produce a negative relationship. These results are intuitively easy to understand. Under perfect competition today's investment decision depends exclusively on the expected path of the price of capital and the expected profitability of capital. However, the latter does not depend on the level of the capital stock. Hence an increase in price uncertainty raises the level of investment since the marginal profitability of capital is convex with respect to price. On the other hand, under imperfect competition the marginal profitability of capital depends on the level of capital stock – an increase in the stock of capital reduces profitability. When this is combined with asymmetric costs of adjustment (i.e. when it is more expensive to reduce capital than to increase it, a weak version of irreversibility) it is better to have a shortage of capital than too much of it. Thus, an increase in uncertainty reduces investment. However, the relationship between investment and uncertainty is not robust to the various factors upon which it depends – see Paraskevopoulos et al. (1991) for an extension to a loose oligopoly and Driver and Moreton (1992) for an evaluation of the literature.

Appendix 5.3 Further Reading on the Demand for Money

In this book the demand for real money balances is a function of real income, the interest rate and real wealth. How does this compare with theoretical specifications of the demand for money?

The existence of money has been explained since Aristotle in terms of its functions as a medium of exchange, store of value, unit of account and means of deferred payments. Money is supposed to facilitate transactions by avoiding the 'double coincidence of wants' and therefore there is a presumption that a monetary economy (an economy in which money is used) is more efficient than a barter economy. In other words, the introduction of money in a barter economy can make all individuals better off (it is welfare-improving) thereby making the equilibrium of a monetary economy Pareto optimal. However, despite being intuitively simple this proposition has been much harder to prove than it sounds. Samuelson (1958) used an intertemporal optimization framework based on an overlapping-generations model to explain that paper money can be valued because it facilitates existing trade and expands its volume by creating new possibilities. However, if apart from money there are other assets that serve as a store of value and yield a higher return than money, which is the case in the real world, then money is not valued.

The difficulty in explaining the use of money has led to the development of models in which it is assumed that money must be used in exchange on the premise that 'money buys goods, goods buys money, but goods do not buy goods'. This assumption is known as the 'Clower constraint' or 'cash-in-advance constraint' (Clower, 1967). An alternative approach is to introduce money directly into the utility function (Sidrauski, 1967). However, before we look at such a general equilibrium framework let us examine partial equilibrium approaches to the demand for money.

Since Keynes the theory of the demand for money has been expressed in terms of the three motives for holding money, namely the transactions, precautionary and speculative motives. The first gives rise to a demand for money from the use of money in making regular payments. The precautionary motive leads to a demand for money to meet unforeseen contingencies. Finally, the speculative motive leads to a demand for money that arises from the uncertainty about the value of assets that yield a higher return than money.

In Keynes's General Theory the demand for money is split into two functions, namely the transactions demand and the speculative demand for money. The former depends on nominal income, while the latter depends on the interest rate. However, the speculative demand for money for an individual is an 'all-or-nothing' demand. Assuming two assets, money and bonds, the individual decides whether to keep her entire wealth in the form of money or bonds by comparing the current with the expected 'normal' interest rate. If the current rate is lower than normal and hence bond prices are higher than normal, the individual would expect interest rates to rise and accordingly bond prices to fall. To avoid capital losses the individual would keep all her wealth in cash. On the other hand, if the current rate is higher than the normal rate and therefore bond prices are below normal, the individual would expect interest rates to fall and therefore would keep her entire wealth in bonds – the demand for money is zero. Assuming that individuals have different normal levels for the interest rate the aggregate speculative demand for money would be an inverse continuous function of the rate of interest.

Apart from the unsatisfactory feature that the micro-speculative demand for money is all-or-nothing, the other main problem with the Keynesian formulation is that people should revise their normal rate if the current rate persistently deviates from it. Thus in a long period of low rates the speculative demand for money should gradually disappear. These deficiencies have been remedied by Tobin (1958), who argued that individuals are risk-averse and hold as a result a diversified portfolio, that is a mixture of the riskless asset (cash) and the risky asset (bonds) rather than an all-or-nothing demand for money. The optimal mix between bonds and cash is derived by optimizing the utility function of an individual, which maps combinations of risk and return subject to the wealth constraint. Changes in the interest rate induce marginal portfolio restructuring by changing the optimum mix between risk and return. Therefore the demand for money would be an inverse continuous function of the interest rate at the micro-level, too. This function does not depend on the concept of the expected 'normal' interest rate and therefore will continue to exist even if interest rates remain low for a long period. Furthermore, the speculative demand for money also depends on the level of wealth.

Despite its attraction, Tobin's portfolio theory cannot explain the demand for demand deposits (cash and cheque accounts that bear no interest), only the demand for time deposits (which are interest-bearing accounts). The reason is that both demand and time deposits are safe assets, but the latter bear interest while the former do not. Thus there is no reason why people should wish to hold demand deposits in their diversified portfolios in the presence of time deposits.

The explanation of demand deposits arises from the medium of exchange function of money and involves a trade-off between the amount of interest an individual would earn by holding such deposits and the cost in terms of wasted time in trips to banks, brokerage fees and inconvenience for having to worry about such things. The total cost of holding cash is equal to the 'brokerage cost' (i.e. the cost of each withdrawal times the number of withdrawals) and the foregone interest. The average holding of cash balances is equal to half the size of a cash withdrawal. The 'inventory theoretic approach' to the transactions demand for money gives rise to the 'square root formula' by minimizing the total cost of holding cash with respect to the number of withdrawals (Baumol, 1952; Tobin, 1956). The demand for money depends positively on income and negatively on the interest rate, with elasticities

0.5 and −0.5 respectively. However, when account is taken of the constraint that the number of withdrawals has to be an integer number the income elasticity of the demand for money rises in the range 0.5 to 1, while the interest elasticity falls in the range −0.5 to zero (see Barro, 1976).

The precautionary demand for money arises from uncertainty regarding the size or pattern of payments that an individual may incur. The problem can be posed as one of balancing the marginal cost of being illiquid and therefore being unable to make a payment that may be incurred with the marginal benefit of receiving extra interest. The optimal precautionary demand for money can be obtained from an inventory approach (Whalen, 1966). The determinants of the precautionary demand for money are the interest rate, the cost of illiquidity and the degree of uncertainty. The higher the interest rate, the greater the foregone interest and therefore the smaller the demand for money. The higher the cost of illiquidity, the larger the demand for money. The higher the degree of uncertainty, the greater the probability of being caught without cash and therefore the larger the demand for money.

All the above approaches are based on a partial equilibrium analysis. What are the determinants of the demand for money in a general equilibrium framework? Lucas and Stokey (1987) derive a demand for money that depends on the interest rate within a 'cash-in-advance' constraint by distinguishing between goods bought with cash and goods being bought on credit. An increase in inflation changes the relative price of these goods and affects the demand for money. However, it is unlikely that the distinction between credit and cash goods is independent of inflation.

An alternative approach is to consider the effects of uncertainty within a Clower constraint (see Krugman et al., 1985). This gives rise to a precautionary demand for money in a general equilibrium analysis because having more money gives the individual more flexibility in choosing consumption. The demand for money is a function of the interest rate and inflation. While an increase in the interest rate leads to a decrease in the demand for money, the effect of inflation is ambiguous. Nevertheless, under a large degree of risk aversion it can be shown that the demand for money depends negatively on the rate of inflation. However, the drawback in this framework is that individuals cannot exchange bonds for cash when in need for money for contingencies.

In Romer (1986, 1987) individuals can exchange bonds for cash as frequently as they wish but at a fixed cost per transaction. The assumption that money must be used in transactions – the Clower constraint – is imposed in a continuous time overlapping-generations model. Individuals receive at the beginning of their life an endowment of goods and money. This wealth can be kept in the form of either money or bonds.

Money does not bear any interest and therefore its return is equal to the negative of the inflation rate. Bonds pay a real interest rate and therefore the opportunity cost of holding money is the nominal interest rate. Consumers maximize an intertemporal utility function, which depends on consumption and the cost of transacting bonds into cash subject to the wealth constraint. They choose how much to consume and save and how to allocate their wealth between bonds and money over time.

Firms produce the output of the economy using a constant returns to scale technology without, however, employing any labour. This means that firms effectively receive the endowment of the young and put it into productive storage, issuing in exchange bonds. This production process determines the real interest rate in the economy. Consumers deposit with the banks the bonds they have received from the firms and exchange them for cash when they need it to buy the goods from the firms. Firms use the money they receive from the sale of goods to consumers to redeem the bonds that are kept in the banks. Thus banks exchange bonds for money with firms, and money for bonds with individuals. The government issues money at a constant rate, which is endowed to every new generation.

The demand for money obtained in this model for the individual is a generalization of the Baumol–Tobin inventory theoretic approach to a general equilibrium framework. The micro-demand for money depends negatively on the nominal interest rate, with elasticity -0.5 (the square root formula), but is a linear function of consumption. The aggregate demand for money is also a decreasing function of inflation because inflation affects consumption and the number of trips to the bank.

What is the effect of open market operations in this model? Money is neutral in steady state. However, there are small real dynamic effects in the transition to the steady state (i.e. the path of real variables is affected). On the other hand, an increase in the rate of growth of money rather than an open market operation increases savings and capital. This result contrasts sharply with the alternative approach to the Clower constraint, which entails putting money directly into either the utility or the production function (Sidrauski, 1967). In this case money is superneutral. The steady-state levels of capital and consumption are independent of the rate of growth of money. The first-order conditions are the same as in the Ramsey model without money. But is it appropriate to put money directly into the utility function? As Blanchard and Fischer (1990, p. 192) have pointed out, the answer depends on whether this formulation is equivalent to an optimization in which individuals face a Clower constraint with a Baumol–Tobin transactions technology. Of course such a question is analytically intractable except in very simple cases (see Feensta, 1986).

Part II

Aggregate Supply

6

Model 6   The Dynamics of Economic Policy in an Inflationary Economy

In this model we relax the assumption that prices are fixed by incorporating into the model developed so far a wage-price sector. The analysis concerns an inflationary economy, that is an economy in which inflation in the long run (i.e. in steady state) is stationary, but not zero. This is our first attempt to provide a simultaneous determination of output and prices (inflation). Furthermore, this model allows us to analyse how a demand or supply shock affects both output and inflation. One of the main objectives of the analysis is to investigate further the causes of business cycles, to examine how a government can influence the targets of economic policy, namely output and inflation, and to explore the possibility of a trade-off between them.

There are two dynamically evolving variables in this model: expected (or anticipated) inflation and private sector wealth. In the short run both variables are fixed. The long run is defined by two conditions. First, expected inflation is stationary and has fully adjusted to actual inflation (i.e. expectations are realized). Second, the budget, including the inflation tax, is balanced and hence private sector wealth is stationary. The dynamics of the system arise from the adjustment of expected to actual inflation and the change in the value of private sector wealth associated with the finance of the budget.

6.1 Assumptions

The relaxation of the assumption that prices are fixed implies that the economy operates on the upward sloping segment of the aggregate supply curve in figure 1.1. Any changes in aggregate demand therefore affect both output and prices. We assume that there are three inputs of production: labour, imported raw materials (e.g. oil) and physical capital. The price of imported raw materials is exogenously determined. Physical capital is assumed to be fixed. Therefore any changes in investment expenditure do not alter the capital stock of the economy, but simply affect aggregate demand. It is assumed that there is no technological change and labour productivity growth is zero. These last two assumptions together imply that the level of capacity output in the economy is fixed.

In the assets markets we assume that there are only two assets: money and government bonds. Both are the liabilities of the government. Furthermore, it is assumed that there are no interest payments on public sector debt. This assumption ensures the linearity of the model and thus greatly simplifies the analysis.

6.2 The Model

The model consists of equations (6.1a) to (6.1j), and (6.2a) and (6.2b)

$$D = C + I + G \tag{6.1a}$$

$$C = c_y YD + c_v \frac{V}{P} ; \quad 0 < c_y, c_v < 1 \tag{6.1b}$$

$$YD = (1 - t_y)Y - p^e(m + b) \tag{6.1c}$$

$$I = I_y Y + I_r(r - p^e); \quad I_y > 0 > I_r \tag{6.1d}$$

$$D = Y \tag{6.1e}$$

$$m = \frac{M}{P} = M_y Y + M_r r + M_v(m + b) \tag{6.1f}$$

$$M_y > 0 > M_r; \quad 0 < M_v < 1$$

$$V = M + B \tag{6.1g}$$

$$w = w_u(u - \bar{u}) + w_p p^e \tag{6.1h}$$

$$w_u < 0; \quad 0 \le w_p \le 1$$

$$p = \beta w + (1 - \beta)pm; \quad 0 < \beta \le 1 \tag{6.1i}$$

$$u = \bar{u} + u_y(Y - \bar{Y}); \quad u_y < 0 \tag{6.1j}$$

$$\dot{m} + \dot{b} = G - t_y Y - p(m + b) \tag{6.2a}$$

$$\dot{p}^e = \gamma(p - p^e); \quad 0 \le \gamma \le 1 \tag{6.2b}$$

where

$b \quad = \dfrac{B}{P} = $ real stock of government bonds;

$B \quad = $ nominal stock of government bonds;

$m \quad = \dfrac{M}{P} = $ real money supply;

M = nominal stock of money;

P = price of output, measured at factory gate prices;

P $= \dfrac{\Delta P}{P}$ = proportionate rate of change of factory gate prices (i.e. actual inflation rate);

p^e = expected (or anticipated) rate of inflation;

PM = price of imported raw materials expressed in domestic currency;

pm $= \dfrac{\Delta PM}{PM}$ = proportionate rate of change of the price of raw materials;

v $= \dfrac{V}{P}$ = real private sector wealth;

V = private sector wealth in nominal terms (i.e. valued at current prices);

u = unemployment rate;

$\bar{u}$ = natural rate of unemployment (i.e. frictional unemployment);

w $= \dfrac{\Delta W}{W}$ = proportionate rate of change of wages (actual wage inflation rate);

$\bar{Y}$ = full capacity level of output or potential output.

A dot over a variable (˙) denotes its time derivative. All other symbols have their usual meaning.

Equations (6.1a) to (6.1j) define the short-run (instantaneous) equilibrium and equations (6.2a) and (6.2b) describe the dynamics of the system. The short-run equilibrium model is divided into three sectors: the real sector, which consists of equations (6.1a) to (6.1e); the monetary sector, equations (6.1f) and (6.1g); and the wage-price sector, equations (6.1h) to (6.1j).

Allowing prices to vary makes no difference to the specification of the real sector of the economy, with one exception, real investment expenditure, I. The latter was until now a function of the nominal interest rate. With flexible prices, however, real investment expenditure depends on the real interest rate, which is defined as the nominal interest rate minus the expected rate of inflation, $r - p^e$. Thus, if the interest rate that banks charge on loans is 10 per cent (this is the nominal rate) and expected inflation is 3 per cent, the real interest rate is only 7 per cent. An increase in the real interest rate deters investment. Hence, I_r in model 6 measures the sensitivity of real investment expenditure with respect to the real interest rate. If, *ceteris paribus*, anticipated inflation rises, the real interest rate is reduced and firms can finance more capital expenditure. Thus, in the above example, if anticipated inflation rises from 3 to 5 per cent, while the nominal interest rate remains unchanged, the real cost of borrowing is reduced from 7 to 5 per cent. In line with model 5, we also make investment a function of demand, proxied by the level of output.

If the private sector is holding money or bonds in an inflationary economy (i.e. a non-zero steady-state rate of inflation), then it is incurring a capital loss. This is usually called the inflation tax. The relationship of real disposable income to the inflation tax is derived as follows.

The real disposable income of the private sector as a whole (personal and company sector) is defined as the sum of planned consumption, C, planned investment, I, and planned savings, S. In equilibrium the latter is equal to the planned change in wealth

$$S = \dot{v}^d \tag{6.3a}$$

Thus, real disposable income is defined as

$$YD \equiv C + I + S = C + I + \dot{v}^d. \tag{6.3b}$$

The planned change in wealth (savings) is obtained by differentiating with respect to time the definition of private sector wealth

$$\dot{v} = \frac{(\dot{M} + \dot{B})P - \dot{P}(M + B)}{P^2} \tag{6.3c}$$

Since in steady state

$$\dot{v} = \dot{v}^d, \quad p = p^e = \frac{\dot{P}}{P} \tag{6.3d}$$

planned savings are equal to

$$\dot{v}^d = \frac{(\dot{M} + \dot{B})}{P} - \frac{M + B}{P} p^e \tag{6.3e}$$

However, the first term on the right hand side of (6.3e) is given by the budget constraint

$$\frac{(\dot{M} + \dot{B})}{P} = G - t_y Y \tag{6.3f}$$

Furthermore, G can be replaced in the above relationship by the equilibrium condition in the goods market (6.1e), i.e.

$$G = Y - C - I \tag{6.3g}$$

Making use of these two expressions and the definition of real disposable income (6.3b), equation (6.3e) can be written as

$$YD \equiv C + I + \dot{v}^d = (1 - t_y)Y - (m + b)p^e \tag{6.3h}$$

Hence, real disposable income, equation (6.1c), is defined as the sum of real factor incomes (i.e. income or output), Y, less income taxes, which are assumed to be proportional to real income, $t_y Y$, less expected capital losses on financial wealth due to inflation (the *expected inflation tax on wealth*), $(m + b)p^e$.

When prices are allowed to vary, the demand for money is explicitly a function of the price level. If prices double, the amount of money needed to finance transactions, meet unforeseen contingencies and store value also doubles. This means that the whole demand for money function is multiplied by the level of prices. The expression $m = M/P$ is called *real money balances*. Equation (6.1f) asserts that real money balances depend positively on real income and negatively on the nominal interest rate. In model 6 the coefficient M_y measures the sensitivity of *real money balances* with respect to real income. Similarly, the coefficient M_r measures the sensitivity of *real money balances* with respect to the nominal interest rate. The emphasis on real money balances means that if the price level changes, the demand for money also changes. This is what distinguishes model 6 from the models developed so far.

In continuous time models real wealth enters the private sector's demand functions instantaneously, but this does not imply that the wealth accumulation process is also instantaneous. Clearly wealth cannot be spent or allocated among assets before it is accumulated. This is ensured by appropriate parameter restrictions in the asset demand functions. The asset demand functions are derived from a utility optimization problem in which a given size of wealth is allocated among competing assets

$$\frac{M}{P} = M\left(Y, r, \frac{V}{P}\right) \tag{6.4a}$$

$$\frac{B}{P} = B\left(Y, r, \frac{V}{P}\right) \tag{6.4b}$$

By totally differentiating these asset demand functions and summing them up we obtain

$$\mathrm{d}\,\frac{M}{P} + \mathrm{d}\,\frac{B}{P} = \mathrm{d}\,\frac{V}{P} = (M_y + B_y)\mathrm{d}Y + (M_r + B_r)\mathrm{d}r$$

$$+ (M_v + B_v)\mathrm{d}\,\frac{V}{P} \tag{6.4c}$$

The top line of (6.4c) shows that the left hand side is the total differential of real private sector wealth, as can be verified from (6.1g). For equation (6.4c) to hold the following conditions must be satisfied

$$M_r + B_r = 0 \tag{6.5a}$$

$$M_y + B_y = 0 \tag{6.5b}$$

$$M_v + B_v = 1 \qquad\qquad (6.5c)$$

where M_i and $B_i (i = r, \ y$ and $v)$ are the partial derivatives of the demand functions for money and bonds with respect to the interest rate, real income and real wealth. These parameter restrictions are called the *adding-up stock constraints*. The first two constraints imply that a change in the interest rate or income results simply in a reallocation of assets. Thus, an increase in the interest rate results in an increase in the demand for bonds, which is met instantaneously by a corresponding reduction in the demand for money. An increase in income raises the transactions demand for money, but this is achieved instantaneously only by reducing the holdings of bonds. However, over time this extra demand for one asset can also be achieved through savings. The third constraint implies that an increase in real private sector wealth by £1000 leads to an increase in the demand for assets by £1000 (i.e. the total increase in wealth is allocated among the two competing assets).

The consumption function is derived from a utility optimization problem in which a given level of disposable income or life-time resources has to be allocated between consumption and savings. The following *adding-up flow constraints* restrict the parameters of the consumption and savings functions

$$C_r + S_r = 0 \qquad\qquad (6.6a)$$

$$C_y + S_y = 1 \qquad\qquad (6.6b)$$

where C_i and $S_i (i = r, y)$ are the partial derivatives of consumption and savings with respect to the interest rate, real income and real wealth respectively. The first constraint implies that an increase in savings, due to a rise in the interest rate, can be achieved instantaneously only by reducing consumption. The second constraint implies that an increase in income of £100 will be spent as additional consumption or held as additional savings (i.e. the total increase in income is allocated between consumption and savings).

Since wealth is fixed at any point in time, only one asset demand function is independent. The demand for the other asset is determined by the wealth constraint. We follow the usual assumption of dropping the bond market and concentrate instead on the money market.

Equation (6.1h) is an expectations-augmented Phillips curve. The rate of growth of wages depends negatively on the unemployment rate and positively on the expected rate of (price) inflation. The coefficient w_u measures the extent to which wage inflation is affected by demand conditions in the labour market. The lower the level of demand for labour, the higher the unemployment rate and the lower the rate of wage inflation.

The coefficient w_p measures the extent to which an increase in expected inflation raises, *ceteris paribus*, wage inflation. A value of $w_p < 1$ can be interpreted as *money illusion*, i.e. that workers are fooled by changes in nominal magnitudes and therefore do not appreciate the corresponding changes in real magnitudes. The fooling arises because workers accept a cut in the expected real wage rate, although all other economic conditions remain unchanged. It may be that workers can be fooled at any particular time, but they cannot be fooled all the time by the same thing. Therefore, such behaviour can be ruled out on the grounds of irrationality, because it implies changes in the expected real wage rate despite unchanged demand conditions in the labour market. For example, other things being equal, an increase in the expected rate of inflation by 3 per cent implies that wage inflation must increase by 3 per cent if workers do not suffer from money illusion. An increase in wages by 3 per cent means that the expected real wage rate remains unchanged. Therefore, absence of money illusion implies that it is changes in the *expected real wage rate* that respond to excess demand/supply in the labour market rather than changes in the *nominal wage rate*. We assume that $w_p < 1$ in the short run, but equal to unity in the long run.

In empirical estimates of equation (6.1h) a value of $w_p < 1$ may not necessarily imply money illusion. Expected (price) inflation is a function, among other things, of actual (price) inflation. If expected inflation in the wage equation, which is an unobserved variable, is replaced by a function of actual inflation, which is observed, then the coefficient w_p measures a composite effect and not just the effect of expected inflation on wage inflation. In this case a value of $w_p < 1$ may imply lags in the adjustment of expected to actual inflation and/or some form of inertia of wage inflation to actual inflation. Such inertia may arise if wage negotiations are bound by *overlapping staggered labour contracts*, i.e. contracts that do not expire simultaneously and last for more than one period, say three-year contracts.

Equation (6.1i) describes the formation of prices (factory gate prices) as a fixed mark-up on average variable unit cost on the assumption of an oligopolistic structure of the economy. The latter consists of wages and the price of imported raw materials. The coefficient β measures the contribution of wages to total cost. The residual $(1 - \beta)$ measures the contribution of imported raw materials to total cost and is a measure of the degree of *supply side openness* or *imported inflation* in the economy.

Equation (6.1j) is a representation of Okun's law, according to which excess supply (demand) in the labour market is related to excess supply (demand) in the goods market. If output, Y, is below its potential, $\bar{Y}$, then unemployment is higher than the natural rate, $\bar{u}$. The economy is slowing down or is already in recession. If, on the other hand, output is above its potential, then unemployment is lower than the natural rate. In this case the economy is expanding too quickly, with obvious bottle-necks in the labour market, and therefore inflation is rising. The coefficient u_y measures the extent to which unemployment falls as demand in the goods market rises. This is a short-term relationship because it is derived for a given level of capital stock.

The dynamics of the system are described by equations (6.2a) and (6.2b). The first is the familiar government budget constraint expressed in real terms. It asserts that the government issues bonds or prints money to finance the excess of its expenditure on goods and services, G, over its tax receipts, which are assumed for simplicity to be proportional to real income, $t_y Y$, and the *inflation tax*, that is the loss due to inflation on the part of private sector financial wealth that is the liability of the government, $p(m + b)$. This term has been called inflation tax because the government does not have to issue as much bonds or money as it would have been required to had inflation not eroded private sector financial wealth. It must be stressed that the inflation tax exists only in an *inflationary economy*, that is, in an economy in which inflation is not zero in steady state (i.e. $p \neq 0$).

The government budget constraint is expressed in real terms. Total government expenditure (i.e. the sum of government expenditure on goods and services and transfer payments) is increased in proportion to prices. If prices double, total government expenditure and hence *psbr* also doubles. Furthermore, the specification of (6.2a) implies that tax revenues increase in the same proportion as prices. In the real world this implies that tax thresholds are adjusted each year according to inflation, so that in real terms the private sector pays the same amount. If this does not hold, and the private sector pays more taxes as inflation rises, then we call this *fiscal drag*. The specification of the government budget constraint in (6.2a) assumes the absence of a fiscal drag.

Finally, equation (6.2b) describes how expectations about inflation are formed. Here an adaptive expectations scheme is adopted, with the coefficient γ measuring the speed at which anticipated inflation adjusts to actual inflation. The scheme can be explained better in discrete time

$$p^e = p^e_{-1} + (1 - \gamma)(p - p^e_{-1}) \quad 0 \leq \gamma \leq 1 \tag{6.7a}$$

where p^e is the expected rate of inflation in period $t + 1$ with information at time t. Denoting by E the mathematical expectation, expected inflation is defined as

$$E_t p_{t+1} = p^e \tag{6.7b}$$

Similarly, p^e_{-1} is this period's expected (or anticipated) inflation rate with information at $t - 1$; and p is this period's actual inflation rate (the latest available inflation figure). The adopted convention for expected inflation is that the time subscript denotes the time the forecast was made. The term $(p - p^e_{-1})$ is the forecast error for this period made with information in the last period, or the unanticipated rate of inflation. According to the adaptive expectations hypothesis, if the previous forecast was an underestimate (i.e. $p - p^e_{-1} > 0$), the current forecast, p^e, is revised upwards from its previous level, p^e_{-1} by a fixed proportion of the forecast error. If the previous forecast was an overestimate, (i.e. $p - p^e_{-1} < 0$), the current forecast is revised downwards. The extent of the revision depends on the parameter γ. If $\gamma = 1$, people do not adjust their expectations at all. Their expectation of inflation is always equal to last period's, irrespective of the actual behaviour of inflation. If $\gamma = 0$, people adjust their expectations to the full extent of the forecast error. This implies that this period's expected rate of inflation is equal to last period's actual inflation rate.

$$p^e = p_{-1} \tag{6.7c}$$

This special case when $\gamma = 0$ is also known as *static expectations*.

Equation (6.7a) can also be written as

$$p^e = \gamma p^e_{-1} + (1 - \gamma)p_{-1} \tag{6.7d}$$

which implies that the expected rate of inflation is an average of last period's expected and actual inflation. The solution to (6.7a) is obtained by repeated substitutions of the lagged expected inflation rate

$$p^e = (1 - \gamma)\sum_{i=0}^{\infty} \gamma^i p_{-i-1} \quad (1 - \gamma)\sum_{i=0}^{\infty} \gamma^i = 1 \tag{6.7e}$$

This implies that expected inflation is an average of past inflation rates, with the recent past more heavily weighted than the distant past. In steady state (6.7a) implies that expectations have adjusted, i.e.

$$p^e = p^e_{-1} = p \tag{6.7f}$$

To close the system we have to assume the type of policy that is pursued by the central bank. Two such policies are considered. First, the government uses as a control the *nominal supply of money* to target *real money balances*. This implies that the government is operating the following feedback rule:

$$M = mP \tag{6.8a}$$

The target is to keep real money balances constant. This policy, referred to as *monetary targeting* in an inflationary economy or simply *monetarist*, means that the central bank is increasing (decreasing) the nominal supply of money to offset any increase (decrease) in the price level so that real money balances remain unchanged. In an inflationary economy this defines a *neutral monetary policy*. If real money balances increase (decrease), then monetary policy is easy (tight). This definition of neutral monetary policy corresponds closer to the real world where inflation is never zero, even in economies like Germany and Japan. According to Tobin a target for real money balances is consistent with a policy of responding to the 'needs of trade'. Assuming that the policy is successful we can substitute (6.8a) into (6.1f) and (6.1g).

Second, the government uses as a control the *nominal stock of domestic government bonds* to target the *real stock of bonds*. This implies that the government is operating the following feedback rule:

$$B = bP \tag{6.8b}$$

The target is to keep the real stock of government bonds fixed. This policy implies that the government is increasing (decreasing) the nominal stock of government bonds to offset any increase (decrease) in the price level, so that the real stock of government bonds remains fixed. We call such a policy *debt targeting* or simply *bondist*. Assuming that the policy is successful we can substitute (6.8b) to eliminate B. Which of the two policies is pursued depends, among other things, on the method of financing the budget.

6.3 Short-run (Instantaneous) Equilibrium

The system can be reduced to the *IS-LM* sub-model and the reduced form of the wage-price sector. Substitute (6.1c) into (6.1b) and that along with (6.1d) into (6.1a). Finally, substitute the resulting equation into (6.1e). We thus obtain the *IS* curve. The *LM* curve is obtained by substituting (6.1g) into (6.1f). Substitute (6.1j) into (6.1h) and that into (6.1i) to obtain the reduced form of the wage-price sector. This is usually called the short-run Phillips curve (*SP*) because it is derived for a given value of expected inflation which is a predetermined variable in the short run. We thus obtain

$$Y = \kappa G + \kappa I_r(r - p^e) + (\kappa C_v - \kappa C_y p^e)(m + b) \tag{6.9a}$$

$$m = M_y Y + M_r r + M_v(m + b) \tag{6.9b}$$

$$p = \beta w_u u_y(Y - \bar{Y}) + \beta w_p p^e + (1 - \beta)pm \tag{6.9c}$$

where

$$\kappa = \frac{1}{1 - c_y(1 - t_y) - I_y} > 0 \tag{6.10}$$

is the simple fiscal multiplier of model 2 modified to take account of the fact that we have incorporated output as a determinant of investment. The condition that (6.10) is positive implies that the *IS* curve has the usual negative gradient.

The dynamics of the system are described by equations (6.2), which are reproduced here for convenience:

$$\dot{m} + \dot{b} = G - t_y Y - p(m + b) \tag{6.2a}$$

$$\dot{p}^e = \gamma(p - p^e) \quad 0 \leq \gamma \leq 1 \tag{6.2b}$$

The model has been reduced into two separate subsystems (6.9) and (6.2). The first subsystem determines the short-run (instantaneous) equilibrium and the second the dynamically evolving variables. The subsystem of equations (6.9) is the static model and determines, at any point in time, income, Y, the interest rate, r, and inflation, p, in terms of (a) the dynamically evolving variables – expected inflation, p^e, real wealth, v; (b) the instruments of fiscal and monetary policy, namely government expenditure, G, and the tax rate, t_y, and real money balances or real stock of government stocks, m or b, according to the monetary policy pursued; and (c) the exogenous variables – (the rate of change of) the price of raw materials in domestic currency, pm, and real capacity output, $\bar{Y}$. This can be written as

$$Y = Y(v, p^e; \quad G, b(\text{or } m); \quad \bar{Y}, pm) \tag{6.11a}$$

$$r = r(v, p^e; \quad G, b(\text{or } m); \quad \bar{Y}, pm) \tag{6.11b}$$

$$p = p(v, p^e; \quad G, b(\text{or } m); \quad \bar{Y}, pm) \tag{6.11c}$$

The system of equations (6.11) and (6.2) works in an iterative manner. First, the reduced form system (6.11) determines the short-run (instantaneous) equilibrium values of output, interest rate and inflation, for given values of the dynamically evolving variables. The short-run equilibrium values are then substituted into (6.2) to determine the values of expected inflation and real money balances (or real stock of domestic bonds). These new values of the dynamically evolving variables are then substituted back into (6.11) to determine the new short-run equilibrium values of output, interest rate and inflation. The process continues until expected inflation is equal to actual inflation and the budget, including the inflation tax, is balanced. In order to analyse how the system evolves through time we need to study the short-run comparative statics with respect to the predetermined variables. This is the subject to which we turn in the next section.

Equation (6.9c) is a representation of the *SP* curve and is depicted in figure 6.1b. The *SP* curve shows the prices (inflation) at which firms are willing to supply their output. The higher the prices, the greater the output that firms are willing to supply. Therefore, the *SP* curve is positively sloped. An increase in income lowers unemployment, raises wage inflation and consequently raises (price) inflation as firms respond by passing the increased cost on to prices. The gradient of the *SP* curve is obtained by partially differentiating (6.9c) with respect to Y:

$$\frac{\partial p}{\partial Y} = \beta w_u u_y > 0. \tag{6.12}$$

The *SP* curve is obtained for a given value of expected inflation. This is a dynamically evolving variable and hence is fixed in the short run.

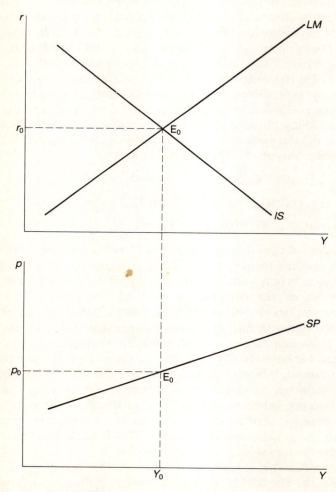

Figure 6.1   Short-run equilibrium

The position of the *SP* curve also depends on the exogenous variables, namely capacity output and inflation in imported raw materials. The greater the response of wages to demand conditions in the labour market, w_u, or the greater the reduction in unemployment, for a given increase in aggregate demand, u_y, the steeper is the *SP* curve. Furthermore, the more supply side closed the economy is (i.e. as β tends to unity), the steeper the *SP* curve. A very steep *SP* curve implies that a movement along the curve, for whatever reason (e.g. fiscal or monetary stimulus), will be translated in the short run into more inflation with little effect on output. In the limiting case of a vertical *SP* curve the effect on output is zero and the whole effect is on inflation. Conversely, in the limiting case of a horizontal *SP* curve the effect on inflation is zero and the whole effect is on output.

Short-run (instantaneous) equilibrium is attained at the intersection of the *IS* and *LM* curves in figure 6.1a. Corresponding to the equilibrium level of income Y_0 there is inflation p_0 (see figure 6.1b).

6.4 Short-run Comparative Statics

The short-run comparative statics are analysed by totally differentiating system (6.9).

$$\begin{bmatrix} 1 & -\kappa I_r & 0 \\ M_y & M_r & 0 \\ -\beta w_u u_y & 0 & 1 \end{bmatrix} \begin{bmatrix} \mathrm{d}Y \\ \mathrm{d}r \\ \mathrm{d}p \end{bmatrix} =$$

$$\begin{bmatrix} D_v(\mathrm{d}m + \mathrm{d}b) + D_p \mathrm{d}p^e + \kappa \mathrm{d}G \\ (1 - M_v)\mathrm{d}m - M_v \mathrm{d}b \\ \beta w_u \mathrm{d}p^e + (1 - \beta)\mathrm{d}pm \end{bmatrix} \tag{6.13a}$$

or in matrix notation

$$\mathbb{B}Y = \mathbb{A} \tag{6.13b}$$

where

$$D_v = \kappa(C_v - C_y p^e) > 0 \tag{6.14a}$$

$$D_p = -\kappa(I_r + C_y v) > 0. \tag{6.14b}$$

Equation (6.14a) shows the effect of private sector wealth on aggregate demand. It can be seen that the total effect can be decomposed into a positive wealth effect, κC_v, and a negative income effect, $\kappa C_y p^e$.

The positive wealth effect arises from the exogenous rise in real money balances or real stock of bonds, which increases wealth and therefore consumption. The negative income effect arises from the effect of inflation tax on real disposable income. As real private sector wealth rises the inflation tax is increased and real disposable income is reduced, thus inducing a negative effect on aggregate demand. Assuming that the positive wealth effect dominates the negative income effect, we impose the restriction that the overall effect is positive.

Equation (6.14b) is the effect of expected inflation on aggregate demand. This effect can be decomposed into two effects: a positive substitution effect ($-\kappa I_r$) and a negative income effect ($-\kappa C_y(m + b)$). The substitution effect arises from the influence of expected inflation on the real interest rate. An increase in expected inflation lowers the real interest rate, which in turn stimulates demand. The income effect arises from the influence of expected inflation on real disposable income through the inflation tax. An increase in expected inflation raises the inflation tax, reduces real disposable income and depresses consumption and hence demand. It is assumed that the substitution effect dominates the income effect.

Given our earlier assumptions the determinant of $\mathbb{B}$, denoted by $\det\mathbb{B}$, is unambiguously negative:

$$\det\mathbb{B} = M_r + \kappa M_y I_r < 0 \tag{6.15}$$

Short-run Effects of Fiscal Policy: Increase in Government Expenditure

The effects of a change in government expenditure are obtained from (6.13) by letting $dG \neq 0$ and setting the differentials of all other exogenous or predetermined variables equal to zero

$$Y_g \equiv \frac{\partial Y}{\partial G} = \frac{1}{1 - c_y(1 - t_y) - I_y + M_y \dfrac{I_r}{M_r}} > 0 \tag{6.16a}$$

$$r_g \equiv \frac{\partial r}{\partial G} = -\frac{M_y}{M_r} Y_g > 0 \tag{6.16b}$$

$$P_g \equiv \frac{\partial p}{\partial G} = \beta w_u u_y Y_g > 0 \tag{6.16c}$$

All multipliers are unambiguously positive. Therefore, an increase in government expenditure raises output, interest rate and inflation, in the short run. Figure 6.2 illustrates this point. Initial equilibrium is at E_0 with income Y_0, interest rate r_0 and inflation p_0. The increase in government expenditure shifts the *IS* curve to $IS(G_1)$ and equilibrium is established at E_1. Income, inflation and the interest rate are all higher in the new equilibrium.

The economic rationale is discussed with the help of box 6.1. The increase in government expenditure stimulates demand and income – route (a). The higher income increases the demand for money. The nominal interest rate rises to clear the assets markets. The increase in the nominal interest rate implies an equivalent increase in the real interest rate because expected inflation is fixed in the short run. This crowds out investment expenditure, thus moderating the initial stimulus of government expenditure – route (b). The increase in income lowers unemployment as firms expand output by employing more labour. Tighter labour market conditions, reflected in lower unemployment, lead to higher wage inflation as firms have to pay higher wages to keep their own workers from going to rival firms and to attract more labour in order to increase output. This leads to higher inflation as firms respond to the increased cost of production by raising prices – route (c).

Box 6.1 The transmission of fiscal policy (government expenditure) in the short run

$$G\uparrow \Rightarrow D\uparrow \Rightarrow Y\uparrow \Rightarrow \begin{cases} YD\uparrow \Rightarrow D\uparrow \Rightarrow Y\uparrow & \text{(a)} \\ M^d\uparrow \Rightarrow r\uparrow \Rightarrow (r - p^e)\uparrow \Rightarrow I\downarrow \Rightarrow Y\downarrow & \text{(b)} \\ u\downarrow \Rightarrow w\uparrow \Rightarrow p\uparrow & \text{(c)} \end{cases}$$

Equation (6.16a) is the fiscal multiplier of model 3 modified because income is a determinant of investment. Therefore, the short-run effect on income/output in an inflationary environment is the same as in model 3, in which prices are fixed. This is a direct consequence of the assumed *'neutral' monetary policy*. The fiscal stimulus (increase in government expenditure) results in higher prices. However, the central bank increases the nominal supply of money to keep real balances unchanged. This is the reason why, as a result of the fiscal expansion, the *LM* curve does not shift in figure 6.2. If the central bank is, instead, operating a *tight* policy of keeping the nominal money supply fixed, then higher prices, resulting from the fiscal stimulus, erode real money balances and the *LM* curve shifts upwards and to the left. In this case the nominal interest rate is certain to rise even more than under neutral monetary policy.

A cursory look at equation (6.16b) reveals that under neutral monetary policy the extent of the interest rate rise is the product of the fiscal multiplier on income, Y_g, times the slope of the *LM* curve. Therefore, the steeper the *LM* curve or the higher the fiscal multiplier, the greater the effect on the interest rate. This is the same result that was reached in model 3.

Similarly, it is obvious from (6.16c) that the effect of fiscal policy on inflation, under neutral monetary policy, is simply the product of the gradient of the *SP* curve times the fiscal multiplier, Y_g. The steeper the *SP* curve or the higher the income multiplier, the greater is the inflationary impact of fiscal policy.

Short-run Effects of Monetary Policy: Increase in Real Money Balances

The effects of a change in real money balances are obtained from (6.13) by letting d$m \neq 0$ and setting the differentials of all other exogenous and predetermined variables equal to zero:

$$Y_m \equiv \frac{\partial Y}{\partial m} = \frac{\dfrac{I_r}{M_r}}{1 - c_y(1 - t_y) - I_y + M_y \dfrac{I_r}{M_r}} > 0 \tag{6.17a}$$

$$r_m \equiv \frac{\partial r}{\partial m} = \frac{1}{M_r}(1 - M_y Y_m) < 0 \tag{6.17b}$$

$$p_m \equiv \frac{\partial p}{\partial m} = \beta w_u u_y Y_m > 0 \tag{6.17c}$$

Equation (6.17a) is unambiguously positive, implying that an increase in real money balances raises income/output in the short run. Furthermore, this expression is equal to the money multiplier of model 3 modified, as in the case of the fiscal multiplier, because income is a determinant of investment.

Equation (6.17b) provides the short-run effect of real money balances on the nominal (and real) interest rate. Assuming a low income sensitivity of the demand for money, the term in the parentheses will be positive and thus the effect of real money balances on the interest rate will be negative. This is the usual assumption that also applies in the context of model 3.

Equation (6.17c) provides the short-run effect of real money balances on the inflation rate. This is unambiguously positive, implying that an increase in real money balances raises the inflation rate in the short run. It is obvious from (6.17c) that the effect of monetary policy on inflation is simply the product of the gradient of the *SP* curve times the effect of real money balances on income, i.e. the money multiplier. Thus, the higher the money multiplier, Y_m, or the steeper the *SP* curve, the greater is the inflationary impact of monetary policy.

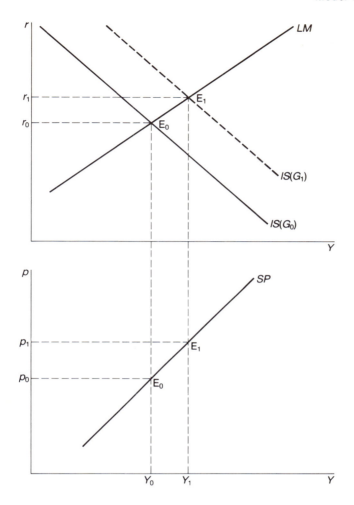

Figure 6.2 The short-run effects of an increase in real government expenditure

Therefore, an increase in real money balances raises output and inflation and lowers the nominal (and real) interest rate. The short-run effects of monetary policy are illustrated in figure 6.3. Initial long-run equilibrium is at E_0, with income Y_0, interest rate r_0 and inflation rate p_0. An increase in real money balances from m_0 to m_1 shifts the *LM* curve to the right from *LM* (m_0) to *LM* (m_1). The nominal and real interest rate falls (since expected inflation is fixed) and this stimulates investment and income. The latter reduces unemployment, as firms employ more labour to increase production. As unemployment falls, labour becomes scarce and firms have to pay higher wages to attract the labour services they need. Firms respond, through mark up pricing, by passing on to prices the increased wage cost. The new short-run equilibrium is attained at E_1 in which inflation and output rise to p_1 and Y_1 respectively and the interest rate falls to r_1. Box 6.2 provides a schematic view of the transmission mechanism of monetary policy in the short run.

Box 6.2 Transmission of monetary policy in the short run

$$m\uparrow \Rightarrow r\downarrow \Rightarrow (r - p^e)\downarrow \Rightarrow I\uparrow \Rightarrow Y\uparrow \Rightarrow u\downarrow \Rightarrow w\uparrow \Rightarrow p\uparrow$$

It is important to compare the channels through which fiscal and monetary policies create inflation. Both an increase in the supply of money and an increase in government expenditure induce inflation by stimulating aggregate demand. Thus, neither fiscal nor monetary policy has a direct effect on inflation. They both work indirectly through aggregate demand. The greater the effect on demand is, the greater the inflationary impact. The effect on demand, on the other hand, depends on the fiscal and money multipliers of model 3, Y_g and Y_m, as well as on the extent of the fiscal and monetary stimulus, dG and dm. Hence,

$$dp = p_g dG + p_m dm \qquad (6.18a)$$

$$= \beta w_u u_y Y_g dG + \beta w_u u_y Y_m dm \qquad (6.18b)$$

If the fiscal stimulus is exactly offset by a corresponding contraction in monetary policy, then the overall inflationary impact depends on the size of the two income multipliers. Thus, if $dG = -dm$, then

$$\frac{dp}{dm} \gtreqless 0, \quad \text{provided that } Y_m \gtreqless Y_g \qquad (6.18c)$$

Although (6.18c) makes a mathematical point, it should be borne in mind that the increase in government expenditure is not strictly speaking comparable to a reduction in real money balances. Although both are measured in pounds, G represents demand for goods and services, while m represents liquidity, that is a form in which wealth can be held. In other words, there is no reason why the authorities should wish to set $dG = -dm$.

Short-run Effects of Monetary Policy: Increase in the Real Stock of Bonds

The effects of a change in the real stock of bonds are obtained from (6.13) by letting $db \neq 0$ and setting the differentials of all other exogenous and predetermined variables equal to zero:

$$\frac{\partial Y}{\partial b} = \frac{1}{\det\mathbb{B}}\,(D_v M_r - \kappa I_r M_v) > 0, \quad \text{if (6.19b) holds;} \tag{6.19a}$$

$$C_v - C_y p^e > \frac{I_r}{M_r} M_v \tag{6.19b}$$

$$\frac{\partial r}{\partial b} = \frac{1}{\det\mathbb{B}}\,(D_v M_y + M_v) > 0 \tag{6.19c}$$

$$\frac{\partial p}{\partial b} = \beta w_u u_y \frac{\partial Y}{\partial b} > 0, \quad \text{if (6.19b) holds} \tag{6.19d}$$

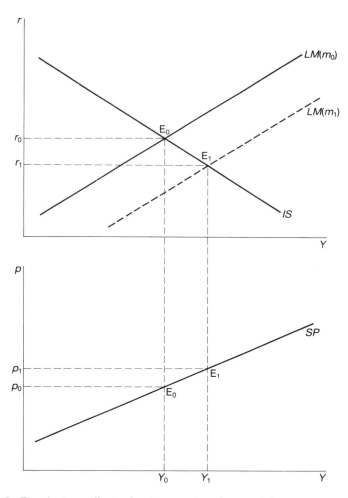

Figure 6.3   The short-run effects of an increase in real money balances

An increase in the real stock of government bonds raises the interest rate, but has an ambiguous effect on output and inflation. If, however, (6.19b) holds, then both output and inflation rise. This is a much stricter condition than (4.24), which was encountered in the context of fixed prices. For inflation and output to rise in an inflationary economy the wealth effect in consumption must exceed: (a) the wealth effect in the demand for money by a factor that measures the relative effectiveness of fiscal to monetary policy; and (b) the effect of the inflation tax on consumption. It is the second effect that is absent in the case when prices are fixed.

Figure 6.4 highlights the effects of an increase in the real stock of government bonds. Initial equilibrium is at E_0 with output Y_0, interest rate r_0 and inflation p_0. The increase in the real stock of government bonds from b_0 to b_1 shifts the *IS* curve to IS_1, on the assumption that the positive wealth effect in consumption dominates the negative income effect associated with the inflation tax (i.e. on the assumption that (6.14a) holds). The increase in b also shifts the *LM* curve upwards and to the left to LM_1, since an increase in wealth increases the demand for money and with fixed real money balances the interest rate must rise to clear the assets markets. The ambiguity with respect to the effect on income arises from the fact that the *IS* curve shifts to the right and the *LM* curve to the left. Thus, whether income would rise or fall depends on the relative shifts of the *IS* and *LM* curves. Income and inflation will rise if the shift in the *IS* curve is larger than the shift in the *LM* curve. The condition for such relative shifts is given by (6.19b). On the assumption that this condition is satisfied equilibrium will be established at E_1. Income, inflation and the interest rate are all higher. The effect on the interest rate is unambiguous because the *IS* shifts to the right and the *LM* to the left.

Short-run Effects of Expected Inflation

The effects of a change in expected inflation are obtained from (6.13) by letting $dp^e \neq 0$ and setting the differentials of all other exogenous and predetermined variables equal to zero

$$Y_p \equiv \frac{\partial Y}{\partial p^e} = \frac{1}{\det \mathbb{B}} M_r D_p > 0, \quad \text{if (6.14b) holds;} \tag{6.20a}$$

$$r_p \equiv \frac{\partial r}{\partial p^e} = -\frac{M_y}{M_r} Y_p > 0, \quad \text{if (6.14b) holds;} \tag{6.20b}$$

$$p_p \equiv \frac{\partial p}{\partial p^e} = \beta \left(w_u u_y Y_p + w_p \frac{1}{\det \mathbb{B}} (M_r + \kappa M_y I_r) \right) > 0 \tag{6.20c}$$

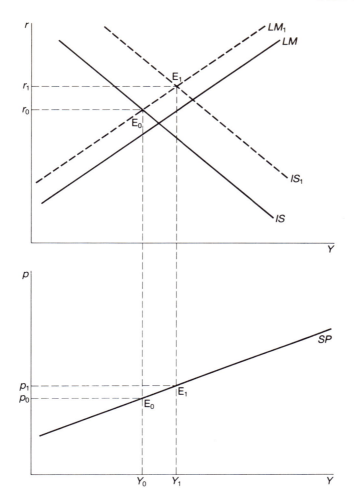

Figure 6.4   The short-run effects of an increase in the real stock of government bonds

An increase in expected inflation will raise inflation, but has an ambiguous effect on output and the interest rate. The ambiguity arises from the fact that the *IS* curve may shift either to the left or to the right depending on the relative strength of the substitution and income effects of expected inflation. An increase in expected inflation lowers the real interest rate, the substitution effect, and therefore stimulates investment. However, at the same time real disposable income is reduced because of a higher inflation tax, the income effect. If the substitution effect dominates the income effect, as is assumed in (6.14b), then the *IS* curve will shift to the right, thereby raising output. Since the *LM* curve remains unchanged the interest rate will also rise. The reason is that a higher income will increase the demand for money and with fixed real money balances the interest rate will rise to clear the assets markets. If, on the other hand, the income effect of expected inflation dominates the substitution effect, then the *IS* curve will shift to the left, thereby lowering income and the interest rate. However, as we shall see in section 6.11, for the economy to be stable the substitution effect must outweigh the income effect. Thus, in a stable economy an increase in expected inflation raises output and the interest rate.

Figure 6.5 illustrates the effects of an increase in expected inflation on the assumption that (6.14b) holds. Initial long-run equilibrium is at

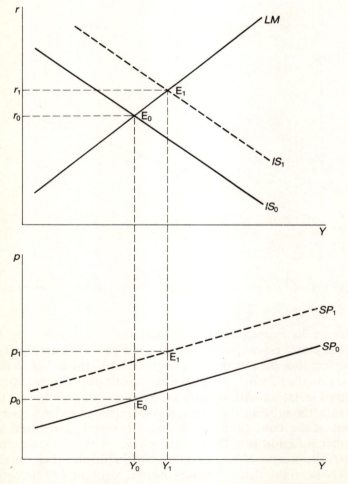

Figure 6.5 The short-run effects of an increase in the expected rate of inflation

E_0, with income Y_0, interest rate r_0 and inflation p_0. The increase in expected inflation shifts the *IS* curve to the right from IS_0 to IS_1 and, with unchanged *LM*, output and the interest rate rise. The increase in output lowers unemployment, pushes wages up and therefore increases the inflation rate. This is the traditional demand channel that we have analysed in the context of a fiscal or monetary stimulus. However, an autonomous increase in the expected rate of inflation has one more additional inflationary effect. It shifts the *SP* curve upwards and to the left from SP_0 to SP_1. At any given level of income, an increase in expected inflation raises actual inflation. The reason is that an increase in expected inflation, *ceteris paribus*, raises wage inflation, and firms pass the increased wage cost on to prices. Final short-run equilibrium is attained at E_1, with income Y_1, interest rate r_1 and inflation rate p_1. Box 6.3 provides a schematic view of the transmission mechanism of expected inflation in the short run.

Box 6.3 The transmission of anticipated inflation in the short run

$$p^e\uparrow \Rightarrow \begin{cases} (r - p^e)\downarrow \Rightarrow I\uparrow \Rightarrow Y\uparrow \Rightarrow u\downarrow \Rightarrow w\uparrow \Rightarrow p\uparrow \\ (m + b)p^e\uparrow \Rightarrow YD\downarrow \Rightarrow Y\downarrow \Rightarrow u\uparrow \Rightarrow w\downarrow \Rightarrow p\downarrow \\ w\uparrow \Rightarrow p\uparrow \end{cases}$$

Short-run Effects of Imported Inflation through Raw Materials

The effects of a change in the rate of inflation of imported raw materials are obtained from (6.13) by letting $dpm \neq 0$ and setting the differentials of all other exogenous variables equal to zero:

$$\frac{\partial Y}{\partial pm} = 0 \tag{6.21a}$$

$$\frac{\partial r}{\partial pm} = 0 \tag{6.21b}$$

$$\frac{\partial p}{\partial pm} = 1 - \beta > 0. \tag{6.21c}$$

An increase in the rate of inflation of imported raw materials raises domestic inflation, but leaves output and the interest rate unchanged in the short run. These results are discussed with the help of figure 6.6. Initial equilibrium is at E_0 with income Y_0, interest rate r_0 and inflation p_0. The rate of inflation of imported raw materials rises from pm_0 to pm_1. This shifts the *SP* curve upwards by the degree of the supply side openness of the economy, $1 - \beta$. At any given level of output, the cost

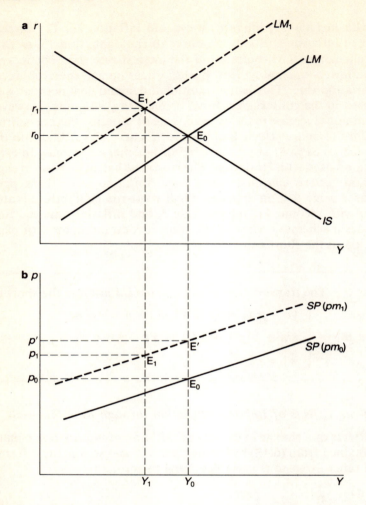

Figure 6.6   The short-run effects of an increase in the rate of inflation of imported raw materials

of production increases as a result of higher prices in raw materials. Firms respond to the increased cost of production, through mark-up pricing, by raising prices. In the short run, expected inflation is fixed. Thus, despite the increase in actual inflation, expected inflation remains unchanged. This implies that the *IS* curve does not shift. Furthermore, under *neutral monetary policy* real money balances remain intact despite rising prices, because the central bank increases the nominal supply of money as prices rise. This implies tha the *LM* curve does not shift. Since both the *IS* and the *LM* curves remain in their original positions it follows that the effect on output and the interest rate is zero. New short-run equilibrium is established at E′ in figure 6.6b with inflation equal to p', and at E_0 in figure 6.6a with output Y_0 and interest rate r_0.

If the central bank follows a *tight monetary policy* of keeping the *nominal supply of money fixed*, then rising prices erode the value of real money balances. The *LM* curve shifts upwards to LM_1 as there is an excess demand for money. Accordingly, the nominal (and real) interest rate rises to r_1 and this lowers output to Y_1. New short-run equilibrium is attained at E_1 in figure 6.6a and b, with higher inflation, p_1. Therefore, an increase in the price of imported raw materials, like oil, causes *stagflation*, i.e. higher inflation and recession. Note that inflation under tight monetary policy is lower than under neutral monetary policy, at p_1 and p' respectively. The reason is that under tight monetary policy the economy slows (lower income), thereby dampening the rate of inflation.

Short-run Effects of Capacity Output

The effects of a change in capacity output are obtained from (6.13) by letting $d\bar{Y} \neq 0$ and setting the differentials of all other exogenous variables equal to zero:

$$\frac{\partial Y}{\partial \bar{Y}} = 0 \tag{6.22a}$$

$$\frac{\partial r}{\partial \bar{Y}} = 0 \tag{6.22b}$$

$$\frac{\partial p}{\partial \bar{Y}} = -\beta w_u u_y < 0 \tag{6.22c}$$

In model 6 capacity output, $\bar{Y}$, is an exogenous variable. However, in the real world it depends on the capital stock, which in turn depends on investment. Higher investment expenditure increases the stock of capital and therefore capacity output. In model 7 we extend the analysis to endogenize capacity output along these lines. Here, we simply examine the effects of an exogenous change in capacity output. An increase in capacity output lowers inflation, but leaves output and the interest rate unchanged. These results are discussed in the context of figure 6.7. Initial equilibrium is at E_0. The increase in capacity output from $\bar{Y}_0$ to $\bar{Y}_1$ shifts the *SP* curve downwards. Increased labour productivity lowers the cost of production and inflation falls. However, the *IS* curve does not shift despite falling inflation because expected inflation is fixed in the short run. The *LM* curve does not shift either, because under *neutral monetary policy* the central bank reduces the nominal supply of money as prices gradually fall. New short-run equilibrium is attained at E' in figure 6.7b with lower inflation, p', and at E_0 in figure 6.7a with unchanged output and the interest rate.

If the central bank operates a *tight monetary policy* of keeping the nominal supply of money fixed, then real money balances increase as prices fall. This causes a downward shift in the *LM* curve to LM_1. There is an excess supply of money and the nominal (and real) interest rate falls to r_1. This, in turn, stimulates output to Y_1. New short-run equilibrium is established at E_1 with lower inflation, lower interest rate and higher output.

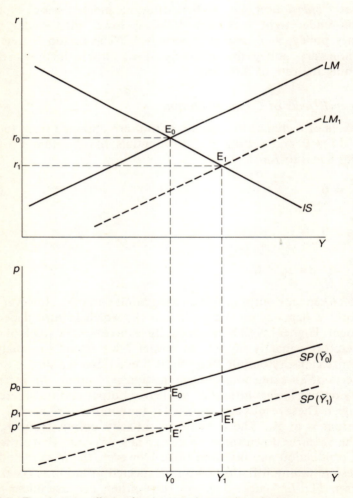

Figure 6.7   The short-run effects of an increase in capacity output

6.5 Long-run (Steady-state) Equilibrium

In the context of model 6 the economy is in long-run equilibrium (i.e. steady state) when two conditions are met. First, expected inflation is stationary. Second, the government does not print any more money or issue more bonds to finance its budget deficit. These conditions are derived by setting the left hand side of the dynamic equations (6.2) equal to zero, i.e.

$$\dot{p}^e = 0, \quad \dot{m} + \dot{b} = 0 \tag{6.23}$$

It follows from (6.2) and (6.23) that in long-run equilibrium inflationary expectations are realized; that is, expected inflation is stationary and equal to actual inflation and the budget deficit is equal to the inflation tax, or the budget is balanced including the inflation tax in tax revenues:

$$p = p^e \tag{6.24}$$

$$G - t_y Y = p(m + b) \tag{6.25a}$$

Using (6.24) and assuming absence of money illusion in the long run (i.e. $w_p = 1$) the system of equations (6.9) defines long-run equilibrium:

$$Y = \kappa G + \kappa I_r(r - p) + (\kappa C_v - \kappa C_y p)(m + b) \tag{6.25b}$$

$$m = M_y Y + M_r r + M_v(m + b) \tag{6.25c}$$

$$(1 - \beta)p = \beta w_u u_y(Y - \bar{Y}) + (1 - \beta)pm \tag{6.25d}$$

Equations (6.25b) and (6.25c) are the long-run IS' and LM' curves. These differ from the short-run curves in that inflationary expectations are adjusted. In the (Y, r) space both curves have the same slope as in the short run.

It is instructive, at this stage, to examine the nature of the long-run equilibrium when the level of unemployment is equal to the natural rate (i.e. $u = \bar{u}$). In this case it is obvious from (6.1j) that the level of output is equal to its potential (i.e. $Y = \bar{Y}$). In addition, it follows from (6.1h) that wage inflation is equal to price inflation (i.e. $w = p$). Then it follows from (6.1i) that

$$p = pm \tag{6.25e}$$

In other words, when the goods and the labour markets are in equilibrium the inflation rate is equal to the exogenously given inflation of the rest of the world, the rate of change of imported raw materials. However, in the context of model 6 this is not a condition for steady state and therefore the country can have a higher or lower inflation rate than the rest of the world. If this is made an extra long-run equilibrium condition, then, since *pm* is already expressed in domestic currency, it follows that

$$p = pm^* - \dot{e} \tag{6.25f}$$

where pm^* is the rate of inflation of imported raw materials expressed in foreign currency (say, dollars) and $\dot{e}$ is the rate of change of the exchange rate, which in turn is defined as the foreign price of domestic currency, e.g. dollars per pound. In this case the country can have a higher (lower) inflation rate than the rest of the world if its exchange rate depreciation (appreciation) absorbs the difference. The experience of many countries, like a number of Latin American countries, Israel and Turkey, to name just a few, shows that this situation can go on for many years, and therefore the analysis of model 6 becomes relevant even if such a steady-state condition is not imposed.

Equation (6.25d) defines the long-run Phillips curve, denoted by *LP*. The *LP* curve shows the prices at which firms are willing to supply their output when inflationary expectations are fully adjusted (i.e. when $p^e = p$). The *LP* curve is depicted in figure 6.8b for given values of inflation in imported raw materials, *pm*, and potential output, $\bar{Y}$. Points along the *LP* curve show combinations of output and inflation along which expected inflation is equal to actual inflation. In the area to the right of the *LP* curve actual inflation is higher than anticipated inflation and in the area to the left of the *LP* curve anticipated inflation is higher than actual inflation.

The gradient of *LP* curve is obtained by partially differentiating (6.25d) with respect to *Y*:

$$\frac{\partial p}{\partial Y} = \frac{\beta w_u u_y}{1 - \beta} > 0 \tag{6.26}$$

The *LP* curve is positively sloped. An increase in output/income raises the demand for labour and consequently unemployment falls. Tighter labour market conditions lead to a higher wage inflation as firms have to raise wages to keep their work force from joining rival firms and to attract more workers to increase production. The higher cost of production forces firms to raise prices. The argument so far is the same as that developed to justify a positively sloped *SP* curve. In the long run there are two more forces that operate. Workers observe the higher inflation and adjust their expectations of inflation upwards. In the next round of wage negotiations workers ask for higher wages to protect their real wage rate from being eroded by higher prices. This leads to a wage–price spiral through higher expected inflation. Firms respond to increased wage cost by raising prices and workers demand higher wages because of expectations of higher prices. When the adjustment is complete and expected

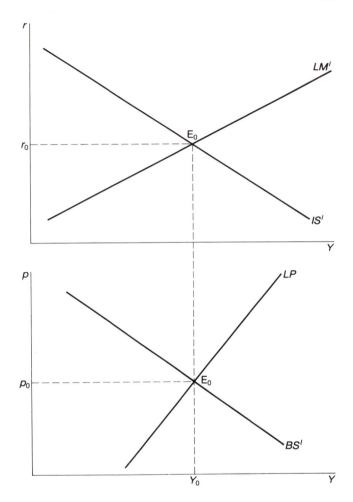

Figure 6.8 Long-run equilibrium

inflation is equal to actual inflation the economy converges to a long-run equilibrium.

The *LP* curve is steeper than the *SP* curve since the numerator of (6.26) is the gradient of the *SP* curve (see 6.12) and the denominator is less than unity, provided β is less than unity. An *LP* curve steeper than the *SP* curve implies that the output–inflation trade-off is smaller in the long than in the short run. In other words, a given stimulus in output produces much higher inflation in the long than in the short run. The economic reason for a steeper *LP* curve is that, for any given stimulus in output, inflation is higher in the long than in the short run because of the wage–price spiral that arises from adjustment of expected inflation.

It is obvious from (6.26) that the *LP* curve will be vertical if the economy is supply side closed; that is, if it does not import any raw materials (i.e. $\beta = 1$). In this case any stimulus to output is unsustainable. Output is only temporarily increased, while in the long run it returns to its original level. Inflation, on the other hand, rises in the long run to an even higher rate than in the short run.

The position of the *LP* curve depends on imported inflation and potential output. An increase in the rate of imported inflation shifts the curve upward and to the left, implying that, at the same level of output, the rate of inflation will be higher, the greater is the rate of imported inflation. An increase in the level of potential output reduces inflation, for any given level of output.

Equation (6.25a) defines the budget surplus curve, denoted by BS^{l}. The BS^{l} curve, plotted in figure 6.8b, shows in the (Y, p) plane combinations of income and inflation along which the budget is balanced, in the sense that taxes and the inflation tax cover government expenditure. This curve is negative sloped

$$\left.\frac{\partial p}{\partial Y}\right|_{bs=0} = -t_y \frac{1}{m+b} < 0 \qquad (6.27a)$$

An increase in income raises taxes and creates a budget surplus. For the budget to be balanced the inflation rate must fall so that the inflation tax is reduced. An increase in real government expenditure shifts the BS^{l} curve to the right, since, at the same level of income, an increase in real government expenditure causes a budget deficit and inflation must rise to increase the inflation tax to restore balance in the budget.

$$\left.\frac{\partial p}{\partial G}\right|_{bs=0} = \frac{1}{m+b} > 0 \qquad (6.27b)$$

An increase in real money balances or the real stock of government bonds rotates the BS^{l} curve anti-clockwise with respect to the income axis, since, at the same level of income, inflation must fall to offset the rise in m or b so that the inflation tax remains unchanged and consequently the budget is again balanced.

$$\left.\frac{\partial p}{\partial m}\right|_{bs=0} = \left.\frac{\partial p}{\partial b}\right|_{bs=0} = \frac{t_y Y - G}{(m+b)^2} < 0 \qquad (6.27c)$$

The system of four equations in (6.25) determines four endogenous variables: the long-run equilibrium level of output, Y, interest rate, r, inflation, p, and real stock of bonds, b, or money, m, according to whether the central bank is targeting m or b. The long-run equilibrium is defined for given values of the policy instruments: government expenditure, G, the income tax rate, t_y, real money balances, m, or the real stock of government bonds, b, and the set of exogenous variables, capacity output, $\bar{Y}$, and inflation in imported raw materials, pm. Figure 6.8 shows a long-run equilibrium for a given set of values of the policy instruments and exogenous variables. As usual, equilibrium in the goods and assets markets is established at the intersection of the IS' and LM' curves, point E in figure 6.8a. This determines the long-run equilibrium level of output and interest rate, Y_0 and r_0 respectively. The long-run equilibrium rate of inflation is attained at the intersection of the LP and BS' curves, point E_0 in figure 6.8b. At the level of income Y_0 inflation is p_0 and the budget is balanced in the sense that government expenditure is equal to tax revenues and the inflation tax. If there is a change in a policy instrument or an exogenous variable, a new long-run equilibrium will be established, provided the economy is stable. This is the task of the next section.

6.6 Long-run Comparative Statics

In this section we study the long-run effects of a change in a policy instrument or an exogenous variable. These effects depend upon the type of monetary policy pursued by the central bank. When the central bank operates a neutral monetary policy of keeping real money balances fixed, the endogenous variables are Y, r, p and b. With this policy regime the long-run comparative statics are analysed by totally differentiating (6.25):

$$
\begin{bmatrix}
t_y & 0 & p & m+b \\
-\beta w_u u_y & 0 & 0 & 1-\beta \\
M_y & M_r & M_v & 0 \\
1 & -\kappa I_r & -D_v & -D_p
\end{bmatrix}
\begin{bmatrix}
dY \\
dr \\
db \\
dp
\end{bmatrix}
=
\begin{bmatrix}
dG - p\,dm \\
(1-\beta)dpm \\
(1-M_v)dm \\
\kappa dG + D_v dm
\end{bmatrix}
$$

or

$$\mathbb{B}Y = \mathbb{A} \tag{6.28}$$

The determinant of $\mathbb{B}$, denoted by $\det\mathbb{B}$, is given by

$$\det\mathbb{B} = \beta w_u u_y \delta_{21} + (1-\beta)\delta_{24} > 0 \tag{6.29}$$

where δ_{ij} is the minor determinant associated with element (i,j). δ_{24} is unambiguously positive. If

$$C_v > \frac{I_r}{M_r}M_v - \frac{p}{v}I_r, \quad \text{then } \delta_{21} > 0 \tag{6.30}$$

This is a much stricter condition than (4.24), which was encountered in the context of fixed prices. In a non-inflationary economy (i.e. $p = 0$), but with flexible rather than fixed prices, condition (6.30) collapses to (4.24). Thus, a stronger wealth effect is required in an inflationary than in a non-inflationary economy. Notice also how (6.30) differs from (6.19b), which is a condition required for stability.

Even if the economy is supply side closed (i.e. $\beta = 1$) and recalling that we have assumed absence of money illusion in the long run (i.e. $w_p = 1$), the determinant of $\mathbb{B}$ is positive provided (6.30) holds true.

When the central bank operates a policy of debt targets, that is keeping the real stock of government bonds fixed, the endogenous variables of the system are Y, r, p and m. The long-run effects of a change in a policy instrument or exogenous variable are analysed by:

$$
\begin{bmatrix}
t_y & 0 & p & m+b \\
-\beta w_u u_y & 0 & 0 & 1-\beta \\
M_y & M_r & M_v - 1 & 0 \\
1 & -\kappa I_r & -D_v & -D_p
\end{bmatrix}
\begin{bmatrix}
dY \\
dr \\
dm \\
dp
\end{bmatrix}
=
\begin{bmatrix}
dG - p\,db \\
(1-\beta)dpm \\
-M_v db \\
\kappa dG + D_v dm
\end{bmatrix}
$$

or

$$\mathbb{B}\mathbb{Y} = \mathbb{A} \tag{6.31}$$

The determinant of $\mathbb{B}$ is given by

$$\det\mathbb{B} = \beta w_u u_y \delta_{21} + (1-\beta)\delta_{24} > 0 \tag{6.32}$$

provided δ_{21} is positive. This will be the case if

$$C_v > \frac{I_r}{M_r}(M_v - 1) - \frac{p}{v} I_r \tag{6.33}$$

This is a less strict condition than (6.30) because the first term on the right hand side is negative rather than positive. In a non-inflationary economy (i.e. $p = 0$) in which, nevertheless, prices are flexible, condition (6.33) will always be satisfied. Given that δ_{24} is unambiguously positive it follows that the determinant of $\mathbb{B}$ is positive even in a supply side closed economy (i.e. $\beta = 1$), provided (6.33) holds.

6.7 Long-run Effects of Fiscal Policy under Bond Finance

The long-run effects of a bond-financed increase in government expenditure are obtained from (6.28) by letting only $dG \neq 0$ and setting all other differentials in $\mathbb{A}$ equal to zero:

$$\left.\frac{\partial Y}{\partial G}\right|_{dm=0} = \frac{1}{\det \mathbb{B}} (1 - \beta)\Delta_{24}^1 > 0 \tag{6.34a}$$

$$\left.\frac{\partial p}{\partial G}\right|_{dm=0} = \frac{1}{\det \mathbb{B}} \beta w_u u_y \Delta_{21}^4 > 0 \tag{6.34b}$$

or

$$\left.\frac{\partial p}{\partial G}\right|_{dm=0} = \frac{\beta w_u u_y}{1 - \beta} \left.\frac{\partial Y}{\partial G}\right|_{dm=0} > 0 \quad \text{since } \Delta_{24}^1 = \Delta_{21}^4 \tag{6.34b}$$

$$\left.\frac{\partial r}{\partial G}\right|_{dm=0} = \frac{1}{\det \mathbb{B}} (\beta w_u u_y \Delta_{21}^2 + (1 - \beta)\Delta_{24}^2) \gtrless 0 \tag{6.34c}$$

$$\left.\frac{\partial b}{\partial G}\right|_{dm=0} = \frac{1}{\det \mathbb{B}} (\beta w_u u_y \Delta_{21}^3 + (1 - \beta)\Delta_{24}^3) \gtrless 0 \tag{6.34d}$$

$$C_v > \frac{I_r}{M_r} M_v - (1 - C_y)p \tag{6.34e}$$

where Δ_{ij}^s is the minor determinant associated with element (i, j) of the fourth-order determinant that results from $\det \mathbb{B}$ by replacing the s column by $\mathbb{A}$.

An increase in government expenditure financed by bonds raises output and inflation in the long run, provided (6.34e) holds. However, it has an ambiguous effect on wealth and the interest rate. These results are discussed in the context of figure 6.9. Initial long-run equilibrium is at A with output Y_0, interest rate r_0 and inflation p_0. The increase in government expenditure raises output, the interest rate and inflation to Y_s, r_s and p_s in the short run, with equilibrium at B. The short-run equilibrium is characterized by unchanged expected inflation and wealth and a budget deficit. In the short run output rises as the increase in government expenditure stimulates aggregate demand. The interest rate rises too, as the increase in income leads to an increased demand for money. The higher income lowers unemployment, raises the rate of wage inflation and pushes inflation up. In the short run, as output rises and actual inflation exceeds expected inflation, we are in the area to the right of the LP curve. Along the SP_0 curve anticipated inflation is only p_0^e, whereas at B actual inflation is p_s $(p_s > p_0^e)$.

Over time the dynamically evolving variables, expected inflation and real bonds, start adjusting. The increase in inflation raises expected inflation and this shifts the SP curve upwards and to the left, setting up the wage–price spiral: a rise in expected inflation raises wages, which raises prices with a further feedback on expected inflation. As wage contracts are renegotiated they incorporate the higher actual inflation

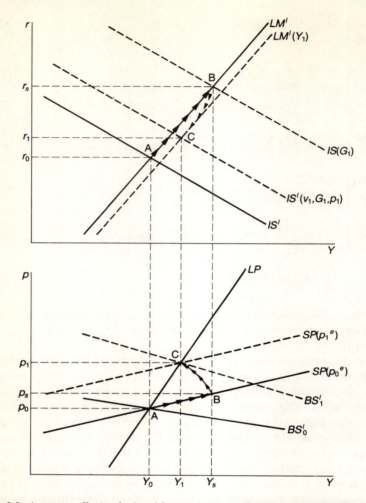

Figure 6.9   Long-run effects of a bond finance increase of government expenditure

into anticipated inflation. However, in staggered labour contracts anti-cipated inflation is always lower than actual inflation because only a fraction of contracts are renegotiated at any point in time. Workers and firms under all other contracts that still have some time to run observe the higher actual inflation rate but are unable to do anything about it. As anticipated inflation rises, the *SP* curve shifts up. This means that, at any given level of output, wages are adjusted upwards as anticipated inflation is increased, which pushes, through mark-up pricing, actual inflation up further. For a time we move along a higher SP curve on which actual inflation exceeds the newly revised anticipated inflation. The adjustment process continues, with the *SP* curve shifting consecutively upwards. Long-run equilibrium is established at C. The SP curve gradually shifts to $SP(p_1^e)$, along which anticipated inflation is p_1^e. Point C represents long-run equilibrium because actual inflation is p_1, which is also equal to anticipated inflation, p_1^e. In the long-run equilibrium expected inflation has fully adjusted to actual inflation and the budget is again balanced.

The ambiguity with respect to the effect of government expenditure on the interest rate arises from the uncertain effect of expected (and actual) inflation on demand (recall that expected and actual inflation are equal in steady state). We can thus apply the analysis related to (6.14b) to steady state. The rise in inflation lowers the real interest rate and this stimulates demand – the substitution effect. However, the rise in inflation also raises the inflation tax and this depresses demand through the effect of lower disposable income on consumption – the income effect. On the assumption that the substitution effect dominates the income effect the IS' curve shifts gradually to the right.

Even if it is assumed that the inflation effect on demand is positive it is not certain that the IS curve will ultimately shift to the right, because there is uncertainty regarding the effect of inflation on real wealth. The initial increase in government expenditure raises *psbr* and the budget is in deficit. The government issues more bonds to cover the deficit, but whether this will lead to a higher or lower real stock of government bonds (and hence real wealth) in the new steady state depends on the effect of excess demand on prices. If the effect on prices is small, the erosion of real bonds is small and in the new steady state real bonds are higher. This shifts the IS' curve further to the right as consumption is stimulated through increased wealth. However, the rise in wealth also increases the demand for money and, with real money balances fixed, the LM' curve shifts to the left. Therefore, on the assumption that the substitution effect of a rise in inflation dominates the income effect and that the effect of excess demand on prices is relatively small, wealth and the interest rate will both rise.

If, on the other hand, the effect of excess demand on prices is large, the value of real bonds is eroded and in the new steady state real wealth is lower. This reverses the rightward shift of the IS' curve as consumption is decreased. The reduction in real wealth implies that the demand for money is diminished and this shifts the LM' curve to the right. In this case the effect on the interest rate is ambiguous, since the LM' curve shifts to the right and the position of the IS' curve in the new long-run equilibrium may be lower or higher relative to the initial equilibrium. As we shall see in section 6.11, the economy is stable under bond finance if the effect of expected inflation on demand is positive and the wealth effect on consumption, adjusted for the effect of inflation tax, is positive and stronger than the wealth effect on the demand for money by a factor that measures the effectiveness of fiscal policy relative to monetary policy. This means that if real wealth falls then the *IS* curve will shift to the left relative to its short-run equilibrium position and that the shift in the *IS* curve is larger than the shift in the *LM* curve. Accordingly, the interest rate falls relative to its short-run equilibrium.

This situation is depicted in Figure 6.9. New long-run equilibrium is attained at C with higher output, inflation and interest rate relative to the initial long-run equilibrium. The expansion in output is less, whereas inflation rises more in the long than in the short run. Finally, the interest rate falls in the long-run relative to the short-run equilibrium. The BS' curve shifts to the right as a result of the increase in government expenditure. Assuming that real wealth falls in the new steady state, the BS' curve rotates clockwise to BS'_1. At C, the budget is again balanced.

In figure 6.9 the arrowed line ABC illustrates a possible adjustment path from one long-run equilibrium to another. The adjustment path depends on the coefficient γ, which measures the speed of adjustment of inflationary expectations and the slope of the *SP* curve. The slower the speed of adjustment (i.e. the lower the γ), or the flatter the SP curve, the

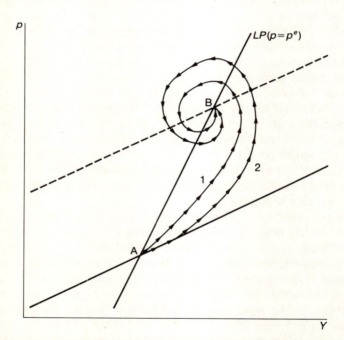

Figure 6.10   Possible dynamic paths under alternative hypotheses about the speed of adjustment of expectations, γ 1, fast adjustment ($\gamma = 1$); 2, slow adjustment ($\gamma = 0.5$)

longer it takes for the economy to reach its new long-run equilibrium (i.e. the longer the loop). During the adjustment of a longer loop, output and inflation initially rise together, but then inflation continues to rise whereas output falls. Figure 6.10 illustrates two alternative adjustment paths to long run equilibrium. Line 1 is drawn for $\gamma = 1$, and line 2 is drawn for $\gamma = 0.5$.

Supply Side Closed Economy

If the economy is supply side closed (i.e. $\beta = 1$), and therefore it does not depend on imported raw materials for the production of its output, then the effects of government expenditure under bond finance are given by:

$$\left.\frac{\partial Y}{\partial G}\right|_{dm=0} = 0 \tag{6.35a}$$

$$\left.\frac{\partial p}{\partial G}\right|_{dm=0} = \frac{1}{\det \mathbb{B}} \beta w_u u_y \Delta_{21}^4 > 0 \tag{6.35b}$$

$$\left.\frac{\partial r}{\partial G}\right|_{dm=0} < 0 \tag{6.35c}$$

$$\left.\frac{\partial b}{\partial G}\right|_{dm=0} < 0 \tag{6.35d}$$

$$C_v > \frac{I_r}{M_r} M_v - (1 - C_y)p \tag{6.35e}$$

An increase in government expenditure under bond finance raises inflation and lowers wealth and the interest rate, while it leaves output unchanged in the long run. For inflation to rise condition (6.35e) must be satisfied. All other results hold unambiguously. Condition (6.35e) differs from (4.24) by the last term on the right hand side. Since this term is negative, (6.35e) is more easily satisfied in an inflationary than in a non-inflationary economy.

Figure 6.11 highlights these results. In a supply side closed economy with absence of money illusion in the long run (i.e. $w_p = 1$) the *LP* curve is vertical, say at Y_0. Initial equilibrium is at A. The increase in government expenditure stimulates demand and output rises in the short run to Y_s, with higher inflation, p_s, and higher interest rate, r_s. The economy moves from A to B as the *IS* curve shifts to the right. At B the budget is in deficit.

Through time, however, expected inflation is catching up with the more quickly rising actual inflation. This gradually shifts the *SP* curve upwards. A vertical *LP* curve means that the inflationary consequences

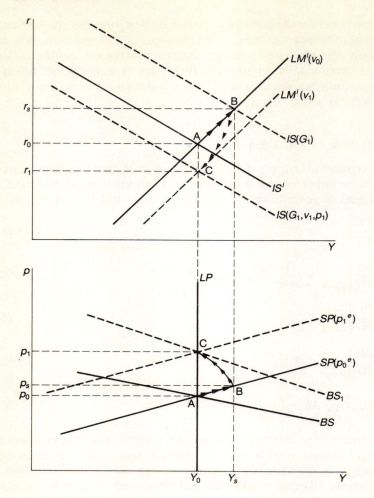

Figure 6.11   Long-run effects of a bond finance increase of government expenditure in a supply side closed economy

of the fiscal stimulus are greater than with an upward sloping *LP* curve. This makes the erosion of real wealth through higher prices an unambiguous result, while it is ambiguous in a supply side open economy. The fall in real wealth reverses the rightward shift of the *IS* curve, causing an output contraction, and also shifts the *LM* curve downwards. The interest rate falls as the demand for money is reduced, because of lower income and wealth. The economy moves through time from B to C. Output returns to its initial equilibrium, Y_0, the interest rate falls to r_1 and inflation rises to p_1. Therefore, following a fiscal stimulus in the form of an increase in government expenditure, output initially expands and then contracts. In the new long-run equilibrium output is unchanged. The interest rate rises in the first phase of the adjustment process and then falls. In the new long-run equilibrium it is lower than the initial steady state. Inflation rises in the long run more than in the short run.

6.8 Long-run Effects of Fiscal Policy under Money Finance

The long-run effects of a money-financed increase in government expenditure are obtained from (6.31) by letting only $dG \neq 0$ and setting all other differentials in $\mathbb{A}$ equal to zero:

$$\left.\frac{\partial Y}{\partial G}\right|_{db=0} = \frac{1}{\det \mathbb{B}} (1 - \beta)\Delta_{24}^1 > 0 \tag{6.36a}$$

$$\left.\frac{\partial p}{\partial G}\right|_{db=0} = \frac{1}{\det \mathbb{B}} \beta w_u u_y \Delta_{21}^4 > 0 \tag{6.36b}$$

or

$$\left.\frac{\partial p}{\partial G}\right|_{db=0} = \frac{\beta w_u u_y}{1 - \beta} \left.\frac{\partial Y}{\partial G}\right|_{db=0} > 0 \quad \text{since } \Delta_{24}^1 = \Delta_{21}^1 \tag{6.36b}$$

$$\left.\frac{\partial r}{\partial G}\right|_{db=0} = \frac{1}{\det \mathbb{B}} (\beta w_u u_y \Delta_{21}^2 + (1 - \beta)\Delta_{24}^2) \gtrless 0 \tag{6.36c}$$

$$\left.\frac{\partial b}{\partial G}\right|_{db=0} = \frac{1}{\det \mathbb{B}} (\beta w_u u_y \Delta_{21}^3 + (1 - \beta)\Delta_{24}^3) \gtrless 0 \tag{6.36d}$$

An increase in government expenditure financed through money raises output and inflation unambiguously, but it has an ambiguous effect on (real) wealth and the interest rate. The difference between bond and money finance is that in the former output and inflation rise provided (6.34e) holds, whereas in the latter this result is unambiguous.

These findings are discussed with the help of figure 6.12. Initial long-run equilibrium is at A, with income, interest rate, inflation and real money balances equal to Y_0, r_0, p_0 and m_0, respectively. This is a long-run equilibrium because expected inflation is equal to actual inflation and the budget is balanced. The increase in government expenditure from G_0 to G_1 shifts the *IS* curve, other things being equal, to $IS(G_1)$. The increased real money balances needed to finance the extra government spending move the *LM* to the right. In the short run (i.e. at the same level of expected inflation and real money balances), output and inflation increase to Y_s and p_s respectively and the interest rate falls to r_s. Short-run equilibrium is attained at B.

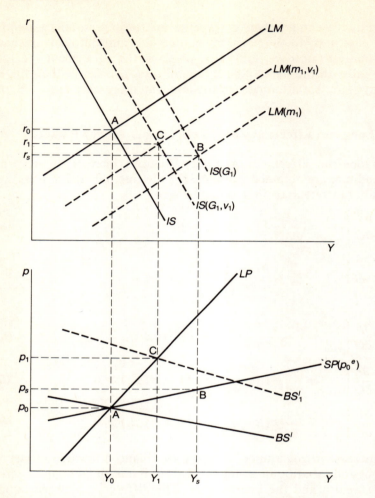

Figure 6.12   Long-run effects of a money finance increase in government expenditure

In the dynamic adjustment to the new steady state the increase in actual inflation raises expected inflation and this sets in motion the wage–price spiral, in exactly the same way as in bond finance. The rise in expected inflation shifts the *SP* curve up gradually and the economy adjusts from B to C.

Although according to our analysis the economy moves from A to B and then to C, this is a conceptual decomposition rather than a dynamic adjustment. The reason is that in the real world the move from A to B is not instantaneous. The most likely effect is that the interest rate initially falls as there is an excess supply of money, and then gradually rises as the demand for money is increased because of rising income. Furthermore, the initial interest rate decline is reversed because real money balances are reduced owing to higher prices and increased tax revenues. The last lowers the dependence of the deficit on printing money.

The gradual erosion of real money balances means that the LM curve shifts up and real wealth most likely falls. Long-run equilibrium is attained at C with higher income and inflation, Y_1 and p_1 respectively, and possibly a lower interest rate, r_1. In the short run output rises, but in the long run most of the initial stimulus is lost. Inflation rises in the long run more than in the short run. The interest rate initially falls and then rises. In the new steady state it may end up higher but most likely it will be lower relative to the initial steady state. The BS' curve shifts to the right as a result of the increase in government expenditure and rotates clockwise in response to reduced wealth. At C, the budget is again balanced.

Supply Side Closed Economy

If the economy is supply side closed (i.e. $\beta = 1$), and therefore does not depend on imported raw materials for the production of its output, then the effects of government expenditure under money finance are given by:

$$\frac{\partial Y}{\partial G}\bigg|_{db=0} = 0 \tag{6.37a}$$

$$\frac{\partial p}{\partial G}\bigg|_{db=0} = \frac{1}{\det\mathbb{B}} \mathbb{B} w_u u_y \Delta_{21}^4 > 0 \tag{6.37b}$$

$$\frac{\partial r}{\partial G}\bigg|_{db=0} > 0 \tag{6.37c}$$

$$\frac{\partial b}{\partial G}\bigg|_{db=0} < 0 \tag{6.37d}$$

An increase in government expenditure under money finance raises inflation and the interest rate, lowers real wealth and leaves output unchanged in the long run. The only difference between money and bond finance is that the interest rate rises in the former, while it falls in the latter.

These results are discussed in the context of figure 6.13. In a supply side closed economy (i.e. $\beta = 1$) with absence of money illusion in the long run (i.e. $w_p = 1$), the LP curve is vertical. Initial long-run equilibrium is at A. In the short run (i.e. with fixed expected inflation and real wealth), the increase in government expenditure raises output and inflation and lowers the interest rate. The economy moves from A to B

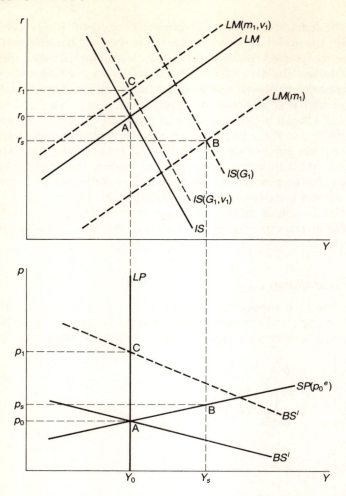

Figure 6.13 Long-run effects of a money finance increase in government expenditure in a supply side closed economy

as the *IS* and *LM* curves move to the right to $IS(G_1)$ and $LM(m_1)$, respectively.

Through time expected inflation adjusts to higher actual inflation and this sets in motion the wage–price spiral. The *SP* curve gradually shifts up. In parallel to the adjustment of expected inflation, real money balances (and hence wealth) also adjust to the budget deficit. At the beginning real money balances rise and then decline because the initial fiscal stimulus is translated into higher prices rather than higher output and this erodes the real value of money balances (and hence real wealth). The *LM* curve shifts up as real money balances are reduced to $LM(m_1, v_1)$ and the rightward shift of the *IS* curve is partially reversed. Long-run equilibrium is established at C, with an unchanged level of income and higher inflation, p_1. The interest rate rises to r_1. The budget is again balanced.

6.9 Long-run Effects of Monetary Policy

If the instrument of monetary policy is real money balances, the long-run effects of monetary policy are obtained from (6.28) by letting only $dm \neq 0$ and setting all other differentials in $\mathbb{A}$ equal to 0. If, on the other hand, the instrument of monetary policy is the real stock of bonds, the long-run effects of monetary policy are obtained from (6.31) by letting only $db \neq 0$ and setting all other differentials in $\mathbb{A}$ equal to zero. Assuming that monetary policy is conducted by changes in real money balances its long-run effects are:

$$\frac{\partial Y}{\partial m} = \frac{1}{\det \mathbb{B}} (1 - \beta) p\kappa (-I_r) > 0 \tag{6.38a}$$

$$\frac{\partial p}{\partial m} = \frac{1}{\det \mathbb{B}} \beta w_u u_y p\kappa (-I_r) > 0 \tag{6.38b}$$

or

$$\frac{\partial p}{\partial m} = \frac{\beta w_u u_y}{1 - \beta} \frac{\partial Y}{\partial m} > 0 \tag{6.38b}$$

$$\frac{\partial r}{\partial m} = \frac{1}{\det \mathbb{B}} (\beta w_u u_y (pD_p - vD_v) - (1 - \beta)(t_y D_v + p)) < 0 \tag{6.38c}$$

$$\frac{\partial b}{\partial m} = \frac{1}{\det \mathbb{B}} (\beta w_u u_y \Delta_{21}^3 + (1 - \beta)\Delta_{24}^3) \gtrless 0 \tag{6.38d}$$

$$C_v > -\frac{p}{v} I_r \tag{6.38e}$$

An increase in real money balances raises output and inflation, lowers the interest rate and has an ambiguous effect on real wealth in the long run. Expansionary monetary policy lowers the interest rate on the assumption that (6.38e) holds, a condition that is easily satisfied in the real world. In a non-inflationary economy (i.e. $p = 0$) this condition is always satisfied.

It makes no difference if the instrument of monetary policy is real money balances or the real stock of bonds because it can easily be verified that the effects on output, inflation and the interest rate are

$$\frac{\partial Y}{\partial m} = -\frac{\partial Y}{\partial b}, \quad \frac{\partial p}{\partial m} = -\frac{\partial p}{\partial b}, \quad \frac{\partial r}{\partial m} = -\frac{\partial r}{\partial b} \qquad (6.39)$$

These results are discussed with the help of figure 6.14. Initial long-run equilibrium is at A with the budget balanced and expected inflation equal to actual inflation. The increase in real money balances shifts the *LM* curve to $LM(m_1)$. The economy moves in the short run from A to B

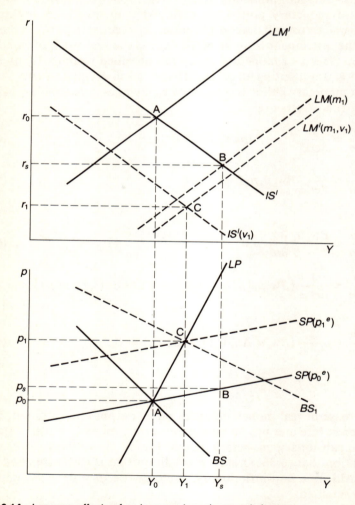

Figure 6.14   Long-run effects of an increase in real money balances

with higher output and inflation, Y_s and p_s respectively, and lower interest rate, r_s.

As expected inflation adjusts to higher actual inflation the *SP* curve moves up because the wage–price spiral is set in motion: higher expected inflation raises wage inflation. This raises actual inflation, which in turn raises expected inflation. This cycle is repeated until expected inflation catches up with actual inflation.

Although the long-run effect of monetary expansion on wealth is ambiguous the most likely effect is a drop in (real) wealth owing to higher prices. This will shift the *LM* curve to the right as the demand for money is reduced. Other things being equal, the interest rate will fall further. However, the decline in the value of wealth will shift the *IS* curve to the left to $IS(v_1)$. The new long-run equilibrium is attained at C with output Y_1, interest rate r_1 and inflation p_1. In the new steady state output falls relative to the short-run equilibrium, B, but rises relative to the initial steady state. Inflation rises in the new long-run equilibrium more than in the short-run. However, the interest rate may be higher or lower relative to the short-run equilibrium, but is lower relative to the initial steady state.

Supply Side Closed Economy

If the economy is self-sufficient in raw materials for the production of its output (i.e. $\beta = 1$) and there is no money illusion in the long run, the effects of monetary policy are given by:

$$\frac{\partial Y}{\partial m} = 0 \tag{6.40}$$

$$\frac{\partial p}{\partial m} = \frac{1}{\det \mathbb{B}} \, w_u u_y p\kappa(-I_r) > 0 \tag{6.40b}$$

$$\frac{\partial r}{\partial m} = \frac{1}{\det \mathbb{B}} \, w_u u_y (pD_p - vD_v) < 0 \tag{6.40c}$$

$$\frac{\partial b}{\partial m} = \frac{1}{\det \mathbb{B}} \, w_u u_y \Delta_{21}^3 \gtrless 0 \tag{6.40d}$$

$$C_v > -\frac{p}{v} I_r \tag{6.40e}$$

An increase in real money balances leaves output unchanged, raises inflation, lowers the interest rate and has an ambiguous effect on wealth. For the interest rate to fall condition (6.40e) must hold. Thus, the same condition applies for both an open and a closed economy. The only qualitative difference between a supply side open and closed economy is that in the former output expands, while in the latter it remains unchanged.

Figure 6.15 illustrates this point. Initial equilibrium is at **A**. The increase in real money balances shifts the *LM* curve to the right to *LM*(m_1). The economy moves in the short run from A to B. Output expands in the short run to Y_s, the interest rate falls to r_s and inflation rises to p_s. Although the long-run effect on wealth is ambiguous the most likely outcome is a fall in real wealth. This possibility is stronger in the case of a closed rather than an open economy because prices rise

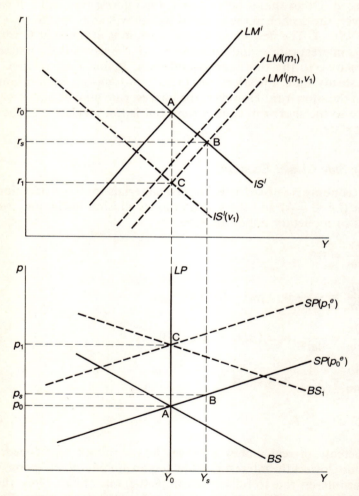

Figure 6.15 Long-run effects of an increase in real money balances in a supply side closed economy

more in the latter. As a result of the decline in real wealth the *IS* curve shifts to the left to $IS(v_1)$ and the *LM* curve to the right. Long-run equilibrium is established at C.

6.10 Long-run Effects of Imported Inflation through Raw Materials

The long-run effects of a change in the rate of inflation of imported raw materials under a neutral monetary policy are obtained from (6.28) by letting only d*pm* ≠ 0 and setting all other differentials in $\mathbb{A}$ equal to zero:

$$\frac{\partial Y}{\partial pm} = \frac{1}{\det\mathbb{B}} (1 - \beta)(\kappa v I_r M_v + p M_r D_p - v M_r D_v) < 0 \qquad (6.41a)$$

$$\frac{\partial p}{\partial pm} = \frac{1}{\det\mathbb{B}} (1 - \beta)\Delta_{24}^4 > 0 \qquad (6.41b)$$

$$\frac{\partial r}{\partial pm} = \frac{1}{\det\mathbb{B}} (1 - \beta)(p M_y D_p - t_y M_v D_p - v M_y D_v - v M_v) < 0 \qquad (6.41c)$$

$$\frac{\partial b}{\partial pm} = \frac{-1}{\det\mathbb{B}} (1 - \beta)(t_y M_r D_p + \kappa v M_y I_r + v M_r) < 0 \qquad (6.41d)$$

$$C_v > \frac{I_r}{M_r} M_v - \frac{p}{v} I_r \qquad (6.41e)$$

An increase in the rate of inflation of imported raw materials raises domestic inflation and lowers real wealth unambiguously. Assuming that (6.41e) holds, output falls, thus leading to stagflation. On the further assumption that the last term in parentheses in (6.41c) is negative, the interest rate declines.

These results are discussed with the help of figure 6.16. Initial equilibrium is at A. The increase in the price of imported raw materials shifts the *SP* and *LP* curves upwards and to the left to $SP(pm_1)$ and $LP(pm_1)$ respectively. In the short run (with expected inflation and real wealth fixed) the economy moves from A to B in figure 6.16b, but remains at A in figure 6.16a. This, as we have seen in the short-run analysis, is a consequence of the neutral monetary policy pursued by the central bank. Thus, in the short run output and the interest rate remain unchanged, but inflation rises to p_s.

In the transition to the new steady state, expected inflation adjusts to the rising actual inflation and the *SP* curve moves upwards. In the new long-run equilibrium expected inflation is equal to actual inflation and the economy converges to C with an even higher inflation than in the short run, p_1.

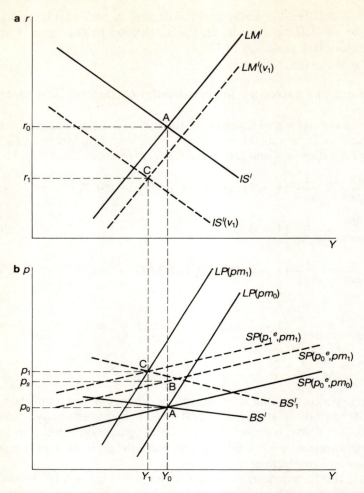

Figure 6.16 Long-run effects of an increase in the price of imported raw materials under neutral monetary policy

Although the government increases the nominal supply of money to maintain intact the value of real money balances, real wealth falls because higher prices erode the value of government bonds. The decline in real wealth shifts the *LM* curve to the right, as the demand for money is reduced, and the *IS* curve to the left. The last term in parentheses in (6.41c) ensures that the *IS* curve shifts to the left, resulting in a fall in the interest rate.

The leftward shift of the *IS* curve and the rightward shift of the *LM* curve are not sufficient to produce a decline in output. The contractionary effect resulting from the leftward shift of the *IS* curve may be offset by the expansionary effect of lower interest rates. Condition (6.41e) ensures that the shift in the *IS* curve is larger than the shift in the *LM* curve and therefore income declines. The *BS'* curve rotates clockwise in response to the assumed decline in real wealth. At C, the budget is again balanced because of higher inflation, despite lower income.

If the central bank is following a tight rather than a neutral monetary

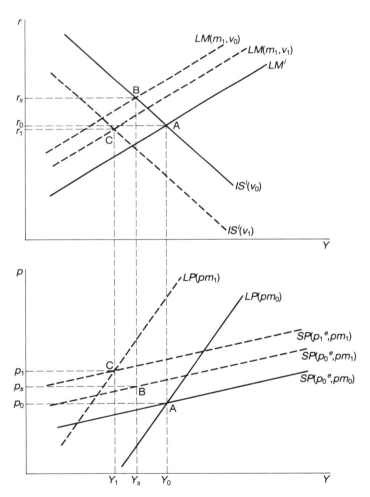

Figure 6.17 Long-run effects of an increase in the (rate of change of the) price of imported raw materials under tight monetary policy

policy (i.e. keeping nominal rather than real money balances fixed), then an increase in the price of imported raw materials raises inflation, lowers output (stagflation), lowers real wealth and has an ambiguous effect on the interest rate.

These results are highlighted in figure 6.17. The increase in the price of imported raw materials shifts the *SP* and *LP* curve to the left and inflation rises in the short run to p_s as the cost of production is increased. A tight monetary policy means that real money balances are eroded even in the short run. Accordingly, the *LM* curve shifts to the left to $LM(m_1, v_0)$ and the economy moves from A to B. The interest rate rises to r_s and therefore output is diminished to Y_s.

In the transition to the new steady state, expected inflation adjusts to higher actual inflation and the *SP* curve shifts to the left. Therefore inflation continues to rise. In the new long-run equilibrium the economy converges to C, where expected and actual inflation are equal to each other. Real wealth falls in the long run and this shifts the *LM* curve to the right to $LM(m_1, v_1)$. Under the same assumptions as with neutral monetary policy the *IS* curve will shift to the left. The effect on the interest rate is ambiguous, while output falls further in the long run on the assumption that (6.41e) holds. There is no doubt that the interest rate falls in the long run compared with the short run.

6.11 Stability Analysis

The stability of the system when the central bank operates a neutral monetary policy is examined through (6.2) by making b the endogenous variable and setting $\dot{m} = 0$

$$\dot{b} = G - t_y Y - pv \tag{6.42a}$$

$$\dot{p}^e = \gamma(p - p^e) \tag{6.42b}$$

With this type of monetary policy we also investigate fiscal policy under bond finance. The short-run equilibrium values for income and inflation, given by (6.11), become (ignoring all other policy instruments and exogenous variables):

$$Y = Y(b, p^e) \tag{6.43a}$$

$$p = p(b, p^e) \tag{6.43b}$$

Linearizing (6.43) around the long-run equilibrium values of income, $\bar{Y}$, and real stock of bonds, $\bar{b}$, using a Taylor series expansion and ignoring all terms higher than first-order, we get

$$Y(b, p^e) = Y(\bar{b}, \bar{p}^e) + Y_b(b - \bar{b}) + Y_p(p^e - \bar{p}^e) \tag{6.44a}$$

$$p(b, p^e) = p(\bar{b}, \bar{p}^e) + p_b(b - \bar{b}) + p_p(p^e - \bar{p}^e) \tag{6.44b}$$

Substituting (6.44) into (6.42) and remembering that in steady state

$$\bar{p} = p(\bar{b}, \bar{p}^e), \quad \bar{p}^e = \bar{p}, \quad \bar{Y} = Y(\bar{b}, \bar{p}^e), \quad G = t_y \bar{Y} + pv$$

the system can be written as follows

$$\begin{bmatrix} \dot{p}^e \\ \dot{b} \end{bmatrix} = \begin{bmatrix} \gamma(p_p - 1) & \gamma p_b \\ -(t_y Y_p + p_p v) & -(t_y Y_b + p_b v) \end{bmatrix} \begin{bmatrix} p^e - \bar{p} \\ b - \bar{b} \end{bmatrix} \tag{6.45a}$$

or in matrix notation

$$\dot{\mathbb{X}} = \mathbb{A} \mathbb{X}^e \tag{6.45b}$$

For the stability of the system we require that the trace of $\mathbb{A}$, denoted by $\text{tr}\mathbb{A}$, must be negative and the determinant of $\mathbb{A}$, denoted by $\det\mathbb{A}$, must be positive:

$$\text{tr}\mathbb{A} = \gamma(p_p - 1) - t_y Y_b - p_b v < 0 \tag{6.46a}$$

$$\det\mathbb{A} = p_b(t_y Y_p + p_p v) - (p_p - 1)(t_y Y_b + p_b v) > 0 \tag{6.46b}$$

A sufficient condition for the trace to be negative is that

$$0 < p_p < 1, \quad Y_b > 0 \quad \text{and} \quad p_b > 0 \tag{6.47a}$$

From our short-run comparative statics, relationships (6.19) and (6.20), we know that p_p is unambiguously positive and $Y_b > 0$, $p_b > 0$, if (6.14a) and (6.19b) hold true.

A sufficient condition for $\det\mathbb{A} > 0$ is that

$$Y_p > 0, \quad p_b > 0, \quad Y_b > 0 \quad \text{and} \quad 0 < p_p < 1 \tag{6.47b}$$

From our short-run comparative statics, relationships (6.20) and (6.19), we know that (6.47b) is satisfied if (6.19b) and (6.14b) hold true. Combining all sufficient conditions together we see that the system is stable under bond finance and, in general, when m is the instrument of monetary policy, if

$$0 < p_p < 1, \quad D_v > 0, \quad C_v - C_y p^e > M_v \frac{I_r}{M_r}, \quad D_p > 0 \tag{6.48}$$

i.e. if the effect of expected inflation on actual inflation is positive and less than unity; the wealth effect on consumption, adjusted for the effect of inflation tax, is positive and stronger than the wealth effect in the demand for money by a factor that measures the effectiveness of fiscal policy relative to monetary policy; and the effect of expected inflation on demand is positive.

It is easy to understand why the system is unstable if $p_p > 1$. In this case actual inflation rises by more than expected inflation. Thus, a given increase in expected inflation, say by 5 per cent, causes actual inflation to increase by more than 5 per cent. This will lead to a further increase in expected inflation, which will then feedback through the wage–price spiral to even higher actual inflation, thus ultimately causing hyperinflation. This is clearly an unstable situation.

The reason why a strong wealth effect on the demand for money will also lead to instability under bond finance is also easy to understand. Suppose that the effect of excess demand on prices is small. Then the increase in real wealth, associated with the finance of the budget deficit, shifts the *LM* curve to the left more than it shifts the *IS* curve to the right, resulting in a large increase in the interest rate, which causes substantial crowding out. Income declines because the reduction in demand owing to the higher interest rate outweighs the stimulus to demand because of increased wealth. The income decline leads to an enlarged budget deficit, which forces the government to issue even more bonds, thus further increasing wealth. This exacerbates the crowding out and income continues to fall. This is clearly an unstable situation because income cannot rise to the level that is sufficient to balance the budget.

The stability of the system under money finance is examined through (6.22) by making dm an endogenous variable and setting $db = 0$. Following a similar procedure to that under bond finance we arrive at

$$\begin{bmatrix} \dot{p}^e \\ \dot{m} \end{bmatrix} = \begin{bmatrix} \gamma(p_p - 1) & \gamma p_m \\ -(t_y Y_p + p_p v) & -(t_y Y_m + p_m v) \end{bmatrix} \begin{bmatrix} p^e - \bar{p} \\ m - \bar{m} \end{bmatrix} \tag{6.49}$$

Since Y_m and p_m are unambiguously positive (see relationship 6.17), a sufficient condition for tr$\mathbb{A} < 0$ is that $p_p < 1$. Since p_m and Y_m are unambiguously positive a sufficient condition for det$\mathbb{A} > 0$ is that $p_p < 1$ and $D_p > 0$. Thus, the system is stable under money finance if

$$0 < p_p < 1, \quad D_p > 0 \tag{6.50}$$

i.e. if the effect of expected inflation on actual inflation is positive and less than unity; and the effect of expected inflation on demand is positive.

A comparison of the stability conditions under bond and money finance reveals that the latter is always stable if the former is stable. Money finance requires only that $p_p < 1$ and $D_p > 0$, whereas bond finance requires in addition that the wealth effect on consumption dominates that on the demand for money.

The reason why money finance is more stable than bond finance is easy to understand if we assume that the wealth effect on consumption, but not on the demand for money, is zero. The increase in real money balances reduces the interest rate, thus stimulating demand, even though there is no stimulus from wealth. This ensures that income rises to balance the budget. Bond finance, on the other hand, results in lower income because the higher interest rate causes crowding out.

6.12 Conclusions and Limitations of Model 6

In model 6 a wage-price sector is integrated into the model developed so far. The dynamics of the system are described by the adjustment of expected to actual inflation and the wealth-accumulation process associated with balancing the budget through a first-order system of two differential equations. The dynamic process has been decomposed into two stages. In the first stage expected inflation and (real) wealth are treated as predetermined. For a given level of expected inflation and wealth, the *IS-LM* and *SP* curves determine, at each point in time, the short-run (momentary) equilibrium level of output, interest rate and inflation. In the second stage output, inflation and the interest rate determine, through the first-order differential equation system, the next level of expected inflation and wealth. To this new level of expected inflation and wealth there corresponds a new short-run equilibrium of output, interest rate and inflation, which in turn induces a new level of expected inflation and wealth, and so on. Assuming that the system is stable, it will converge to a steady state in which expected inflation is equal to actual inflation and the budget is balanced, including the inflation tax. The stability of the system depends on how movements in expected inflation and wealth affect the short-run equilibrium values of output, interest rate and actual inflation. We analyse this equation through short-run comparative statics.

In the short run, a fiscal or monetary expansion stimulates output, but at the cost of also increasing inflation. Easy fiscal policy leads to higher interest rates, thus inducing an expansion of the public sector at the expense of the private sector (crowding out). In contrast, easy monetary policy leads to lower interest rates and therefore to a contraction of the public sector share in GNP.

In the long run, most of the initial stimulus to output from either fiscal or monetary policy is lost. Output increases, but by less than in the short run, while inflation rises more. These results hold for a supply side open economy. In a supply side closed economy output returns to its original steady-state level and all initial stimulus is lost. Similarly, fiscal and/or monetary policy can be used to reduce inflation at the cost of an output loss. This loss is large for a supply side open economy, whereas it is only transient for a closed economy. The long-run effects of fiscal policy depend on the method of finance. Money finance is more stable than bond finance.

Although it is unrealistic to assume that the economy is supply side closed (i.e. $b = 1$), the analysis is relevant because it illustrates the case in which there is a feedback effect from the rest of the world that eliminates the exploitation of a long-run trade-off between output and inflation in the home economy.

The inflation cost of a given long-run output expansion depends on the type of monetary policy pursued in the adjustment towards a new steady state. A neutral monetary policy associated with either expansionary fiscal or monetary policy is more inflationary than a tight one.

An adverse supply shock (e.g. an increase in the price of imported raw materials) leads to stagflation.

The most serious limitation of this model is that although part of the analysis deals with a supply side open economy it is closed on the demand side. This creates an asymmetry. There is no trade with the rest of the world and therefore there is no adjustment through either the exchange rate or wealth if there is a balance of payments disequilibrium. This drawback is rectified in models 8 and 9.

Despite these limitations the model is useful in providing one possible explanation of price stickiness and in showing that shocks in demand can have persistent effects on output. Furthermore, the model analyses the interrelationship of the main macroeconomic variables in business cycles.

7

Model 7   A Simulation Model of Output and Inflation with Asset Accumulation

The analysis of model 6 has taken important steps forward in enhancing our understanding of the forces that determine output and inflation simultaneously. However, the approach we have used so far has a serious drawback. The short-run analysis – short-run comparative statics – covers too short a time for any practical purposes. The reason is that real wealth and expected inflation cannot remain fixed in an environment in which prices are changing. On the other hand, the long-run analysis – steady-state comparative statics – covers too long a time for practical considerations. Most econometric models show that seven to ten years is not an unreasonably long time for the system to converge to long-run equilibrium. Although ten years may not be an unduly long time for investment projects or programmes of structural change, it is certainly too long a time for stabilization purposes, given also that the term of office of a single government is, at most, five years. A government may be unwilling to embark on a stabilization programme whose effects will be felt far beyond its term of office. The economic cycle, induced by a stabilization policy, cannot be incompatible with the political cycle; otherwise there is a risk that the stabilization policy will not be adopted by the government.

For all practical purposes, then, our interest lies in the dynamic effects of a policy over a period of one to five years. Even if the system has not converged to steady state we want to know whether a large proportion of the total effect, say 70–80 per cent, of a given policy has worked itself out within such a time-scale. This type of analysis cannot be accomplished with analytical models like model 6. Simulation models, which are numerical replicas of the analytical models, provide perhaps the best vehicle for studying the dynamic response of the system to a policy change over a given time period, say five years. Furthermore, simulation models are uncompromising in that they do not sacrifice reality for the benefit of obtaining unambiguous results in comparative statics. In this respect non-linearities, such as those that emerge from interest payments on government debt, are important both in the dynamic adjustment path and in the new steady state. Most neutrality propositions in debates on economic policy rest on the assumption that the model is linear. However, the real world is non-linear!

In this model we concentrate on the dynamic and long-run effects of fiscal policy under alternative finance rules. We study the dynamic and long-run effects of open market operations and supply shocks. Finally, we consider the role of non-linearities in both the dynamic adjustment and the new steady state.

There are four sources of dynamics in this model. The first is wealth accumulation dynamics arising from the financing of the budget deficit. The second is dynamics arising from the adjustment of expected to actual inflation. These two sources of dynamics are the ones we considered in the context of model 6. However, in model 7 we also allow for dynamics arising from a differential speed of adjustment between the goods and assets markets. Furthermore, the model is structured to incorporate dynamics arising from a distributed lag effect of the explanatory variables on the system, although these are not used in the exercises reported here, for simplicity.

7.1 Assumptions

The assumption that there are no interest payments on government debt is relaxed. This brings us back to model 5 but with one important difference: namely that prices are not fixed. In all other respects we continue with the assumptions made in model 6. In particular, it is assumed that there are only two assets: money and government bonds. These are fixed-price–variable-coupon with one quarter to maturity. We assume that the goods market clears sluggishly, whereas the assets markets clear instantly. On the production side, we assume that there are three factors of production: labour, imported raw materials and capital. The last is assumed to be fixed. Potential output is fixed and labour productivity growth is zero.

We continue with the approach initiated in chapter 6 of considering aspects of the open economy, provided that these do not complicate the analysis. This is achieved by treating these variables, in the first instance, as exogenous to the system. This allows examination, to a first degree of approximation, of the effects on the economic system of a change in, say, the price of oil. An examination of the full implications of the openness of the economy (i.e. of endogenizing these variables) is undertaken in models 8 and 9. In the present model we draw a distinction between producer (output) prices measured at the factory gate and the consumer price index. The latter allows for the consumption of domestically produced output as well as imported goods, which are both final and intermediate, because certain raw materials, like oil, are used by consumers as well as by industry.

7.2 The Model

The model is assumed to be quarterly and consists of equations (7.1) to (7.18).

$$D = C + I + G \tag{7.1}$$

$$C = \mathfrak{U}(\delta_{CY})\left\{\alpha_{CY}YD + \alpha_{Copi}(1 - HRT)\left(\frac{OPI}{CPI}\right)\right\}$$
$$+ \alpha_{Cr}\mathfrak{U}(\delta_{Cr})(r - cpi^e) + \alpha_{Cv}\mathfrak{U}(\delta_{Cv})\frac{V_{-1}}{CPI} + \alpha_{CC}C_{-1} + \gamma_C \tag{7.2}$$

$$\alpha_{Cr} < 0, \quad 0 < \alpha_{CY}, \quad \alpha_{Copi}, \quad \alpha_{Cv}, \quad \alpha_{CC} < 1$$

$$I = \alpha_{IY}\mathfrak{U}(\delta_{IY})Y + \alpha_{Ir}\mathfrak{U}(\delta_{Ir})(r - p^e)$$
$$- \alpha_{IK}K_{-1} + \alpha_{II}I_{-1} + \gamma_I \tag{7.3}$$

$$\alpha_{IY} > 0, \quad \alpha_{Ir} > 0, \quad 0 < \alpha_{IK}, \quad \alpha_{II} < 1$$

$$Y = D \tag{7.4}$$

$$YD = (1 - SRT)P\frac{Y}{CPI} \tag{7.5}$$

$$OPI = ((1 + r_{-1})^{1/4} - 1)B_{-1} \tag{7.6}$$

$$\frac{M}{CPI} = \alpha_{MY}\mathfrak{U}(\delta_{MY})Y + \alpha_{Mv}\mathfrak{U}(\delta_{Mv})\frac{V_{-1}}{CPI} + \alpha_{Mr}\mathfrak{U}(\delta_{Mr})r + \gamma_M \tag{7.7}$$

$$\alpha_{MY} > 0, \quad \alpha_{Mr} < 0, \quad 0 < \alpha_{Mv} < 1$$

$$PSBR = PG + (1 - HRT)OPI - PT + \gamma_{PSBR} \tag{7.8}$$

$$T = SRT\,Y \tag{7.9}$$

$$M = M_{-1} + \alpha_{monfin}PSBR + \Delta MB \tag{7.10}$$

$$0 < \alpha_{monfin} < 1$$

$$B = B_{-1} + (1 - \alpha_{monfin})PSBR + \Delta OMO \tag{7.11}$$

$$V = M + B + PK \tag{7.12}$$

$$w = \alpha_{wy}\mathfrak{U}(\delta_{wy})(y - \bar{y}) + \alpha_{wY}\mathfrak{U}(\delta_{wY})(Y - \bar{Y})$$
$$+ \alpha_{wcpi^e}\mathfrak{U}(\delta_{wcpi^e})cpi^e + \gamma_w \tag{7.13}$$

$$\alpha_{wy} > 0, \quad 0 \le \alpha_{wcpi^e} \le 1$$

$$P = \alpha_{PW} W + (1 - \alpha_{PW})\frac{PIW}{e} + \alpha_{PY}(y - \bar{y}) + \gamma_P \qquad (7.14)$$

$$0 \le \alpha_{PW} \le 1, \quad \alpha_{PY} > 0$$

$$CPI = \alpha_{CPIP} P + (1 - \alpha_{CPIP})PM \qquad (7.15)$$

$$0 \le \alpha_{CPIP} \le 1$$

$$PM = (\alpha_{PMPW} PW + (1 - \alpha_{PMPW})PIW)/\mathfrak{U}(\delta_{PMe})e \qquad (7.16)$$

$$0 \le \alpha_{PMPW} \le 1$$

$$p^e = p^e_{-1} + \alpha_{p^e p}(p_{-1} - p^e_{-1}) \qquad (7.17)$$

$$cpi^e = cpi^e_{-1} + \alpha_{p^e p}(cpi_{-1} - cpi^e_{-1}) \qquad (7.18)$$

$$0 \le \alpha_{p^e p} \le 1$$

	Variable definition	Initial steady-state value
B	= (nominal) stock of government bonds, at current prices	50
C	= real consumer expenditure	65
CPI	= consumer price index	1
cpi	= actual inflation rate (as measured by the change in the consumer price index), i.e. $cpi = \dfrac{CPI - CPI_{-1}}{CPI_{-1}}$	0
cpi^e	= expected inflation rate in period t, as with information available at $t-1$	0
D	= aggregate demand	100
e	= exchange rate, foreign price of domestic currency, i.e. units of foreign currency per unit of domestic currency	1
G	= real government expenditure	25
HRT	= higher rate of income tax on other personal income	0.6
I	= real gross investment expenditure	10
K	= capital stock	200
M	= (nominal) money stock, currency in circulation (notes and coin)	10
MB	= autonomous monetary base, at current prices	0

OMO	= open market operations instrument	0
OPI	= other personal income (interest income), in nominal terms	2.0768
P	= producer price index	1
p	= actual inflation rate (as measured by the producer price index, i.e. $$p = \frac{P - P_{-1}}{P_{-1}}$$	0
p^e	= expected inflation in period t, with information in $t-1$	
PIW	= world price of imported raw materials, in foreign currency	1
PM	= price of imports, in domestic currency	1
$PSBR$	= public sector borrowing requirement, at current prices	0
PW	= price of imported final goods, in foreign currency	1
r	= interest rate (yield) on government bonds	0.1
SRT	= standard rate of income tax	0.25
T	= total tax revenues, in real terms	25
V	= stock of private sector wealth, at current prices	300
W	= nominal wage rate	1
w	= actual wage inflation, i.e. change in the nominal wage rate, $$w = \frac{W - W_{-1}}{W_{-1}}$$	0
Y	= domestic output, real income	100
y	= rate of growth of output (GDP), i.e. $y = \dfrac{Y - Y_{-1}}{Y_{-1}}$	0
$\bar{Y}$	= potential (or capacity) output	100
$\bar{y}$	= rate of growth of potential (or capacity) output, i.e. $\bar{y} = \dfrac{\bar{Y} - \bar{Y}_{-1}}{\bar{Y}_{-1}}$	0
YD	= real disposable income	75

$$u(\delta)X = \sum_{i=0}^{3} \delta_i X_{-i} / \sum_{i=0}^{3} \delta_i \text{ is a unitary moving}$$

average operator.

In the exercises reported below $\mathfrak{U}(\delta) = (1\,0\,0\,0)$, that is the total effect is distributed instantaneously.

Coefficient	Value
α_{CY}	0.35
α_{Copi}	0.5
α_{Cr}	-25
α_{Cv}	0.065
α_{CC}	0.5
γ_C	-10.75
α_{IY}	0.0775
α_{Ir}	-25
α_{IK}	0.05
α_{II}	0.0
γ_I	14.75
α_{MY}	0.075
α_{Mr}	-100
α_{Mv}	0.01
γ_M	9.5
γ_{PSBR}	0.04
α_{monfin}	1.0
α_{wy}	0.5
α_{wY}	0.0001
α_{wcpi^e}	1.0
γ_w	0.0
α_{PW}	0.85
α_{Py}	0.5
γ_P	0.0
α_{CPIP}	0.85
α_{PMPW}	0.7
$\alpha_{p^e p}$	0.5

The model is similar in many respects to model 5 and therefore the reader is referred to that model for detailed discussion of its specification. Here, only fundamental differences are stressed. The major difference between models 5 and 7 stems from the relaxation of the assumption that prices are fixed. Two price indices are considered: the producer (output) price index, *P*, and the consumer price index, *CPI*. The former measures prices at factory gates (i.e. before items such as VAT are added) and reflects cost considerations and profit margins, which in turn depend upon the pricing policy of the firms. The reason we prefer the producer price index rather than the conventional GDP-deflator is that the latter excludes imports and therefore ignores imported inflation, which is an important aspect of the inflationary process in an increasingly interdependent world. The consumer price index reflects the true cost to households because it recognizes that imports (both final and intermediate) enter the baskets of consumers along with domestically produced goods. *CPI* therefore includes domestic as well as imported inflation.

The implication of relaxing the assumption that prices are fixed is that all nominal variables have to be deflated by the appropriate price index. Thus, in the consumption function unearned income in the form of interest income, *OPI*, is deflated by the consumer price index to provide a measure of real purchasing power of other personal income, *OPI/CPI*. If other personal income doubles, but the consumer price index also doubles, consumers are not better off and accordingly their consumption expenditure remains unchanged. Private sector wealth is also deflated by the consumer price index. Nominal wealth enters the consumption function with a lag, reflecting the fact that consumer decisions are based on wealth at the beginning of the period, since consumers cannot spend wealth that has not yet been accumulated. Nominal wealth is deflated by the consumer price index of the current period, V_{-1}/CPI. The reason for this is that in deciding this period's consumption, households look at the real value of their wealth in the current period. Thus, if accumulated wealth at the beginning of the period stands at £300 billion, but prices rise by 2 per cent in the current quarter, consumers make decisions on how much to spend in the current quarter on the basis that their real wealth is worth only £294.1 billion.

In line with model 6, it is the real interest rate that determines the effect of the terms of credit on consumer expenditure, $r - cpi^e$. Thus, if the interest rate is raised by 1 per cent, but expected inflation also rises by 1 per cent, the real cost to consumers is the same and therefore consumption remains unchanged.

Investment expenditure (7.3) has the same specification as in model 5, the only difference being that it is the real rather than the nominal interest rate that matters.

A subtlety that arises from the distinction between the producer price index and the consumer price index, is the way real disposable income is calculated (7.5). If nominal factor incomes double, but the producer price index (or more appropriately the GDP-deflator) also doubles, one would have expected that real disposable income should have remained unchanged. However, this is not necessarily so. The real value of disposable income is calculated by the consumer price index, since this measures inflation in the goods that the consumer is buying. The consumer price index includes imported goods, final and intermediate, like oil. If domestic prices remain unchanged, but the price of imports doubles, then assuming that imports represent half of the basket of goods that comprise the consumer price index, the real value of disposable income is reduced by a third.

Other personal income *in nominal terms* (7.6) is the interest that accrues to bond holders times the stock of *nominal* government debt in existence.

The specification of the demand for money function (7.7a) is as in model 5, with the only difference being that with variable prices the stock of money is deflated by the consumer price index. If prices double, the demand for money also doubles. Instead of disaggregating the demand for money by households and firms and deflating each one separately, we deflate it, for simplicity, by the consumer price index. This assumption is justified on the grounds that the demand for money by households is much larger than that by firms. Private sector wealth, as in the case of consumption, is deflated by the consumer price index. In addition, nominal wealth enters the demand for money with a lag, since households cannot allocate wealth to money and bonds before it is accumulated. However, once wealth is accumulated, it is the proportions of the *real* value that are to be kept in competing assets that have to be decided upon.

In this model the *modus operandi* of monetary policy is through the money supply (the instrument of policy) while the interest rate is the endogenous variable. Since, at any given point in time, wealth is given, only the demand for one asset is independent, the other being determined by the wealth constraint. In this model, in line with model 5, the demand for bonds is obtained as a residual.

With variable prices, the government budget constraint is specified in nominal terms (7.8). For simplicity, the producer price index is used to transform real into nominal prices. Equation (7.9) gives taxes on factor incomes in *real terms*. The government finances its *nominal budget deficit* either through printing money or by issuing bonds (7.10 and 7.11). This is implemented by choosing the values of $\alpha_{monfin} = 1$ and $\alpha_{monfin} = 0$ respectively. The definition of private sector wealth *in nominal terms* is given in equation (7.12).

The wage–price sector is described by equations (7.13) to (7.17). This is where model 7 breaks away from model 5. The specification of the wage–price sector is along the lines of model 6. Thus, equation (7.13) is an expectations augmented Phillips curve, in which unemployment has been eliminated through Okun's law. In model 7 we measure excess demand as the difference between the rate of growth and the level of actual over potential output, $y - \bar{y}$ and $Y - \bar{Y}$, respectively. The latter measures the degree of *hysteresis*. If the level effect is absent, the economy is characterized by hysteresis, meaning that any level of output, no matter how low, is consistent with steady inflation. With hysteresis an economy can experience an acceleration of inflation even in the middle of a depression.

The producer price index, P (7.14), is determined through a variable mark-up on unit variable cost. Since there are only two variable factors of production, labour and imported raw materials, the producer price index is an average of the wage rate and the domestic price of imported raw materials. The foreign price of imported raw materials is converted into domestic currency through the exchange rate, e. Hence, imported inflation is introduced into the economy through one of the following routes or any particular combination of them. An increase in the *foreign* price of imported raw materials, or a depreciation of the exchange rate, raises the price of raw materials in *domestic currency* and therefore increases the cost of domestically produced goods. The coefficient $1 - \alpha_{PW}$ measures the extent to which a country depends on imported raw materials and is a measure of the *degree of supply side openness* of the economy. The mark-up varies with demand conditions in the goods market. Firms adjust their profit margins upwards where there is excess demand for their product, and vice versa. This is measured by the coefficient α_{PY}.

The consumer price index is defined in equation (7.15) as an arithmetic average of the producer price index, P, and imported final and intermediate goods expressed in domestic currency, PM. The reason we include intermediate goods in CPI is that certain raw materials, like oil, are used directly by consumers too. This opens another avenue through which imported inflation affects the economy. If the price of imported final goods is increased, this raises the consumer price index and reduces real disposable income, the real value of other personal income, real money balances and the real value of private sector wealth, even when the price of domestic output remains unchanged. The increase in CPI raises expected inflation and induces domestic inflation through higher wages. The coefficient α_{CPIP} measures the proportion of domestic output in the basket of goods that comprise the consumer price index. The coefficient $1 - \alpha_{CPIP}$ measures the proportion of foreign goods in CPI and is a measure of *the degree of demand side openness* of the economy.

Equation (7.16) defines the price of imported goods in domestic currency, PM, as an arithmetic average of final goods, PW, and intermediate goods, PIW, in proportion $\alpha_{PMPW}/(1 - \alpha_{PMPW})$. The price of imported goods is given in foreign currency and is converted to domestic currency through the exchange rate. The effect of the foreign price of imported goods or the exchange rate on the domestic price of imports is distributed through time. This reflects a policy of foreign companies to absorb temporarily through reduced profit margins some of the effect of higher prices or any appreciation of the exchange rate in pricing their products for exports. Such a pricing policy may be dictated by oligopolistic behaviour in export markets, in which firms try to keep their share of the market. The sum of coefficients δ_{PMe} is equal to unity, reflecting the fact that foreign companies can only temporarily absorb such price effects and that in the long run prices are fully adjusted.

Finally, equations (7.17) and (7.18) specify an adaptive expectations scheme for expected inflation in the producer and consumer price index, in which the speed of adjustment is measured by the coefficient $\alpha_{p^e p}$. In the basic set of parameter values this coefficient assumes the value 0.5.

7.3 Monetary Policy

We now consider the impact, dynamic and steady-state effects of a straight increase in the nominal supply of money and an open market purchase. The impact effect of a monetary action is to change income and consequently the budget is no longer balanced. The subsequent effects of monetary policy depend on the method of budget finance. We consider a policy of monetary targets and debt targets.

A straight increase in the nominal supply of money is unrealistic because it is equivalent to a helicopter drop. In the real world an increase in the nominal supply of money is implemented either through an open market purchase or to finance increased subsidies. The latter means that disposable income rises to the same extent as the money supply. Although this can easily be implemented in the context of model 7, we do not consider such an exercise because we want to retain compatibility with the multiplier analysis of the analytical models and because a straight increase in the supply of money is easier to understand. On the other hand, as a realistic exercise of easy monetary policy we consider an open market purchase. The two exercises have the same qualitative results.

Increase in the Nominal Money Supply

Box 7.1 provides a schematic view of the main channels through which an increase in the *nominal* supply of money affects the economy. We assume that the central bank, which operates a policy of monetary targets, allows the nominal money supply to increase by, say, £1 billion, and then re-imposes monetary targets at this higher level. This implies that any changes in *PSBR*, caused by the increase in the money supply, will induce further changes in the stock of government bonds.

In box 7.1, routes (a) to (c) are the same as in model 5, with the only difference being that other personal income and wealth are deflated by the consumer price index. The increase in the nominal money supply creates, at the initial level of income, interest rate, prices and wealth, an excess supply of money. Since we assume that the assets markets clear instantly whereas the goods market clears sluggishly, the *nominal* interest rate falls to equilibrate the asset market. This reduces the real interest rate, since prices and hence expected inflation are initially unchanged, which in turn stimulates investment and hence income – channel (a).

Box 7.1 The transmission of monetary policy (increase in money supply)

$$(r - p^e)\downarrow \Rightarrow I\uparrow \Rightarrow D\uparrow \Rightarrow Y\uparrow \tag{a}$$

$$M\uparrow \Rightarrow \begin{cases} r\downarrow \Rightarrow \begin{cases} \dfrac{OPI}{CPI}\downarrow \Rightarrow C\downarrow \Rightarrow D\downarrow \Rightarrow Y\downarrow & \text{(b)} \\[2ex] \dfrac{V}{CPI}\uparrow < \dfrac{V}{CPI}\downarrow \Rightarrow C\downarrow \Rightarrow D\downarrow \Rightarrow Y\downarrow & \text{(c)} \end{cases} \end{cases}$$

$$(a) > ((b) + (c)) \Big\} u\downarrow \Rightarrow w\uparrow \Rightarrow p\uparrow \Rightarrow \begin{cases} \dfrac{OPI}{CPI}\downarrow \Rightarrow C\downarrow \Rightarrow Y\downarrow \\[2ex] \dfrac{V}{CPI}\downarrow \Rightarrow C\downarrow \Rightarrow Y\downarrow \\[2ex] \dfrac{M}{CPI}\downarrow \Rightarrow r\uparrow \Rightarrow I\downarrow \Rightarrow Y\downarrow \end{cases}$$

The fall in the nominal interest rate reduces, at the initial level of government bonds, real other personal income, which forces households to cut consumption and cause income contraction - channel (b). The decline in the interest rate reduces interest payments on government debt and *PSBR* falls. Under a policy of monetary targets, the government retires debt from the market and this diminishes private sector real wealth, which in turn depresses consumption and income – channel (c).

Thus, there is one expansionary force, channel (a), and two contractionary forces, channels (b) and (c). However, at the initial phase of the adjustment process, channel (a) dominates channels (b) and (c) and therefore income rises. This reduces unemployment, as firms hire more labour to increase production, and pushes wages up, as labour shortages increase. Firms pass on to prices the increased cost of production and this increases actual and expected inflation. Higher prices reduce real other personal income and real wealth and therefore reinforce the contractionary effects of channels (b) and (c). At the same time, higher prices reduce real money balances and this reverses the interest rate adjustment process. The combined effect of all these forces is a fall in income.

An illustration of the transmission of monetary policy is provided by simulating model 7 numerically under monetary targets (i.e. keeping the nominal money supply fixed after the shock) and debt targets (i.e. keeping the nominal stock of government bonds fixed). The increase in the money supply is implemented via £1 billion increase in autonomous monetary base, *MB*, in the first period only. Under a policy of monetary targets this has the effect of increasing the nominal money supply, *M*, by £1 billion permanently. The effects of this policy action on *PSBR* are felt through changes in the nominal stock of government bonds. Under debt targets the money supply, *M*, does not increase permanently by £1 billion because the finance of the budget induces further changes in the money supply. To simulate a policy of monetary and debt targets we set $\alpha_{monfin} = 0$ and $\alpha_{monfin} = 1$, respectively.

Figures 7.1 to 7.4 present the effects on output/income, interest rate, real wealth and prices (consumer price index) of simulating model 7 under monetary targets and debt targets. For comparisons the initial steady state is also included. Under monetary targets, income rises for the first four quarters and then declines continuously (figure 7.1). In the new steady state income is lower than the original long run equilibrium. Under debt targets, income also rises initially. The initial rise in income is due in both cases to the immediate fall in the interest rate, which stimulates consumption and investment. The upswing of the cycle lasts for only two quarters under debt targets, compared with four quarters under monetary targets. Furthermore, at its peak, income under monetary

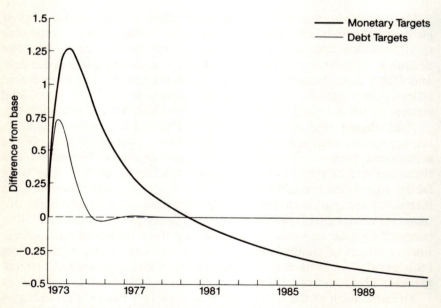

Figure 7.1   Output response to a step increase in the money supply

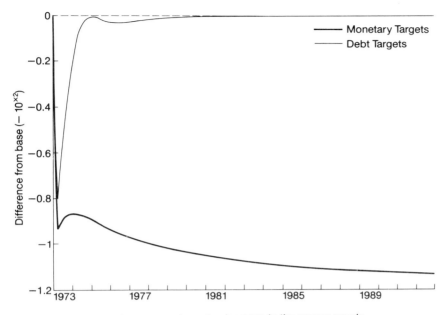

Figure 7.2   Interest rate response to a step increase in the money supply

targets is almost twice as high as under debt targets (£1.3 and £0.75 billion respectively). This is because of a larger fall in the interest rate under monetary targets than under debt targets. Finally, income returns to its original long-run equilibrium under debt targets, whereas it falls by £0.4 billion under monetary targets. This is caused by the different behaviour of real wealth, which returns to its original long-run equilibrium under debt targets, but falls under monetary targets. The system converges to its long-run equilibrium within three years under debt targets, whereas it takes 19 years to converge under monetary targets.

Figure 7.2 depicts the dynamic adjustment of the interest rate to the money supply shock. The impact effect is a fall in the interest rate from 10 per cent to 9 per cent under monetary targets and to 9.2 per cent under debt targets. This is caused by the initial excess supply of money in the assets markets and the assumption that these markets clear instantly whereas the goods market clears sluggishly. Under debt targets, the interest rate quickly returns to its original level. This is because of the government cutting the money supply in response to the initial fall in *PSBR*, which in turn is caused by the smaller interest payments on government debt.

Under monetary targets, the interest rate after its initial fall recovers for the next three quarters. This is because of the rise in income, which

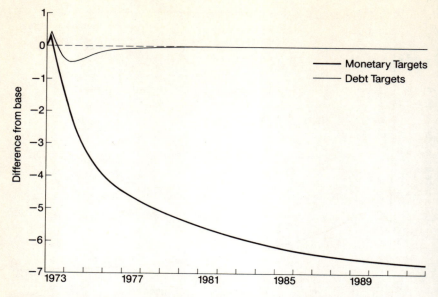

Figure 7.3   Real wealth response to a step increase in the money supply

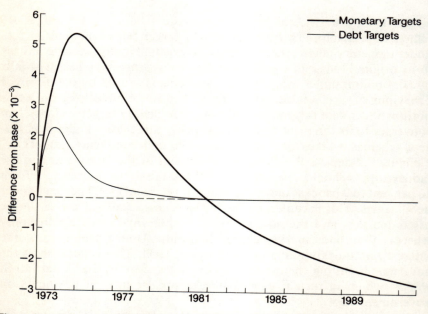

Figure 7.4   Response of consumer prices to a step increase in the money supply

increases the demand for money. However, after the lapse of five quarters the interest rate declines, until it converges to 8.9 per cent in its new long-run equilibrium after 14 years. This is because of lower income and real wealth in the new steady state, which implies smaller demand for money.

Figure 7.3 illustrates the dynamic adjustment of real wealth to the money supply shock. The impact effect is a small rise in real wealth under both rules. However, under debt targets real wealth converges to its original long-run equilibrium, owing to the cut in the money supply, which exactly offsets the initial increase. Under monetary targets real wealth falls continuously, until in the new long-run equilibrium it is £6.7 billion lower than the original steady state. This is because of the government retiring debt from the market as interest payments on existing debt are reduced in response to falling *PSBR*.

The dynamic adjustment of prices is illustrated in figure 7.4. The consumer price index rises initially for seven quarters under monetary targets, but then continuously declines and in the new steady state is lower than in the original. Under debt targets, the consumer price index rises for the first year and then declines until it returns to its original steady state.

Open Market Purchase

Box 7.2 provides a schematic view of the transmission mechanism of an open market purchase under monetary and debt targets. An open market purchase implies that the central bank buys government bonds. This increases the supply of money and reduces the stock of bonds by the same amount (£1 billion) in the first period. Under monetary targets the open market purchase results in a permanent increase in the money supply by £1 billion. The finance of the budget means that the nominal stock of government bonds is reduced by more than £1 billion after the initial shock. Under debt targets, on the other hand, the stock of bonds is permanently reduced by £1 billion, whereas the money supply is increased by less than £1 billion after the initial shock.

The transmission of an open market purchase is the same under monetary and debt targets, with one exception. The initial fall in the interest rate causes a reduction in *PSBR*, as interest payments on existing government debt are lower. With monetary targets the government retires debt from the market and this diminishes the real value of wealth, which depresses consumption and therefore income – channel (c1). With debt targets the government reduces the supply of money and this raises the interest rate. This, in turn, depresses aggregate demand (consumption and investment) and lowers income – channel (c2).

Box 7.2 The transmission of monetary policy (open market purchase) under monetary and debt targets

$$(r - p^e)\downarrow \Rightarrow I\uparrow \Rightarrow D\uparrow \Rightarrow Y\uparrow \qquad \text{(a)}$$

$$\Delta M\uparrow = -\Delta B\downarrow \Rightarrow r\downarrow \Rightarrow \left\{ \frac{OPI}{CPI}\downarrow \Rightarrow C\downarrow \Rightarrow D\downarrow \Rightarrow Y\downarrow \qquad \text{(b)} \right.$$

$$\frac{PSBR}{P}\downarrow \Rightarrow \left\{ \begin{array}{l} \dfrac{B}{P}\downarrow \Rightarrow \dfrac{V}{CPI}\downarrow \Rightarrow C\downarrow \Rightarrow Y\downarrow \quad \text{(c1)} \\[2ex] \dfrac{M}{P}\downarrow \Rightarrow r\uparrow \Rightarrow D\downarrow \Rightarrow Y\downarrow \qquad \text{(c2)} \end{array} \right.$$

$$(a) > ((b) + (c)) \left. \right\} u\downarrow \Rightarrow w\uparrow \Rightarrow p\uparrow \Rightarrow \left\{ \begin{array}{l} \dfrac{OPI}{CPI}\downarrow \Rightarrow C\downarrow \Rightarrow Y\downarrow \\[2ex] \dfrac{V}{CPI}\downarrow \Rightarrow C\downarrow \Rightarrow Y\downarrow \\[2ex] \dfrac{M}{CPI}\downarrow \Rightarrow r\uparrow \Rightarrow I\downarrow \Rightarrow Y\downarrow \end{array} \right.$$

Figures 7.5 to 7.8 show the dynamic response of income/output, the interest rate, real wealth and prices to an open market purchase of £1 billion under monetary targets and debt targets. The open market purchase is implemented by simulating the model with an increase of £1 billion in *MB* and a decrease of £1 billion in *OMO* for the first period only. This produces a permanent increase in the nominal money supply by £1 billion under monetary targets. With debt targets, on the other hand, the nominal stock of government bonds is reduced permanently by £1 billion, whereas the supply of money is increased only on impact by £1 billion.

The dynamic response of income, interest rate, real wealth and prices to an open market purchase is pretty much the same as a straight increase in the money supply. The only difference is the behaviour of real wealth. With a straight increase in the money supply there is an initial rise in real wealth. With the open market purchase, on the other hand, there is an immediate fall in real wealth. This slightly moderates the rise in income during the upswing of the business cycle, leaving the rest of the adjustment pretty much the same as with the straight increase in the money supply. With debt targets a straight increase in the money supply results in an unchanged trajectory for the stock of government bonds, whereas an open market purchase results in a permanent decrease in bonds by £1

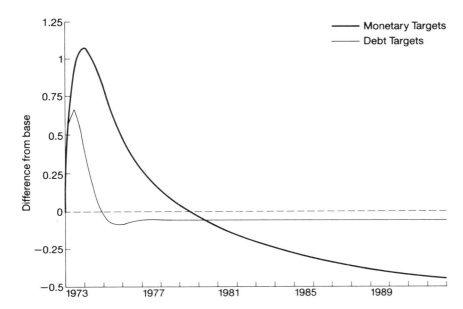

Figure 7.5   Output response to an open market purchase

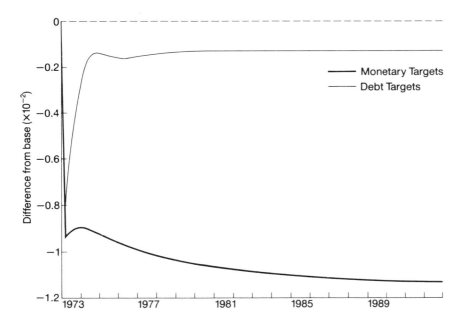

Figure 7.6   Interest rate response to an open market purchase

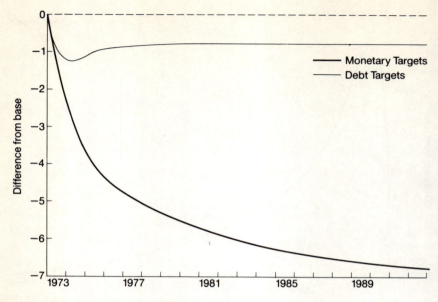

Figure 7.7 Real wealth response to an open market purchase

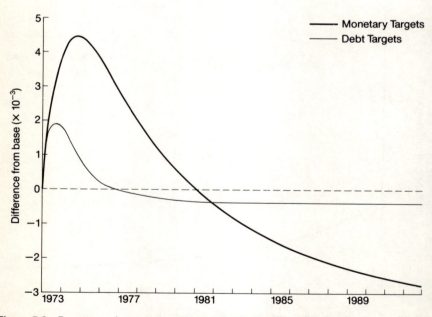

Figure 7.8 Response of consumer prices to an open market purchase

billion. This produces a small reduction in real wealth in the new steady state under an open market purchase (figure 7.7). This, in turn, decreases the demand for money and the interest rate remains lower in the new steady state; through depressed consumption it also lowers income.

7.4 Fiscal Policy under Bond and Money Finance

Box 7.3 provides a schematic view of the main channels through which an increase in government expenditure affects the economic system under bond finance. Channels (a) to (e) are the same as in model 5, with the only difference being that all nominal variables are deflated by the appropriate price index. The increase in government expenditure raises aggregate demand. At the initial level of income/output there is an excess demand in the goods market, to which firms respond by increasing output and consequently factor incomes. This has two effects. First, it raises real disposable income, which stimulates consumption and through another cycle leads to a further increase in income – channel (a). This is the traditional channel analysed in the context of model 2. It holds true even with variable prices. What is required for government expenditure to have a stimulative effect on the economy through this channel is that there still be some spare capacity in the economy. In other words, we are

---

Box 7.3 The transmission of fiscal policy (government expenditure) under bond finance

$$
G\uparrow \Rightarrow
\begin{cases}
D\uparrow \Rightarrow Y\uparrow \Rightarrow
\begin{cases}
YD\uparrow \Rightarrow C\uparrow \Rightarrow D\uparrow \Rightarrow Y\uparrow & \text{(a)} \\
I\downarrow \Rightarrow D\downarrow \Rightarrow Y\downarrow & \text{(b)}
\end{cases} \\
\dfrac{M^d}{CPI}\uparrow \Rightarrow r\uparrow \Rightarrow
\begin{cases}
OPI/CPI\uparrow \Rightarrow C\uparrow \Rightarrow Y\uparrow & \text{(c)}
\end{cases} \\
\dfrac{PSBR}{P}\uparrow \Rightarrow \dfrac{B}{P}\uparrow \Rightarrow \dfrac{V}{CPI}\uparrow \Rightarrow
\begin{cases}
\dfrac{V}{CPI}\uparrow \Rightarrow C\uparrow \Rightarrow Y\uparrow & \text{(d)} \\
C\uparrow \Rightarrow D\uparrow \Rightarrow Y\uparrow & \text{(e)}
\end{cases}
\end{cases}
$$

$$
\left. ((a)+(c)+(d)+(e)) > (b) \right\} u\downarrow \Rightarrow w\uparrow \Rightarrow p\uparrow \Rightarrow
\begin{cases}
\dfrac{OPI}{CPI}\downarrow \Rightarrow C\downarrow \Rightarrow Y\downarrow \\
\dfrac{V}{CPI}\downarrow \Rightarrow C\downarrow \Rightarrow Y\downarrow \\
\dfrac{M}{CPI}\downarrow \Rightarrow r\uparrow \Rightarrow I\downarrow Y\downarrow
\end{cases}
$$

on the horizontal or upward-sloping segment of the aggregate supply curve, but not on the vertical part. If we are on the vertical segment, firms respond to the excess demand in the goods market by raising prices and not output.

The second effect of the increase in income is to raise the demand for real money balances as more money is needed to finance an increased volume of transactions. Since a regime of monetary targets in a static model implies fixed money supply, there is an initial excess demand for money and the rate of interest rises to equilibrate the assets markets. This leads to crowding out of private investment expenditure and to an income contraction – channel (b). This is the crowding-out effect that was first introduced in model 3. What is important in the context of model 7 is that this crowding-out effect will occur irrespective of whether the stimulus of government expenditure would lead to a rise in income through channel (a). The reason is that even if there is no income expansion, excess demand in the goods market will lead to increased prices. Since the transactions demand for money is proportional to the price level, an increase in the latter will lead to higher interest rates and consequently to crowding out.

The interest rate rise, apart from leading to crowding out, has two more effects. First, at the initial stock of government bonds it leads to higher other personal income in nominal and real terms. This induces households to spend more on consumption and as a result income rises – channel (c). In the context of model 7 this channel is not as important as it is in model 5, because the rise in prices tends to offset the increase in nominal other personal income. The second effect of the interest rate rise is to increase interest payments on existing government debt. Under bond finance the government increases the stock of bonds and this raises nominal and real private sector wealth, which stimulates consumption and therefore income – channel (d). In the context of model 7 this channel is not as important as it is in model 5, because the rise in prices tends to offset the rise in nominal wealth.

At the initial level of prices and income, the increase in government expenditure results in an enlarged budget deficit, which raises the public sector borrowing requirement in real terms. Under bond finance the government issues more bonds to finance the deficit and this increases real private sector wealth. The latter has two effects. First, it leads to an increase in the demand for money, which requires a larger rise in the interest rate than was implied by channel (a). This intensifies the effects that work through channels (b) to (d). The second effect of the increase in real private sector wealth is to stimulate consumption and therefore income – channel (e).

Thus, there are four expansionary forces that dominate the single contractionary force emanating from channel (b), and therefore income rises. As firms hire more labour to increase production, unemployment falls and wages rise. Firms pass the increased cost of production on to prices, and this increases the rate of actual and expected inflation. Increased prices reduce real other personal income, real private sector wealth and real money balances. The first two tend to offset the expansionary effects of channels (c) and (d), whereas the third increases the upward pressure on interest rates.

Box 7.4 provides a schematic view of the channels through which an increase in government expenditure affects the economic system under money finance. Channel (a) is the same as under bond finance. The main difference between bond and money finance arises out of the behaviour of the interest rate. Under money finance the government increases the

---

Box 7.4 The transmission of fiscal policy (government expenditure) under money finance

$$YD\uparrow \Rightarrow C\uparrow \Rightarrow D\uparrow \Rightarrow Y\uparrow \qquad \text{(a)}$$

$$D\uparrow \Rightarrow Y\uparrow \Rightarrow \left\{ \begin{array}{l} \\ \dfrac{M^d}{CPI}\uparrow \end{array} \right.$$

$$\Downarrow$$

$$G\uparrow \Rightarrow \left\{ \begin{array}{l} \\ \\ \end{array} \right. \qquad r\downarrow > r\uparrow \Rightarrow \left\{ \begin{array}{l} I\uparrow \Rightarrow D\uparrow \Rightarrow Y\uparrow \qquad \text{(b)} \\ OPI/CPI\downarrow \Rightarrow C\downarrow \Rightarrow Y\downarrow \qquad \text{(c)} \\ \dfrac{V}{CPI}\downarrow \Rightarrow C\downarrow \Rightarrow Y\downarrow \qquad \text{(d)} \end{array} \right.$$

$$\dfrac{PSBR}{P}\uparrow \Rightarrow \dfrac{M}{CPI}\uparrow \Rightarrow \left\{ \begin{array}{l} \\ \Uparrow \end{array} \right.$$

$$\dfrac{V}{CPI}\uparrow \Rightarrow \left\{ \begin{array}{l} \dfrac{M^d}{CPI}\uparrow \\ \\ C\uparrow \Rightarrow D\uparrow \Rightarrow Y\uparrow \qquad \text{(e)} \end{array} \right.$$

$$((a) + (b) + (e)) > ((c) + (d)) \left. \begin{array}{l} \\ \\ \\ \end{array} \right\} u\downarrow \Rightarrow w\uparrow \Rightarrow p\uparrow \Rightarrow \left\{ \begin{array}{l} \dfrac{OPI}{CPI}\downarrow \Rightarrow C\downarrow \Rightarrow Y\downarrow \\ \dfrac{V}{CPI}\downarrow \Rightarrow C\downarrow \Rightarrow Y\downarrow \\ \dfrac{M}{CPI}\downarrow \Rightarrow r\uparrow \Rightarrow I\downarrow \Rightarrow Y\downarrow \end{array} \right.$$

supply of real money balances to cover the increased real public sector borrowing requirement. At the initial level of income and interest rates, this creates an excess supply of money and the interest rate falls to equilibrate the assets markets. This is in sharp contrast with bond finance, which implies an interest rate rise. The fall in the interest rate under money finance has three main effects. First, it stimulates investment and therefore leads to an income expansion – channel (b). Second, the interest rate fall reduces interest payments on the existing stock of government debt and thus real other personal income declines, which in turn induces households to spend less on consumption. This leads to income contraction – channel (c). Third, a reduced debt service implies that the government retires debt from the market and this diminishes real private sector wealth, which in turn leads households to spend less on consumption. This leads to a decline in income – channel (d).

As in model 5, the initial stimulus of government expenditure leads to an increase in the demand for money through the income expansion that it entails – channel (a). This tends to offset the initial excess supply of money and reverses the interest rate adjustment process. This effect is strengthened by the increase in the demand for money resulting from the initial rise in private sector wealth, which is caused by the increase in the supply of money.

A comparison of the transmission mechanism of government expenditure under bond and money finance shows that the main difference lies in the behaviour of the interest rate, which rises under bond finance but falls under money finance. This is the same conclusion that we reached in the context of model 5 and therefore this result is robust, whether prices are fixed or variable.

In the context of model 5 wealth is certain to rise under both modes of finance, although the rise is greater under bond finance. In model 7, however, the increase in *real* private sector wealth is ambiguous. The contraction of real wealth due to the fall in the interest rate (channel d) may outweigh the increase in real wealth due to the increase in real money balances. In this case the long-run income expansion under money finance will be lower than in model 5.

A comparison of the transmission mechanism of a fiscal expansion under bond and money finance is provided by simulating model 7. The fiscal expansion takes the form of a permanent increase in government expenditure by £1 billion throughout the 20-year horizon. Figures 7.9 to 7.12 present the results of this simulation under bond and money finance for output/income, interest rate, real wealth and the consumer price index.

Income/output rises faster under money than under bond finance (figure 7.9). Almost complete adjustment takes place within one year under money finance, whereas with bond finance the system has not yet

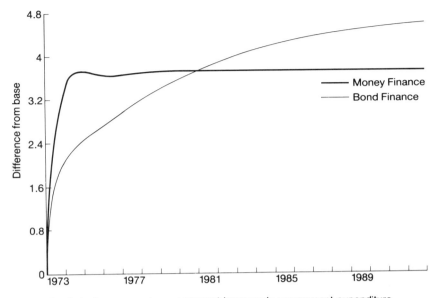

Figure 7.9 Output response to a permanent increase in government expenditure

converged after 20 years. The income multiplier is higher for the first eight years under money finance and lower thereafter. The long-run multiplier is 3.7 with money finance, whereas after 20 years it is 4.6 with bond finance. The time-profile of the income multiplier from model 7 has the same basic characteristics as in model 5, in which prices are fixed; i.e. bond finance is more expansionary than money finance in the long run and less expansionary in the short run.

The interest rate (figure 7.10) falls on impact under money finance and continues to slide until it reaches a new steady state after seven years. In the long run it is 1.4 percentage points lower. With bond finance, on the other hand, the interest rate rises gradually until in the new steady state it is 0.7 percentage points higher. The interest rate adjustment in model 7 is similar to that in model 5 with one exception: under money finance in model 5 there is short-run overshooting of the long-run equilibrium, whereas in model 7 the adjustment is monotonic. In spite of this difference the basic result that money finance leads to lower interest rates, whereas bond finance leads to higher, is valid in both models.

The adjustment of real wealth is portrayed in figure 7.11. After a tiny fall in the first period, real wealth rises monotonically with bond finance but it takes a long time to converge. After 20 years it has not yet fully converged and it has risen by £7.1 billion. With money finance, on the

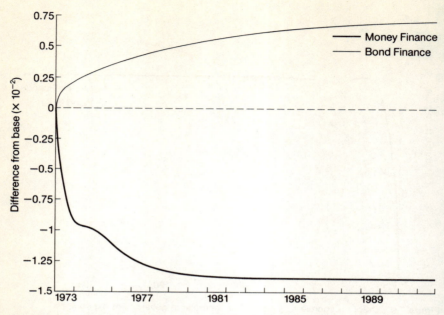

Figure 7.10   Interest rate response to a permanent increase in government expenditure

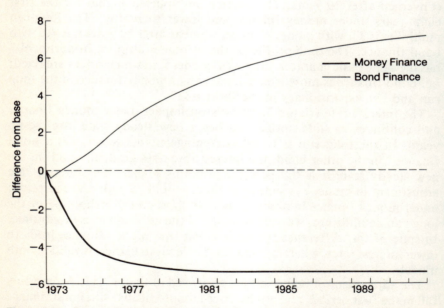

Figure 7.11   Real wealth response to a permanent increase in government expenditure

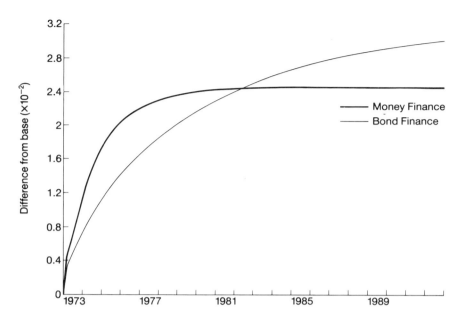

Figure 7.12   Response of consumer prices to a permanent increase in government expenditure

other hand, real wealth falls continuously until in the new steady state it is £5.4 billion lower. Almost complete adjustment takes place within five years. The adjustment under bond finance is similar in models 5 and 7. The effect of flexible prices is to prolong the adjustment process. However, with money finance the adjustment is qualitatively different: in model 5 real wealth rises, while in model 7 it falls.

The dynamic adjustment of prices is illustrated in figure 7.12. The consumer price index initially rises more quickly under money than under bond finance. This is caused by the greater stimulus to demand under money finance, which then feeds through the wage-price spiral. The adjustment of prices is complete within ten years with money finance, whereas with bond finance the system has not fully converged after 20 years. The reason for the slow adjustment with bond finance lies in the fact that, because of crowding out, the system relies solely on the wealth effect to reach its long-run equilibrium and this works very slowly. In addition, the fact that prices are flexible prolongs the adjustment period because the budget deficit is enlarged. In the new steady state the consumer price index rises by 2.5 per cent with money finance, whereas after 20 years it has risen by 3.1 per cent with bond finance.

7.5 An Adverse Supply Shock – Oil Price Rise

A proper analysis of an oil price rise requires the framework of models 8 and 9, in which the role of exports and imports on demand is considered. Nevertheless, even without such an effect the results of this model are interesting.

Box 7.5 presents a schematic view of the main channels through which an increase in the price of imported raw materials, e.g. oil, affects the economic system under monetary targets of keeping the nominal supply of money fixed. The initial effect is to raise the unit variable cost of production, which forces firms to increase output prices, P. At the same time, since oil enters the consumer price index there is a direct effect, in addition to the effect of prices, on the consumer price index. This raises the actual and expected rate of inflation, which in turn feeds back through wages to prices. The rise in prices has three effects. First, it reduces real other personal income, which induces households to spend less on consumption, and therefore income declines – channel (a). Second, the price rise reduces real wealth, which again depresses consumption and income – channel (b). Third, since the nominal stock of money is kept unchanged, real money balances are reduced and the interest rate rises to equilibrate the assets markets.

Box 7.5 The transmission of an oil price rise under monetary targets

$$\frac{OPI}{CPI}{\downarrow} \Rightarrow C{\downarrow} \Rightarrow Y{\downarrow} \qquad \text{(a)}$$

$$PIW{\uparrow} \Rightarrow P{\uparrow} \text{ and } CPI{\uparrow} \Rightarrow \begin{cases} \\ \dfrac{V}{CPI}{\downarrow} \Rightarrow C{\downarrow} \Rightarrow Y{\downarrow} \qquad \text{(b)} \\ \\ \dfrac{M}{CPI}{\downarrow} \Rightarrow r{\uparrow} \Rightarrow \begin{cases} (r - p^e){\uparrow} \Rightarrow I{\downarrow} \Rightarrow Y{\downarrow} \ \text{(c)} \\ \dfrac{OPI}{CPI}{\uparrow} \Rightarrow C{\uparrow} \Rightarrow Y{\uparrow} \quad \text{(d)} \end{cases} \end{cases}$$

$$Y{\downarrow} \text{ and } r{\uparrow} \Rightarrow \frac{PSBR}{P}{\uparrow} \Rightarrow \frac{B}{P}{\uparrow} \Rightarrow \frac{V}{CPI}{\uparrow} \Rightarrow C{\uparrow} \Rightarrow Y{\uparrow} \qquad \text{(e)}$$

The interest rate rise has three effects. First, for a given rate of expected inflation, it raises the real interest rate. However, as prices increase, the rate of expected inflation also rises and this introduces some ambiguity as to the final effect on the real interest rate. The most likely effect is an increase in the real interest rate. This deters investment and leads to a decline in income – channel (c). The combined effect of channels (a) to (c) results in, at the initial phase of the adjustment process, a recession. We thus find that an oil price rise leads to *stagflation*, the coexistence of inflation and recession. Second, the interest rate rise increases interest payments on the existing stock of government bonds and this results in higher nominal other personal income – channel (d) – which counters the effect of channel (a). The former tends to dominate the latter through time, as the interest rate follows a monotonic adjustment to a higher level in the new steady state. Third, the rise in the interest rate, combined with the decline in income, leads to a budget deficit and, with a regime of monetary targets, the stock of government bonds increases to finance the budget. This increases real wealth, which stimulates consumption and therefore income – channel (e). This channel will dominate, through time, the contractionary forces and steer the economy out of the initial recession.

Box 7.6 The transmission of an oil price rise under debt targets

$$\frac{OPI}{CPI}\!\downarrow \Rightarrow C\!\downarrow \Rightarrow Y\!\downarrow \tag{a}$$

$$PIW\!\uparrow \Rightarrow P\!\uparrow \text{ and } CPI\!\uparrow \Rightarrow \left\{ \right.$$

$$\frac{V}{CPI}\!\downarrow \Rightarrow C\!\downarrow \Rightarrow Y\!\downarrow \tag{b}$$

$$(r - p^e)\!\downarrow \Rightarrow I\!\uparrow \Rightarrow Y\!\uparrow \tag{c}$$

$$Y\!\downarrow \Rightarrow \frac{PSBR}{P}\!\uparrow \Rightarrow \frac{M}{CPI}\!\uparrow \Rightarrow r\!\downarrow \Rightarrow \left\{ \frac{OPI}{CPI}\!\downarrow \Rightarrow C\!\downarrow \Rightarrow Y\!\downarrow \right. \tag{d}$$

$$\frac{B}{P}\!\downarrow \Rightarrow \frac{V}{CPI}\!\downarrow \Rightarrow C\!\downarrow \Rightarrow Y\!\downarrow \tag{e}$$

Box 7.6 provides a schematic view of the channels through which an oil price rise affects the economy under debt targets of keeping the nominal stock of government bonds fixed. As with monetary targets, the initial effect is a rise in prices and a fall in real other personal income and real wealth – channels (a) and (b). The combined effect of these channels drives the economy into recession in the initial stage of the adjustment process. Thus, under both monetary and debt targets the effect of an oil price rise is to cause stagflation.

The fall in income means that the budget is in deficit and the government prints money to finance it. This reduces the nominal interest rate and most likely diminishes the real interest rate too. The latter stimulates investment and helps the economy to get out of the recession – channel (c). However, the fall in the interest rate has two more effects that are contractionary – channels (d) and (e). Real other personal income is reduced as interest payments on government debt diminish, and real wealth also falls as the government retires debt from the market.

The main difference between monetary and debt targets is that channels (a) and (b) reinforce channels (d) and (e) under debt targets, whereas they work in opposite directions under monetary targets. This, in turn, follows from the adjustment of the interest rate, which falls under debt targets but rises under monetary targets.

A comparison of the effects of an oil price rise is illustrated by simulating model 7 with a permanent increase in the price of imported raw materials, *PIW*, to 1.1 from 1, a 10 per cent increase. Figures 7.13 to 7.16 present the results of this simulation under monetary targets and debt targets for income/output, interest rate, real wealth and prices.

With monetary targets, income declines for the first three years and then rises (figure 7.13). Thus, a 10 per cent increase in the price of oil

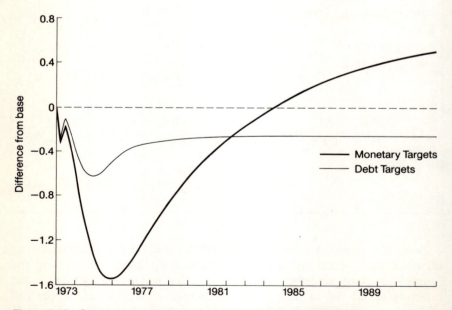

Figure 7.13 Output response to a permanent increase in the price of oil

creates a transient recession. Income returns to its original level after 11 years and then rises even further. The economy has not fully converged to a new steady state after 20 years. At the trough of the recession income is 1.6 per cent lower. With debt targets, income declines for only two years and then partially recovers to a lower new steady state, reached in seven years. In the trough of the recession income falls by only 0.6 per cent. Thus, the recession is larger and lasts longer under monetary than under debt targets. However, the economy more than recovers in the long run under monetary targets, whereas with debt targets the recovery is only partial.

The interest rate rises monotonically under monetary targets, whereas it falls under debt targets (figure 7.14). The behaviour of the interest rate under the two rules explains the difference in the size and duration of the initial recession.

Real wealth falls for the first two years under monetary targets and then recovers (figure 7.15). With debt targets, real wealth slides continuously until in the new steady state, reached in seven years, it is £11.1 billion lower. The different behaviour of wealth under the two rules explains why income more than recovers under monetary targets whereas the recovery is only partial with debt targets. The difference in the behaviour of wealth, on the other hand, is due to higher interest rates under monetary targets, which entail an increased stock of bonds, and

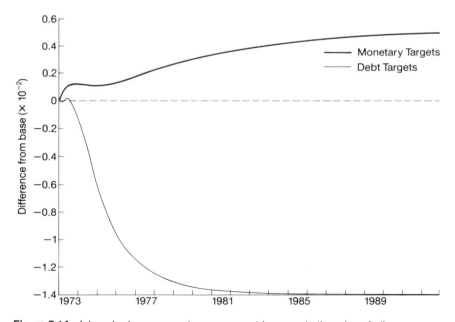

Figure 7.14   Interest rate response to a permanent increase in the price of oil

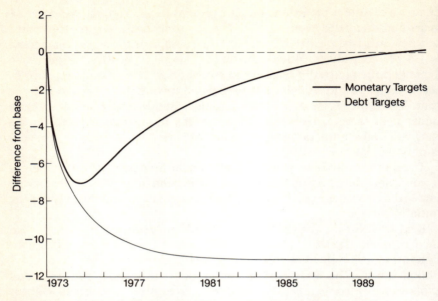

Figure 7.15   Real wealth response to a permanent increase in the price of oil

lower interest rates with debt targets.

The consumer price index (figure 7.16) rises at the same rate during the first year, but then it rises more quickly under debt targets until year 11 and more slowly thereafter. This reflects the difference in the adjustment of income under the two rules. Since monetary targets imply a longer and more severe recession, prices rise more slowly from year 2 to year 11. After that, the income recovery is greater under monetary targets and therefore prices rise more quickly.

7.6 The Role of Interest Payments

Model 7 differs from model 6 in that it includes interest payments on government debt and deals with a non-inflationary economy. Interest payments introduce an important non-linearity to the model and in this section we examine its implications. We drop from model 7 other personal income and taxes associated with it, its effect on consumption and *PSBR*. To retain the scaling of the underlying equations we adjust the constant of these equations.

Figures 7.17 to 7.20 present the dynamic income multipliers of the original model 7 and its variant without interest payments, under bond

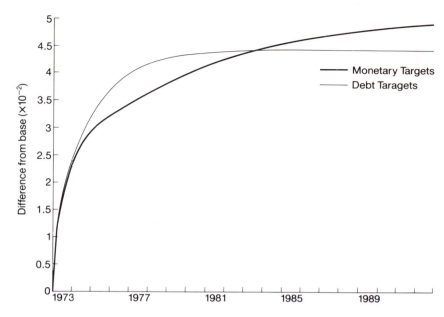

Figure 7.16 Response of consumer prices to a permanent increase in the price of oil

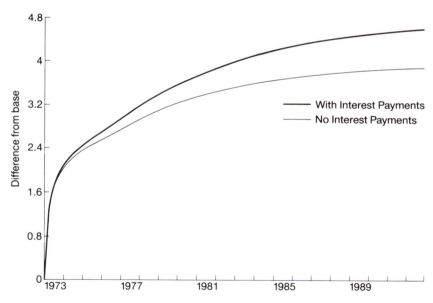

Figure 7.17 The role of non-linearities: output response to a permanent increase in government expenditure under bond finance for the linear and non-linear models

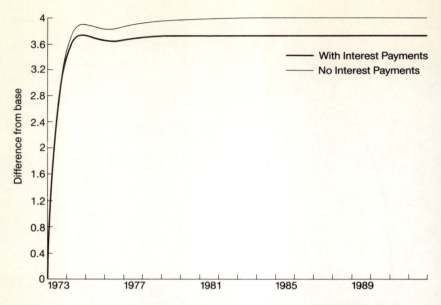

Figure 7.18   The role of non-linearities: output response to a permanent increase in government expenditure under money finance for the linear and non-linear models

finance and money finance, of a permanent £1 billion increase in government expenditure, an open market purchase and an oil price rise.

It can easily be shown that in a non-inflationary economy with flexible prices, but without interest payments, the government expenditure multiplier is equal to the inverse of the marginal tax rate irrespective of the mode of finance. Given that in model 7 the standard tax rate is 0.25, the steady-state income multiplier is 4. From figure 7.17 it follows that when interest payments are excluded the income multiplier under bond finance tends to 4 but very slowly. After 20 years it is 3.9. With the original model that includes interest payments the corresponding multiplier is 4.6. Thus, the non-linearity introduced by interest payments causes an increase of 18 per cent in the long-run income multiplier. Under money finance, however, the steady-state income multiplier without interest payments converges to 4 within ten years, whereas with interest payments it converges to 3.7 (see figure 7.18). This represents a reduction of 7.5 per cent in the steady-state multiplier.

The income multiplier of £1 billion open market purchase, with monetary targets re-imposed after the shock, is illustrated in figure 7.19. The steady-state multiplier with interest payments is −0.4, whereas without interest payments it is 0. The reason why income falls more than

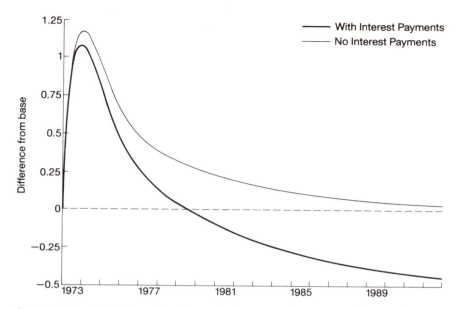

Figure 7.19   The role of non-linearities: output response to an open market purchase under monetary targets for the linear and non-linear models

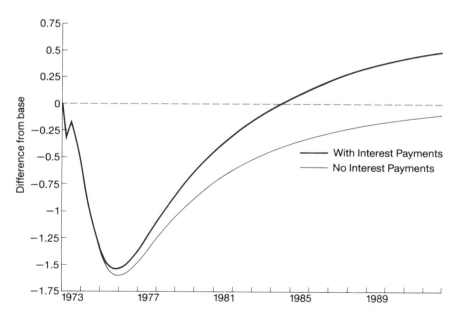

Figure 7.20   The role of non-linearities: output response to a permanent increase in the price of oil under monetary targets for the linear and non-linear models

the original steady state is that as the interest rate falls the government retires more debt from the market because of lower interest payments. This reduces real wealth, which depresses consumption and therefore income.

The income multiplier of a 10 per cent rise in the price of oil under monetary targets is illustrated in figure 7.20. The initial effect is a recession, but with interest payments income more than recovers in the long run, whereas with the model that excludes interest payments income returns to its original steady state. The reason why income exceeds in the long run the original steady state is that as the interest rate rises more bonds have to be issued to cover the additional interest payments, and this causes wealth to rise, which in turn stimulates consumption and therefore income.

7.7 Sensitivity of Fiscal Policy Multipliers to Parameter Variation

In this section the approach of model 5 is adopted for testing the robustness of the results to parameter variation. This is essential since the model depends on the chosen initial set of parameter values. The sensitivity analysis has two objectives: (a) to provide a quantitative measure of the extent of the sensitivity of fiscal multipliers to parameter variation; (b) to provide a ranking of the coefficients according to the multipliers' sensitivity to their perturbation.

Table 7.1 presents the impact and steady-state fiscal multipliers under bond and money finance when certain critical parameters are perturbed. These are the interest sensitivity of consumption, investment and demand for money; the wealth effect on consumption and demand for money; the effect of excess demand and expected inflation on wage inflation; and the effect of actual inflation on expected inflation. The multipliers are computed by doubling and halving each of these coefficients separately. When a coefficient is perturbed the constant in that equation is adjusted to retain the scaling of the equation. The impact multiplier is the average of the first four quarters and the steady-state multiplier is the average for year 20 whenever the system has not fully converged. As in model 5, a measure of the sensitivity of each multiplier to a given parameter change is the corresponding elasticity, defined in (5.18). If the multiplier is insensitive to a given parameter perturbation then the elasticity is near zero.

The results in table 7.1 indicate a number of points. First, the multipliers are insensitive to all perturbed parameters. The maximum sensitivity of the steady-state and impact multipliers occurs under the perturbation of the interest sensitivity of the demand for money, with elasticities of 0.112 and 0.228 respectively. This implies that for a

Table 7.1 Sensitivity of fiscal multipliers to parameter variation

Perturbed coefficient		Bond finance		Money finance	
		Multiplier	Elasticity	Multiplier	Elasticity
Basic model	Impact	1.75		2.63	
	Steady-state	4.62		3.75	
Interest sensitivity of consumption, C_r					
Doubled, $C_r = -50$	Impact	1.71	0.023	2.92	0.110
	Steady-state	4.65	0.006	3.84	0.024
Halved, $C_r = -12.5$	Impact	1.77	0.023	2.44	0.144
	Steady-state	4.60	0.009	3.66	0.048
Interest sensitivity of investment, I_r					
Doubled, $I_r = -50$	Impact	1.73	0.011	2.84	0.080
	Steady-state	4.64	0.004	3.80	0.013
Halved, $I_r = -12.5$	Impact	1.76	0.011	2.50	0.099
	Steady-state	4.61	0.004	3.71	0.021
Interest sensitivity of demand for money, M_r					
Doubled, $M_r = -200$	Impact	1.83	0.046	2.36	0.103
	Steady-state	4.49	0.028	3.78	0.008
Halved, $M_r = -50$	Impact	1.60	0.171	2.93	0.228
	Steady-state	4.88	0.112	3.73	0.011
Wealth effect on consumption, C_v					
Doubled, $C_v = 0.13$	Impact	1.66	0.051	2.48	0.057
	Steady-state	4.56	0.013	3.63	0.032
Halved, $C_v = 0.0325$	Impact	1.81	0.069	2.72	0.068
	Steady-state	4.55	0.030	3.82	0.037
Wealth effect on demand for money, M_v					
Doubled, $M_v = 0.02$	Impact	1.76	0.006	2.64	0.004
	Steady-state	4.64	0.004	3.75	0
Halved, $M_v = 0.005$	Impact	1.75	0	2.63	0
	Steady-state	4.61	0.004	3.75	0
Excess demand on wage inflation, w_y					
Doubled, $w_y = 0.5$	Impact	1.67	0.046	2.55	0.030
	Steady-state	4.70	0.017	3.62	0.035
Halved, $w_y = 0.125$	Impact	1.79	0.046	2.68	0.038
	Steady-state	4.52	0.043	3.82	0.037
Expected inflation on wage inflation, w_p					
Halved, $w_p = 0.5$	Impact	1.77	0.023	2.65	0.015
	Steady-state	4.51	0.048	3.82	0.037
Actual inflation on expected inflation, p_p					
Doubled, $p_p = 1$	Impact	1.78	0.017	2.66	0.011
	Steady-state	4.65	0.006	3.75	0

perturbation equal to 100 per cent in this coefficient the steady-state multiplier changes by only 11.2 per cent and the impact multiplier changes by 22.8 per cent. Second, for the coefficients that affect the real sector and the monetary sector of the economy, the steady-state multipliers are less sensitive than the impact multipliers. For the coefficients that affect the aggregate supply the opposite is true: the impact multipliers are less sensitive than the steady-state multipliers. The reason is that the main effect of these coefficients works through prices, and these are changing gradually. Third, the ranking of the coefficients according to the sensitivity they cause to the steady-state multipliers under bond finance is as follows (with the percentage indicating the extent of the multiplier change as measured by the elasticity): (1) the interest sensitivity of the demand for money (11.2 per cent); (2) the effect of expected inflation on wage inflation (4.8 per cent); (3) the effect of excess demand on wage inflation (4.3 per cent); (4) the wealth effect on consumption (3.0 per cent); (5) the interest sensitivity of consumption (0.9 per cent); (6) the effect of actual on expected inflation (0.6 per cent); (7) the interest sensitivity of investment and the wealth effect on the demand for money (0.4 per cent). The equivalent ranking under money finance is as follows: (1) the interest sensitivity of consumption (4.8 per cent); (2) the effect of expected inflation and excess demand on wage inflation and the wealth effect on consumption. All these three effects cause the same multiplier change (3.7 per cent). In third and fourth places come the interest sensitivity of investment (2.1 per cent) and the interest sensitivity of the demand for money (1.1 per cent). Finally, the multiplier elasticities of the wealth effect on the demand for money and the effect of expected on actual inflation are zero.

7.8 Concluding Comments

In this model the dynamic response of the economy to monetary policy, fiscal policy under alternative finance rules and an oil price rise are examined.

An expansionary monetary policy, through a straight increase in the money supply or an open market purchase, temporarily stimulates income. The overall effects depend on whether the government is following monetary or debt targets. The initial stimulus is bigger with monetary than with debt targets. However, the long-run effect of monetary targets is a decline in income, whereas that of debt targets is either zero or a much smaller decline. The long-run decline in income is due to the non-linearities introduced by interest payments on government debt. In the absence of such payments income returns to its original steady state.

A fiscal stimulus (e.g. an increase in government expenditure) under money finance is more expansionary in the short run (i.e. a period of five years) and less expansionary in the long run than bond finance. This implies that for stabilization purposes money finance is preferable to bond finance. However, this result is not unambiguous and depends on the government's policy objectives. Money finance is more expansionary than bond finance in the short run, but it also creates more inflation. This is a direct consequence of the fact that both methods of finance create inflation by stimulating aggregate demand. Thus, there is a trade-off between inflation and growth, and whether money or bond finance is preferable depends on the relative importance that the authorities attach to inflation and growth. This choice depends, among other things, on the state of the economy in the business cycle. If the economy is in recession, then the authorities attach more importance to growth than to inflation, and vice versa if the economy is in a boom.

Without interest payments, money finance is as expansionary as bond finance in the long run. With interest payments, bond finance is more expansionary than money finance. This is the same conclusion reached in the context of model 5, in which prices are fixed. Hence, this result is robust, whether prices are fixed or variable. In this model only fiscal policy matters, even with the absence of money illusion, provided the economy is non-inflationary and supply side open. This follows from the fact that long-run equilibrium is attained when the budget is balanced. Hence, a fiscal expansion requires that income must rise sufficiently to generate enough taxes to balance the budget. If the economy is non-inflationary and supply side closed there are two long-run equilibrium conditions (a vertical Phillips curve and a vertical budget surplus line in the (Y, p) space) and the system is most likely unstable.

An oil price rise in the short run creates stagflation, i.e. inflation and recession. The extent and duration of the recession and the inflationary impacts of the oil price rise depend on whether the authorities follow monetary or debt targets. The recession is much deeper and lasts longer with monetary than with debt targets, but inflation is lower with the former than with the latter in the short to medium term. In the long run, however, income more than recovers with monetary targets, whereas with debt targets the recovery is only partial. The non-linearities that are introduced by interest payments are again important. With monetary targets the economy returns to its original steady state without interest payments, whereas it exceeds the initial steady state with interest payments.

Appendix 7.1 Further Reading on the Wage–Price Sector

The wage–price sector in this book characterizes prices as responding slowly to changes in aggregate demand (prices are sticky). The explanation that is offered for this price stickiness is that expected inflation adjusts gradually to actual inflation, which in turn depends on excess demand in the goods market, expected inflation and imported inflation. The latter arises either from changes in the prices of imported goods and raw materials or from the exchange rate. This price behaviour is the result of the interaction of wages and prices. The hypothesis about wages is that they respond to disequilibrium in the labour market. Prices, on the other hand, are based on a variable mark-up of average cost on the assumption that firms act in a monopolistic environment. Finally, the mark-up depends on excess demand in the goods market. However, this justification of price stickiness is only one among many others, as we shall see, and is invoked as a convenient simplification for analytical purposes rather than as a statement of how the real world works. Nevertheless, despite this drawback the postulated behaviour of prices fits the stylized facts mentioned in the introduction. For convenience these are reproduced here.

- Changes in nominal GNP are strongly correlated with changes in output (real GNP), but have little correlation with inflation (measured, for example, by the GNP-deflator). The implications are, first, that shocks in nominal demand have persistent effects on output and, second, that prices are sticky.
- Innovations in money supply are positively correlated with innovations in output. This suggests that changes in money supply may have large effects on output.
- There is very little correlation between real wages and output or employment and this is procyclical rather than counter-cyclical.
- Changes in the demand for labour produce large fluctuations in employment and small changes in the real wage rate. This means that wages are sticky. Unemployment is largely involuntary and the unemployed are unhappier than those who are employed.

These stylized facts differ across industries (see Bresnahan, 1989; Carlton, 1986; Cecchetti, 1986; Stigler and Kindahl, 1970), across different historical periods and across countries (see, e.g., Gordon, 1982, 1983; Sachs, 1980). Furthermore, there are three different types of price stickiness describing inertia or serial correlation, rate-of-change or hysteresis effects and level or Phillips-curve effects (see Gordon, 1990, for estimates of these three different types of price stickiness across time and countries).

Within the Keynesian tradition, the explanation of these stylized facts has proceeded along four different lines. Theories differ in whether they concentrate on real or nominal rigidity in the goods or the labour market. Thus the range of possibilities can be represented on 2×2 matrix describing the type of market (goods or labour) and the type of rigidity (real or nominal) – see Gordon (1990) and Mankiw (1990) for a summary and an evaluation of these theories.

Theories of Real Wage Rigidity in the Labour Market

Early attempts of providing an explanation of aggregate price stickiness concentrated on the labour market. The most prominent amongst them is the 'implicit contract' theory developed simultaneously by Azariadis (1975), Baily (1974) and Gordon (1974). The original attraction of the theory stemmed from the belief that it was providing the microfoundations of wage stickiness. However, it was soon realized that although the theory, at least in its initial formulation, could explain the rigidity of the real wage rate, it could not explain greater fluctuations in employment (or unemployment) than those predicted by the perfectly competitive market (i.e. the Walrasian model) (see Akerlof and Miyazaki, 1980; Grossman and Hart, 1981).

According to the implicit contract theory workers are risk-averse and therefore they would like to stabilize the fluctuations in their income (the real wage rate) due to unanticipated shocks in demand. However, workers have only limited access to capital markets and cannot obtain insurance against income fluctuations from conventional insurance companies. Firms are less risk-averse and have greater access to capital markets than workers. They maximize profits while minimizing the variability of the income of their labour force, thereby offering to workers such an insurance in their wage–employment package. The typical firm can be thought of as having two departments: a production and an insurance department. The former would provide a wage-employment package according to the competitive market forces (the Walrasian equilibrium). In this package both the real wage rate and employment fluctuate in response to demand shocks. The insurance department of the firm modifies this package by offering a stable take-home pay in both 'good' and 'bad' states of nature (provided that both are observable and verifiable by firms and workers) by asking workers to pay a premium only in good states. Thus, although the Walrasian real wage rate is volatile, the take-home pay is stable. However, there is no unemployment since the Walrasian real wage fluctuates to clear the labour market at each point in time. The observed fluctuations in employment and unemployment cannot therefore be greater than those predicted by the Walrasian model. This result is consistent with the findings of Arrow and Debreu that insurance contracts improve the functioning of competitive economies by making them Pareto efficient – see Azariadis (1979) and Azariadis and Stiglitz (1983) for surveys of this literature.

If, however, firms are risk-averse rather than risk-neutral as was assumed in the original version of the implicit contract theory, and they are better informed about the state of the world than workers (i.e. there is asymmetric information), then the implicit contract model can explain 'non-Walrasian' unemployment (Azariadis, 1983; Grossman and Hart, 1983); for a survey of the asymmetric information version of the implicit contract theory see Hart (1983). The reason is the following. If firms are risk-averse, they have an incentive to lower the real wage rate in bad states. If information is also asymmetric, then firms have an incentive always to claim that states are bad. Thus, in this case the contract cannot specify that wages would depend on the state of the economy. Instead, the contract should specify that wages should be lowered if the firm reduces employment since this is observable by workers as well as firms. Therefore, employment will fall in bad states by more than the Walrasian equilibrium because this is the only way the firm can reduce the real wage rate.

This result is not robust, however. The asymmetric information theory of implicit contracts can result in overemployment or underemployment depending on the nature of the utility function and the degree of risk aversion of firms (see Stiglitz, 1986). For example, if firms are risk-neutral, then there is under or overemployment as leisure is an inferior or normal good. If firms are infinitely risk-averse, whereas workers have a finite degree of risk aversion, then underemployment results. However, even when the theory explains underemployment this is not consistent with observed behaviour: unions do not seem to say to management: 'we will be willing to accept a further wage cut if you prove, by throwing more of us out of work, that the state of nature is so bad', but rather 'we will be willing to accept a further wage cut if you reduce your planned level of lay-offs' (Stiglitz, 1986, pp. 173–4). Furthermore, this approach creates many problems as to how the contract ought to be drafted.

The asymmetric information theory of implicit contracts has a number of other drawbacks, too. First, even when the theory explains greater variability in unemployment than the Walrasian equilibrium this is achieved at the expense of greater variability in the real wage rate. This is not only counterfactual, but opposite to the original version of the theory of symmetric information with firms being less risk averse than workers. Second, the theory has the unappealing implication that in some cases workers are equally well off when employed or unemployed and that in others they are better off unemployed than employed. Third, and this is a criticism common to all real wage rigidity theories, the implicit contract theory does not explain why, if workers care about their real income, they do not insist on full indexation of wage contracts to nominal GNP. The share of labour in GNP remains constant if the growth rate of the nominal wage rate is indexed to the growth rate of nominal GNP. This point Gordon (1990) has called the 'indexation puzzle'. Indexation to nominal GNP overcomes the problems of CPI indexation, namely that full CPI indexation is not optimal in the presence of supply shocks (Gray, 1976; Fischer 1977a).

An early attempt at providing an explanation of labour market behaviour based on microfoundations was the collection of papers in the Phelps (1970) volume. These papers explain unemployment as being voluntary and therefore provide a basis for the new-classical macroeconomics. When shocks in demand reduce the equilibrium real wage rate workers voluntarily quit their jobs to search for higher wages. This approach may explain why the natural rate of unemployment is not zero, but it cannot explain lay-offs. Furthermore, it predicts that voluntary quits vary procyclically, while evidence suggests exactly the opposite (Okun 1981, chapter 2).

It is a common belief among many academic economists, practitioners, politicians and the general public that real wage rigidity is caused by, or is at least connected with, labour unions. Models that explore the role of labour unions in real wage rigidity are based on bargaining between workers and firms over wages and employment. In some of these models the labour union is assumed to maximize the expected utility of its 'representative member' on the implicit assumption that all members are treated equally by the firm and the union. In other models the union maximizes the expected utility of the 'median voter' on the assumption that workers differ in terms of seniority – see Oswald (1985) and Pencavel (1985) for some of these problems, surveys of the literature and extended bibliographies.

Although bargaining can be over wages and employment, in reality actual labour contracts appear to set a wage and to leave the employment decision to the firm. The most influential model in this category is the 'right-to-manage', according to which the firm and the union bargain over the real wage rate and then employment is chosen by the firm so as to maximize profits (Nickell, 1982). An extreme version of this model is the early approach of the 'monopoly-union', according to which the union chooses the real wage rate unilaterally and the firm maximizes profits taking as given that wage rate (Dunlop, 1944).

A monopoly-union that maxmizes the expected utility of its representative member would choose that level of the real wage rate at which the highest indifference curve of the union between real wages and employment is tangent to the firm's labour demand curve. The reason is that the labour demand curve can be thought of as the locus of maximum points of the firm's isoprofit curves between real wages and employment for given values of the real wage rate (i.e. the locus of points along which the marginal revenue product of labour is equal to the wage).

As Leontief (1946) first pointed out, this optimal combination of the real wage rate and employment chosen by a monopoly-union is inefficient, in the sense that both the firm and the union can be made better off (i.e. there can be a Pareto improvement) by a lower real wage rate that leads to higher employment. The condition for efficient bargains is that these are points of tangency between the isoprofit curves of the firm and the indifference curves of the union. This locus is called the 'contract curve' and is upward-sloping in the real wage–employment space. Thus there is no incentive for the union to choose a point on the labour demand curve either in conjunction with the firm (right-to-manage approach) or unilaterally (monopoly-union approach). Both would be better off by bargaining over both the real wage rate and employment and choosing a point on the contract curve.

Which point on the contract curve should they choose? The answer depends on the relative bargaining power of the firm and the union (i.e. who calls the tune). If the union is relatively powerful, the equilibrium may be close to the zero profit of the firm or to a 'fair' division of net revenue between the firm and the union. If, on the other hand, the firm is relatively powerful, the outcome may be close to the competitive equilibrium, which is one of the end-points of the contract curve, namely the point at which the isoprofit and the indifference curves have zero slope. The relative power (or equity) locus is downward-sloping in the real wage–employment space. Equilibrium is established at the intersection of the upward-sloping contract curve with the downward-sloping relative power curve.

In this framework, McDonald and Solow (1981) show that large fluctuations in employment can be associated with small variations in the real wage rate on the assumption that product market conditions are more sensitive to business cycles than the reservation wage. The importance of this assumption can be seen as follows. Suppose that economic conditions worsen (i.e. the economy enters the downswing of the business cycle). Then for any given real wage rate the efficient contract implies lower employment. However, at the same time the labour market conditions deteriorate and for every level of employment the efficient contract implies that the reservation wage is lower. The assumption implies that the former effect dominates the latter and the contract curve shifts to the left.

The reason why this model produces real wage rigidity can be seen as follows. The effect of efficient bargaining is to lead the firm to hire more workers than it would like at the negotiated wage rate. However, higher wages and employment favour the union while lower wages favour the firm. If economic conditions worsen, employment is reduced and the firm gains while the union loses. The effect of bargaining is to transfer some of that gain from the firm to the union by raising the real wage rate. However, this may be partly or wholly offset by the effect of the cyclical variation in demand on the wage rate, thereby producing wage rigidity, while the effect on employment is magnified (i.e. both the contract curve and the relative power curve shift to the left).

If the labour market is segmented into a unionized part and a competitive part, then aggregate demand shocks will affect the two sectors differently. Obviously, a negative demand shock would force wages down more in the competitive than in the unionized sector. Hence, the differential wage between the two sectors would widen during recessions, but so would the fluctuations in employment. The unionized sector would experience smaller wage variability but larger employment fluctuations than the competitive sector (McDonald and Solow, 1985).

There are a number of problems with the explanation of the union's approach of real wage rigidity. First, the real wage rigidity result is not robust. It depends on the assumption of an isoelastic demand with a constant marginal cost curve. Second, since the firm and the union are involved in repeated bargaining, reputation considerations may force the firm to give up short-run profits for better contracts in the future, thereby increasing real wage flexibility (Espinosa and Rhee, 1987). Third, membership considerations imply a dynamic model and this may induce more real wage flexibility than the static model (Gottfries and Horn, 1987). Fourth, as Blanchard and Fischer (1990, chapter 9) argue, if the union cares about employment, why does it bargain only over the real wage rate and not also over employment? Fifth, at least in the USA there is evidence of price stickiness before unions became important (Gordon, 1990). Finally, there is the issue of what Gordon calls the 'indexation puzzle': why unions do not agree contracts with full indexation of the growth rate of the nominal wage rate with the growth rate of nominal GNP.

If the bargaining power of workers does not come from powerful trade unions, where does it arise from? An insight into this problem comes from the 'insider–outsider' models (see Lindbeck and Snower, 1986, 1987, 1988; and Solow, 1985). The labour market consists of incumbent employees (insiders) and unemployed workers (outsiders). In these models the determination of wages is considered as the outcome of a bargain between insiders and employers, while outsiders are unable to influence either the wage rate or the level of employment. Insiders have bargaining power that arises from turnover costs, such as costs of hiring, firing and training. Incumbent employees exploit these turnover costs in bargaining with employers without taking into consideration the interests of outsiders, and raise wages above the clearing market level, thereby creating unemployment. The bargaining power of insiders makes it possible for them to extract a share of the product market rents earned by firms. Real wage rigidity is an optimal behaviour in these models because turnover costs make it costly for employers to replace their incumbent employees with unemployed workers. Outsiders are unable to gain employment by offering their labour services at a lower wage because insiders cooperate among themselves and threaten firms with collective action, harass new entrants and make it, in general, unpleasant for outsiders to underbid and gain jobs. Insiders can maximize their bargaining power by forming unions. The implications of insider–outsider models for wages and employment are similar to those obtained under the theory of unions. Insider–outsider models can generate 'hysteresis' effects and have been used by Blanchard and Summers (1986) and Layard and Nickell (1986) to explain high and persistent unemployment in Europe in the 1980s.

The most promising theory of unemployment is the 'efficiency wage hypothesis' developed in the 1980s. The main idea is that the productivity of workers depends on the wage paid. In this case firms may be unwilling to lower the real wage rate in the face of excess supply of labour if the increase in costs due to falling productivity exceeds the gains from lower wages. It is therefore possible that profit-maximizing firms may pay a real wage that is higher than the Walrasian equilibrium and that would explain real wage stickiness, unemployment and large fluctuations in employment in the presence of unexpected shocks. The basic efficiency wage result can be illustrated in a perfectly competitive environment in which the production function depends on the number of workers and their effort, which in turn is a positive function of the real wage rate. The optimal wage, called the 'efficiency wage' because it minimizes labour costs per efficiency unit, satisfies the condition that the elasticity of effort with respect to the real wage is unity. Each firm will hire workers up to the point where the value of its marginal product equals the efficiency wage (see Solow, 1979). This basic model has been extended by adding to the effort function the unemployment rate, unemployment benefits and the average wage rate – see Katz (1988), Stiglitz (1986), Weiss (1990) and Yellen (1984) for surveys of the literature.

The explanation of wage stickiness is important, but it rests on the assumption that productivity depends on wages (the effort function), which is postulated rather than derived. There are at least five versions of the efficiency wage hypothesis that differ in terms of the explanation they offer for the relationship between productivity and wages. The original idea is usually attributed to Leibenstein (1957) in his theory of development economics. He postulated a relationship between, on the one hand, the level of nutrition and productivity and, on the other hand, the level of wages. The second theory emphasizes labour turnover costs, which are wholly or partly borne by firms as long as workers are more risk-averse than firms (see Arnott and Stiglitz, 1982; Hashimoto, 1981; Phelps, 1970; Stiglitz, 1982). In this case, the lower the wage rate, the higher the rate of labour turnover and the lower the labour productivity. The rationale can be seen as follows. If a firm is paying a wage rate that is lower than that paid by other firms (the equilibrium wage), then this firm will experience a higher quit rate by workers who are searching for higher wages. Since total labour cost depends on the wage bill (the product of the wage rate times employment) and the training cost, which in turn is a positive function of the quit rate, it follows that these costs are minimized at the equilibrium wage rate. In this economy unemployment will be created for any shock in the economy that requires a reduction of the real wage rate, as no firm has an incentive to adjust its real wage rate first, since to do so would invite a higher quit rate. Hence, unemployment follows from a coordination failure.

The third version of the efficiency wage hypothesis (quality-efficiency wage model) assumes that labour is not homogeneous and firms are unable, because of imperfect information, to attract the right quality of labour force unless they pay higher wages (see Stiglitz, 1976; Weiss, 1980). The fourth version of the theory is based on 'shirking', according to which firms, because of imperfect monitoring regarding the actions of a non-homogeneous labour force, pay higher wages to induce workers not to shirk (see Calvo, 1979; Salop, 1979; Shapiro and Stiglitz, 1984). The fifth explanation of the positive relationship between productivity and wages is based on sociological factors (see Akerlof, 1984; Akerlof and Yellen, 1987). In these models a decrease of the real wage rate is considered as 'unfair' among workers who as a result reduce their effort. Accordingly, firms do not lower the real wage rate in the face of an excess supply of labour.

The advantage of the efficiency wage hypothesis is that it can explain not only real wage rigidity, unemployment and large fluctuations in employment in the presence of unexpected shocks, but also queues for high paid jobs, the procyclical fluctuation of the quit rate, segmented labour markets and why unemployment may hit some groups more than others. The last, for example, can be explained by invoking the fact that various groups differ in their relationship between wage and productivity. The theory, therefore, can explain patterns of observed unemployment and many aspects of micro labour market behaviour. Although all versions of the theory can explain the above results, their policy implications differ substantially. For example, in the shirking version an increase in unemployment benefits will result in higher wages and higher unemployment as the opportunity cost of being fired when caught shirking is reduced and therefore firms have to pay even higher wages to induce workers not to shirk. However, in the quality-efficiency version the effect of unemployment benefits on wages and unemployment is ambiguous and depends on parameter values.

The main objection to the efficiency wage hypothesis is based on the argument that more elaborate pay schemes could be designed to overcome the coordination failure implicit in all versions of the theory. In the labour turnover version workers could be forced to pay all of their training costs and therefore receive only their reservation wage, which would lead to a Walrasian equilibrium. Similarly, in the case of imperfect monitoring, workers could be forced to post a bond, which they would forfeit if they were found shirking. In the case of the quality-efficiency version, contracts could be tied with performance bonds, which the workers could forfeit if it turned out that they were not as good as they claimed. These issues have given rise to more elaborate models, like the 'moral hazard' model in which firms have an incentive to charge individuals for training that they do not provide. Other models are based on the observation that individuals do not have sufficient wealth to post bonds or that they are more risk-averse than firms. These issues are not yet resolved because critics counter-argue that some effective bonding is observed in the real world in the form of low-wage apprenticeships and performance-related pay schemes, in which a proportion of wages or salaries is related to the company's earnings.

Similar criticisms have been raised to sociological theories of the efficiency wage, which are based on the premise of 'fairness'. Why is it fair for some workers to keep their jobs at the same wage rate, while others are losing their jobs? The challenge for the proponents of the sociological version of the efficiency wage theory is to explain rather than assume 'fairness'.

Finally, as with all theories of real wage rigidity the puzzle is why workers do not agree contracts with full GNP indexation.

Theories of Real Price Rigidity

Real price rigidity models attempt to explain why firms would choose to keep their profit margins (i.e. the relationship between price and cost) constant in the face of unexpected shocks, or to keep constant the prices of their products relative to those of their competitors or to the general price level (i.e. a form of relative prices) (see Okun, 1975). These models draw a distinction between auction and customer markets and originate from the analyses of Alchian (1969) and Phelps and Winter (1970). In auction markets prices would change to equate demand and supply at any point in time, whereas customer markets are characterized by price stickiness. The presence of search costs explains why firms build long-lasting relationships with customary suppliers and are willing to pay a premium over the competitive price. Similarly, search costs discourage customers from identifying whether intertemporal price changes apply to all firms or only to their preferred one. These costs make customers willing to pay a premium above the competitive price. On the other hand, for the sake of preserving such long-lasting relationships firms are prepared to absorb transient increases in costs and apply mark-up pricing, in which temporary increases in demand do not lead to frequent price adjustment. Moreover, Okun argues that customers would accept as fair any increase in prices due to a permanent increase in costs, but not an increase due to changes in productivity or changes in demand, which are generally regarded as transient. This sort of behaviour would explain price stickiness. The attraction of this theory is that it is intuitively appealing.

This approach suffers from a number of drawbacks. First, the argument of customer dissatisfaction is not sufficient to justify deviation from competitive pricing. Customer dissatisfaction arising in periods of boom would, on average, be offset in periods of recession. Second, the theory leaves unexplained what is regarded as 'fair'. Third, why do firms not revert to pricing practices that are based on full indexation of their costs to the nominal GNP?

Theories of Nominal Price Stickiness

Recently, attention has switched from the labour to the goods market with the emphasis placed on nominal price rigidity. If price rigidity is to be explained by optimizing behaviour then the framework of monopolistic competition is more appropriate than that of perfect competition, since in the former firms are allowed to set up prices. However, the mere introduction of imperfect competition is not sufficient to explain price stickiness and, moreover, money is neutral as under perfect competition (see Blanchard and Kiyotaki, 1987; Fischer, 1988; Kiyotaki, 1985; Rotemberg, 1987). For an imperfectly competitive firm, shifts in demand can produce two alternative extreme combinations of price–output response. At one end of the spectrum, the price can remain unchanged with the whole adjustment being borne by output under the assumption of constant marginal cost (i.e. a flat marginal cost curve) and isoelastic demand. At the other end of the spectrum, a decrease in demand would leave the profit-maximizing level of output unchanged with the whole adjustment being borne by the price if the marginal cost is reduced in proportion to the marginal revenue.

In between these two extremes both the price and output would change in response to shifts in demand, but whether most of the adjustment would fall on price or output depends on the following factors. The relaxation of the assumption of either an isoelastic demand function or a flat marginal cost curve would introduce some degree of price adjustment. An upward-sloping marginal cost curve would allow for some price adjustment, even with an isoelastic demand curve. On the other hand, a linear demand curve, even with a flat marginal cost curve, would also allow for some price adjustment. In the Blanchard and Kiyotaki model the marginal cost curve is flat under the twin assumptions of a constant marginal disutility of work and constant returns to labour in production. If either the marginal disutility of work increases with the amount of work or there are decreasing returns to labour in production, or both, then the marginal cost curve is upward-sloping, implying some price adjustment. Furthermore, even with an isoelastic demand curve and a flat marginal cost curve there would be some price adjustment if the marginal cost was reduced (i.e. if the curve shifted down). Thus, the justification of price stickiness suggests that the explanation ought perhaps to be sought in the sticky adjustment of marginal cost, and this, in turn, points to factors in the labour market and material prices.

Furthermore, in the Blanchard and Kiyotaki model money is neutral because there is complete symmetry across producers. In response to a decrease in money, which decreases aggregate demand and therefore the demand of each firm, an attempt by each producer to reduce its relative price leads, because of the assumption of symmetry, to unchanged relative prices in the new equilibrium. Hence, money is neutral and therefore there is no explanation of price stickiness despite the framework of imperfect competition. Nevertheless, output is lower and the price is higher relative to perfect competition.

To make further progress in explaining aggregate price stickiness we must introduce barriers to nominal price adjustment at the micro-level through adjustment costs, 'menu costs' (see Akerlof and Yellen, 1985; Mankiw, 1985). These menu costs include not only the costs of listing new prices, but also the costs of informing customers, customer annoyance at changing prices and the administrative cost of taking the decision to change prices. In the presence of such menu costs it is optimal for firms not to change prices and to allow output and employment to fluctuate in response to shifts in demand. But these costs by their very nature must be small and therefore the question arises as to how they can account for the large fluctuations in output and employment observed in industrialized countries such as the USA or the UK. The important point is that even small menu costs can produce large fluctuations in output and employment and create nominal aggregate price rigidity. Firms in a monopolistic environment who face a fall in demand will only cut prices if the extra profit exceeds the menu cost. However, any cut in prices will lead to a welfare gain, in terms of the sum of the consumer and producer surplus, exactly because output under imperfect competition is lower than that under perfect competition. Thus, small menu costs deter firms from cutting their prices although doing so would be socially optimal. Moreover, if some firms do not adjust their prices then it is likely that other firms will not adjust either, thereby spreading the price rigidity.

The menu cost approach suffers from three main criticisms and therefore cannot provide an adequate explanation of price stickiness. First, for small menu costs to generate large fluctuations in output and employment the condition that the marginal disutility of work is small is equivalent to the condition that the labour supply is very flat (see Blanchard and Fischer, 1990, chapter 8). This, in turn, requires a very strong intertemporal substitution effect of leisure, which is counterfactual. Second, if there are social losses during recessions because of a failure to reduce prices, symmetry suggests that these should be offset during booms because of a failure to increase prices. Thus, since the mean output remains unchanged, the welfare cost of price rigidity is an increase in the variance of output, which surely must be a second-order effect. Hence, as Ball and Romer (1989a) and Gordon (1990) have pointed out, the menu cost approach to price rigidity cannot conclusively reduce welfare and therefore explain large fluctuations in output and employment as a deviation from perfect competition, because it involves the comparison of two second-order effects. Third, price rigidity is explained by postulating costs of adjustment of changing prices. If, however, there are costs in adjusting output, as in the theory of investment or inventory, then it is not sure whether the balance of adjustment falls on prices or output.

The above analysis of menu costs is static. The introduction of dynamics means that the issue is no longer whether but rather how often prices will adjust. This depends on the functional form of the price rules used by firms. These fall within two broad categories: 'state-dependent' and 'time-dependent' rules. The former indicate that the price changes whenever it deviates a particular percentage from the desired price, while the latter indicates that price changes occur at fixed intervals because of explicit or implicit contracts with suppliers, the labour force and clients.

The first state-dependent rules were derived for a monopolist who faces demand shocks that take the form of a random walk without drift under fixed costs of adjusting prices (Barro, 1972). In this case the optimal policy is to set the price that maximizes profits for a given value of the demand shock and then to re-adjust it whenever future realizations of shocks (or to be precise the change in a shock) exceed a certain 'floor' or 'ceiling'. The determination of the lower and upper bounds, called *S–s*, from which this literature derives its name, depends on a comparison of the opportunity cost of not adjusting the price (i.e. having the 'wrong' price) with the cost of changing it. Explicit analytic solutions have not been derived except under very restrictive assumptions, such as the one made in the Barro model that demand shocks follow a random walk, instead of serial correlation as observed in business cycles.

The Barro model cannot explain aggregate price stickiness and the stylized facts because money is neutral. Although this is the result of the particular assumptions made, their relaxation makes the *S–s* approach analytically intractable and therefore there are as yet no further firm results – see also Blanchard and Fischer (1990, chapter 8), Caplin and Spulber (1987) and Sheshinski and Weiss (1983) for some attempts at extending this approach.

Theories of Nominal Wage Rigidity

The alternative approach to explaining aggregate price stickiness is to explore time-dependent rules based on explicit or implicit contracts. Initial attempts emphasized overlapping staggered contracts in the labour market (Fischer, 1977b; Phelps and Taylor, 1977; Taylor, 1980). A contract specifies a fixed nominal wage for the duration of the contract. Staggered labour contracts reflect the absence of synchronization in the renewal of these contracts and therefore imply that in different firms wages change at different times. In these models prices in the goods market are flexible, but wages are sticky. The labour market fails to clear because at any point in time wages are given and therefore employment is determined by fluctuations in the demand for labour. In the Fischer model the nominal wage is set for the duration of the contract with the aim of maintaining a constant real wage rate on the basis of price expectations that are formed rationally. In the Taylor model the wage rate is affected by past wages because of an overhang of unexpired contracts and expectations of both future wages and demand conditions in the labour market. Again expectations are formed rationally. The attraction of models on staggered contracts is that their assumptions are realistic, reflecting observed behaviour in developed economies.

The contribution of these models was to clarify the role of rational expectations in producing the 'policy irrelevance proposition' in models of market clearing. Sargent and Wallace (1975) had previously shown that if expectations are formed rationally in a model of market clearing, then output is invariant to the money supply rule chosen by the monetary authorities, the policy irrelevance proposition. However, this conclusion results from the assumption of continuous market clearing rather than the assumption of rational expectations. In the Fischer and Taylor models, in which there is wage stickiness, monetary policy affects output in the short run despite the presence of rational expectations.

More recently, Blanchard (1986) generalized these models by extending the staggering to price decisions too. In a monopolistic environment in the goods and the labour markets workers attempt to maintain their real wage rate, while firms attempt to maintain their mark-ups of prices over wages. Expectations are formed rationally, but under staggering of price and wage decisions shifts in aggregate demand, caused, for example, by changes in nominal money supply, have long-lasting effects on output. The aggregate price level responds slowly to these nominal shocks, thereby producing a wage–price spiral in the adjustment to long-run equilibrium. Furthermore, on the assumption that the economy is hit predominantly by aggregate demand shocks, there is no correlation between the real wage rate and output. In this model, therefore, there is scope for stabilization policy.

In the Blanchard–Fischer–Taylor models staggering is not explained and the timing of price changes is exogenous. Therefore the question arises as to why firms and unions adopt staggering when they would be better off under synchronization. Ball and Romer (1989b) investigate the conditions under which synchronization and staggering are optimal and an equilibrium. They assume that synchronization is socially optimal, but market failure leads to staggering. The model is an extension of Blanchard's, in which the timing of staggering is made endogenous and there is an incentive for staggering because it is assumed that there are firm-specific shocks that arrive at different times for different firms. Ball and Romer reach two major conclusions. First, staggering is inefficient, but it can be an equilibrium provided there are firm-specific shocks of any size. The reason is that 'a firm's decision to adjust at different times from others contributes, through its effect on the behaviour of the price level, to movements in relative prices and real aggregate demand that harm all firms. In a large economy, each price setter ignores these effects because it takes the behaviour of the price level as given' (Ball and Romer, 1989b, p. 180). Second, multiple equilibria are possible and therefore both synchronization and staggering can be an equilibrium.

There are three drawbacks with nominal wage stickiness based on staggered contracts. First, these models cannot explain the diversity of stylized facts across time, across industries and across countries. Second, the approach lacks microfoundations. Staggered price and wage decisions are unexplained and they are not derived from optimizing behaviour. As Barro (1977) has pointed out, this approach leaves open the question as to why, if fluctuations in output and employment are costly, firms and unions do not write contracts that avoid such costs. Third, in most of these models the predicted behaviour of the real wage rate is not consistent with the stylized facts described above. In particular, with a fixed nominal wage rate a negative disturbance in demand lowers the price level and raises the real wage rate, thereby suggesting a counter-cyclical behaviour of the real wage rate. However, as we have seen the evidence suggests that the real wage rate fluctuates procyclically.

It follows from the above survey that there is not yet available a satisfactory theory of wage–price stickiness that can explain all stylized facts in the labour and the goods markets. Nevertheless, these theories are useful in clarifying the issues and suggesting the ways for future research.

Part III

The Open Economy

8

Model 8 An Open Economy Model with Fixed Exchange Rates

The analysis in this model concerns an open economy on both the demand and the supply sides under fixed exchange rates. A demand side open economy is one that trades with the rest of the world in final goods (i.e. it exports part of its output to the rest of the world and imports some of the output produced by the rest of the world). Households and firms decide, *ceteris paribus*, on whether to buy domestically produced goods or foreign goods on the basis of their relative prices. Similarly, foreign households or firms decide to import goods or buy their own products on the basis of relative prices. Other things being equal, if domestic goods become more expensive relative to foreign goods, domestic households and firms switch to foreign products and foreigners switch to their own products. Accordingly, our imports rise and our exports fall. The ratio of relative prices expressed in domestic currency is a measure of the country's competitiveness or real exchange rate.

A supply side open economy is one that relies on imported raw materials for the production of its output. Under a system of fixed exchange rates the central bank is obliged to buy or sell whatever amount of foreign currency is demanded or supplied at a fixed price. The extent to which a central bank can support a fixed exchange rate system depends on the amount of foreign reserves it holds (i.e. the stock of foreign currency held by the central bank on behalf of the private sector) or its ability to borrow foreign currency from abroad (either from other central banks and the International Monetary Fund or directly from the foreign private sector). Assuming no borrowing, foreign reserves are the accumulation of all previous current account balances. If the country exports more than it imports in terms of goods and services, then it is earning (accumulating) foreign currency. If, on the other hand, the country runs a deficit in the current account, then it is losing (decumulating) foreign currency.

Assuming that the government is not engaged in imports/exports, an increase in foreign reserves means that the wealth of the private sector is rising and a decrease that wealth is falling. Nevertheless, the central bank has a choice regarding the form in which wealth is held. In this model the central bank may decide to increase (decrease) money or bonds (both of which are the liabilities of the government) by the change in foreign reserves. If all net foreign currency that is earned by the private sector increases wealth in the form of money, then the central bank is *monetizing* the change in foreign reserves. If, on the other hand, private sector wealth is increased in the form of government bonds, then the central bank is *sterilizing* the change in foreign reserves. The degree of sterilization has important implications for the efficacy of monetary and fiscal policy. The aim of this chapter is to analyse the implications of the combined choice of sterilization and method of budget finance: (a) for the stability and effectiveness of fiscal and monetary policy; and (b) for various shocks in exogenous variables, namely oil price and world trade.

8.1 Assumptions

The analysis, as in the previous chapter, concerns a non-inflationary economy; that is, an economy in which the steady-state rate of inflation is zero. Inflation is produced in the transition from one long-run equilibrium to the other. Although inflation is zero in steady state the price level and relative prices are different between two steady states. The emphasis in this chapter is on the response of the economy to changes in the price level and relative prices rather than inflation rates. In the framework of this and the next chapter neutral monetary policy means that the nominal supply of money remains fixed. Changes in the price level, induced in the transition to a new steady state, cause changes in real money balances, which in turn have further repercussions for the dynamic adjustment path and the new steady state.

The economy is producing a single good, which is an imperfect substitute for the internationally traded good. There are three inputs of production: labour, imported raw materials and capital. The latter is fixed. Potential output is also fixed and the rate of growth of labour productivity is zero. The model used in this chapter is model 7, extended only to reflect the openness of the economy on the demand side. In order to concentrate on the interaction of the degree of sterilization with the method of budget finance we abstract from the non-linearities of interest payments on government debt. These were considered in model 7 and it was shown that in their presence the method of budget finance affects both the dynamic path and the new steady state.

8.2 The Model

The model is assumed to be quarterly and consists of equations (8.1) to (8.24).

$$D = C + I + G + X - Q \tag{8.1}$$

$$C = \mathcal{U}(\delta_{CY})\left\{\alpha_{CY}YD + \alpha_{Copi}(1 - HRT)\left(\frac{OPI}{CPI}\right)\right\}$$
$$+ \alpha_{Cr}\mathcal{U}(\delta_{Cr})(r - cpi^e) + \alpha_{Cv}\mathcal{U}(\delta_{Cv})\frac{V_{-1}}{CPI} + \alpha_{CC}C_{-1} + \gamma_C \tag{8.2}$$

$$\alpha_{Cr} < 0, \quad 0 < \alpha_{CY}, \quad \alpha_{Copi}, \quad \alpha_{Cv}, \quad \alpha_{CC} < 1$$

$$I = \alpha_{IY}\mathcal{U}(\delta_{IY})Y + \alpha_{Ir}\mathcal{U}(\delta_{Ir})(r - p^e)$$
$$- \alpha_{IK}K_{-1} + \alpha_{II}I_{-1} + \gamma_I \tag{8.3}$$

$$\alpha_{IY} > 0, \quad \alpha_{Ir} < 0, \quad 0 < \alpha_{IK}, \quad \alpha_{II} < 1$$

$$COMP = \frac{Pe}{PW} \tag{8.4}$$

$$Q = \alpha_{QY}\mathcal{U}(\delta_{QTFE})TFE + \alpha_{QCOMP}\mathcal{U}(\delta_{QCOMP})COMP$$
$$+ \alpha_{QQ}Q_{-1} + \gamma_Q \tag{8.5}$$

$$0 < \alpha_{QTFE}, \quad \alpha_{QQ} < 1, \quad \alpha_{QCOMP} > 0$$

$$X = \alpha_{XWT}\mathcal{U}(\delta_{XWT})WT + \alpha_{XCOMP}\mathcal{U}(\delta_{XCOMP})COMP$$
$$+ \alpha_{XX}X_{-1} + \gamma_X \tag{8.6}$$

$$0 < \alpha_{XWT}, \quad \alpha_{XX} < 1, \quad \alpha_{XCOMP} < 0$$

$$Y = D \tag{8.7}$$

$$YD = (1 - SRT)P\frac{Y}{CPI} \tag{8.8}$$

$$OPI = ((1 + r_{-1})^{1/4} - 1)B_{-1} \tag{8.9}$$

$$\frac{M}{CPI} = \alpha_{MY}\mathcal{U}(\delta_{MY})Y + \alpha_{Mv}\mathcal{U}(\delta_{Mv})\frac{V_{-1}}{CPI} + \alpha_{Mr}\mathcal{U}(\delta_{Mr})r + \gamma_M \tag{8.10}$$

$$\alpha_{MY} > 0, \quad \alpha_{Mr} < 0, \quad 0 < \alpha_{Mv} < 1$$

$$PSBR = PG + ((1 + r_{-1})^{1/4} - 1)B_{-1} - PT \tag{8.11}$$

$$T = SRTY + HRT\frac{OPI}{CPI} \tag{8.12}$$

$$M = M_{-1} + \alpha_{monfin}\,PSBR + (1 - \alpha_{ster})\Delta RES + \Delta MB \tag{8.13}$$

$$0 \leq \alpha_{monfin}, \quad \alpha_{ster} \leq 1$$

$$B = B_{-1} + (1 - \alpha_{monfin})PSBR + \alpha_{ster}\Delta RES + \Delta OMO \tag{8.14}$$

$$CB = PX - PMQ \tag{8.15}$$

$$\Delta RES = CB \tag{8.16}$$

$$V = M + B \tag{8.17}$$

$$w = \alpha_{wy}\mathfrak{U}(\delta_{wy})\,(y - \bar{y}) + \alpha_{wY}\mathfrak{U}(\delta_{wY})\,(Y - \bar{Y})$$

$$\quad + \alpha_{wp^e}\mathfrak{U}(\delta_{wcpi^e})cpi^e + \gamma_w \tag{8.18}$$

$$\alpha_{wy} > 0, \quad 0 \leq \alpha_{wcpi^e} \leq 1$$

$$P = \alpha_{PW}W + (1 - \alpha_{PW})\frac{PIW}{e} + \alpha_{PY}(y - \bar{y}) + \gamma_P \tag{8.19}$$

$$0 \leq \alpha_{PW} \leq 1, \quad \alpha_{PY} > 0$$

$$CPI = \alpha_{CPIP}P + (1 - \alpha_{CPIP})PM \tag{8.20}$$

$$0 \leq \alpha_{CPIP} \leq 1$$

$$PM = (\alpha_{PMPW}PW + (1 - \alpha_{PMPW})PIW)/\mathfrak{U}(\delta_{PMe})e \tag{8.21}$$

$$0 \leq \alpha_{PMPW} \leq 1$$

$$p^e = p^e_{-1} + \alpha_{p^ep}(p_{-1} - p^e_{-1}) \tag{8.22}$$

$$cpi^e = cpi^e_{-1} + \alpha_{p^ep}(cpi_{-1} - cpi^e_{-1}) \tag{8.23}$$

$$0 \leq \alpha_{p^ep} \leq 1$$

$$TFE = C + I + G + X \tag{8.24}$$

Variable definition		Initial steady-state value
B	= (nominal) stock of government bonds, at current prices	50
C	= real consumer expenditure	65
CB	= current balance in domestic currency	0
$COMP$	= index of competitiveness	1
CPI	= consumer price index	1

	Variable definition	Initial steady-state value
cpi	= actual inflation rate (as measured by the change in the consumer price index), i.e. $cpi = \dfrac{CPI - CPI_{-1}}{CPI_{-1}}$	0
cpi^e	= expected inflation rate in period t, with information available at $t - 1$	0
D	= aggregate demand	100
e	= exchange rate, foreign price of domestic currency, i.e. units of foreign currency per unit of domestic currency	1
G	= real government expenditure	25
HRT	= higher rate of income tax on other personal income	0.6
I	= real gross investment expenditure	10
K	= capital stock	200
M	= (nominal) money stock, currency in circulation (notes and coin)	10
MB	= autonomous monetary base, at current prices	0
OMO	= open market operations instrument	0
OPI	= other personal income (interest income), in nominal terms	2.0768
P	= producer price index	1
p	= actual inflation rate (as measured by the producer price index, i.e. $p = \dfrac{P - P_{-1}}{P_{-1}}$	0
p^e	= expected inflation in period t, with information in $t - 1$	
PIW	= world price of imported raw materials, in foreign currency	1
PM	= price of imports, in domestic currency	1
$PSBR$	= public sector borrowing requirement, at current prices	0
PW	= price of imported final goods, in foreign currency	1
Q	= real imports of goods and services in domestic currency	25
r	= interest rate (yield) on government bonds	0.1

Variable definition		Initial steady-state value
RES	= level of foreign exchange reserves in domestic currency	40
SRT	= standard rate of income tax	0.25
T	= total tax revenues, in real terms	25
TFE	= real total final expenditure	125
V	= stock of private sector wealth, at current prices	300
W	= nominal wage rate	1
w	= actual wage inflation, i.e. change in the nominal wage rate,	

$$w = \frac{W - W_{-1}}{W_{-1}}$$

0

X	= real exports of goods and services in domestic currency	25
Y	= domestic output, real income	100
y	= rate of growth of output (GDP),	

i.e. $y = \dfrac{Y - Y_{-1}}{Y_{-1}}$

0

| $\bar{Y}$ | = potential (or capacity) output | 100 |
| $\bar{y}$ | = rate of growth of potential (or capacity) output, | |

i.e. $\bar{y} = \dfrac{\bar{Y} - \bar{Y}_{-1}}{\bar{Y}_{-1}}$

0

| *YD* | = real disposable income | 75 |

$$\mathcal{U}(\delta)X = \sum_{i=0}^{3} \delta_i X_{-i} \bigg/ \sum_{i=0}^{3} \delta_i \text{ is a unitary moving average operator.}$$

In the exercises reported below $\mathcal{U}(\delta) = 1\ 0\ 0\ 0$, that is the total effect is instantaneous.

Coefficient	Value	Coefficient	Value
α_{CY}	0.35	α_{XX}	0.25
α_{Copi}	0.5	γ_X	23.75
α_{Cr}	−25	α_{MY}	0.075
α_{Cv}	0.065	α_{Mr}	−100
α_{CC}	0.5	α_{Mv}	0.01
γ_C	−10.75	γ_M	9.5
α_{IY}	0.0775	α_{monfin}	1.0

Coefficient	Value	Coefficient	Value
α_{Ir}	-25	α_{ster}	1.0
α_{IK}	0.05	α_{wy}	0.5
α_{II}	0.0	α_{wp^e}	1.0
γ_I	14.75	γ_w	0.0
α_{QTFE}	0.1	α_{PW}	0.85
α_{QCOMP}	15	α_{Py}	0.5
α_{QQ}	0.75	γ_P	0.0
γ_Q	-21.25	α_{CPIP}	0.85
α_{XWT}	0.20	α_{PMPW}	0.7
α_{XCOMP}	-25	$\alpha_{p^e p}$	0.5

All equations are the same as in model 7, with the following exceptions, all of which arise from the demand side openness of the economy. Equation (8.1) defines aggregate demand in real terms as the sum of consumption, investment, government expenditure on goods and services and exports, less imports of goods and services. The difference between export and import volumes is also called net exports.

Equation (8.5) specifies imports of goods and services at constant prices as a positive function of total final expenditure, and competitiveness. Total final expenditure is the sum of consumption, investment, government expenditure and exports (8.24). The rationale of making imports a function of total final expenditure is the following. Imports are demanded by households and the government for consumption and by firms for capital goods and raw materials. When factor incomes increase, the demand for imports by households rises. Thus, an increase in consumer expenditure leads, *ceteris paribus*, to a rise in imports. When demand is picking up, either in the domestic economy or abroad, firms expand their capacity by ordering capital goods at home and abroad, thereby boosting imports. Hence, an increase in gross fixed capital formation (investment) or exports leads, other things being equal, to a rise in imports. Finally, an increase in government expenditure also leads to a rise in imports.

Competitiveness is defined in equation (8.4) as the ratio of domestic to foreign prices converted into domestic currency. Thus, an increase in the price of domestically produced goods or a rise in the exchange rate leads to a loss in competitiveness. On the other hand, an increase in the price of foreign goods leads to a gain in competitiveness. Imports depend on competitiveness. Other things being equal, a loss in competitiveness results in higher imports. The effect of competitiveness and total final expenditure on imports lasts for more than one period through an autoregressive process.

Equation (8.6) defines exports of goods and services as a function of world trade and competitiveness. A rise in world trade is consistent with an increase in foreign demand, which leads to higher exports, *ceteris paribus*. A loss in competitiveness results in lower exports, other things being equal, as foreign demand is switching into their own home output.

Equation (8.15) defines the trade account of the balance of payments at current prices as the difference between the value of exports and the value of imports. Under a fixed exchange rate system a surplus (deficit) in the trade balance implies an increase (decrease) in foreign reserves (8.16).

A surplus in the trade account increases private sector wealth. Since the central bank is holding the foreign reserves that the private sector has earned it must give back to the private sector the equivalent in the form of money or bonds. If the central bank keeps the money supply unchanged and allows the stock of bonds to rise by the surplus in the trade account, then the effect of foreign reserves on the money supply is sterilized. If, on the other hand, the central bank keeps the stock of bonds fixed and allows the monetization of foreign reserves, then there is no sterilization. This choice is reflected in the value of α in equations (8.13) and (8.14). If $\alpha_{ster} = 1$, there is sterilization. The money supply remains unchanged according to (8.13), while the whole of the change in reserves is absorbed in the stock of government bonds (8.14). If $\alpha_{ster} = 0$, there is no sterilization. According to (8.13) the change in foreign reserves raises the money supply, while the stock of bonds remains unchanged (8.14).

In all exercises reported below interest payments on government debt are exogenized.

8.3 Monetary Policy

In an open economy with fixed exchange rates the effects of monetary policy depend on the method of budget finance and the degree of sterilization of foreign reserves. Easy monetary policy stimulates the economy and results in a budget surplus and a trade account deficit. If the central bank operates a policy of monetary targets then private sector wealth falls as the government retires debt from the market in response to the budget surplus. If, on the other hand, the central bank follows a bondist rule (i.e. it has a debt target), then the supply of money declines, moderating or even offsetting the initial increase. Similarly, the central bank has another choice regarding the monetization of the trade account deficit. If a sterilization policy is pursued, the money supply remains unchanged and private sector wealth declines as the central bank retires government debt from the market. Without sterilization the initial increase in the supply of money is reversed as the country runs a trade account deficit. Thus, four cases can be distinguished: monetary targets with and without sterilization and debt targets with and without sterilization. In order to keep the number of cases analysed to a minimum we consider only the two extremes: monetary targets with sterilization and debt targets without sterilization.

Box 8.1 provides a schematic view of the main channels through which expansionary monetary policy in the form of an open market purchase affects the economy. A policy of monetary targets with sterilization implies that after the initial increase in the supply of money and the equivalent reduction in the stock of government bonds the money supply remains unchanged. On the other hand, a debt target without sterilization implies that after the initial reduction the stock of government bonds remains unchanged.

Channels (a) to (f) are the same as in model 7 and therefore need only a brief comment. An open market purchase results in a cut in the nominal and real interest rate, which stimulates demand and therefore output – channel (a). The decrease in the nominal interest rate implies lower interest payments on existing government debt and thus smaller real other personal income. This depresses consumption, demand and hence

---

Box 8.1 The transmission of monetary policy (open market purchase) under monetary and debt targets with and without sterilization

$$(r - p^e)\downarrow \Rightarrow I\uparrow \Rightarrow D\uparrow \Rightarrow Y\uparrow \tag{a}$$

$$\Delta M\uparrow = -\Delta B\downarrow \Rightarrow r\downarrow \Rightarrow \begin{cases} \dfrac{OPI}{CPI}\downarrow \Rightarrow C\downarrow \Rightarrow D\downarrow \Rightarrow Y\downarrow \tag{b} \end{cases}$$

$$\dfrac{PSBR}{P}\downarrow \Rightarrow \begin{cases} \dfrac{B}{P}\downarrow \Rightarrow \dfrac{V}{CPI}\downarrow \Rightarrow C\downarrow \Rightarrow Y\downarrow \tag{c1} \\[2em] \dfrac{M}{P}\downarrow \Rightarrow r\uparrow \Rightarrow D\downarrow \Rightarrow Y\downarrow \tag{c2} \end{cases}$$

$$(a) > ((b) + (c))\Big\} u\downarrow \Rightarrow w\uparrow \Rightarrow p\uparrow \Rightarrow \begin{cases} \dfrac{OPI}{CPI}\downarrow \Rightarrow C\downarrow \Rightarrow Y\downarrow \tag{d} \\[1.5em] \dfrac{V}{CPI}\downarrow \Rightarrow C\downarrow \Rightarrow Y\downarrow \tag{e} \\[1.5em] \dfrac{M}{CPI}\downarrow \Rightarrow r\uparrow \Rightarrow I\downarrow \Rightarrow Y\downarrow \tag{f} \end{cases}$$

$$Y\uparrow \Rightarrow \qquad Q\uparrow$$
$$\Big\} Y\downarrow \text{ and } CB\downarrow \Rightarrow \Delta RES\downarrow \Rightarrow \begin{cases} \dfrac{B}{P}\downarrow \Rightarrow \dfrac{V}{CPI}\downarrow \Rightarrow C\downarrow \Rightarrow Y\downarrow \tag{g1} \\[1.5em] \dfrac{M}{P}\downarrow \Rightarrow r\uparrow \Rightarrow D\downarrow \Rightarrow Y\downarrow \tag{g2} \end{cases}$$
$$P\uparrow \Rightarrow COMP\uparrow \Rightarrow X\downarrow \text{ and } Q\uparrow$$

output – channel (b). The decrease in the interest rate and the increase in income lead to a budget surplus. With a policy of monetary targets the central bank retires government debt from the market, thereby diminishing real private sector wealth and hence consumption, demand and output – channel (c1). If the central bank follows a debt target, the budget surplus leads to a reduction in the money supply, which moderates the initial stimulus of easy monetary policy – channel (c2).

Irrespective of whether the central bank follows monetary or debt targets at the initial phase of the adjustment process income rises (i.e. channel (a) exceeds the combined effect of (b) and (c)) and this leads to lower unemployment and rising wage and price inflation. Higher prices reduce real other personal income, real private sector wealth and real money balances. The first two forces reduce consumption, demand and output – channels (d) and (e) – and strengthen the contractionary effects of channels (b) and (c). The reduction in real money balances reverses the interest rate adjustment process, thereby curtailing investment and output – channel (f).

The initial increase in income boosts imports and leads to a trade (and current) account deficit. Furthermore, the increase in domestic prices leads to a loss in competitiveness and consequently to a cut in exports and a rise in imports. This further deteriorates the trade account deficit and leads to a continued loss in reserves. Moreover, the rise in imports and fall in exports reduces even more the stimulus to output. Thus, easy monetary policy is less expansionary in a demand side open economy than in a closed economy because of the decline in net exports (exports minus imports).

If the central bank sterilizes the effect of the drain in reserves on the money supply, the stock of government debt is reduced, thereby diminishing real private sector wealth and hence demand and output – channel (g1). This adds further to the contractionary forces of channels (b) to (f), lowering the initial stimulus of easy monetary policy and accelerating the reversal process. If, on the other hand, the central bank does not follow a sterilization policy, the loss in reserves decreases the money supply and reverses the initial fall in the interest rate, thus cutting investment and output – channel (g2).

The effects of easy monetary policy with and without sterilization are highlighted in figure 8.1. Since the economy is non-inflationary and in steady state the inflation rate is always equal to zero, the *SP* and *LP* curves are drawn in the prices–output space (P, Y) rather than the inflation–output space (p, Y).

In figure 8.1c the *BS* curve shows the budget surplus/deficit as a positive function of income. The budget surplus is defined as taxes minus government spending and is therefore the opposite of PSBR. The *BS* curve is a positive function of income because an increase in income

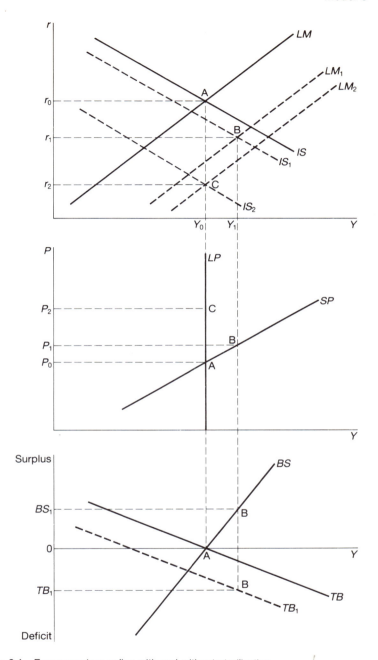

Figure 8.1 Easy monetary policy with and without sterilization

raises taxes and improves the financial position of the government. An increase in government expenditure or transfer payments will shift the *BS* curve down and to the right, since at any given level of income the budget surplus is reduced or the deficit is enlarged. A cut in the income tax rate will rotate the *BS* curve clockwise, because at any given level of income taxes are reduced and the budget surplus diminishes. The *TB* curve in figure 8.1c shows the trade (or current account) balance as a decreasing function of income. A rise in income increases imports and lowers the trade balance. A loss in competitiveness caused by either an appreciation in the exchange rate or higher domestic prices will shift the *TB* curve to the left, since, at any given level of income, imports will rise and exports will fall, thereby deteriorating the trade balance. An increase in world trade will shift the *TB* curve upwards and to the right as at any given level of income exports will rise and the trade balance will improve. An increase in real private sector wealth will shift the *TB* curve to the left as imports rise and the trade balance deteriorates.

Initial long-run equilibrium is at A with output, interest rate and prices Y_0, r_0 and P_0 respectively, and the budget and the trade account balanced. The increase in the supply of money shifts the *LM* curve to the right to LM_1 and output expands. The stimulus in demand pushes prices up in the short run along the initial *SP* curve. Net exports decline as income rises and higher prices harm competitiveness, causing a leftward shift in the *IS* curve to IS_1. In the short run the interest rate falls to r_1 and output expands to Y_1 as equilibrium is attained at B. Prices rise to P_1 along the *SP* curve to B. The rise in income increases tax revenues, resulting in a budget surplus equal to BS_1. The loss in competitiveness due to higher prices shifts the *TB* curve to the left to TB_1. The rise in income and the loss in competitiveness cause a deficit in the trade account equal to TB_1.

If the central bank, after the increase in the money supply, re-imposes its monetary target and sterilizes the effect of the loss in reserves on the money supply, private sector wealth is reduced as the stock of government bonds decreases in response to the budget surplus and the trade deficit. The decline in wealth shifts the *LM* curve further to the right to LM_2 and the *IS* curve to the left to IS_2, with long-run equilibrium at C. The interest rate falls to r_2 and output returns to its initial equilibrium Y_0. Prices rise to P_2 as the *SP* curve adjusts upwards to C.

If, on the other hand, the central bank does not sterilize the effect of the loss in reserves on the money supply and follows a bondist rule, according to which the stock of government bonds remains unchanged, the money supply is reduced in response to the budget surplus and the trade deficit, while private sector wealth is fixed. In this case the *LM* curve gradually returns to its original position and equilibrium is attained back at A.

An illustration of the transmission mechanism of monetary policy is provided by simulating Model 8 numerically under monetary targets with sterilization (i.e. keeping the nominal money supply fixed after the shock) and under debt targets without sterilization (i.e. keeping the nominal stock of government bonds fixed after the shock). The increase in the nominal supply of money is implemented via an open market purchase of £1 billion of government bonds by the central bank. This increases the supply of money and reduces the stock of bonds by £1 billion in the first period. Under monetary targets with sterilization the open market purchase results in a permanent increase in the nominal supply of money by £1 billion. The budget surplus and the sterilization of the current account deficit imply that the stock of government bonds is reduced by more than £1 billion after the initial shock. In the other extreme case of a debt target without sterilization the stock of nominal bonds is permanently reduced by £1 billion and the money supply is increased by less than £1 billion after the initial shock. There are two intermediate cases. The first is monetary targets without sterilization. This implies that the central bank retires debt from the market in response to the budget surplus, thereby causing a decline in wealth, but allows the money supply to shrink in response to the loss in reserves associated with the trade deficit. The second intermediate case is a debt target with sterilization. This implies that the central bank allows the money supply to decrease in response to the budget surplus and retires government debt from the market, thus causing a decline in wealth in response to the loss in reserves associated with the trade deficit.

Figures 8.2 to 8.5 show the dynamic response of output, prices (consumer price index), interest rate and real wealth to an open market purchase of £1 billion of government bonds by the central bank under the two extreme cases of monetary targets with sterilization and bond targets without sterilization. Under monetary targets with sterilization output rises for the first four quarters and then gradually returns to its initial steady state monotonically (figure 8.2). With debt targets without sterilization output rises for the first three quarters and then returns to its initial steady state on an oscillatory adjustment path. Furthermore, at its peak output rises more with monetary targets with sterilization than with debt targets without sterilization (the multipliers are 0.50 and 0.34 respectively). The upswing of the business cycle is caused in both cases by the fall in the interest rate in the first phase of the dynamic adjustment, which stimulates domestic demand (consumption and investment). The system converges more quickly to its long-run equilibrium with debt targets without sterilization.

Figure 8.3 depicts the dynamic adjustment path of prices. Under monetary targets with sterilization, prices rise more and for a longer period than under debt targets without sterilization, before they return

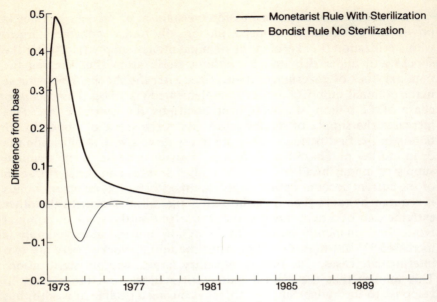

Figure 8.2   Output response to an open market purchase

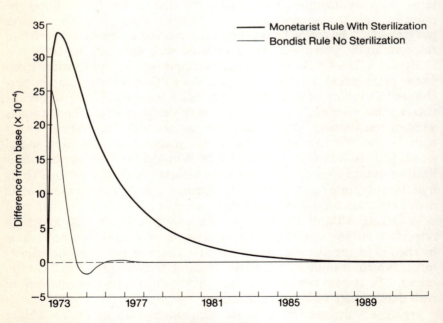

Figure 8.3   Prices response to an open market purchase

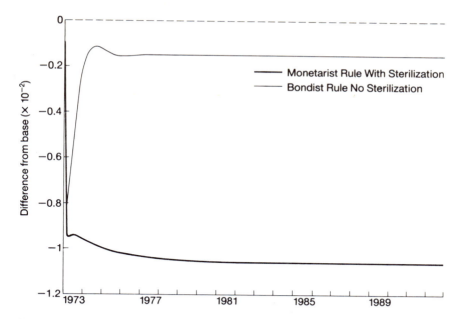

Figure 8.4   Interest rate response to an open market purchase

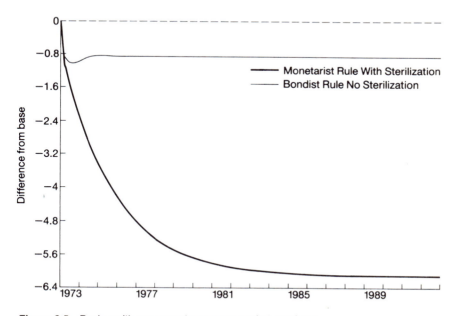

Figure 8.5   Real wealth response to an open market purchase

to the initial steady state. The behaviour of prices reflects with a few lags the conditions of demand in the goods market.

Figure 8.4 depicts the dynamic adjustment of the interest rate. The immediate effect of the open market purchase is a fall in the interest rate in response to the initial excess supply of money. The drastic fall in the interest rate is caused by the different speeds of adjustment of the assets markets and the goods market. The former clear instantly whereas the latter clears sluggishly. The income expansion causes a budget surplus and a trade deficit with a loss in reserves. With monetary targets with sterilization the surplus in the budget and the loss in reserves lead to a decline in real wealth (figure 8.5). In the new steady state real wealth falls by £6 billion. The demand for money is reduced as wealth and income decline and the interest rate falls further to equilibrate the assets markets (figure 8.4). In the new steady state the interest rate is 1 per cent lower than the original long-run equilibrium.

With debt targets without sterilization real wealth falls by almost £1 billion, the extent of the open market purchase (see figure 8.5). The central bank reverses the expansion of the money supply in response to the budget surplus and the loss in reserves associated with the trade deficit, and therefore the interest rate returns towards its initial steady state (see figure 9.4). In the case of a straight increase in the money supply (i.e. a helicopter drop) rather than an open market purchase, real wealth remains unchanged and the interest rate returns exactly to its initial steady state.

8.4 Fiscal Policy under Bond and Money Finance

An expansionary fiscal policy creates a stimulus to the economy, with higher prices and a deficit in the budget and the trade account. The effectiveness of fiscal policy depends on the method of budget finance and the degree of sterilization of foreign reserves. The nominal money supply is increased if the government finances the budget deficit through money, but is decreased if the central bank does not sterilize the loss in reserves. The nominal stock of government bonds remains unchanged. In the other extreme case the nominal stock of money remains fixed and the government finances the budget deficit through bonds, while the central bank sterilizes the loss in reserves.

Box 8.2 provides a schematic view of the main channels through which an increase in government expenditure affects the economy under bond finance with and without sterilization. Channels (a) to (h) are the same as in model 7 and need only a brief comment. The increase in government expenditure stimulates demand and hence output – channel (a). The rise in income leads to an increase in the demand for money, thereby

Box 8.2 The transmission of fiscal policy (government expenditure) under bond finance with and without sterilization

$$G\uparrow = \begin{cases} D\uparrow \Rightarrow Y\uparrow \Rightarrow \begin{cases} YD\uparrow \Rightarrow C\uparrow \Rightarrow D\uparrow \Rightarrow Y\uparrow & \text{(a)} \\ \dfrac{M^d}{CPI}\uparrow \Rightarrow r\uparrow \Rightarrow \begin{cases} I\downarrow \Rightarrow D\downarrow \Rightarrow Y\downarrow & \text{(b)} \\ OPI/CPI\uparrow \Rightarrow C\uparrow \Rightarrow Y\uparrow & \text{(c)} \end{cases} \end{cases} \\ \dfrac{PSBR}{P}\uparrow \Rightarrow \dfrac{B}{P}\uparrow \Rightarrow \dfrac{V}{CPI}\uparrow \Rightarrow \begin{cases} \dfrac{V}{CPI}\uparrow \Rightarrow C\uparrow \Rightarrow Y\uparrow & \text{(d)} \end{cases} \end{cases}$$

$$C\uparrow \Rightarrow D\uparrow \Rightarrow Y\uparrow \qquad \text{(e)}$$

$$((a)+(c)+(d)+(e)) > (b) \Big\} u\downarrow \Rightarrow w\uparrow \Rightarrow p\uparrow \Rightarrow \begin{cases} \dfrac{OPI}{CPI}\downarrow \Rightarrow C\downarrow \Rightarrow Y\downarrow & \text{(f)} \\ \dfrac{V}{CPI}\downarrow \Rightarrow C\downarrow \Rightarrow Y\downarrow & \text{(g)} \\ \dfrac{M}{CPI}\downarrow \Rightarrow r\uparrow \Rightarrow I\downarrow \Rightarrow Y\downarrow & \text{(h)} \end{cases}$$

$$Y\uparrow \Rightarrow \qquad Q\uparrow$$
$$\Big\} Y\downarrow \text{ and } CB\downarrow \Rightarrow \Delta RES\downarrow \Rightarrow \begin{cases} \dfrac{B}{P}\downarrow \Rightarrow \dfrac{V}{CPI}\downarrow \Rightarrow C\downarrow \Rightarrow Y\downarrow & \text{(i1)} \\ \dfrac{M}{P}\downarrow \Rightarrow r\uparrow \Rightarrow D\downarrow \Rightarrow Y\downarrow & \text{(i2)} \end{cases}$$
$$P\uparrow \Rightarrow COMP\uparrow \Rightarrow X\downarrow \text{ and } Q\uparrow$$

resulting in higher interest rates. This crowds out investment expenditure – channel (b). Higher interest rates imply increased interest payments on existing government debt, thus boosting other personal income, consumption, demand and output – channel (c). Other things being equal, higher interest rates lead to a budget deficit, which implies a further increase in the stock of government debt. This increases real private sector wealth, thus stimulating consumption and output – channel (d). The increase in government expenditure results in an enlarged deficit and a rise in government debt and hence in private sector wealth. This stimulates consumption – channel (e) – and intensifies the forces that operate in channels (b) to (d).

The rise in output leads to lower unemployment and higher wage and price inflation. Rising prices erode the value of real other personal income, real wealth and real money balances. The first two reduce the initial stimulus by decreasing consumption, thus setting in motion the contractionary phase of the adjustment process – channels (f) and (g). The reduction in real money balances puts a further upward pressure on the interest rate, cutting investment and output – channel (h).

The rise in income increases imports and creates a trade deficit. This is deteriorated by a further rise in imports and a cut in exports owing to a loss in competitiveness resulting from higher domestic prices. The decline in net exports reduces the stimulus of fiscal policy. Thus, as with monetary policy, fiscal policy is less expansionary in an open than a closed economy. Easy fiscal policy creates crowding out, not only via higher interest rates but also through a loss in competitiveness.

If the central bank sterilizes the drain on reserves arising from the trade deficit, private sector wealth will fall as the government reduces its debt from the market. This leads to a cut in consumption and output – channel (i1). If, on the other hand, the central bank does not sterilize the effect of the loss in reserves, the money supply will decrease and the interest rate will rise even higher – channel (i2). This may lead to instability as the interest rate may rise *ad infinitum*.

Figure 8.6 illustrates the effects of an increase in government expenditure under bond finance with sterilization. Initial long-run equilibrium is at A with the budget and the trade account balanced. The increase in government expenditure shifts the *IS* and the *BS* curves to the right. Therefore output expands and the budget turns into deficit. The rise in income boosts imports and creates a trade account deficit. The loss in competitiveness shifts the *TB* curve to the left. Hence, the trade account deficit worsens as the loss in competitiveness retards exports and further increases imports. The reduction in net exports reverses the rightward shift of the *IS* curve, thus moderating the income expansion. In an open economy the degree of crowding out of a fiscal expansion is exacerbated through a reduction in net exports because of a loss in competitiveness. Short-run equilibrium is attained at B, with higher income, Y_1, and higher interest rate, r_1. Part of the fiscal stimulus will be translated into higher prices, P_1, as the economy moves in the short run along the *SP* curve to B. The budget deficit is equal to BS_1 and the trade deficit to TB_1, in the short run.

The effect on real private sector wealth is ambiguous because the fiscal stimulus implies the issue of government bonds and therefore a rise in wealth. However, the trade deficit leads to a drain in reserves and, assuming that the central bank follows a sterilization policy, private sector wealth falls. If the drain on reserves outweighs the issue of new government debt, wealth will fall, and vice versa. If wealth falls, the *IS* curve will shift back to the left and the *LM* curve to the right, and the economy moves to a new long-run equilibrium at C. Income falls relative to the short run. The budget deficit will rise to BS_2. The *TB* curve will shift back to the right as wealth declines and the deficit will shrink to TB_2. In the new steady state the trade deficit is equal to the budget deficit.

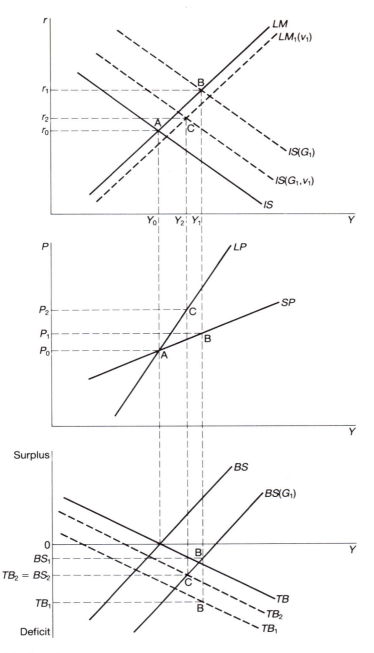

Figure 8.6 Bond finance with sterilization

Box 8.3 The transmission of fiscal policy (government expenditure) under money finance with and without sterilization

$$G\uparrow \Rightarrow \begin{cases} D\uparrow \Rightarrow Y\uparrow \Rightarrow \begin{cases} YD\uparrow \Rightarrow C\uparrow \Rightarrow D\uparrow \Rightarrow Y\uparrow & \text{(a)} \\[2ex] \dfrac{M^d}{CPI}\uparrow \\ \quad\Downarrow \end{cases} \\[6ex] \dfrac{PSBR}{P}\uparrow \Rightarrow \dfrac{M}{CPI}\uparrow \Rightarrow \begin{cases} r\downarrow > r\uparrow \Rightarrow \begin{cases} I\uparrow \Rightarrow D\uparrow \Rightarrow Y\uparrow & \text{(b)} \\ OPI/CPI\downarrow \Rightarrow C\downarrow \Rightarrow Y\downarrow & \text{(c)} \\ \dfrac{V}{CPI}\downarrow \Rightarrow C\downarrow \Rightarrow Y\downarrow & \text{(d)} \end{cases} \\[6ex] \dfrac{V}{CPI}\uparrow \Rightarrow \begin{cases} \dfrac{M^d}{CPI}\uparrow \\[1ex] C\uparrow \Rightarrow D\uparrow \Rightarrow Y\uparrow & \text{(e)} \end{cases} \end{cases} \end{cases}$$

$$((a)+(b)+(e)) > ((c)+(d)) \Big\} \ u\downarrow \Rightarrow w\uparrow \Rightarrow p\uparrow \Rightarrow \begin{cases} \dfrac{OPI}{CPI}\downarrow \Rightarrow C\downarrow \Rightarrow Y\downarrow & \text{(f)} \\[2ex] \dfrac{V}{CPI}\downarrow \Rightarrow C\downarrow \Rightarrow Y\downarrow & \text{(g)} \\[2ex] \dfrac{M}{CPI}\downarrow \Rightarrow r\uparrow \Rightarrow I\downarrow \Rightarrow Y\downarrow & \text{(h)} \end{cases}$$

$$\begin{matrix} Y\uparrow \Rightarrow & Q\uparrow \\ & \\ P\uparrow \Rightarrow COMP\uparrow \Rightarrow X\downarrow \text{ and } Q\uparrow \end{matrix} \Big\} \ Y\downarrow \text{ and } CB\downarrow \Rightarrow \Delta RES\downarrow \Rightarrow \begin{cases} \dfrac{B}{P}\downarrow \Rightarrow \dfrac{V}{CPI}\downarrow \Rightarrow C\downarrow \Rightarrow Y\downarrow & \text{(i1)} \\[2ex] \dfrac{M}{P}\downarrow \Rightarrow r\uparrow \Rightarrow AD\downarrow \Rightarrow Y\downarrow & \text{(i2)} \end{cases}$$

Box 8.3 provides a schematic view of the transmission mechanism of an increase in government expenditure under money finance with and without sterilization. The main difference between bond and money finance arises from the behaviour of the interest rate, which rises in the former and falls in the latter. Under bond finance the interest rate rises gradually as the demand for money is increased in response to higher income and wealth. Under money finance the interest rate falls at the initial stage of the adjustment process in response to the excess supply of money associated with the finance of the increased government expenditure. Later on, the demand for money increases in response to rising income and wealth. This leads to a reversal of the interest rate adjustment process. The different effects of the mode of finance on the interest rate mean that channels (b) to (d) are exactly opposite under bond and money finance. In all other respects bond and money finance have qualitatively the same effects.

The fiscal stimulus leads to a trade account deficit and a loss in reserves irrespective of the mode of finance. At the initial phase of the adjustment process money finance is more expansionary than bond finance because the interest rate provides an additional stimulus in the former, whereas it retards the expansion in the latter. This means that the loss in reserves is larger under money than bond finance. If the government finances the budget deficit through money and the central bank sterilizes the effect of the loss in reserves on the money supply, the economy may be unstable because the reduction in wealth may increase the downward pressure on the interest rate. If, on the other hand, the government finances the budget deficit through bonds and the central bank does not sterilize the loss in reserves, then the money supply will decrease, thus accelerating the contractionary phase of the adjustment process through a faster rise of the interest rate. The economy may again be unstable because lower income implies a higher budget deficit, leading to ever-increasing wealth and necessitating an ever-increasing interest rate.

Figure 8.7 highlights the effects of an increase in government expenditure under money finance without sterilization. Initial equilibrium is at A with the budget and the trade account balanced. The increase in government expenditure shifts the *IS* and *BS* curves to the right to IS_1 and BS_1, stimulating output and creating a budget deficit. The central bank finances this deficit by printing money and the *LM* curve shifts to the right to LM_1. In the short run the economy moves to B with higher output, Y_1, lower interest rate, r_1, higher prices, P_1, and a budget deficit equal to BS_1. Higher prices lead to a loss in competitiveness and the *TB* curve shifts to the left to TB_1. The income expansion causes a trade deficit because of rising imports (a movement along the *TB* curve). The deficit worsens because of the leftward shift of the *TB* curve, associated with the loss in competitiveness. The short-run trade deficit is TB_1.

If the central bank does not sterilize the loss in reserves, the money supply shrinks and the *LM* curve shifts to the left to LM_2. The decrease in wealth associated with the reduction in the money supply shifts the *IS* curve to the left to IS_2 and the *TB* curve to the right to TB_2. The economy moves to a new long-run equilibrium at C, with lower income relative to B, Y_2, higher prices, P_2, lower trade deficit, TB_2, and a higher budget deficit, BS_2. The effect on the interest rate is ambiguous since both the *IS* and the LM curves move to the left. In the new steady state wealth is stationary and this implies that the trade deficit matches the budget deficit.

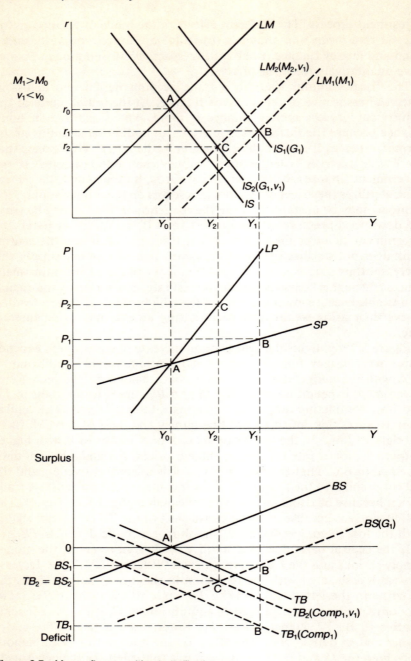

Figure 8.7 Money finance without sterilization

The dynamic adjustment of the economy is not from A to B and then to C in figure 8.7. This is only a conceptual decomposition. An illustration of the transmission mechanism and the time profile of fiscal policy is provided by simulating model 8 numerically under bond finance with sterilization and money finance without sterilization. The former implies that the nominal supply of money remains fixed, while the latter implies that the stock of government bonds in nominal terms is fixed. The two intermediate cases of bond finance without sterilization and money finance with sterilization are also examined because they illustrate that these policies lead to instability.

Figures 8.8 to 8.11 show the dynamic response of output, prices (consumer price index), interest rate and wealth under bond finance with sterilization and money finance without sterilization. Output rises rapidly under both policies and then declines to give the same steady-state multiplier of 0.6 in five years (see figure 8.8). The upswing of the business cycle lasts a bit longer and the stimulus is stronger under money finance without sterilization than under bond finance with sterilization. The dynamic multiplier under money finance without sterilization rises to 1.20, whereas the peak occurs at 0.85 under bond finance with sterilization. More than 90 per cent of the overall adjustment occurs under both policies within the first two years.

In the new steady state prices rise by 0.8 per cent under both policies

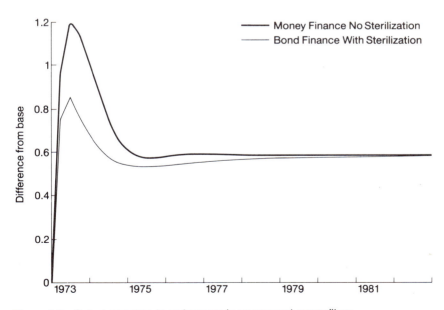

Figure 8.8 Output response to an increase in government expenditure

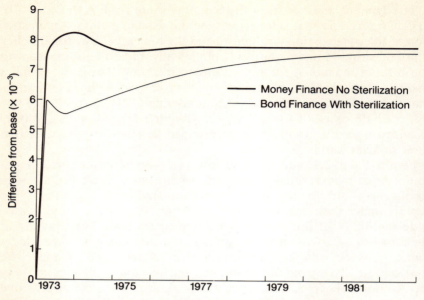

Figure 8.9   Prices response to an increase in government expenditure

(see figure 8.9). However, prices rise faster under money finance without sterilization than under bond finance with sterilization. By the end of the first year prices rise by more than 0.8 per cent with the former and less than 0.6 per cent with the latter. The behaviour of prices reflects demand conditions in the goods market under the two policy regimes.

The reason why the stimulus in output is greater under money finance without sterilization than under bond finance with sterilization lies in the behaviour of the interest rate (see figure 8.10). The former causes an immediate fall in the interest rate equal to 65 basis points by the end of the first year, while the latter causes a slight increase in the interest rate. The interest rate falls under money finance without sterilization in response to the increase in the money supply, while it rises under bond finance without sterilization because of the increase in income and wealth.

Under money finance without sterilization real private sector wealth falls to its steady state value very rapidly, whereas under bond finance with sterilization it falls on impact, but then gradually rises (see figure 8.11). In the new steady state wealth is higher by £3 billion. The decline in wealth under money finance without sterilization is due to the loss in foreign reserves associated with the trade account deficit. This more than offsets the rise in wealth resulting from the finance of the budget

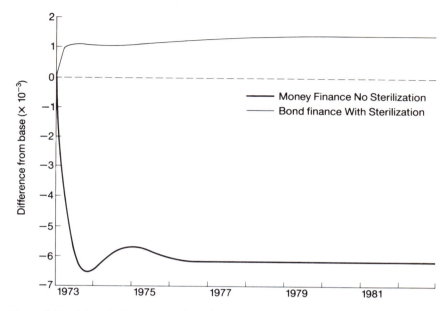

Figure 8.10   Interest rate response to an increase in government expenditure

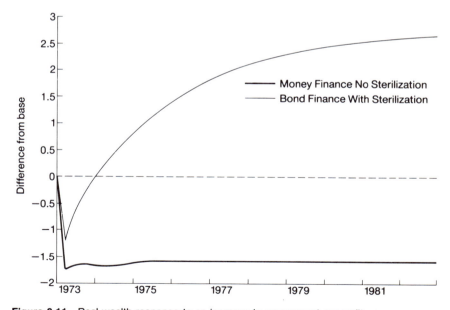

Figure 8.11   Real wealth response to an increase in government expenditure

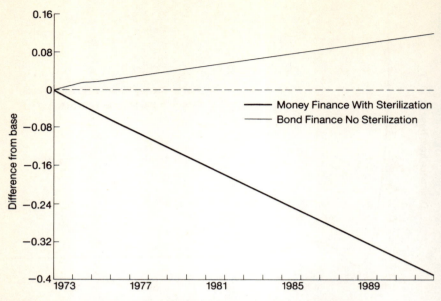

Figure 8.12   Interest rate response to an increase in government expenditure

deficit. The rise in wealth under bond finance with sterilization is due to the finance of the budget deficit, which more than offsets the decline in wealth associated with the loss of foreign reserves.

Figures 8.12 and 8.13 show the dynamic adjustment of interest rate and wealth under money finance with sterilization and bond finance without sterilization. The former implies that the supply of money is allowed to increase to provide finance to the budget deficit, but the stock of bonds is diminished as a response of the trade deficit. On the other hand, bond finance without sterilization implies that the government issues more bonds to finance the budget deficit, but the supply of money is reduced by the central bank as a result of the trade deficit. Both policies are unstable. The interest rate and wealth fall *ad infinitum* under money finance with sterilization. The initial drop in the interest rate is due to the excess supply of money. However, the trade deficit leads to a decline in wealth as the central bank retires debt from the market. This causes a further drop in the interest rate as the demand for money is decreased. The fall in the interest rate further stimulates income and the trade deficit worsens. Wealth declines even more because of the increased loss in reserves and this leads to a further drop in the interest rate as the demand for money is decreased, and so on. The economy is unstable!

The interest rate and wealth rise *ad infinitum* under bond finance

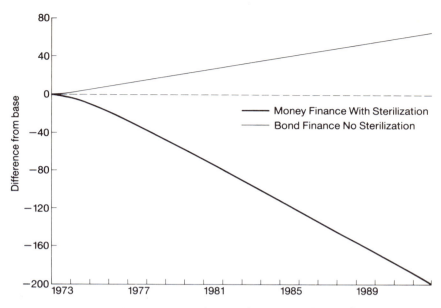

Figure 8.13   Real wealth response to an increase in government expenditure

without sterilization. The initial rise in wealth is due to the finance of the budget deficit through bonds. This increases the demand for money and the interest rate rises to equilibrate the assets markets. The initial income expansion causes a trade deficit and the central bank contracts the supply of money in response to the loss in reserves. This forces the interest rate up, causing an income decline and an enlarged budget deficit. Wealth rises as the government issues more bonds to finance the budget deficit, causing a further increase in the interest rate and so on. The economy is unstable!

8.5 An Adverse Supply Shock – Oil Price Rise

An increase in the price of raw materials, such as oil, causes stagflation and a deficit in the budget and the trade account. If the policy-makers follow a policy of monetary targets with sterilization, the nominal money supply remains fixed and the stock of government bonds increases as a result of the budget deficit, but decreases in response to the trade deficit. The most likely effect is a decline in wealth as the trade deficit outweighs the budget deficit. If the policy-makers follow a policy of debt targets without sterilization, the nominal stock of bonds remains fixed and the

---

Box 8.4 The transmission of an oil price rise under monetary targets with and without sterilization

$$\frac{OPI}{CPI}\downarrow \Rightarrow C\downarrow \Rightarrow Y\downarrow \qquad \text{(a)}$$

$$PIW\uparrow \Rightarrow P\uparrow \quad \text{and} \quad CPI\uparrow \Rightarrow \qquad \frac{V}{CPI}\downarrow \Rightarrow C\downarrow \Rightarrow Y\downarrow \qquad \text{(b)}$$

$$\frac{M}{CPI}\downarrow \Rightarrow r\uparrow \Rightarrow \begin{cases} (r-p^e)\uparrow \Rightarrow I\downarrow \Rightarrow Y\downarrow & \text{(c)} \\ \\ \dfrac{OPI}{CPI}\uparrow \Rightarrow C\uparrow \Rightarrow Y\uparrow & \text{(d)} \end{cases}$$

$$Y\downarrow \quad \text{and} \quad r\uparrow \Rightarrow \frac{PSBR}{P}\uparrow \Rightarrow \frac{B}{P}\uparrow \Rightarrow \frac{V}{CPI}\uparrow \Rightarrow C\uparrow \Rightarrow Y\uparrow \qquad \text{(e)}$$

$$PIW\uparrow \Rightarrow \text{oil bill } \uparrow \qquad\qquad\qquad \frac{B}{P}\downarrow \Rightarrow \frac{V}{CPI}\downarrow \Rightarrow C\downarrow \Rightarrow Y\downarrow \quad \text{(f1)}$$

$$\left.\begin{array}{c} \\ \\ \end{array}\right\} Y\downarrow \text{ and } CB\downarrow \Rightarrow \Delta RES\downarrow \Rightarrow \begin{cases} \\ \\ \end{cases}$$

$$P\uparrow \Rightarrow COMP\uparrow \Rightarrow X\downarrow \qquad\qquad\qquad \frac{M}{P}\downarrow \Rightarrow r\uparrow \Rightarrow D\downarrow \Rightarrow Y\downarrow \quad \text{(f2)}$$

---

supply of money is increased as a result of the budget deficit, but decreased because of the trade deficit. The most likely effect is a contraction in the money supply.

Box 8.4 presents a schematic view of the main channels through which an increase in the price of oil affects the economy under monetary targets with and without sterilization. The transmission mechanism is in many respects the same as that in model 7 and the reader is referred there for more details. The initial effect of an oil price rise is to raise domestic prices. This reduces real other personal income and real wealth, thereby lowering consumption and income – channels (a) and (b). The increase in prices erodes real money balances, creating an excess demand for money, and the interest rate rises to clear the assets markets. Given the higher speed of adjustment of financial markets, relative to the goods market, the increase in the nominal interest rate implies a rise in the real rate too. The latter deters investment and causes income contraction – channel (c). Other things being equal, the rise in the interest rate increases real other personal income – channel (d) – moderating the contractionary effect of channel (a). The rise in domestic prices results in a loss in competitiveness and leads to lower net exports, thereby

Box 8.5 The transmission of an oil price rise under debt targets with and without sterilization

$$\frac{OPI}{CPI}\downarrow \Rightarrow C\downarrow \Rightarrow Y\downarrow \qquad\qquad\qquad (a)$$

$$PIW\uparrow \Rightarrow P\uparrow \quad \text{and} \quad CPI\uparrow \Rightarrow \begin{cases} \\ \\ \dfrac{V}{CPI}\downarrow \Rightarrow C\downarrow \Rightarrow Y\downarrow \qquad\qquad\qquad (b) \end{cases}$$

$$\left(r - p^e\right)\downarrow \Rightarrow I\uparrow \Rightarrow Y\uparrow \qquad\qquad (c)$$

$$Y\downarrow \Rightarrow \frac{PSBR}{P}\uparrow \Rightarrow \frac{M}{CPI}\uparrow \Rightarrow r\downarrow \Rightarrow \begin{cases} \dfrac{OPI}{CPI}\downarrow \Rightarrow C\downarrow \Rightarrow Y\downarrow \qquad\qquad (d) \\ \\ \dfrac{B}{P}\downarrow \Rightarrow \dfrac{V}{CPI}\downarrow \Rightarrow C\downarrow \Rightarrow Y\downarrow \qquad (e) \end{cases}$$

$$PIW\uparrow \Rightarrow \text{oil bill}\uparrow \qquad \begin{cases} \dfrac{B}{P}\downarrow \Rightarrow \dfrac{V}{CPI}\downarrow \Rightarrow C\downarrow \Rightarrow Y\downarrow \quad (f1) \end{cases}$$

$$\Big\} Y\downarrow \text{ and } CB\downarrow \Rightarrow \Delta RES\downarrow \Rightarrow \begin{cases} \\ \dfrac{M}{P}\downarrow \Rightarrow r\uparrow \Rightarrow D\downarrow \Rightarrow Y\downarrow \quad (f2) \end{cases}$$

$$P\uparrow \Rightarrow COMP\uparrow \Rightarrow X\downarrow$$

depressing output. The combined effect of channels (a) to (d), along with the decline in net exports, creates a recession and therefore the initial effect of an oil price rise is *stagflation*, i.e. stagnation and inflation.

With a policy of monetary targets, the fall in income and the rise in the interest rate lead to a budget deficit and therefore to higher private sector wealth. This stimulates consumption and income – channel (e). The rise in the oil price means that initially the oil bill is enlarged, thereby causing a trade deficit. This is exacerbated by the loss in competitiveness resulting from higher prices. If the central bank sterilizes the drain on foreign reserves, real private sector wealth declines, thus causing a further income contraction – channel (f1). If, on the other hand, the central bank does not sterilize the loss in reserves, the money supply diminishes and the interest rate rises, again making the recession worse – channel (f2). However, as the recession deepens imports fall, therefore halting the deterioration of the trade deficit.

Box 8.5 provides a schematic view of the channels through which an oil price rise affects the economy under a debt target of keeping the nominal stock of government bonds fixed with and without sterilization. As with monetary targets, the oil price rise increases prices and this erodes the real value of other personal income and real private sector wealth. The rise in the price of oil increases domestic prices and through a loss in competitiveness reduces net exports. This, together with the decline in wealth, causes a recession – channels (a) and (b). The recession creates a budget deficit, and with a policy of keeping the nominal stock of government bonds fixed, the money supply is partly raised and the interest rate falls to clear the assets markets. This has two effects. First, it moderates the recession by lowering the real interest rate. Second, it lowers other personal income and wealth – channels (d) and (e).

If the central bank sterilizes the loss in reserves wealth falls, and this deepens the recession – channel (f1). If, on the other hand, the central bank does not sterilize the loss in reserves the money supply shrinks, the interest rate rises and income falls – channel (f2).

The transmission and the time profile of the effects of an oil price rise are highlighted by simulating model 8 numerically under monetary targets with sterilization and debt targets without sterilization. Figures 8.14 to 8.17 show the dynamic response of output, prices, interest rate and wealth to these two policy regimes. A permanent 10 per cent oil price rise causes stagflation, output falls and prices rise. In the new steady state output is lower by 3 per cent with both types of policy (see figure 8.14). More than 90 per cent of the overall adjustment occurs within the first two years after the shock. Output falls slightly more slowly under

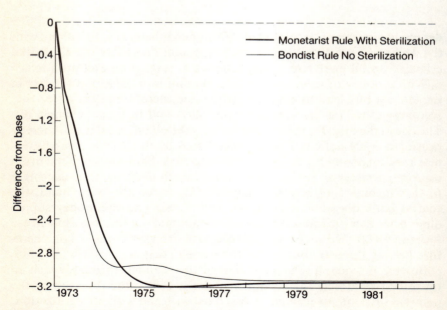

Figure 8.14 Output response to an oil price rise

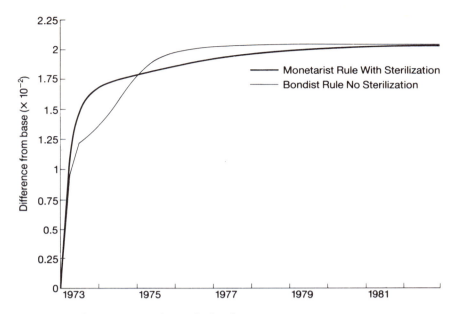

Figure 8.15 Prices response to an oil price rise

a regime of monetary targets with sterilization than under debt targets without sterilization. Consequently, prices rise at a slower pace with the former than with the latter. However, in the new steady state prices are 2 per cent higher with both policies (see figure 8.15). The slower pace of the rise in prices in the transition to the new steady state under monetary targets with sterilization implies that the loss in competitiveness is also smaller. This has a feedback effect on output because of the effect of competitiveness on net exports.

The interest rate gradually falls with monetary targets and sterilization in response to an excess supply of money, which is caused by the decline in income and wealth (see figure 8.16). As the adjustment of income and wealth is gradual so is the adjustment of the interest rate. On the other hand, with debt targets without sterilization the interest rate rises in the first year of the shock by 90 basis points because the money supply diminishes in response to the trade deficit and the consequent loss in reserves. The rapid rise of the interest rate in the first year results from the instant clearance of financial markets, compared to the sluggish clearance of the goods market. Hence, as the supply of money is reduced the interest rate rises to clear the money market. However, as the recession deepens and income and wealth decrease, the demand for money is reduced and the interest rate falls.

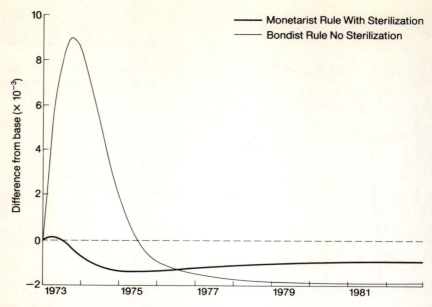

Figure 8.16   Interest rate response to an oil price rise

Real private sector wealth is diminished with both policies (see figure 8.17). Nevertheless, wealth falls more quickly during the first phase of the adjustment process with monetary targets and sterilization than with debt targets without sterilization.

If the central bank follows a policy of monetary targets without sterilization, the economy is unstable. This policy implies that the central bank issues bonds to cover the budget deficit and wealth is increased, while the money supply shrinks in response to the trade deficit. The reduction in the money supply raises the interest rate and the economy falls into deeper recession, which enlarges the budget deficit. Hence wealth rises, driving the interest rate up as the demand for money is increased. This leads to a further rise in wealth and so on. The economy is unstable!

If the central bank follows a policy of debt targets with sterilization, the economy is again unstable. This policy implies that the central bank increases the supply of money in response to the budget deficit, while the stock of bonds is reduced in response to the trade deficit. The increase in the supply of money reduces the interest rate and stems the decline in income. The trade deficit worsens and wealth is reduced even more. The decline in income and wealth induce a further fall in the interest rate. This accelerates the decline in wealth and so on. The economy is unstable!.

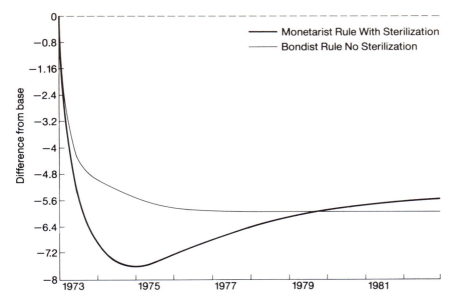

Figure 8.17 Real wealth response to an oil price rise

8.6 World Trade Shock – Increase in Foreign Demand

The effects of a world trade shock are in many respects similar to those of a government expenditure shock. A boost in world trade stimulates the economy by raising exports, and pushes prices up. The behaviour of the interest rate and wealth depends on the type of monetary policy pursued. With monetary targets and sterilization the interest rate and wealth fall. With debt targets and no sterilization the interest rate and wealth rise. The effects of world trade so far are the same as with government expenditure. The difference arises from the behaviour of the trade balance and the budget. With an increase in government expenditure the budget and the trade account are thrown into deficit, whereas with a world trade shock both are driven into surplus.

Figures 8.18 to 8.21 show the dynamic response of the economy to a permanent increase of 1 per cent in world trade under a monetarist rule with sterilization and a bondist rule (debt target) without sterilization. Output rises, overshooting in the short run its long-run equilibrium (figure 8.18). Although in the new steady state the increase in output is the same with both policies, in the short run a bondist rule without sterilization is more expansionary than a monetarist rule with sterilization. This is because of the behaviour of the interest rate, which falls in

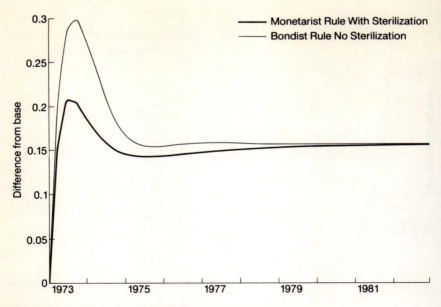

Figure 8.18   Output response to an increase in world trade

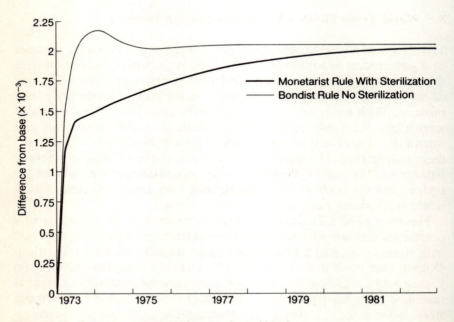

Figure 8.19   Prices response to an increase in world trade

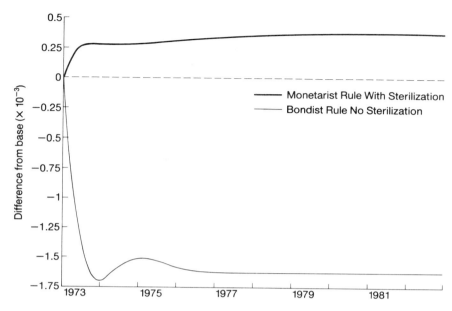

Figure 8.20 Interest rate response to an increase in world trade

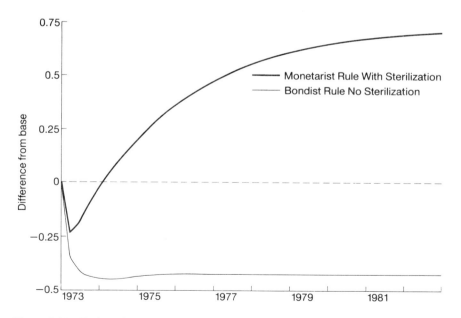

Figure 8.21 Real wealth response to an increase in world trade

the latter and rises in the former. The stimulus in the economy is caused by a boost in exports. Prices rise in response to tightening conditions in the goods and labour markets (figure 8.19). Although in the new steady state prices rise to the same extent under both policies, in the short run debt targets without sterilization cause higher inflation than monetary targets with sterilization because the former is more expansionary than the latter.

The boost in world trade stimulates exports and creates a trade surplus and the rise in income causes a budget surplus. With monetary targets and sterilization the stock of government bonds increases in response to the trade surplus, but decreases in view of the surplus in the budget. Since the former dominates the latter, wealth is increased (figure 8.21). This increases the demand for money and the interest rate rises to clear the assets markets (figure 8.20). With debt targets and no sterilization the money supply increases in response to the trade surplus, but decreases as a result of the budget surplus (figure 8.21). As with the previous case, the former dominates the latter and the money supply is increased. The excess supply of money reduces the interest rate (figure 8.20).

A policy of monetary targets without sterilization is unstable because it leads to a spiral of higher interest rates and wealth. A policy of debt targets with sterilization is also unstable because it leads to a spiral of lower interest rates and wealth.

8.7 Conclusions

Under a regime of fixed exchange rates the issue of whether a central bank should sterilize the effect of foreign reserves on the money supply is interlinked with the financial policy associated with the budget. Both a policy of monetary targets without sterilization and a policy of debt targets with sterilization are unstable under a shock caused by a change in government expenditure, oil price or world trade. The only exception is a shock caused by a change in monetary policy. In this case the economy is always stable irrespective of the way the sterilization policy is combined with the financial policy of the budget. Fiscal policy is stable if money finance is not combined with sterilization and if bond finance is. In the case of a shock caused by either the price of oil or world trade the economy is stable if a policy of monetary targets is pursued along with sterilization and a policy of debt targets without sterilization.

Easy monetary policy can only temporarily stimulate the economy, but in doing so it also raises prices. The interest rate and real wealth fall. If after the shock the central bank re-imposes its policy of debt targets without sterilization, the trade account deteriorates and the initial budget surplus turns into deficit. In the new steady state the trade deficit matches the budget deficit. If, on the other hand, the central bank re-imposes after the monetary shock its monetary targets with sterilization, the deficit in the trade account and the budget are only transient. In the new long-run equilibrium both the trade account and the budget are again balanced.

Easy fiscal policy raises output and prices in both the short and the long run. The stimulus in the short run is greater than in the long run. The trade account deteriorates and the budget turns into deficit in both the transition and the new steady state. In the new long-run equilibrium the trade deficit is equal to the budget deficit. Money finance without sterilization is more expansionary than bond finance with sterilization in the short run because the former leads to lower interest rates, while the latter causes higher interest rates.

A permanent oil price rise creates stagflation, lowers real wealth and causes trade and budget deficits. In the new steady state the trade deficit is equal to the budget deficit. With a policy of debt targets without sterilization output falls more quickly than with monetary targets with sterilization in the short run, although the long-run effect is the same, because the interest rate rises in the initial phase of the adjustment process in the former and falls in the latter. In the new steady state the interest rate is lower with both policies.

A boost in world trade raises output and prices in both the short and the long run, although the short-run stimulus exceeds the long-run. The trade account and the budget turn into surplus. In the new steady state the trade surplus matches the budget surplus. A policy of debt targets without sterilization is more expansionary than a policy of monetary targets with sterilization in the short run, although the long-run effect is the same, because the former leads to lower interest rates and wealth, whereas the latter leads to higher interest rates and wealth.

9

Model 9 An Open Economy Model with Flexible Exchange Rates

In this model the assumption that the economy is closed in the assets markets is relaxed. Domestic residents can hold foreign bonds. In this framework the determinants of the exchange rate are explained and its role in the macroeconomy is analysed. In a fully open economy (on the assets and the goods markets) output and inflation depend not only on domestic fiscal and monetary policy, but also on the policies of the major trading partners. The policy mix at home and abroad affects the exchange rate and the current account balance. The latter has a feedback effect on private sector wealth, with repercussions on output, inflation, the exchange rate and the current account balance.

In this chapter the emphasis is in the interactions of the exchange rate with the rest of the main macroeconomic variables in response to a change in economic policy or other exogenous variables in a non-inflationary economy. The dynamic adjustment of the economy from one steady state to the other is affected by the way expectations in the foreign exchange market are formed. In this context we compare and contrast model-consistent (or rational) expectations with exchange rate expectations that are consistent with balancing the current account in the long run.

9.1 Assumptions

The assumptions underlying this economy are the same as in model 8 with the following differences. There are three assets: money, domestic government bonds and foreign bonds. Foreigners do not hold any domestic money or domestic bonds, but domestic residents can allocate their portfolios to all three assets. Domestic and foreign bonds are regarded as perfect substitutes so that the only difference is the currency in which they are denominated. Domestic residents then switch between domestic and foreign bonds on the basis of expectations of appreciation or depreciation of the currency.

9.2 The Model

The model is assumed to be quarterly and consists of equations (9.1) to (9.27).

$$D = C + I + G + X - Q \tag{9.1}$$

$$C = \mathfrak{U}(\delta_{CY})\left\{\alpha_{CY} YD + \alpha_{Copi}(1 - HRT)\left(\frac{OPI}{CPI}\right)\right\}$$

$$+ \alpha_{Cr}\mathfrak{U}(\delta_{Cr})(r - cpi^e) + \alpha_{Cv}\mathfrak{U}(\delta_{Cv})\frac{V_{-1}}{CPI} + \alpha_{CC}C_{-1} + \gamma_C \tag{9.2}$$

$$\alpha_{Cr} < 0, \quad 0 < \alpha_{CY}, \alpha_{Copi}, \alpha_{Cv}, \alpha_{CC} < 1$$

$$I = \alpha_{IY}\mathfrak{U}(\delta_{IY})Y + \alpha_{Ir}\mathfrak{U}(\delta_{Ir})(r - p^e)$$

$$- \alpha_{IK}K_{-1} + \alpha_{II}I_{-1} + \gamma_I \tag{9.3}$$

$$\alpha_{IY} > 0, \quad \alpha_{Ir} < 0, \quad 0 < \alpha_{IK}, \alpha_{II} < 1$$

$$COMP = \frac{Pe}{PW} \tag{9.4}$$

$$TFE = C + I + G + X \tag{9.5}$$

$$Q = \alpha_{QTFE}\mathfrak{U}(\delta_{QTFE})TFE + \alpha_{QCOMP}\mathfrak{U}(\delta_{QCOMP})\,COMP$$

$$+ \alpha_{QQ}Q_{-1} + \gamma_Q \tag{9.6}$$

$$0 < \alpha_{QTFE}, \alpha_{QQ} < 1, \alpha_{QCOMP} > 0$$

$$X = \alpha_{XWT}\mathfrak{U}(\delta_{XWT})WT + \alpha_{XCOMP}\mathfrak{U}(\delta_{XCOMP})\,COMP$$

$$+ \alpha_{XX}X_{-1} + \gamma_X \tag{9.7}$$

$$0 < \alpha_{XWT}, \alpha_{XX} < 1, \alpha_{XCOMP} < 0$$

$$Y = D \tag{9.8}$$

$$YD = (1 - SRT)P\frac{Y}{CPI} \tag{9.9}$$

$$OPI = ((1 + r_{-1})^{\frac{1}{4}} - 1)B_{-1} + ((1 + rw_{-1})^{\frac{1}{4}} - 1)\frac{F_{-1}}{e} \tag{9.10}$$

$$\frac{M}{CPI} = \alpha_{MY}\mathfrak{U}(\delta_{MY})Y + \alpha_{Mv}\mathfrak{U}(\delta_{Mv})\frac{V_{-1}}{CPI} + \alpha_{Mr}\mathfrak{U}(\delta_{Mr})r + \gamma_M \tag{9.11}$$

$$\alpha_{MY} > 0, \quad \alpha_{Mr} < 0, \quad 0 < \alpha_{Mv} < 1$$

$$\frac{F}{e} = \left(\frac{F}{e}\right)_{-1} + CB \tag{9.12}$$

$$r = rw - \left(\frac{\dot{e}}{e}\right)^e \tag{9.13}$$

$$\left(\frac{\dot{e}}{e}\right)^e = \alpha_{ede}\left(1 - \frac{e}{\bar{e}}\right); \alpha_{ede} \geq 0 \tag{9.14a}$$

$$\left(\frac{\dot{e}}{e}\right)^e = \left(\frac{\dot{e}}{e}\right)_{+1} \tag{9.14b}$$

$$CB\left(\frac{\bar{P}\bar{e}}{PW}; \bar{Y}, WT\right) = 0 \tag{9.15a}$$

$$\bar{e} = e_{+1} \tag{9.15b}$$

$$V = M + B + \frac{F}{e} \tag{9.16}$$

$$PSBR = PG + ((1 + r_{-1})^{\frac{1}{4}} - 1)B_{-1} - PT \tag{9.17}$$

$$T = SRT\,Y + HRT\frac{OPI}{CPI} \tag{9.18}$$

$$M = M_{-1} + \alpha_{monfin}PSBR + \Delta MB \tag{9.19}$$

$$0 \leq \alpha_{monfin} \leq 1$$

$$B = B_{-1} + (1 - \alpha_{monfin})PSBR + \Delta OMO \tag{9.20}$$

$$CB = PX - PMQ + ((1 + rw_{-1})^{\frac{1}{4}} - 1)\frac{F_{-1}}{e} \tag{9.21}$$

$$w = \alpha_{wy}\mathcal{U}(\delta_{wy})\,(y - \bar{y}) + \alpha_{wY}\mathcal{U}(\delta_{wY})\,(Y - \bar{Y})$$
$$+ \alpha_{wp^e}\mathcal{U}(\delta_{wcpi^e})cpi^e + \gamma_w \tag{9.22}$$

$$\alpha_{wy} > 0, \quad 0 \leq \alpha_{wcpi^e} \leq 1$$

$$P = \alpha_{PW}W + (1 - \alpha_{PW})\frac{PIW}{e} + \alpha_{PY}(y - \bar{y}) + \gamma_P \tag{9.23}$$

$$0 \leq \alpha_{PW} \leq 1, \quad \alpha_{PY} > 0$$

$$CPI = \alpha_{CPIP}P + (1 - \alpha_{CPIP})PM \tag{9.24}$$

$$0 \leq \alpha_{CPIP} \leq 1$$

$$PM = (\alpha_{PMPW}PW + (1 - \alpha_{PMPW})PIW)/\mathcal{U}(\delta_{PMe})e \tag{9.25}$$

$$0 \leq \alpha_{PMPW} \leq 1$$

$$p^e = p^e_{-1} + \alpha_{p^ep}(p_{-1} - p^e_{-1}) \tag{9.26}$$

$$cpi^e = cpi^e_{-1} + \alpha_{p^e p}(cpi_{-1} - cpi^e_{-1}) \tag{9.27}$$

$$0 \le \alpha_{p^e p} \le 1$$

Variable definition		Initial steady-state value
B	= (nominal) stock of government bonds, at current prices	50
C	= real consumer expenditure	65
CB	= nominal current balance in domestic currency	0
$COMP$	= index of competitiveness	1
CPI	= consumer price index	1
cpi	= actual inflation rate (as measured by the change in the consumer price index), i.e. $cpi = \dfrac{CPI - CPI_{-1}}{CPI_{-1}}$	0
cpi^e	= expected inflation rate in period t, with information available at $t-1$	0
D	= aggregate demand	100
e	= exchange rate, foreign price of domestic currency, i.e. units of foreign currency per unit of domestic currency	1
$\bar{e}$	= expected long-run exchange rate	1
$\left(\dfrac{\dot{e}}{e}\right)^e$	= expected currency appreciation/depreciation	0
F	= nominal net foreign asset position expressed in foreign currency, net holdings of foreign bonds	10
f	= real net foreign asset position (F/P)	10
G	= real government expenditure	25
HRT	= higher rate of income tax on other personal income	0.6
I	= real gross investment expenditure	10
K	= capital stock	200
M	= (nominal) money stock, currency in circulation (notes and coin)	10
MB	= autonomous monetary base, at current prices	0
NX	= net exports, the difference between export and import volumes	0
OMO	= open market operations instrument	0

	Variable definition	Initial steady-state value
OPI	= other personal income (interest income), in nominal terms	2.0768
P	= producer price index	1
p	= actual inflation rate (as measured by the producer price index, i.e. $p = \dfrac{P - P_{-1}}{P_{-1}}$	0
P^e	= expected inflation in period t, with information in $t - 1$	
PIW	= world price of imported raw materials, in foreign currency	1
PM	= price of imports, in domestic currency	1
$PSBR$	= public sector borrowing requirement, at current prices	0
PW	= price of imported final goods, in foreign currency	1
Q	= real imports of goods and services in domestic currency	25
r	= interest rate (yield) on government bonds	0.1
rw	= interest rate (yield) on foreign bonds	0.1
SRT	= standard rate of income tax	0.25
T	= total tax revenues, in real terms	25
TFE	= real total final expenditure	125
V	= stock of private sector wealth, at current prices	300
W	= nominal wage rate	1
w	= actual wage inflation, i.e. change in the nominal wage rate, $w = \dfrac{W - W_{-1}}{W_{-1}}$	0
X	= real exports of goods and services in domestic currency	25
Y	= domestic output, real income	100
y	= rate of growth of output (GDP), i.e. $y = \dfrac{Y - Y_{-1}}{Y_{-1}}$	0
$\bar{Y}$	= potential (or capacity) output	100
$\bar{y}$	= rate of growth of potential (or capacity) output, i.e. $\bar{y} = \dfrac{\bar{Y} - \bar{Y}_{-1}}{\bar{Y}_{-1}}$	0
YD	= real disposable income	75

$$\text{u}(\delta)X = \sum_{i=0}^{3} \delta_i X_{-i} / \sum_{i=0}^{3} \delta_i \text{ is a unitary moving average operator.}$$

In the exercises reported below $\mathfrak{U}(\delta) = 1\,0\,0\,0$, that is the total effect is instantaneous.

Coefficient	Value	Coefficient	Value
α_{CY}	0.35	α_{XX}	0.25
α_{Copi}	0.5	γ_X	23.75
α_{Cr}	−25	α_{MY}	0.075
α_{Cv}	0.065	α_{Mr}	−100
α_{CC}	0.5	α_{Mv}	0.01
γ_C	−10.75	γ_M	9.5
α_{IY}	0.0775	α_{monfin}	1.0
α_{Ir}	−25	α_{ede}	0.9
α_{IK}	0.05	α_{wy}	0.5
α_{II}	0.0	α_{wp^e}	1.0
γ_I	14.75	γ_w	0.0
$\alpha_{Q\,TFE}$	0.1	α_{PW}	0.85
$\alpha_{Q\,COMP}$	15	α_{Py}	0.5
α_{QQ}	0.75	γ_P	0.0
γ_Q	−18.75	α_{CPIP}	0.85
$\alpha_{X\,WT}$	0.20	α_{PMPW}	0.7
$\alpha_{X\,COMP}$	−25	$\alpha_{p^e p}$	0.5

The endogenization of the exchange rate introduces the following changes to model 8. Domestic residents hold three assets: domestic money, M, domestic currency denominated bonds, B, and foreign currency denominated bonds, F. Money bears no interest, whereas domestic and foreign bonds bear interest r and rw respectively. Money and domestic bonds are the liabilities of the government. The supplies of money and government bonds are determined by government finance considerations of budget surpluses or deficits. Foreigners do not hold domestic money or domestic currency denominated bonds. Domestic residents may hold foreign currency denominated bonds, which they acquire or dispose of by running a current account surplus or deficit. Domestic and foreign bonds are considered to be perfect substitutes so that the *uncovered interest rate parity* relationship holds (9.13). This relationship means that in equilibrium the return of domestic bonds is equal to the return of foreign bonds. The latter is equal to the foreign interest rate less the rate of expected appreciation of the domestic currency. The perfect substitutability assumption implies further that the two asset demand functions (domestic and foreign bonds) can be consolidated into one equation.

Nominal private sector wealth is defined in (9.16) as the sum of money, domestic currency denominated bonds and foreign currency denominated bonds. Given the wealth budget constraint and the assumption of perfect asset substitutability only one of the two equilibrium asset conditions is independent (Walras' law), the other being determined residually from the definition of wealth. We follow the usual approach of casting the argument in terms of the money market and consider as redundant the consolidated bond market.

Equation (9.12) asserts that a current account surplus (deficit) leads to the acquisition (disposition) of foreign assets. If the first term on the right hand side is moved to the left, then an alternative explanation of equation (9.12) is that balance of payments equilibrium requires that the capital account is equal to the current account. The value of F measures the net foreign asset position. If $F > 0$, the country is a net creditor to the rest of the world, and if $F < 0$, the country is a net debtor.

The definition of other personal income is adjusted to reflect interest payments on foreign debt (9.10).

We distinguish three different schemes of expectations in the foreign exchange market. First, it is assumed that expectations are rational or model-consistent in the long run, but regressive in the short run. This scheme is captured in equations (9.14a) and (9.15b) and is referred to as *model-consistent expectations*. Economic agents can correctly calculate the effects of economic policy or other exogenous shocks on the expected long-run equilibrium exchange rate, $\bar{e}$. However, what is not known is the exact adjustment path towards the long-run equilibrium. According to equation (9.14a), participants in the foreign exchange market expect the current spot rate to converge to its expected long-run value at a speed $\alpha_{ede} \geq 0$. If the current exchange rate is above its long-run expected value, the currency is overvalued and agents expect it to depreciate. If the current exchange rate is below its long-run expected value, the currency is undervalued and agents expect it to appreciate. The speed at which expectations are adjusted for a given discrepancy between the current and expected long-run exchange rate depends on α_{ede}. A large value of α_{ede} implies fast adjustment. In the limiting case where the adjustment coefficient is zero (i.e. $\alpha_{ede} = 0$), private agents possess static expectations.

The second expectations scheme assumes that the expected long-run exchange rate is computed by the condition that the current account must balance in the long run (9.15a). The current rate converges to its long-run value regressively (9.14a). This scheme is referred to in the rest of this chapter as *current account expectations*.

The third expectations scheme assumes that agents can correctly compute the effects of economic policy or other exogenous shocks on the expected exchange rate and that the adjustment is instantaneous. This scheme is captured by equation (9.14b) and is referred to as *short-run model-consistent expectations*. Obviously, the exchange rate should exhibit greater initial volatility (a bigger 'jump') under short-run than under long-run model-consistent expectations. However, the difference between them is in practice very small. Figure 9.1 plots the difference between the two expectations schemes for the exchange rate in response to a permanent increase in government expenditure under bond finance. As can be seen, the maximum difference occurs when the exchange rate jumps but this is only 1.7×10^{-4}. After the initial jump the difference tapers off as the two schemes produce the same long-run equilibrium. The difference between the two expectations schemes is equally small for all other shocks. Therefore, the analysis in this chapter concentrates on the differences between long-run model-consistent expectations and current account expectations.

To avoid the complexities of non-linearities, in all exercises reported below interest payments on government debt are exogenized.

9.3 Monetary Policy

Easy monetary policy results in the short run in an expansion in output, lower interest rates, exchange rate depreciation, higher prices, budget surplus and lower real wealth, but has an ambiguous effect on the trade

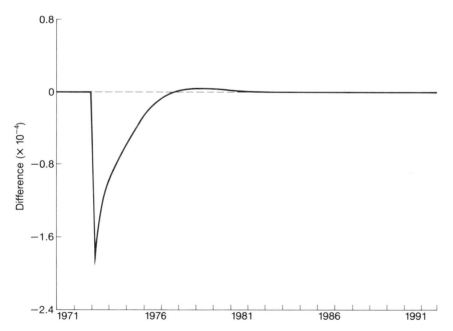

Figure 9.1 The difference between short- and long-run consistent expectations of the exchange rate in response to a permanent increase in government expenditure under bond finance

(and current) balance. In the long run, the stimulus to output peters out. The inflation rate returns to zero although prices are higher. The exchange rate depreciates. The budget turns into a small deficit which is equal to the deficit in the trade account. However, the effect on interest rate and real wealth is ambiguous. The interest rate may remain lower in the long run or return to its initial steady state. Real wealth may rise or fall in the long-run equilibrium.

Box 9.1 provides a schematic view of the main channels through which expansionary monetary policy in the form of an open market purchase affects the economy. An open market purchase leads to a drop in the nominal and real interest rates, which stimulates domestic demand (consumption and investment) and hence output – channel (a). The fall in the interest rate results in an exchange rate depreciation, a gain in competitiveness and an increase in net exports and therefore output – channel (b). Thus, at the initial phase of the adjustment process output expands.

After a while the stimulus to output runs out of steam. The increase in output spurs a fall in unemployment, rising wage and price inflation. Higher prices reduce real money balances and real wealth. The former reverses the initial decline in the interest rate and along with the latter curtails domestic demand – channels (c) and (d).

The expansion in output leads to increased tax revenues and a surplus

---

Box 9.1 The transmission of monetary policy (open market purchase)

$$\Delta M\uparrow = -\Delta B\downarrow \Rightarrow r\downarrow \Rightarrow \begin{cases} (r - p^e)\downarrow \Rightarrow I \text{ and } C\uparrow \Rightarrow D\uparrow \Rightarrow Y\uparrow \quad (a) \\[2em] e\downarrow \Rightarrow COMP\downarrow \Rightarrow NX\uparrow \Rightarrow Y\uparrow \quad\quad\quad (b) \end{cases}$$

$$Y\uparrow \Rightarrow u\downarrow \Rightarrow w\uparrow \Rightarrow p\uparrow \Rightarrow \begin{cases} \dfrac{V}{CPI}\downarrow \Rightarrow C\downarrow \Rightarrow Y\downarrow \quad\quad\quad\quad\quad\quad (c) \\[2em] \dfrac{M}{CPI}\downarrow \Rightarrow r\uparrow \Rightarrow I \text{ and } C\downarrow \Rightarrow Y\downarrow \quad (d) \end{cases}$$

$$Y\uparrow \Rightarrow \begin{cases} CB\downarrow \Rightarrow \dfrac{f}{e}\downarrow \Rightarrow \\[1.5em] \dfrac{PSBR}{P}\downarrow \Rightarrow \dfrac{B}{P}\downarrow \Rightarrow \end{cases} \Bigg\} \dfrac{V}{CPI}\downarrow \Rightarrow C\downarrow \Rightarrow Y\downarrow \quad (e)$$

in the budget. The central bank retires debt from the market and private sector wealth is reduced. If the increase in output and the resultant higher imports outweigh the stimulus to net exports from the gain in competitiveness, the trade account deteriorates. This diminishes the net foreign asset position and lowers real private sector wealth, thereby curtailing consumption and hence output – channel (e). This reinforces the contractionary forces of channels (c) and (d) and contributes to the return of output to its initial steady state.

The effects of monetary policy are illustrated by simulating model 9 numerically under model-consistent and current account expectations. Monetary policy takes the form of an open market purchase of £1 billion of government bonds by the central bank. This increases the (nominal) supply of money by £1 billion in all periods and consequently the interest rate falls (see figure 9.2). Since the assets markets are clearing instantly whereas the goods market clears sluggishly the interest rate drop is very fast. With model-consistent expectations the interest rate falls by 35 basis points (100 basis points is 1 per cent) in the first six months. With current account expectations the interest rate drop is almost three times as large, 90 basis points.

The exchange rate depreciates under both expectations schemes (see figure 9.3). With model-consistent expectations the exchange rate falls by almost 12 per cent in the first three months, whereas in the new long-

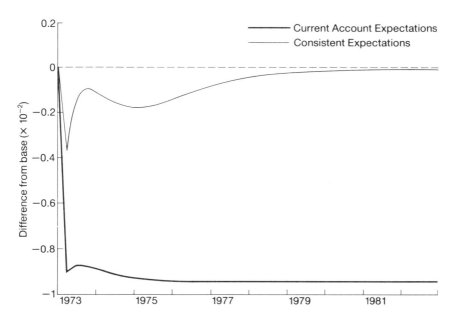

Figure 9.2 Interest rate response to easy monetary policy (open market purchase)

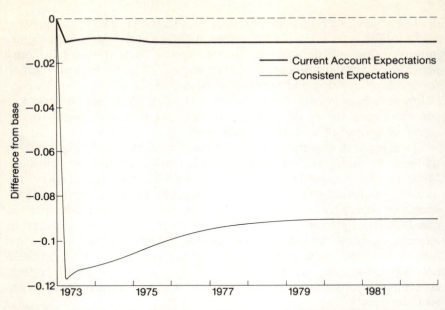

Figure 9.3   Exchange rate response to easy monetary policy (open market purchase)

run equilibrium it depreciates by 9 per cent. Therefore, there is an exchange rate overshoot. With current account expectations the exchange rate converges to its steady state within three months and the depreciation is only 1 per cent. Accordingly, there is a larger gain in competitiveness with model-consistent expectations than with current account expectations. In the first year, competitiveness is improved on average by 5.3 per cent with the former and 0.1 per cent with the latter.

Lower interest rates and enhanced competitiveness stimulate output in the short run (see figure 9.4). With model-consistent expectations output rises in the first year by 4 per cent. By contrast, with current account expectations output rises by only 0.8 per cent. Subsequently, the stimulus dies out quickly. This is owing, to a large extent, to higher prices, which erode the value of wealth and money balances, (see figure 9.5). Inflation rises and peaks at almost 6 per cent in the first year with model-consistent expectations. By contrast, inflation peaks at only 0.75 per cent with current account expectations. The almost ten times larger increase in inflation is due to the bigger stimulus in output and the higher depreciation with model-consistent than with current account expectations. Prices are 10 per cent higher in the new long-run equilibrium under model-consistent expectations and only 1 per cent higher under current account expectations.

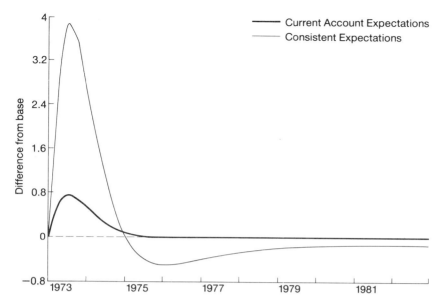

Figure 9.4 Output response to easy monetary policy (open market purchase)

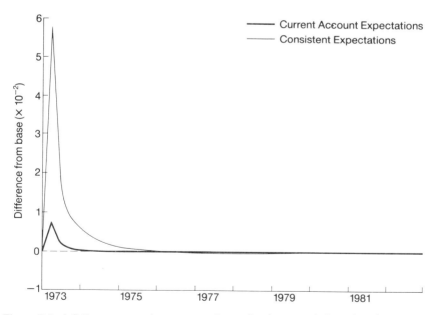

Figure 9.5 Inflation response to easy monetary policy (open market purchase)

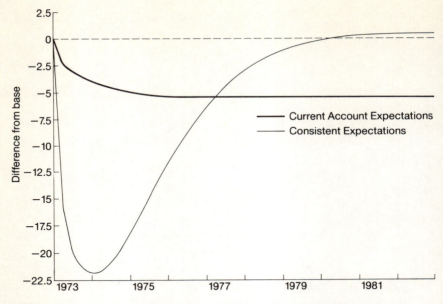

Figure 9.6   Real wealth response to easy monetary policy (open market purchase)

The long-run behaviour of the interest rate depends on real wealth. Wealth declines monotonically with current account expectations (see figure 9.6). In the new steady state it is lower by £5 billion (or 1.7 per cent). On the other hand, with model-consistent expectations wealth falls by £22 billion (or 7.3 per cent) in the first year and then gradually recovers. In the new steady state, real wealth is £0.5 billion higher than in the initial steady state. (Note that in the case of a straight increase in the money supply rather than an open market purchase real wealth returns to its initial value.)

The different behaviour of real wealth under the two expectations schemes results from the effects of monetary policy on the budget and the trade account. The initial stimulus to output increases tax revenues and produces a surplus in the budget under both expectations schemes. However, the surplus at constant prices is equal to £0.8 billion (or 0.8 per cent of GNP) with model-consistent expectations and only £0.16 billion with current account expectations. Furthermore, because of higher inflation the real value of bonds is reduced in the first three years by £9.3 billion with model-consistent expectations and £2.4 billion with current account expectations.

The real trade balance improves in the short run by £1.8 billion (or 1.8 per cent of GNP) with model-consistent expectations, but deteriorates by £0.16 billion with current account expectations. The improvement is due to the large exchange rate depreciation, which outweighs the higher imports resulting from the stimulus in output. On the other hand, the deterioration in the trade balance with current account expectations is due to a small gain in competitiveness that is dominated by the income effect on imports. This leads to a higher real net foreign asset position with model-consistent expectations and a lower position with current account expectations. This is the reason why real wealth recovers with model-consistent expectations, whereas it continues to fall with current account expectations (see figure 9.6).

The decline in real wealth leads to a lower interest rate because the demand for money is diminished with current account expectations. On the other hand, the recovery of real wealth with model-consistent expectations increases the demand for money and pushes the interest rate up to its initial steady state (see figure 9.2).

9.4 Fiscal Policy

Expansionary fiscal policy under bond finance stimulates output in the short run, raises prices and the interest rate, produces a deficit in the budget and the trade balance, but has an ambiguous effect on real wealth and the exchange rate. In the long run, the stimulus to output is largely eroded, but is still positive. The rate of inflation converges to zero. Real wealth rises. The budget deficit is equal to the deficit in the trade account. The interest rate may remain higher in the new steady state or return to its initial long-run equilibrium. The exchange rate may depreciate or appreciate.

Box 9.2 provides a schematic view of the transmission mechanism of an increase in government expenditure under bond finance. The increase in government expenditure spurs demand and hence output – channel (a). The buoyancy in income increases the demand for money and the interest rate rises to equilibrate the assets markets. This crowds out private investment, thereby curtailing the output expansion – channel (b). Under normal conditions, the interest rate rise appreciates the exchange rate, leading to a loss in competitiveness, which lowers net exports and hence output – channel (c). The increase in government expenditure leads to a budget deficit, which is financed by issuing government bonds, thereby raising real wealth. This stimulates consumption and hence output – channel (d) – but it also intensifies the forces that operate in channels (b) and (c).

In the short run, the stimulus to output results in lower unemployment and rising wage and price inflation. Higher prices erode the real value of wealth and money balances. The former depresses consumption and

---

Box 9.2 The transmission of fiscal policy (government expenditure) under bond finance–a schematic approach

$$YD\uparrow \Rightarrow C\uparrow \Rightarrow D\uparrow \Rightarrow Y\uparrow \tag{a}$$

$$D\uparrow \Rightarrow Y\uparrow \Rightarrow \quad\begin{cases} \end{cases} \quad I\downarrow \Rightarrow D\downarrow \Rightarrow Y\downarrow \tag{b}$$

$$G\uparrow \Rightarrow \begin{cases} \end{cases} \qquad \frac{M^d}{CPI}\uparrow \Rightarrow r\uparrow \Rightarrow \begin{cases} \end{cases}$$

$$\frac{PSBR}{P}\uparrow \Rightarrow \frac{B}{P}\uparrow \Rightarrow \frac{V}{CPI}\uparrow \Rightarrow \begin{cases} \end{cases} \qquad e\uparrow \Rightarrow NX\downarrow \Rightarrow Y\downarrow \tag{c}$$

$$C\uparrow \Rightarrow D\uparrow \Rightarrow Y\uparrow \tag{d}$$

$$\frac{V}{CPI}\downarrow \Rightarrow C\downarrow \Rightarrow Y\downarrow \tag{e}$$

$$((a) + (d)) > ((b) + (c)) \Rightarrow u\downarrow \Rightarrow w\uparrow \Rightarrow p\uparrow \Rightarrow \begin{cases} \end{cases}$$

$$\frac{M}{CPI}\downarrow \Rightarrow r\uparrow \Rightarrow I\downarrow \Rightarrow Y\downarrow \tag{f}$$

$$Y\uparrow \Rightarrow CB\downarrow \Rightarrow \frac{f}{e}\downarrow \Rightarrow \frac{V}{CPI}\downarrow \Rightarrow C\downarrow \Rightarrow Y\downarrow \tag{g}$$

---

hence output – channel (e) – while the latter raises the interest rate and cuts investment and output – channel (f).

The rise in income leads to higher imports, resulting in a deficit in the trade (and current) account. This diminishes the real net foreign asset position, thereby lowering wealth and therefore consumption – channel (g).

An illustration of the transmission mechanism of fiscal policy under bond finance is provided by simulating model 9 under model-consistent and current account expectations. Government expenditure is increased by £1 billion (or 1 per cent of GNP) for the whole of the simulation period – 20 years. In the short run, the interest rate rises more with current account expectations than with model-consistent expectations (see figure 9.7). The exchange rate appreciates with the latter by 1.2 per cent within the first three months, whereas it depreciates by 1.5 per cent with current account expectations (see figure 9.8). In the latter scheme an increase in government spending deteriorates in the long run the trade (and current) account, and therefore requires a depreciation of the exchange rate. On the other hand, with model-consistent expectations long-run equilibrium requires that the domestic interest rate returns to the level of the foreign interest rate.

Output rises in the short run, reaching its peak within the first year (see figure 9.9). The stimulus is higher with current account expectations than with model-consistent expectations. The multiplier reaches a peak of 1.3

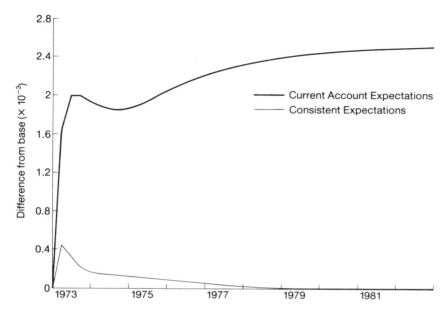

Figure 9.7 Interest rate response to a permanent increase in government expenditure under bond finance

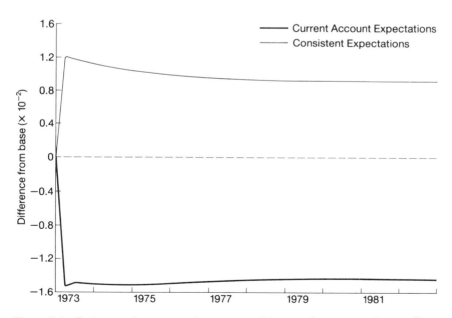

Figure 9.8 Exchange rate response to a permanent increase in government expenditure under bond finance

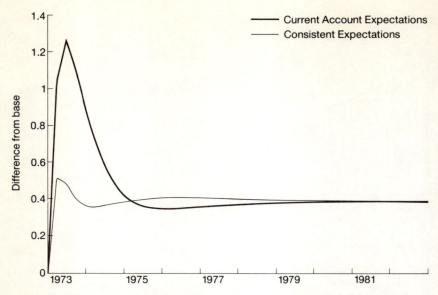

Figure 9.9   Output response to a permanent increase in government expenditure under bond finance

with the former and 0.5 with the latter. The difference is due to the exchange rate, which appreciates with model-consistent expectations, but depreciates with current account expectations, leading to a gain and a loss in competitiveness respectively. Accordingly, the volume of imports increases by £0.55 billion and the volume of exports falls by £0.36 billion in the first year with model-consistent expectations. With current account expectations imports rise by £0.20 billion and exports rise rather than fall by a meagre £0.04 billion. From the second year onwards the volume of exports declines, reaching a steady state of −£0.20 billion. In the long run, the fiscal stimulus is eroded and both expectations schemes converge to a steady-state multiplier of 0.4.

The step-up of production leads to lower unemployment and rising wage and price inflation in the short run (see figure 9.10). However, the smaller increase in output and the appreciation of the exchange rate reduce inflation after the initial shock with model-consistent expectations. In the long-run, inflation converges to zero with both expectations schemes.

In the short run, real wealth rises with model-consistent expectations, overshooting its long-run equilibrium value (see figure 9.11). Real wealth reaches a peak at £2.4 billion in the second year and then gradually declines to £1.2 billion. With current account expectations, real wealth

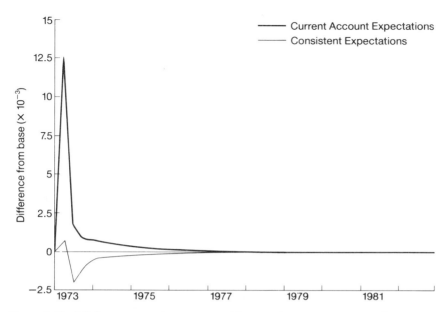

Figure 9.10 Inflation response to a permanent increase in government expenditure under bond finance

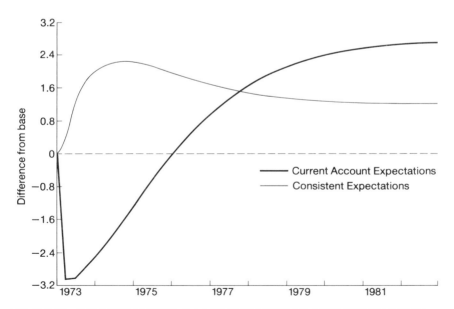

Figure 9.11 Real wealth response to a permanent increase in government expenditure under bond finance

falls in the short run by £3 billion and then rises. In the new steady state wealth is higher with current account than with model-consistent expectations. There are two reasons for this different behaviour of real wealth. First, the real value of domestic bonds is increased under both schemes as the government issues bonds to cover its budget deficit. However, the increase is higher with model-consistent expectations as inflation rises only temporarily. Second, the trade deficit is much higher in the short run with model-consistent expectations because of the loss in competitiveness. Therefore, the real net foreign asset position declines much more with model-consistent than with current account expectations.

Since wealth is increased much more with current account than with model-consistent expectations in the long run, the interest rate has to rise in response to a higher demand for money (see figure 9.7).

If the government increases its expenditure permanently and finances it through money, the economy is unstable. Output expands in both the short and the long run and converges to a new steady state. Inflation rises more in the short than in the long run. It converges to a steady-state rate of inflation that is not zero. However, this is a non-inflationary economy and the only rate of inflation consistent with stability is zero. The instability manifests itself through a continuous exchange rate depreciation and continuous decline in the interest rate. The economy is unstable because real wealth also falls continously as rising prices erode the value of government bonds and the net foreign asset position. The trade account and the budget are balanced in real terms, but not in nominal terms. Furthermore, the deficit in the trade account is not equal to the deficit in the budget, and therefore real wealth is not stationary. The fall in wealth reduces the demand for money and lowers the interest rate. This leads to a further exchange rate depreciation, which increases prices even more. The central bank prints more money and this reduces the interest rate, which depreciates the exchange rate once more. The economy is unstable! Lower interest rates lead to lower exchange rates, which produce higher prices. These erode real money balances and real wealth. The central bank prints money, which along with the reduction in wealth accentuates the fall in the interest rate, and the cycle repeats itself. What needs to be done for the economy to return to a stable path is either for the central bank to stop printing money or for the government to reduce its expenditure to its old level.

9.5 Foreign Monetary Policy Shock – Foreign Interest Rate Rise

An increase in the foreign interest rate depreciates the exchange rate, raises the domestic interest rate and reduces real private sector wealth, but has an ambiguous effect on output and inflation, in the short run. If the country is relatively open on the demand side, then output expands and inflation rises in the short run. If the country is relatively demand side closed, output contracts and inflation falls. In the first case the foreign country, by adopting a tight monetary policy, exports its inflation to the rest of the world. In the second case, the foreign country exports its recession to the rest of the world, a *beggar thy neighbour* policy.

In the long run, the domestic interest rate rises and the exchange rate falls, but the extents of these changes depend on the exchange rate expectations scheme. With model-consistent expectations the domestic interest rate rises to match the level of the foreign interest rate, but with current account expectations the domestic interest rate rise is only partial. The exchange rate depreciates much more with model-consistent than with current account expectations. The effect on output and inflation is only transient. Both return to their initial steady-state values. However, in the new steady state prices are higher with model-consistent than with current account expectations. Real wealth rises in the long run.

Box 9.3 provides a schematic view of the transmission mechanism of foreign monetary policy for a relatively demand side open economy. The increase in the foreign interest rate raises the domestic interest rate and depreciates the exchange rate. The former crowds out investment expenditure and depresses domestic demand – channel (a) – whereas the latter improves competitiveness and stimulates net exports and therefore

---

Box 9.3 Increase in the foreign interest rate

$$rw\uparrow \Rightarrow \begin{cases} r\uparrow \Rightarrow I\downarrow \Rightarrow Y\downarrow & \text{(a)} \\[2mm] \quad COMP\downarrow \Rightarrow NX\uparrow \Rightarrow Y\uparrow & \text{(b)} \\[2mm] e\downarrow \Rightarrow \begin{cases} \dfrac{f}{e}\uparrow \Rightarrow C\uparrow \Rightarrow D\uparrow \Rightarrow Y\uparrow & \text{(c)} \end{cases} \end{cases}$$

$$(a) < ((b) + (c)) \Rightarrow u\downarrow \Rightarrow w\uparrow \Rightarrow p\uparrow \Rightarrow \begin{cases} \dfrac{V}{CPI}\downarrow \Rightarrow C\downarrow \Rightarrow Y\downarrow & \text{(d)} \\[3mm] \dfrac{M}{CPI}\downarrow \Rightarrow r\uparrow \Rightarrow I\downarrow \Rightarrow Y\downarrow & \text{(e)} \end{cases}$$

$$Y\uparrow \Rightarrow \dfrac{PSBR}{P}\downarrow \Rightarrow \dfrac{B}{P}\downarrow \Rightarrow \dfrac{V}{CPI}\downarrow \Rightarrow C\downarrow \Rightarrow Y\downarrow \qquad \text{(f)}$$

output – channel (b). The exchange rate fall increases the real net foreign asset position, raising real wealth and therefore consumption and output – channel (c).

For a relatively demand side open economy, channels (b) and (c) dominate the contractionary effect of channel (a) and output expands. This lowers unemployment and raises wage and price inflation. Higher prices erode the real value of wealth and money balances, thereby helping to reverse the expansionary phase in the long run – channels (d) and (e).

The initial stimulus in income raises tax revenues and produces a surplus in the budget. The central bank retires government debt from the market, thus reducing the value of government bonds. Real wealth falls and consumption declines, thereby reinforcing the contractionary forces of channels (d) and (e).

An illustration of the channels through which an increase in the foreign interest rate affects the domestic economy is provided by simulating model 9 under model-consistent and current account expectations. The experiment involves a permanent increase of 1 per cent in the foreign interest rate that brings the level to 11 per cent from 10 per cent for all 20 years. The increase in the foreign interest rate makes foreign bonds more attractive and this is satisfied, in the short run in which

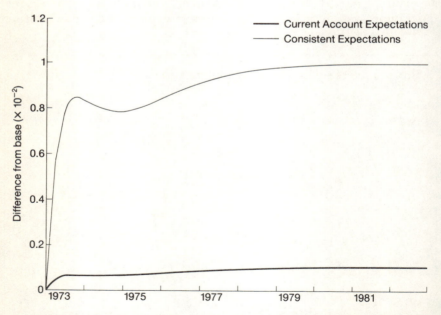

Figure 9.12 Interest rate response to a permanent increase in the foreign interest rate under monetary targets

wealth is fixed, by a portfolio re-allocation of running-down positions in domestic bonds and money balances. The resulting excess demand for money raises the domestic interest rate. With model-consistent expectations the interest rate rises by 85 basis points in the first year (see figure 9.12). The interest rate undershoots its new long-run equilibrium, which entails one-to-one adjustment. Hence, the domestic interest rate rises by 1 per cent in the new steady state. With current account expectations the domestic interest rate adjustment is only partial and involves short-run undershooting of the long-run equilibrium. In the new steady state the interest rate rises by only 10 basis points.

The exchange rate depreciates by 13 per cent on impact and then gradually recovers to converge to a steady-state depreciation of 9.4 per cent with model-consistent expectations (see figure 9.13). On the other hand, with current account expectations the exchange rate adjusts to its new steady state within three months. The depreciation is only 1 per cent.

The depreciation of the exchange rate enhances competitiveness in the first year by 6 per cent with model-consistent expectations and 0.5 per cent with current account expectations. Improved competitiveness stimulates net exports. The volume of exports increases by £1.9 billion and £0.16 billion in the first year of the adjustment process with model-consistent and current account expectations respectively. Similarly, the

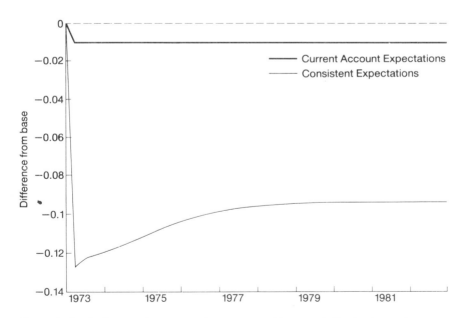

Figure 9.13 Exchange rate response to a permanent increase in the foreign exchange rate under monetary targets

volume of imports falls by £1.6 billion and £0.14 in the first year, respectively. As a result of this adjustment of net exports, output rises by 3 per cent in the first year with model-consistent expectations and 0.25 per cent with current account expectations (see figure 9.14). However, through time higher prices erode the initial gains in competitiveness, thereby reversing the expansionary forces. In the new steady state output returns to its initial value. With model-consistent expectations the adjustment is cyclical. Output falls below its initial steady state for a time as higher inflation more than offsets the initial gains in competitiveness.

Inflation rises at the initial phase of the expansion and then peters out as the stimulus fades away (see figure 9.15). With model-consistent expectations inflation rises to a peak of 2.34 per cent in the first year of the adjustment process, while with current account expectations inflation only rises to a maximum of 0.18 per cent. The difference in inflation is due not only to the higher output expansion with model-consistent expectations, but also to larger depreciation. In the new steady state inflation is back to zero under both expectations schemes, but prices are up by 10.5 per cent with model-consistent expectations and only 1 per cent with current account expectations.

Real wealth falls in the short run and rises in the long run (see figure 9.16). With model-consistent expectations real wealth falls by £20 billion (or 6.7 per cent), on average, in the first year. In the new steady state wealth is £6.4 billion higher than its initial value. With current account expectations wealth falls by £1.6 billion (or 0.5 per cent), on average, during the first year. It then gradually rises and in the new steady state it is £0.7 billion higher than its initial value. The fall of wealth during the first phase of the adjustment process is due to budget surplus caused by the income expansion. This forces the central bank to retire government bonds from the market. Furthermore, the real value of bonds is eroded by higher prices. The decline of wealth is also partly due to lower real money balances. However, through time the surplus in the trade account and the resultant increase in the net foreign asset position outweigh the reduction in the value of domestic bonds and wealth rises. Since the increase in prices and the income expansion are larger with model-consistent than with current account expectations, wealth falls much more under the former than the latter expectations scheme. However, the depreciation is also larger with model-consistent than with current account expectations, and therefore wealth rises more in the long run.

9.6 World Trade Shock – Increase in Foreign Demand

An increase in world trade stimulates output, raises the interest rate and real wealth, and appreciates the exchange rate, but has an ambiguous

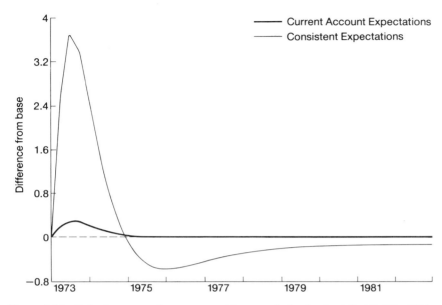

Figure 9.14 Output response to a permanent increase in the foreign interest rate under monetary targets

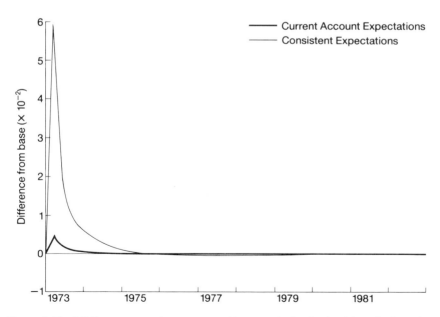

Figure 9.15 Inflation response to a permanent increase in the foreign interest rate under monetary targets

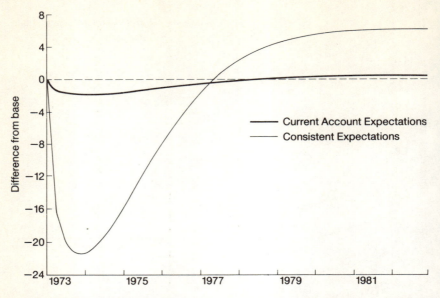

Figure 9.16 Real wealth response to a permanent increase in the foreign interest rate under monetary targets

effect on inflation, in the short run. The stimulus to output tends to raise inflation, but the appreciation in the exchange rate reduces inflation by lowering import prices. If the economy is relatively supply side open, inflation may fall. The trade account and the budget move into surplus in the short run.

In the long run, the stimulus to output is sustained, the inflation rate returns to zero, the exchange rate appreciates and real wealth rises, but not as much as in the short run. The surplus in the budget is equal to the surplus in the trade account. The interest rate may return to its initial level or fall even further.

The transmission mechanism is illustrated by simulating model 9 under the two expectations schemes. The experiment involves a 10 per cent increase in world trade maintained throughout the whole simulation period. The underlying monetary policy is neutral. The central bank controls the nominal supply of money.

The increase in world trade boosts exports and stimulates output (see figure 9.17). The stimulus to output is slightly larger in the short than in the long run. There is no difference between the two expectations schemes as far as the effect on output is concerned.

The rise in income increases the demand for money and the interest

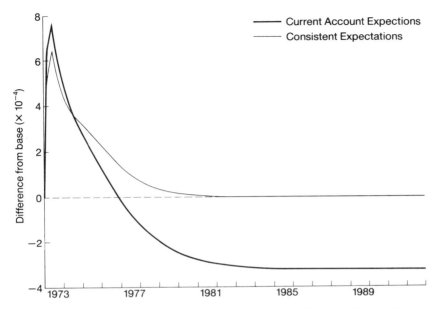

Figure 9.17 Output response to a permanent increase in world trade under monetary targets

rate rises to equilibrate the assets markets (see figure 9.18). The exchange rate appreciates as a direct result of the increase in world trade and the rise in the interest rate (see figure 9.19). With model-consistent expectations the exchange rate overshoots in the short run its long-run equilibrium value. With current account expectations the exchange rate jumps directly to its long-run equilibrium value. Despite that the difference between the two expectations schemes is very small.

Inflation falls in the short run as the effect of the higher exchange rate on import prices outweighs the effect of increased demand on prices, reflecting a relatively supply side open economy (see figure 9.20). Again, there is no significant difference between the inflation trajectories of the two expectations schemes.

Real wealth rises in the short run more than in the long run under both expectations schemes (see figure 9.21). This is because of a short-run fall of inflation. The rise in wealth is caused by the surplus in the trade account, which increases the net foreign position. This outweighs the small decline in the real value of government bonds because of the surplus in the budget. In the long run, the surplus in the trade account tapers off and therefore wealth declines. In the new steady state the small trade surplus equals the budget surplus.

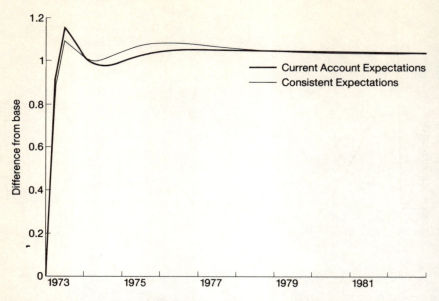

Figure 9.18   Interest rate response to a permanent increase in world trade under monetary targets

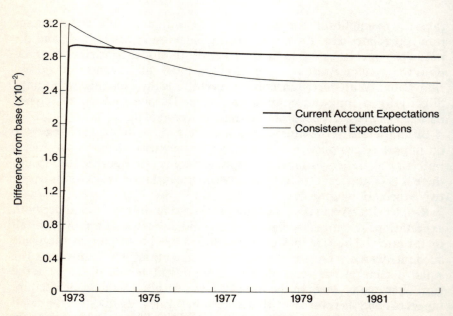

Figure 9.19   Exchange rate response to a permanent increase in world trade under monetary targets

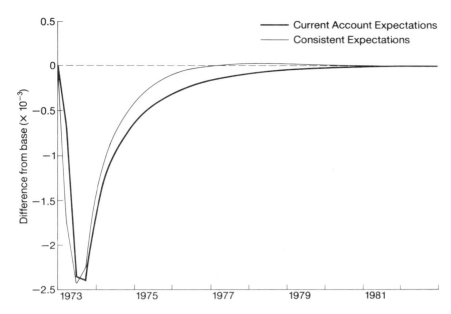

Figure 9.20   Inflation response to a permanent increase in world trade under monetary
targets

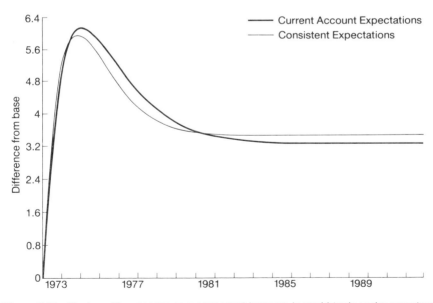

Figure 9.21   Real wealth response to a permanent increase in world trade under monetary
targets

9.7 An Adverse Supply Shock – Oil Price Rise

An increase in the price of oil causes short-run stagflation, exchange rate depreciation, higher interest rates, budget deficit, trade deficit and lower wealth. In the long run, the inflation rate returns to zero, but prices are higher; the output loss is permanent; the exchange rate remains lower; the budget deficit is equal to the trade deficit; real wealth is lower; and the interest rate may return to its initial value or fall.

Box 9.4 provides a schematic view of the main channels through which an increase in the price of oil affects the economy under a policy of monetary targets. The first effect is an increase in both consumer and producer prices. This harms competitiveness and reduces net exports and hence output – channel (a). The loss in competitiveness is partly offset by a fall in the exchange rate. The partial adjustment of the exchange rate is owing to the policy of monetary targets which implies a priority in reducing inflation over avoiding recession.

The increase in consumer prices lowers real wealth and this decreases consumption and output – channel (b). The increase in consumer prices erodes real money balances and therefore, in the short run, the interest rate rises in response to excess demand for money. Since the speed of adjustment of inflation expectations is lower than the speed of clearance of financial markets, the rise in the nominal interest rate implies a short-term increase in the real interest rate. This causes a contraction of domestic demand (consumption and investment) and therefore decreases income – channel (c).

Box 9.4 The transmission of an oil price rise under monetary targets

$$e\downarrow \text{ and } COMP\uparrow \Rightarrow NX\downarrow \Rightarrow Y\downarrow \qquad (a)$$

$$PIW\uparrow \Rightarrow P \text{ and } CPI\uparrow \Rightarrow \left\{ \begin{array}{l} \dfrac{V}{CPI}\downarrow \Rightarrow C\downarrow \Rightarrow Y\downarrow \qquad (b) \\[2ex] \dfrac{M}{CPI}\downarrow \Rightarrow r\uparrow \Rightarrow (r - p^e)\uparrow \Rightarrow C \text{ and } I\downarrow \Rightarrow Y\downarrow \qquad (c) \end{array} \right.$$

$$Y\downarrow \Rightarrow \dfrac{PSBR}{P}\uparrow \Rightarrow \dfrac{B}{P}\uparrow \Rightarrow \dfrac{V}{CPI}\uparrow \Rightarrow C\uparrow \Rightarrow Y\uparrow \qquad (d)$$

$$\left. \begin{array}{l} PIW\uparrow \Rightarrow \text{oil bill}\uparrow \\[2ex] P\uparrow \Rightarrow COMP\uparrow \Rightarrow X\downarrow \end{array} \right\} CB\downarrow \Rightarrow \dfrac{f}{e}\downarrow \Rightarrow \dfrac{V}{CPI}\downarrow \Rightarrow C\downarrow \Rightarrow Y\downarrow \qquad (e)$$

The income contraction leads to lower tax revenues, thus causing a budget deficit. With a policy of monetary targets the central bank sells government bonds to finance the deficit, thereby increasing, other things being equal, real wealth – channel (d). This stimulates demand and moderates the contractionary forces of channels (a) to (c).

Other things being equal, increased oil prices mean that the oil bill is higher, leading the trade account into deficit. Furthermore, the loss in competitiveness results in lower net exports, thereby deteriorating the trade deficit. This reduces the real net foreign asset position of the country, causing, *ceteris paribus*, a decline in real wealth. This depresses consumption and therefore income – channel (e).

An illustration of the transmission mechanism of an oil price rise is provided by simulating model 9 under model-consistent and current account expectations. The experiment involves a permanent 10 per cent increase in the price of oil in all periods of the 20-year simulation. The central bank follows a policy of monetary targets of keeping the nominal supply of money fixed.

Output falls monotonically under both expectations schemes until it reaches a new steady state that is 3 per cent lower than the initial one (see figure 9.22). The decline in output is due to a loss in competitiveness and falling wealth.

Inflation rises more with model-consistent than with current account

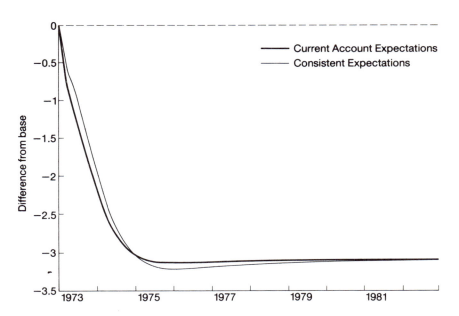

Figure 9.22   Output response to a permanent increase in the price of oil under monetary targets

expectations in the short run, because of greater exchange rate depreciation (see figure 9.23). In the long run, the rate of inflation returns to
zero, but prices are higher. With model-consistent expectations consumer prices are almost 3 per cent higher, while with current account
expectations prices rise by 2.2 per cent.

The exchange rate falls under both expectations schemes (see figure
9.24). With model-consistent expectations there is short-term overshooting in that the exchange rate falls in the short run more than in the
long run. The fall in the exchange rate is due to the decline in income and
the deterioration of the trade account, which implies lower wealth. With
current account expectations the exchange rate falls monotonically to its
new steady state. The fall is caused by the deficit in the trade account.

Real wealth falls under both expectations schemes (see figure 9.25). In
the short run, real wealth overshoots its long-run equilibrium value. The
extent of overshooting is larger and the recovery is greater in the new
steady state with model-consistent than with current account expectations. The decline in wealth in the short and long run is due to the
deterioration of the trade account, which diminishes the real net foreign
asset position. This is partly offset by the increase in the real value of
bonds because of the budget deficit. The fall of real wealth in the short
run is larger under model-consistent than under current account expectations because of higher inflation in the former.

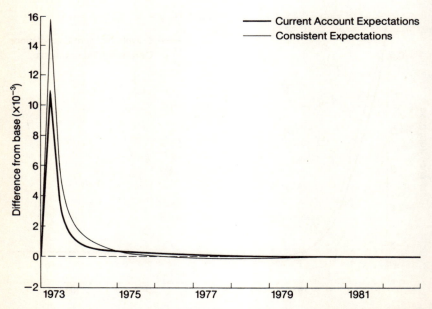

Figure 9.23   Inflation response to a permanent increase in the price of oil under monetary targets

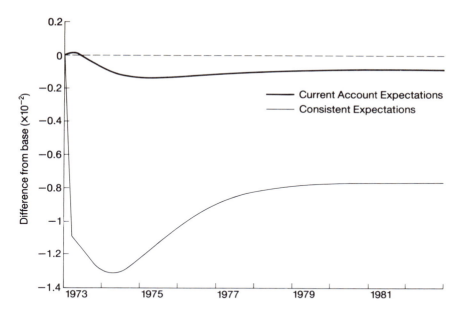

Figure 9.24 Exchange rate response to a permanent increase in the price of oil under monetary targets

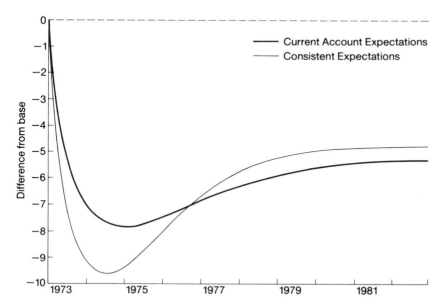

Figure 9.25 Real wealth response to a permanent increase in the price of oil under monetary targets

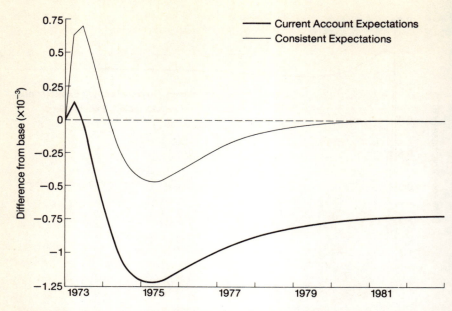

Figure 9.26   Interest rate response to a permanent increase in the price of oil under monetary targets

In the short run, the interest rate rises as higher prices erode real money balances (see figure 9.26). However, through time lower income and wealth reduce the demand for money and the interest rate falls. With model-consistent expectations the interest rate returns to its initial value, whereas with current account expectations the recovery is only partial.

9.8 Conclusions

The expectations formation mechanism in the foreign exchange market is important in determining the dynamic adjustment path of output and inflation to a shock in world trade or oil price, or to a change in economic policy. Exchange rate expectations do not affect the steady-state properties of output and inflation. However, they do affect both the steady-state properties and the dynamic adjustment of the interest rate, exchange rate and real wealth.

In the short run, easy monetary policy stimulates output, raises inflation, lowers the interest rate, depreciates the exchange rate, creates a budget surplus, probably causes a trade deficit and lowers wealth. In the long run, the stimulus to output fades away, inflation returns to zero, the exchange rate depreciates and the budget turns into a small deficit that is equal to the deficit of the trade account. However, the effect on interest rates and wealth is ambiguous.

Expansionary fiscal policy under bond finance stimulates output in the short run, raises prices and the interest rate, produces a deficit in the budget and the trade balance, but has an ambiguous effect on real wealth and the exchange rate. With model-consistent expectations the exchange rate appreciates and real wealth rises. However, with current account expectations the exchange rate depreciates and wealth falls. In the long run, the stimulus to output is largely eroded, but is still positive. The rate of inflation converges to zero. Real wealth rises. The budget deficit is equal to the deficit in the trade account. The interest rate returns to its initial value and the exchange rate is higher in the new steady state with model-consistent expectations. On the other hand, the interest rate remains higher in the new steady state and the exchange rate depreciates with current account expectations.

A permanent increase in government expenditure under money finance is unstable. The interest rate, exchange rate and real wealth fall continously unless the government stops printing money or reduces its expenditure to its previous level. A government can therefore revert to money finance for only a short period of time. It cannot go on indefinitely financing its deficit by printing money.

Assuming a relatively demand side open economy, an increase in the foreign interest rate depreciates the exchange rate, raises the domestic interest rate, reduces real wealth, expands output and raises inflation, in the short run. In the long run, the domestic interest rate rises and the exchange rate falls, but the extent of these changes depends on the exchange rate expectations scheme. With model-consistent expectations the domestic interest rate rises to match the level of the foreign interest rate, but with current account expectations the domestic interest rate rise is only partial. The exchange rate depreciates much more with model-consistent than with current account expectations. The effect on output and inflation is only transient.

An increase in world trade stimulates output, raises the interest rate and real wealth, and appreciates the exchange rate, but has an ambiguous effect on inflation, in the short run. The stimulus to output tends to raise inflation, but the appreciation in the exchange rate reduces inflation by lowering import prices. If the economy is relatively supply side open, inflation may fall. The trade account and the budget move into surplus in the short run. In the long run, the stimulus to output is sustained, the inflation rate returns to zero, the exchange rate appreciates and real wealth rises, but not as much as in the short run. The surplus in the budget is equal to the surplus in the trade account.

An increase in the price of oil causes short run stagflation, exchange rate depreciation, higher interest rates, budget deficit, trade deficit and lower wealth. In the long run, the inflation rate returns to zero, but prices are higher; the output loss is permanent; the exchange rate remains lower; the budget deficit is equal to the trade deficit; real wealth is lower; and the interest rate may return to its initial value or fall.

References

Abel, A. (1979) *Investment and the Value of Capital*. New York: Garland.

Abel, A. (1981) Dynamic adjustment in a putty putty model: implications for testing the putty clay hypothesis. *International Economic Review*, 22, 19–36.

Abel, A. (1983) Optimal investment under uncertainty. *American Economic Review*, 73, 228–33.

Abel, A. (1985) Precautionary savings and accidental bequests. *American Economic Review*, 75, 777–91.

Akerlof, G. (1984) Gift exchange and efficiency wages: four views. *American Economic Review Proceedings*, 74, 79–83.

Akerlof, G. and H. Miyazaki (1980) The implicit contract theory of unemployment meets the wage bill argument. *Review of Economic Studies*, 47, 321–38.

Akerlof, G. and J. Yellen (1985) A near-rational model of the business with wage and price inertia. *Quarterly Journal of Economics*, 100, supplement, 823–38.

Akerlof, G. and J. Yellen (1987) The fair wage effort hypothesis and unemployment. Mimeo, University of California, Berkeley.

Alchian, A. (1969) Information costs, pricing and resource unemployment. *Western Economic Journal*, 7, 109–28.

Allais, M. (1947) *Economie et Interest*. Paris: Imprimerie Nationale.

Ando, A. and F. Modigliani (1963) The life cycle hypothesis of saving: aggregate implications and tests. *American Economic Review*, 53, 55–84.

Arnott, R. and J. Stiglitz (1982) Equilibrium in competitive insurance markets: the welfare effects of moral hazard. Mimeo, Princeton University.

Azariadis, C. (1975) Implicit contracts and underemployment equilibria. *Journal of Political Economy*, 83, 1183–202.

Azariadis, C. (1979) Implicit contracts and related topics: a survey. In Z. Hornstein et al. (eds), *The Economics of the Labour Market*. London: HMSO.

Azariadis, C. (1983) Employment with asymmetric information. *Quarterly Journal of Economics*, 98, 157–72.

Azariadis, C. and J.E. Stiglitz (1983) Implicit contracts and fixed price equilibria. *Quarterly Journal of Economics*, 98, 1–22.

Baily, M. (1974) Wages and employment under uncertain demand. *Review of Economic Studies*, 41, 37–50.

Ball, L. and D. Romer (1989a) Are prices too sticky? *Quarterly Journal of Economics*, 104, 507–24.

316   *References*

Ball, L. and D. Romer (1989b) The equilibrium and optimal timing of price changes. *Review of Economic Studies*, 56, 179–98.

Barro, R. (1972) A theory of monopolistic price adjustment. *Review of Economic Studies*, 34, 17–26.

Barro, R. (1974) Are government bonds net wealth? *Journal of Political Economy*, 82, 1095–117.

Barro, R. (1976) Integer constraints and aggregation in the inventory model of money demand. *Journal of Finance*, March.

Barro, R. (1977) Long term contracting, sticky prices and monetary policy. *Journal of Monetary Economics*, 3, 305–16.

Barro, R.J. and H.I. Grossman (1976) *Money, Employment and Inflation*. Cambridge: Cambridge University Press.

Baumol, W. (1952) The transactions demand for cash. *Quarterly Journal of Economics*, 67, 545–56.

Bernheim, B.D. (1987) Ricardian equivalence: an evaluation of theory and evidence. *NBER Macroeconomics Annual*, 2, 263–303.

Bischoff, C.W. (1969) Hypothesis testing and the demand for capital goods. *Review of Economics and Statistics*, 51, 354–68.

Bischoff, C.W. (1971) Business investment in the 1970s: a comparison of models. *Brookings Papers on Economic Activity*, 1, 13–63.

Blanchard, O.J. (1985) Debt, deficits and finite horizons. *Journal of Political Economy*, 93, 223–47.

Blanchard, O.J. (1986) The wage–price spiral. *Quarterly Journal of Economics*, 101, 543–65.

Blanchard, O.J. and S. Fischer (1990) *Lectures on Macroeconomics*. Cambridge, MA: MIT Press.

Blanchard, O.J. and N. Kiyotaki (1987) Monopolistic competition and the effects of aggregate demand. *American Economic Review*, 77, 647–66.

Blanchard, O.J. and L.H. Summers (1986) Hysteresis and the European unemployment problem. *NBER Macroeconomics Annual*, 1, 15–77.

Brechling, F.P. (1975) *Investment and Employment Decisions*. Manchester: Manchester University Press.

Bresnahan, T.F. (1989) Industries with market power. In. R. Schmalensee and R. Willig (eds), *Handbook of Industrial Organisation*. Amsterdam: North-Holland, 1011–57.

Brown, T.M. (1952) Habit persistence and lags in consumer behaviour. *Econometrica*, 20, 355–71.

Caballero, R.J. (1991) On the sign of the investment–uncertainty relationship. *American Economic Review*, 81, 279–88.

Calvo, G. (1979) Quasi Walrasian theories of unemployment. *American Economic Review*, 69, 102–7.

Campbell, J. and N.G. Mankiw (1987) Are output fluctuations transitory? *Quarterly Journal of Economics*, 102, 857–80.

Campbell, J.Y. and N.G. Mankiw (1989) Consumption, income and interest rates: reinterpreting the time series evidence. *NBER Macroeconomics Annual*, 4, 185–216.

Caplin, A. and D. Spulber (1987) Menu costs and the neutrality of money. *Quarterly Journal of Economics*, 102, 703–26.

Carlton, D.W. (1986) The rigidity of prices. *American Economic Review*, 76, 637–58.

Carroll, C. and L.H. Summers (1989) *Consumption Growth Parallels Income Growth: Some New Evidence*. Cambridge, MA: Harvard University Press.

Cecchetti, S. (1986) The frequency of price adjustment: a study of the newsstand prices of magazines. *Journal of Econometrics*, 31, 255–74.

Clark, J.M. (1917) Business acceleration and the law of demand. *Journal of Political Economy*, 25, 217–35.

Clower, R. (1967) A reconsideration of the microeconomic foundations of monetary theory. *Western Economic Journal*, 6, 1–8.

Craine, R. (1989) Risky business: the allocation of capital. *Journal of Monetary Economics*, 23, 201–18.

Diamond, P.A. (1965) National debt in a neo-classical growth model. *American Economic Review*, 55, 1126–50.

Dreze, J. and F. Modigliani (1972) Consumption decisions under uncertainty. *Journal of Economic Theory*, 5, 308–35.

Driver, C. and D. Moreton (1991) The influence of uncertainty on UK manufacturing investment. *Economic Journal*, 101, 1452–9.

Driver, C. and D. Moreton (1992) *Investment, Expectations and Uncertainty*. Oxford: Blackwell.

Duesenberry, J.S. (1949) *Income, Saving and the Theory of Consumer Behaviour*. Cambridge, MA: Harvard University Press.

Dunlop, J. (1944) *Wage Determination under Trade Unions*. New York: Macmillan.

Eisner, R. and M.I. Nadiri (1968) Investment theory and neo-classical theory. *Review of Economics and Statistics*, 50, 369–82.

Espinosa, M. and C.Y. Rhee (1987) Efficient wage bargaining as a repeated game. Mimeo, Harvard University.

Feensta, R. (1986) Functional equivalence between liquidity costs and the utility of money. *Journal of Monetary Economics*, 17, 271–91.

Fischer, S. (1977a) Wage indexation and macroeconomic stability. In K. Brunner and A. Meltzer (eds), *Stabilisation of the Domestic and International Economy*, Carnegie-Rochester Conference Series on Public Policy, 5. Amsterdam: North Holland, 107–47.

Fischer, S. (1977b) Long term contracts, rational expectations and the optimal money supply rule. *Journal of Political Economy*, 85, 191–205.

Fischer, S. (1988) Recent developments in macroeconomics. *Economic Journal*, 98, 294–339.

Flavin, M.A. (1981) The adjustment of consumption to changing expectations about future income. *Journal of Political Economy*, 89, 974–1009.

Friedman, M. (1957) *A Theory of the Consumption Function*. Princeton, NJ: Princeton University Press.

Frisch, R. (1933) Propagation and impulse problems in dynamic economics. In *Economic Essays in Honour of Gustav Cassel*. London, Macmillan, 171–205.

Gordon, D. (1974) A neo-classical theory of Keynesian unemployment. *Economic Inquiry*, 12, 431–59.

Gordon, R. (1982) Why US wage and employment behaviour differs from that in Britain and Japan. *Economic Journal*, 92, 13–44.

Gordon, R. (1983) A century of evidence on wage and price stickiness in the US, UK and Japan. In J. Tobin (ed.), *Macroeconomics, Prices and Quantities*. Washington, DC: Brookings Institution.

Gordon, R. (1990) What is new-Keynesian economics? *Journal of Economic Literature*, 28, 1175–81.

Gottfries, N. and H. Horn (1987) Wage formation and the persistence of unemployment. *Economic Journal*, 97, 877–86.

Gray, J.A. (1976) Wage indexation: a macroeconomic approach. *Journal of Monetary Economics*, 2, 221–35.

Grossman, S. and O. Hart (1981) Implicit contracts, moral hazard, and unemployment. *American Economic Review*, 71 (papers and proceedings), 301–7.

Grossman, S. and O. Hart (1983) Implicit contracts under asymmetric information. *Quarterly Journal of Economics*, 98, 1223–56.

Haavelmo, T. (1960) *A Study in the Theory of Investment*. Chicago: Chicago University Press.

Hadjimatheou, G. (1987) *Consumer Economics after Keynes*. Brighton: Wheatsheaf.

Hall, R. (1978) Stochastic implications of the life cycle–permanent income hypothesis: theory and evidence. *Journal of Political Economy*, 86, 971–87.

Hall, R. and F.S. Mishkin (1982) The sensitivity of consumption to transitory income: estimates from panel data on households. *Econometrica*, 50, 461–81.

Hart, O. (1983) Optimal labour contracts under asymmetric information: an introduction. *Review of Economic Studies*, 50, 3–36.

Hartman, R. (1972) The effects of price and cost uncertainty and investment. *Journal of Economic Theory*, 5, 258–66.

Hashimoto, M. (1981) Firm-specific human capital as a shared investment. *American Economic Review*, 71, 23–54.

Hausman, J.A. (1973) Theoretical and empirical aspects of vintage capital models. Unpublished PhD thesis, Oxford University.

Hayashi, F. (1982) Tobin's marginal q and average q: a neo-classical interpretation. *Econometrica*, 50, 213–24.

Hayashi, F. (1985) Tests of liquidity constraints: a critical survey. *NBER Working Paper* no. 1720.

Jorgenson, D.W. (1963) Capital theory and investment behaviour. *American Economic Review*, 53, 247–56.

Jorgenson, D.W. (1967) The theory of investment behaviour. In R. Ferber (ed.), *Determinants of Investment Behaviour*. New York: Columbia University Press.

Jorgenson, D.W. (1972) Investment behaviour and the production function. *Bell Journal of Economics*, 3, 220–51.

Jorgenson, D.W. and C.D. Siebert (1968) A comparison of alternative theories of corporate investment behaviour. *American Economic Review*, 58, 681–712.

Katz, L.F. (1988) Some recent developments in labour economics and their implications for macroeconomics. *Journal of Money Credit and Banking*, 20, 507–22.

Kiyotaki, N. (1985) Macroeconomics of monopolistic competition. PhD dissertation, Harvard University.

Kotlikoff, L.J. and L.H. Summers (1981) The role of intergenerational transfers in aggregate capital accumulation. *Journal of Political Economy*, 89, 706-32.

Krugman, P., T. Persson and L. Svenson (1985) Inflation, interest rates and welfare. *Quarterly Journal of Economics*, 100, 677-96.

Layard, R. and S.J. Nickell (1986) Unemployment in Britain. *Economica*, 53, 121-70.

Leibenstein, J. (1957) *Economic Backwardness and Economic Growth*. New York: Wiley.

Leland, H. (1968) Saving and uncertainty: the precautionary demand for saving. *Quarterly Journal of Economics*, 82, 465-73.

Leontief, W. (1946) The pure theory of the guaranteed annual wage contract. *Journal of Political Economy*, 54, 76-9.

Lindbeck, A. and D. Snower (1986) Wage setting, unemployment and insider-outsider relations. *American Economic Review*, 76, 235-9.

Lindbeck, A. and D. Snower (1987) Union activity, unemployment persistence and wage-employment ratchets. *European Economic Review*, 31, 157-67.

Lindbeck, A. and D. Snower (1988) Cooperation, harassment and involuntary unemployment: an insider-outsider Approach. *American Economic Review*, 78, 167-88.

Lucas, R. and N. Stokey (1987) Money and interest in a cash-in-advance Economy. *Econometrica*, 55, 491-514.

McDonald, R. and D.R. Siegel (1985) Investment and the valuation of firms when there is an option to shut down. *International Economic Review*, 26, 331-49.

McDonald, I. and R. Solow (1981) Wage bargaining and employment. *American Economic Review*, 71, 896-908.

McDonald, I. and R. Solow (1985) Wages and employment in a segmented market. *Quarterly Journal of Economics*, 100, 1115-41.

Mankiw, N.G. (1985) Small menu costs and large business cycles: a macroeconomic model of monopoly. *Quarterly Journal of Economics*, 100, 529-39.

Mankiw, N.G. (1990) A quick refresher course in macroeconomics. *Journal of Economic Literature*, 28, 1645-60.

Merton, R. (1969) Lifetime portfolio selection under uncertainty: the continuous time case. *Review of Economics and Statistics*, 51, 247-57.

Modigliani, F. and R.E. Brumberg (1954) Utility analysis and the consumption function. In K.K. Kurihara (ed.), *Post Keynesian Economics*. New Brunswick, NJ: Rutgers University Press.

Nickell, S.J. (1978) *The Investment Decisions of Firms*. Cambridge: Cambridge University Press.

Nickell, S.J. (1982) A bargaining model of the Phillips curve. Discussion paper 105, Centre for Labour Economics, London School of Economics.

Okun, A.M. (1975) Inflation: its mechanism and welfare cost. *Brookings Papers on Economic Activity*, 2, 351-401.

Okun, A.M. (1981) *Prices and Quantities: a Macroeconomic Analysis*. Washington, DC: Brookings Institution.

Oswald, A. (1985) The economic theory of trade unions: an introductory survey. *Scandinavian Journal of Economics*, 87, 160–93.

Pencavel, J. (1985) Wages and employment under trade unionism: micro-economic models and macroeconomic applications. *Scandinavian Journal of Economics*, 87, 197–225.

Paraskevopoulos, D., E. Karakitsos and B. Rustem (1991) Robust capacity expansion under uncertainty. *Management Science*, 37, 787–800.

Phelps, E.S. (1970) *Microeconomic Foundations of Employment and Inflation Theory*. New York: Norton.

Phelps, E.S. and J. Taylor (1977) Stabilizing powers of monetary policy under rational expectations. *Journal of Political Economy*, 85, 163–90.

Phelps, E.S. and S. Winter (1970) Optimal price policy under atomistic competition. In E.S. Phelps (ed.), *The Microeconomic Foundations of Employment and Inflation Theory*. New York: Norton.

Pindyck, R.S. (1988) Irreversible investment, capacity choice and the value of the firm. *American Economic Review*, 78, 969–85.

Precious, M. (1987) *Rational Expectations, Non-market Clearing and Investment Theory*. Oxford: Clarendon Press.

Ramsey, F. (1928) A mathematical theory of saving. *Economic Journal*, 38, 543–59.

Romer, D. (1986) A simple general equilibrium version of the Baumol–Tobin model. *Quarterly Journal of Economics*, 101, 663–86.

Romer, D. (1987) The monetary transmission mechanism in a general equilibrium version of the Baumol–Tobin model. *Journal of Monetary Economics*, 20, 105–22.

Rotemberg, J. (1987) The new-Keynesian microfoundations. *NBER Macroeconomics Annual*, 2, 69–104.

Sachs, J. (1980) The changing cyclical behaviour of wages and prices: 1890–1976. *American Economic Review*, 70, 78–90.

Salop, S. (1979) A model of the natural rate of unemployment. *American Economic Review*, 69, 117–25.

Samuelson, P.A. (1958) An exact consumption-loan model of interest with or without the social contrivance of money. *Journal of Political Economy*, 66, 467–82.

Samuelson, P.A. (1969) Lifetime portfolio selection by dynamic stochastic programming. *Review of Economics and Statistics*, 51, 239–46.

Sargent, T. and N. Wallace (1975) Rational expectations, the optimal monetary instrument and the optimal money supply rule. *Journal of Political Economy*, 83, 241–54.

Shapiro, C. and J.E. Stiglitz (1984) Equilibrium unemployment as a discipline device. *American Economic Review*, 74, 433–44.

Sheshinski, E. and Y. Weiss (1983) Optimum pricing policy under stochastic inflation. *Review of Economic Studies*, 50, 513–29.

Sidrauski, M. (1967) Rational choice and patterns of growth in a monetary economy. *American Economic Review*, 57, 534–44.

Slutzky, E. (1937) The summation of random causes as the source of cycle. *Econometrica*, 312–30.

Solow, R. (1979) Another possible source of wage and stickiness. *Journal of Macroeconomics*, 1, 79–82.

Solow, R. (1985) Insiders and outsiders in wage determination. *Scandinavian Journal of Economics*, 87, 411–28.

Stigler, G. and J.K. Kindahl (1970) *The Behaviour of Industrial Prices*. New York: Columbia University Press.

Stiglitz, J.E. (1976) The efficiency wage hypothesis, surplus labour and the distribution of income in LDCs. *Oxford Economic Papers*, 28, 185–207.

Stiglitz, J.E. (1982) The wage productivity hypothesis: its economic consequences and policy implications. Mimeo, Princeton University.

Stiglitz, J.E. (1986) Theories of wage rigidity. In J. Butkiewicz et al. (eds), *Keynes' Economic Legacy*. New York: Praeger, 159–206.

Taylor, J. (1980) Aggregate dynamics and staggered contracts. *Journal of Political Economy*, 88, 1–24.

Tobin, J. (1956) The interest elasticity of the transactions demand for cash. *Review of Economics and Statistics*, 38, 241–7.

Tobin, J. (1958) Liquidity preference as behaviour towards risk. *Review of Economic Studies*, 25, 65–86.

Tobin, J. (1967) Comments on Jorgenson. In R. Ferber (ed.), *Determinants of Investment Behaviour*. New York: Columbia University Press for NBER.

Tobin, J. and W. Brainard (1977) Asset markets and the cost of capital. In B. Belassa and R. Nelson (eds), *Economic Progress, Private Values and Public Policy: Essays in Honour of W. Fellner*.

Weiss, A. (1980) Job queues and layoffs in labour markets with flexible wages. *Journal of Political Economy*, 88, 526–38.

Weiss, A. (1990) *Efficiency Wages: Models of Unemployment, Layoffs and Wage Dispersion*. Princeton, NJ: Princeton University Press.

Whalen, E.H. (1966) A rationalisation of the precautionary demand for cash. *Quarterly Journal of Economics*, 80, 314–24.

Yellen, J.L. (1984) Efficiency wage models of unemployment. *American Economic Review*, 74, 200–5.

Yoshikawa, H. (1980) On the 'q' theory of investment. *American Economic Review*, 70, 739–43.

Index

ESTAT – PROGRAM
written by R.G. Becker

Introduction

The README file contains instructions on how to back-up the distribution floppy disk, how to install the software on to your hard disk and simple usage instructions. The distributed software contains proprietary material and is provided for the exclusive use of the purchaser. It may not be sold or released for the benefit of a third party. The software and other files in packed and unpacked forms are Copyright © R.G. Becker, 1992. The author and publisher take no responsibility whatever for any loss or damage resulting from the use of this software – this software is employed entirely at the user's own risk.

The ESTAT software as distributed is for IBM PCs and 100 per cent compatibles. The software is known to work with a wide variety of machines from Toshiba portables using Intel 8088 cpus to IBM PS/2s and AT bus machines with 80386 cpus. The use of a floating point coprocessor (80×87) is recommended, but not required. ESTAT can plot to the screen on machines with the Hercules monochrome video card or any machine with VGA, EGA or CGA compatible video cards. The plotting software can also plot to printers which are compatible with the Epson FX or LQ series dot-matrix printers or to HP Laserjet laser printers (and compatibles). The software requires around 500kB free hard disk space and requires around 256kB RAM to run efficiently (it will run less efficiently with less memory).

Backing up the Distribution Disk

The distribution disk contains all the software so to prevent accidental loss you should make a copy of the disk as soon as possible. You can use any of the standard copying programs to copy all the files on the distribution floppy to another disk. If you have a second floppy drive a typical sequence of commands to do this might be

```
format b:
copy A: *.* B:
```

which first formats a disk in drive B and then copies all files from drive A to drive B. The distribution disk should contain the following files

estatexe.pkd
estatdat.pkd
estatprc.pkd
estathlp.pkd
leeexe.pkd
model5.pkd
model7.pkd
model8.pkd
model9.pkd
question.pkd
README
adecode.exe
install.exe

where the files with .pkd extensions are packed files.

Installation

It is assumed that ESTAT will be installed on a hard disk. To install the software and associated files place the back-up copy of the distribution disk into one of the floppy drives (e.g. drive A) and then type the command

A: install   (or B: install if using drive B)

at the DOS prompt. The INSTALL program will then ask various questions about where to place the software and about some default parameters that the ESTAT program wants (such as what kind of printer (if any) you will use with the software). Having determined reasonable answers to these questions INSTALL will proceed to unpack the files on the distribution disk and place these on the hard drive. The following files will be placed on your hard disk in one or more directories (the number of directories depending on the answers to the questions asked by INSTALL):

estat.exe	ESTAT executable
lee.exe	helper program for ESTAT
estat.dat	data file for the book
estat.prc	script file used by ESTAT for the examples
estat.hlp	help file for ESTAT; you can also read this for more information on ESTAT's commands
estat.ini	initialization file created by INSTALL; this ASCII file is read by ESTAT on start-up. INSTALL sets certain parameters using this file. You can edit the file to change the default assumptions made by the INSTALL program.
model5	These are the model files used by ESTAT to carry
model7	out the example simulations. The numbers correspond
model8	to the book chapter in which the models are
model9	introduced.
question.txt	ASCII text file containing suggested exercises.

Beginning

As set up by the INSTALL program, ESTAT is ready to go for the examples. At the DOS prompt just type

    ESTAT

and you will then get a command prompt of the form

    Enter command:

this indicates that ESTAT is waiting for user input. The most important input is, of course, 'quit' – the command that causes ESTAT to return you to the DOS prompt.

To carry out one of the examples just type

    shock1;

and answer the questions. The ESTAT program will then create databases and so forth to carry out a perturbation of the desired model. You can view the results by entering the commands

    plot1;

or

    print1;

to plot or print results on the screen. A comparison experiment can be made by using the command

    shock2;

which is like shock1, but which simulates to a result ss2. The corresponding results can be viewed using

    plot2;
    print2;

or

    plotb;

which will plot results from both ss1 and ss2. To print the differences ss2 − ss1, you can use the printd command. The command shocks carries out both shocks one after another. Finally, the command plothorizon may be used to set up the default plotting start and finish; this will be useful when the trajectories converge to a steady state fairly quickly and most plots will be flat after say 1982 (i.e. not very exciting). If you want to see an anticipated shock you can use the command shock period to set the date at which variable changes occur. This is useful only when the model uses consistent expectations (which can effectively see into the future). Normally the shocks are applied at the start of the simulation period (1973:1) and it is assumed that the past is fixed. If you set the shock date in, say, 1974:1 then (in a CE model) clever agents (in the economy) react to the shock before it occurs; this is an anticipated shock. In the other case we disallow changes to past expectations so the shock is unanticipated. The effect of the shock period command lasts for the next shock only (even if this fails to solve properly).

General Points

It's quite possible that you won't get the hang of using ESTAT right away; it's quite daunting to be faced with a program as complicated as ESTAT when it asks for input and you have no idea what to do. ESTAT is not exactly user-friendly, but you can usually get it back to the command prompt (and the quit command) by typing ;. The program will then either moan about some missing input or will proceed to do something. A further complication is that the program sometimes halts its output to allow you to see what's on the screen. You will then see a prompt at the bottom of the screen

CR/Header/space/Go/Abort/Skip

which means that at this point you can type a single character to

get 1 more line ....CR(carriage return)
get 1 more page ....space bar
get more until a new header line is at the top ....h
go forever (until output ceases) ....g
abort the current action ....a
skip current output ....s.

Similarly when a plot is on the screen you can

transfer the plot to a printer ....p
replot...r
return to command mode....................................Esc key or CR.

Of course you can only plot to a printer if the program has been correctly set up and there is a printer attached to your computer. It should be noted that although ESTAT only knows how to plot on certain printers, ordinary screen printing will work provided that it normally does so.

The majority of commands can be interrupted using Control-C (i.e. press both the control and C keys at the same time); at the next program output you will then be asked if you wish to abort. If you do just enter an a.

Model Variable and Coefficient Names

The example test procedures require you to enter the names of variables and if desired coefficients. The convention used is that Greek letters are spelt as follows: alpha, gamma and delta. Since it is impossible to enter subscripts we have adopted the convention of using the underscore '_' character to denote subscripts and when in the book there are two subscripts we separate these with an underscore as well. Thus the marginal propensity to consume is denoted in our notation as alpha__C__Y. If in doubt about the names of coefficients, etc., you can use the ESTAT commands show model;, show variables; and show coefficients; to see which ones are actually present (only if a model has been loaded, e.g. by a shock1/2 etc.). Remember that for model names case is important, i.e. CPI and cpi are not the same (although they are of course closely related).

Problems

The example software will often be sufficient to accomplish most of the things you may wish to do to the models, but these are not guaranteed to be solvable under all circumstances (e.g. you may shock a variable too much). In these cases the model may be unsolvable for a variety of reasons. The solution procedure may complain about arithmetic errors or too many iterations etc.; in these cases it may be possible to get the model to solve by reducing the shock size. Alternatively it may be possible to get the model to solve by altering the solution method (help solt;) or the method of imposition of consistent expectations (help sre*;). If you think that you feel confident enough to do this then you can repeat the simulation that failed by using the ESTAT command sim s ss1 or sim s ss2. Most of the parameters that may be of use can be set up using the command

    setup;

which asks for the values of the major parameters that affect the carrying out of the shocks. The default values are those initially used by the example procedures.

Colour Plotting

As distributed the example procedures don't plot in colour; it's possible to get the procedures to plot in colour by altering the procedure file ESTAT.PRC using an ASCII editor. The numbers 32767 should be changed to values in the range 0 to 1 less than the number of colours for your video display mode. It's very difficult to determine these numbers in advance so one can try them out using an ESTAT command of the form

    plot Y(ss1):colour cnum;

Zero (0) is almost certainly black (i.e. non-plotting) and NCOLOURS-1 will most likely be bright white, but this depends on the exact set-up of your machine and video card.

Example Commands

shock1	shock a model to ss1 (possibly with parameter changes).
shock2	shock a model to ss2 (possibly with parameter changes).

shock_period	set period at which the shock starts. Lasts for one shock only.
shocks	same as shock1; shock2;
plot1	plot results from ss1
plot2	plot results from ss2
plotb	plot results from ss2 and ss1
print1	print (on screen) results from ss1
print2	print (on screen) results from ss2
printd	print (on screen) results from ss2–ss1
setup	change default convergence criteria
plothorizon	change default plotting horizon

Exercises

Model 5

1   A monetary expansion is more stimulative in the short run with monetary than with debt targets. Why?

2   Compare the short-run and long-run effectiveness of monetary policy in the linear and non-linear models.

3   A fiscal stimulus is more expansionary in the short run but less expansionary in the long run with money than with bond finance. Why? Is this result robust to the linearity assumption of the model?

4   A strong wealth effect in the demand for money relative to consumption makes a bond finance fiscal stimulus unstable. Why?

5   Analyse the interrelationship of the wealth effects in the consumption and the demand for money functions, as well as the interest sensitivity of aggregate demand and the demand for money with respect to the stability of fiscal policy.

Model 7

1   Analyse the transmission of a fiscal stimulus under bond and money finance with adaptive expectations of inflation.

2   Compare the response of the economy to an unanticipated permanent increase in government expenditure under model consistent (or rational) and adaptive expectations of inflation. Prices increase more with adaptive than consistent expectations. Why? Examine the robustness of this result to the method of finance and the linearity assumption of the model.

3   Compare the response of the economy to an anticipated and unanticipated fiscal stimulus under model consistent (or rational) and adaptive expectations.

4   Fiscal policy is more expansionary with money than with bond finance in the short run irrespective of whether inflation expectations are model consistent or adaptive. Why?

5   A fiscal stimulus under bond finance is more expansionary with the non-linear than with the linear model. Why? Check the robustness of this result to the inflation expectations mechanism.

6   A fiscal stimulus under money finance is more expansionary with the linear than with the non-linear model. This is the opposite conclusion to that reached under bond finance. Why? Check the robustness of this result to the inflation expectations mechanism.

7   A monetary stimulus (open market purchase) is more expansionary in the short run with monetary than with debt targets. Why? Is this result robust to the inflation expectations mechanism?

8   The long-term effect of a monetary stimulus (open market purchase) on prices is zero in the linear model with adaptive inflation expectations. Why? Is this result robust to the type of monetary policy pursued by the central bank?

9   A monetary stimulus with model consistent expectations increases prices in the short run but decreases them in the long run. Is this a plausible behaviour? Which parameter values would you change and what values should they assume to alter this result? Compare the results of this exercise with those from exercise 8.

10 An oil price rise causes stagflation, but the recession is shallower with model consistent than with adaptive inflation expectations. Why? Is this result robust to the type of monetary policy?

11 Compare the response of the economy to an anticipated and unanticipated monetary expansion with model consistent and adaptive expectations.

Model 8

1   A fiscal stimulus with money finance and without sterilization is more expansionary in the short run than with bond finance with sterilization. Why? Is this result robust to the inflation expectations mechanism and the linearity assumption of the model?

2   Compare the effects of a fiscal expansion with money finance and without sterilization under model consistent (or rational) and adaptive inflation expectations.

3   A fiscal expansion with money finance and sterilization is unstable. Why? Is this result robust to the inflation expectations mechanism?

4   A fiscal expansion with bond finance without sterilization is unstable. Why? Is this result robust to the inflation expectations mechanism?

5   Compare the effects of an anticipated and unanticipated fiscal expansion under model consistent and adaptive inflation expectations.

6   A monetary expansion is more stimulative in the short run with monetary targets and sterilization than with debt targets and without sterilization.

Why? Is this result robust to the inflation expectations mechanism and the linearity assumption of the model?

7   A monetary stimulus with model consistent expectations raises prices in the short run, but lowers them in the long run. Is this plausible? Which parameters should be changed and what values should they assume to alter this result?

8   Compare the effects of an anticipated and unanticipated monetary expansion with model consistent and adaptive inflation expectations.

9   An oil price rise leads to stagflation, but the recession is shallower and inflation is lower with model consistent than with adaptive inflation expectations. Why? Is this result robust to the type of monetary policy and the linearity assumption of the model?

10   An oil price rise leads to a worse recession in the short run with debt targets without sterilization than with monetary targets with sterilization. Why? Is this result robust to the inflation expectations mechanism?

11   A permanent boost in world trade is more expansionary with debt targets without sterilization than with monetary targets with sterilization. Why? Is this result robust to the inflation expectations mechanism?

12   A permanent boost in world trade is more expansionary and inflation is lower with model consistent than with adaptive inflation expectations. Why? Is this result robust to the type of monetary policy and the linearity assumption of the model?

Model 9

1   A fiscal stimulus is more expansionary with model consistent than with current account expectations in the foreign exchange market. Why?

2   A fiscal expansion with model consistent expectations in the foreign exchange market leads to higher prices in the short run, but lower prices in the long run. Why? Is this plausible? Which parameters should be changed and what values should they assume if prices are to rise in both the short and the long run?

3   A permanent increase in government expenditure financed through money leads to instability. Why?

4   A monetary expansion leads to a short-term stimulus in output, higher prices and lower exchange rate. This result is robust to the expectations formation mechanism for inflation and depreciation/appreciation of the currency and the linearity assumption of the model. Why?

5   Easy monetary policy with model consistent expectations in the foreign exchange market is more expansionary in the short run, but also more inflationary than current account expectations. Why?

6   Compare the effects of an anticipated and unanticipated monetary expansion with model consistent and current account expectations in the foreign exchange market.

7   Tight foreign monetary policy raises output in the home country and increases inflation in the short run. Is this result robust to the expectations formation mechanism and the linearity assumption of the model? Which parameters should be changed and what values should they assume if this result is to be reversed?

8   An increase in world trade stimulates output in the short run, but has an ambiguous effect on inflation. Which parameters are critical for this ambiguity? Are these results robust to the expectations formation mechanism and the linearity assumption of the model?

9   An oil price rise leads to stagflation. Examine the robustness of this result to the type of monetary policy, the expectations formation mechanism and the linearity assumption of the model.

10 Final conclusion: do you agree with the view that one and the same structure is capable of generating vastly diverse results regarding the response of the economy to policy and exogenous shocks depending on the type of monetary policy pursued by the central bank, the formation of expectations and the role of interest payments. Within this structure one single set of parameter values is not capable of producing plausible behaviour in all these cases.